Corporate Mans
Corporate Homi...

A Managers' Guide to Legal Compliance

Corporate Manslaughter and Corporate Homicide

A Managers' Guide to Legal Compliance

Second edition

Michael G Welham

Tottel
publishing

Tottel Publishing Ltd, Maxwelton House, 41–43 Boltro Road, Haywards Heath, West Sussex, RH16 1BJ

© Tottel Publishing Ltd 2008

A CIP Catalogue record for this book is available from the British Library.

ISBN   978 1 84592 259 7

Typeset by Kerrypress Ltd, Luton, Beds

Printed and bound in Great Britain by Athenaeum Press Ltd, Gateshead, Tyne and Wear

Preface

The foundations for the current corporate manslaughter and corporate homicide law began with the Law Commission's report *Legislating the Criminal Code: Involuntary Manslaughter* which was produced in 1996. The report included a draft Bill and set the scene for a corporate offence and two individual offences. It also proposed encompassing all organisations under the banner of 'undertakings'. Management failure was to be the basis and individuals were to be identified and be answerable for the failure.

Four years later the Government adopted the Law Commission proposal and produced *Reforming the Law on Involuntary Manslaughter: the Government's Proposals* in 2000. Again this involved a corporate offence and the two individual offences. However, after consultation and delays the Government produced *Corporate Manslaughter: The Government's Draft Bill for Reform* in 2005. The new law of corporate manslaughter and corporate homicide bears little resemblance to that proposed by the Law Commission in 1996.

The new law is controversial in that directors of small organisations remain susceptible to individual gross negligence manslaughter prosecution, but directors in large organisations will generally not be liable to prosecution. Without doubt it will be claimed that the objective of creating a new law based on the Law Commission concept to provide a level playing field has not been met.

Michael G Welham

www.corporate-manslaughter.net

2007

About the Author

Michael G Welham JP, MPhil, LLM, MSc, Dip OSHM, CFIOSH, MEWI

Michael's career began with military service following which he worked in the offshore oil and gas industry both in the UK and overseas. He joined Britoil Plc (now BP), a major oil and gas exploration and production company and was involved with risk and operational management in onshore and offshore projects. Today Michael is a director of Total Control and is involved with the development of occupational health and safety leadership, risk management and corporate safety systems and training courses with a diverse range of organisations both in the UK and overseas. He has been a magistrate for 15 years.

For 15 years he was with the Health and Safety Executive and was the manager of a team of health and safety inspectors tasked with the enforcement of health and safety legislation, inspections, audits, accident investigation and enforcement action. His team also reviewed safety cases for organisational safety management systems, and emergency planning and procedures for legal compliance.

He was a member of the Health and Safety Executive's 'Manslaughter at Work' Project Group reviewing the impact of the proposed Corporate Manslaughter legislation within the HSE. He utilized his knowledge and experience from the management of HSE investigations in co-operation with the police and CPS for corporate and individual manslaughter prosecutions. He was the HSE manager of a number of joint Police/HSE investigations involving manslaughter prosecutions.

Michael gave evidence in October 2005 to the 11 Members of the Parliamentary Home Affairs and Work and Pensions Sub-Committees in their consideration of the draft Corporate Manslaughter Bill and he is currently, a member of the Institute of Directors – Health and Safety Commission steering group developing the joint IoD/HSC guidance – Leading Health and Safety at Work – Actions for Board Members. He is a member of the Federation of Small Business health, safety and risk management committee. Michael is the co-author of *The Poacher and the Gamekeeper – Leadership for Risk Mitigation in Occupational Health and Safety,* Total Control, 2004.

Introduction

The new law of corporate manslaughter and corporate homicide is probably the most significant piece of health and safety related legislation since the introduction of the Health and Safety at Work etc Act 1974. At this important time there will be many questions as to how the new law will affect organisations, those who manage them, those who work for them and those who are not employed but are affected by their activities. To provide vital information on these issues this book is intended for directors, executives, employers, company secretaries, managers, supervisors, safety officers, trade unionists, lawyers, students as well as the general public. To aid the reader the book is divided into three sections: Part 1 – Corporate and Individual Manslaughter; Part 2 – Corporate Manslaughter and Corporate Homicide; and Part 3 – Directors Responsibilities for Health and Safety.

The birth of the new law began when the Law Commission produced a report *Legislating the Criminal Code: Involuntary Manslaughter,* 1996, Law Commission No 237, HMSO, and set the base line for a new offence for manslaughter in the workplace. It was to be four years before the Government produced a draft Bill in *Reforming the Law on Involuntary Manslaughter: the Government's Proposals* (May 2000). It adopted much of the law Commissions proposals but it was under consultation and redrafting until 2005 when a modified Bill was produced. After due Parliamentary process corporate manslaughter legislation in England and Wales and corporate homicide in Scotland has been introduced in 2007.

A major departure from the original proposals of the Law Commission and the Government is that the new law will only encompass corporations as it is deemed that the current law is sufficiently robust enough to deal with individuals whose actions are within the workplace context. A prime objective of this book is to provide important information for the management of any organisation that could be affected by the proposed new law. There is a need for management to understand the complexities of corporate and individual manslaughter and the dramatic change there will be with the new offence of corporate manslaughter.

The implications for management with the new corporate manslaughter and corporate homicide offences are far reaching because instead of the manslaughter element it will be a case of management failure. It will be the degree of that failure in the cause of death that will determine whether the corporate charge will be laid. In addition, the activities of individuals will be examined and if there is a case of gross negligence then an individual could face manslaughter charges. It is very clear that the new offences will be encompassed in the failure of health and safety management, rather than gross negligence action of an individual. It is worth considering that prosecutions resulting from the well used HSWA 1974, ss 2 and 3 are generally the outcome of some form of management failure.

Management at board or senior level will need to focus on the fact that leadership and ownership of health and safety must be at the highest level of management in every organisation. Responsible management will not want to be placed in a situation of being prosecuted for either corporate or individual offences. Therefore, it is imperative that health and safety is adopted as an integral part of an organisation's day-to-day activities and culture and it is not an afterthought, or considered an unnecessary expense.

The law on health and safety at work is evolving all the time, with new regulations and codes of practice being introduced and updated, and it is not an acceptable defence to plead ignorance of the law. The management of every organisation can take suitable and sufficient steps to manage health and safety in the same way that they manage other aspects of the business such as sales or marketing. To aid management there is a veritable mountain of books, articles and academic reports both official and unofficial relating to the management of health and safety. They range from technical academic editions to practical hands-on material, all providing information for a diverse range of industries and businesses.

Organisations differ in size, location, type and management structure, and they will involve a diverse range of hazards providing a wide range of risks that have to be managed. It follows that the law pertaining to health and safety can also be complex and may not be readily understood by management; after all it is but one tool in the management toolbox. The senior management of many organisations will argue that it is not financially viable to employ a competent health and safety professional. However, that does not preclude utilising the services of a health and safety consultant, providing that person is competent and that means those engaging a consultant will need to ensure that the person is competent. No matter the size of an organisation, be it a multinational company or a self-employed person, the law of health and safety applies and it is a matter for those who create the risk to manage the risk, and failure to do so can result in serious injury or death with an outcome of criminal sanctions.

Having safety management systems in place is no guarantee that criminal sanctions will not be imposed; however, a judge and a jury will, where there have been deaths at work or caused by work activities, take the degree of positive health and safety management into consideration. The number of manslaughter at work cases that have been progressed have been few, and there are more failures than successes, particularly with large organisations but it can be anticipated that there will be a substantial increase in corporate manslaughter prosecutions under the new corporate manslaughter and corporate homicide legislation.

Contents

Contents

Contents

Contents

Contents

Table of Cases

Table of statutes

Table of Statutory Instruments

Part 1

Corporate and Individual Manslaughter

Chapter 1

Deaths at Work – A Case for Reform

Introduction

1.1   Public attention did not become focused on the total lack of corporate liability for deaths which could have been said to be caused by corporate board level failures until a number of disasters took place within a four-year period from 1985–1989. After these tragedies, sufficient priority began to be given to health and safety.

The first case occurred in 1985 when 49 people died in the Bradford City football stadium fire. The wooden stand caught fire, possibly as a result of a cigarette being discarded in rubbish accumulated under the stand over a long period of time.

1.2   In 1987 there were two major tragedies, but it was the first, the sinking of the *Herald of Free Enterprise*, which was to be the catalyst which pushed the failings in corporate liability to the forefront of public attention. The *Herald of*

3

Free Enterprise capsized outside Zeebrugge harbour having sailed with its bow doors open, which allowed the sea to swamp the car deck making the ship unstable. The result was that 154 passengers and 38 crew were killed. The company which owned the ship, P&O European Ferries (Dover) Ltd, was charged with corporate manslaughter, but the case was dismissed.

In the second tragedy in 1987, 31 people died and 60 were injured when fire engulfed Kings Cross underground station. The cause was attributed to a discarded cigarette igniting waste that had accumulated under the escalators.

1.3   The following year, there were again two major tragedies. The Clapham train crash, which killed 37 and injured 500 people, resulted from two trains colliding outside Clapham Junction station. In the same year, an explosion destroyed the Piper Alpha oil platform causing the deaths of 165 crew members.

1.4   In 1989 there were three tragedies. The Purley train crash caused the deaths of five and injuries to 88 passengers when a train driver ignored a red light and crashed into the back of another train. The dredger *Bowbelle* collision with the River Thames pleasure craft the *Marchioness* caused the deaths of 51 and injuries to 80 passengers. Finally in that year the Hillsborough football stadium disaster caused the deaths of 95 and injuries to hundreds of spectators after a large number of people were allowed to enter the stadium at one time in an uncontrolled manner.

1.5   Since that four-year period of disasters there have been other high-profile incidents with loss of life, including the Paddington rail crash involving Great Western Trains, and the Hatfield and Potters Bar rail crashes. The fact remains, however, that only four large companies have faced manslaughter charges in court in England, those being P&O European Ferries (Dover) Ltd, Great Western Trains Ltd, Railtrack, and Balfour Beatty; in Scotland Transco faced a case of corporate culpable homicide; none of these prosecution cases were successful. This has raised much concern not only amongst the families of those killed, but also within the wider public. Large organisations are perceived to be outside the law, with senior managements not being held accountable for their failure to manage. It is considered necessary to raise the stakes where there has been negligence or failure of management to ensure the health and safety of those at work and members of the public affected by those activities when fatal accidents occur. The objective of the new offence of corporate manslaughter and corporate homicide (Scotland) is to enhance health and safety at work and provide sanctions that will have far-reaching consequences for all organisations, and particularly for those in control of them.

The need for reform

1.6   Manslaughter at work has for many years been a topic of increasing public interest. Following some of the major disasters a number of action groups such as Disaster Action, the Herald Families Association and the Marchioness Action Group have been formed, which, along with other established organisations such as Victim Support, the Royal Society for the Prevention of Accidents and the Trade Union Congress have been seeking redress against directors and senior management, the 'controlling minds' of companies.

1.7   The debate on corporate manslaughter has a history extending back a number of years. Garry Slapper[1] identifies the issue of public unrest at the failures in an article in which he states:

'In January, the Piper Alpha Families and Survivors association discontinued their attempt to execute a private prosecution of manslaughter against the oil company Occidental. They were ultimately thwarted by a number of legal obstacles stemming from the fact that since the disaster in 1998, when 167 people died, the company has been sold and changed its name and there have been several significant changes in key personnel. Ivor Glogg, who lost his wife in the *Marchioness* disaster in August 1989, is bringing a private prosecution against South Coast Shipping Company Ltd of Canute Road, Southampton, owners of the *Bowbelle* and the four senior managers. In February, committal proceedings were adjourned for the third time in this case pending judicial review being instituted by the defendants. This case could become only the third trial ever involving a charge of corporate manslaughter but Mr Glogg, who has already spent £20,000 on this matter, has a difficult battle ahead of him as he confronts a corporate defendant which is a subsidiary of the public company Ready Mix Concrete. When an engagement of this sort becomes a war of attrition those who face corporate defendants are plainly prejudiced.'

1 Slapper, G, 'The Legal Regulation for Safety', *Health and Safety at Work,* April 1992.

1.8   It was the lack of action by the Government that focused the attention of victims' groups. In the case of Disaster Action, the umbrella organisation for members of family support groups, they readily identified that a common factor with all the disasters of recent years is that they could all be considered preventable. Their view is that organisations do not take effective action to prevent such disasters because the consequences for either organisations or directors are not sufficiently serious. They point out that no matter how negligent directors in large organisations have been, if legal action is taken it will only be a regulatory offence with an outcome of a minimal sentence and that is restricted to a fine. Disaster Action's opinion[1] has been that the absence of accountability leads to a climate of complacency and sloppy management practices which can result in disaster. This is supported through their opinion that there is a lack of suitable penalties with no real deterrent to prevent companies from risking the lives of the public and their employees. They believe that company directors will only stop putting lives at risk when they know that they and their organisations face the real possibility of criminal sanctions when their activities cause death and injury.

---

1 www.disasteraction.org.uk

1.9 It is very evident that throughout recent years there have been many views and opinions on the corporate manslaughter debate and the whole concept of a new law. Whatever the argument on the rights and wrongs of a corporate manslaughter offence the fact remains that after 30 years of the Health and Safety at Work etc Act 1974 (HSWA 1974), people are still needlessly dying at work. The question that remains is whether the new offence will reduce incidents and disasters and the subsequent loss of life.

The Health and Safety at Work etc Act 1974

1.10 The foundation of current law is the HSWA 1974 which emanated from a committee of six, chaired by Lord Robens.[1] He was chairman of the National Coal Board, a post he held from 1961 until 1972. During that time he had taken to writing personal letters to the widows and mothers of those killed in the pits. During his time deaths at work reduced in number, but he considered that there were still too many accidents. This first-hand knowledge and experience provided him with the credentials needed to chair the committee.

---

1 Allen, B, 'Health and Safety at Work Act: 1974', *Occupational Health Review*, July/August 1999, pp 22–27.

1.11 The committee determined that there was a need to move away from prescriptive legislation to adopt a self-regulating system, which focused on the need to have better systems of safety organisation, management initiatives and more involvement of the workforce. The emphasis was that with health and safety in mind, good management should be normal management, and that effective management would encompass detailed policy and objectives within an effective organisation: a sound and constructive basis for all workplaces. However, there are many commentators who do not see health and safety breaches as being 'real' criminal offences and that may be reflected in the way that the judiciary deal with such offences.

1.12 The HSWA 1974 provides the UK with a framework of legislation placing a duty on employers, the self-employed and employees to conduct their activities in such a way that those who could be affected by the activity of the business are not harmed. This extends to those who are not connected with the activities, such as members of the public.

1.13 It is important to identify whether the HSWA 1974 has fulfilled its objectives. There is some evidence identifying inadequacies in the regulatory offences within the Act, a point raised by the Law Commission[1] who stated:

'... it was suggested that the conduct proscribed by offences under this Act is a failure to comply with a duty, whether or not death or injury resulted: the fact that an employee had died or been seriously injured as a result was immaterial. The courts therefore imposed small fines for those offences, which did not reflect the serious consequences of the offence. Another perceived defect of the 1974 Act was that none of the offences for which it provides were triable only on indictment, even where death had occurred; it is therefore up to the discretion of the magistrates to decide whether or not the case should be prosecuted in the Crown Court.'

---

1 *Legislating the Criminal Code: Involuntary manslaughter*, The Law Commission, Law Com No 237, 199, p 90.

1.14   In the 33 years since the HSWA 1974 was introduced there has been a steady reduction in levels of health and safety failures. However, in recent years it has been seen that the decline in fatal incidents has reached a plateau where levels of incidents are still seen to be unacceptable. The Act provides the tool for the Health and Safety Executive (HSE) and local authorities to carry out their work, which seeks to balance their duties of giving advice, inspecting, undertaking enforcement action and investigating complaints and accidents. It has been claimed that there is no need to change this basic approach, but there is a pressing need for constant vigilance and further action to raise standards. It has also been claimed for a long time that there is a need to provide these enforcement authorities with more resources. Many of the findings of Lord Robens' committee remain valid today through a partnership between government, employers, employees and unions. However, it is identified that there is a need to introduce new energy and a new strategic direction.

Employers' legal obligations

1.15   Employers have an absolute duty under the HSWA 1974 for the care of their employees and those not in their employment who may be affected by their activities. Therefore, there is an obligation to provide a safe place and system of work. By implication, the employer is seen as senior management, the directors or others of similar standing, whatever their title.

1.16   HSWA 1974, s 2(1) states:

'It shall be the duty of every employer to ensure, so far as is reasonably practicable, the health, safety and welfare at work of all his employees.'

HSWA 1974, s 3(1) states:

'It shall be the duty of every employer to conduct his undertaking in such a way as to ensure, so far as reasonably practicable, that persons not in his employment who may be affected thereby are not thereby exposed to risks to their health and safety.'

7

There is no alternative. It is a defined obligation and responsibility for an employer and is not connected to any liability that may arise in respect of injury caused to an employee by a fellow employee in the course of their employment. A breach of the employer's obligation is not just negligence but is the employer's own negligence.

1.17   There are examples of case law which explain the general nature of the employer's obligation, as in the civil law case *Wilson and Clyde Coal Co Ltd v English* [1937] 3 All ER 628, where Lord Wright said:

> '... a duty rests on the employer and which is personal to the employer, to take reasonable care for the safety of his workmen, whether the employer be an individual, a firm, or a company, and whether or not the employer takes any share in the conduct of the operations.'

1.18   Since the ruling, the House of Lords have generally treated the duty as one 'to take reasonable care for his servant's safety in all the circumstances of the case'. This is extended where there are appropriate references to the more specific duties. On the question of duty and liability reference can be made to the case of *Donoghue v Stevenson* [1932] AC 562 where Lord Atkin said:

> 'The duty which is common to all cases where liability is established must logically be based upon some element common to the cases where it is found to exist ... There must be, and is, some general conception of relations giving rise to a duty of care, of which the particular cases found in the books are but instances ... You must take reasonable care to avoid acts or omissions which you reasonably foresee would be likely to injure your neighbour. Who then, in law is my neighbour? The answer seems to be persons who are so closely and directly affected by my act that I ought reasonably to have them in contemplation as being so affected when I am directing my mind to the acts or omissions which are called in question.'

However, Munkman[1] explains that:

> 'these words cannot be, and never were, taken at face value ... the cited passage was an unreliable guide to when liability would be found in new types of case.'

---

1 Munkman, J, *Employers' Liability at Common Law,* (13th edn).

1.19   It can be considered that there are three main areas encompassing a duty of care which were contained in the dictum of Scott in the case of *Vaughan v Ropner & Co Ltd* (1947) 80 LL L Rep 119, when he said:

> 'The three main duties [of the employer] are (1) to provide proper premises in which, and proper plant and appliances by means of which, the work-

man's duty is to be performed; (2) to maintain premises, plant and apparatus in a proper condition; (3) to establish and enforce a proper system of working.'

1.20   It follows that for a corporation to undertake its obligations of a *duty of care* there needs to be a corporate management system for health and safety. This system has to be developed, adopted and driven by senior management and encompasses all aspects of the undertaking with the objective of providing safe methods of working. The precedent rather than the broad principle is today the most reliable guide and it is important to note that the duty is not confined to these matters.

The Management of Health and Safety at Work Regulations 1999

1.21   The Management of Health and Safety at Work Regulations 1999,[7] reg 3 (risk assessment) is also very clear in that it requires every employer to make suitable and sufficient assessment of the risks to the health and safety of his employees and the risks to the health and safety of persons not in his employment. There is also a requirement to introduce suitable control measures and employers must have access to competent health and safety assistance and establish procedures for serious and imminent danger. They are required to make suitable arrangements for contact with external services and provide suitable information to employees as well as providing suitable information to visiting workers. Adequate health and safety training must be provided for employees and employees have a duty to use any equipment and substances in the manner in which they have been trained and instructed. These regulations encompass employers and employees with defined obligations. They are a foundation for management to act upon and non-compliance with any of the regulations could constitute management failure.

---

1 SI 1999/3242.

Parliamentary debates

1.22   The Government takes the lead for all health and safety issues, and it is a subject raised by numerous Ministers, who are lobbied by unions, groups and individuals (the latter often relations of those killed or seriously injured in the workplace). The message is the same, in that they want to see directors or senior management held accountable for failures in undertakings that result in serious incidents and fatalities.

1.23   A number of MPs have been proactive in promoting a corporate manslaughter law, including Ross Cranston MP who in a parliamentary paper[1] states:

> 'many prominent business leaders … are in favour of the new offence. While there is resistance to a new offence in some cases, I have to concede, by lawyers the debate is being won by the proponents of change … the Institute of Directors said that it was happy to support its proposals; in fact it called it step in the right direction … a law of corporate killing would lead to co-operation and information drying up or being destroyed …

---

1 www.Parliament.the-stationery-office.co.uk – Parliamentary Paper 10 Jul 2001: Column 232WH Corporate Killing.

1.24   In March 2004, Frank Doran MP[1] introduced a private draft Corporate Killing Bill into Parliament, which was based on a Transport and General Workers Union draft. The private bill would have created a new offence of corporate killing that would apply to all companies and unincorporated bodies as well as Crown bodies. In his address to the House of Commons on 30 March 2004, he said that:

> 'his Bill would punish management failures of companies where their conduct fell "far below what could reasonably be expected of the corporation in the circumstances".'

---

1 www.frankdoran.org.uk

1.25   The wording came from s 4(1)(b) of the Law Commission's original Draft Involuntary Homicide Bill, that would impose a largely objective test (the subjective element coming in the assessment of the circumstances) so that culpability would not be judged by the company's actual consciousness, intent or other positive mental state at the time of the incident leading to death, but would be assessed by judging what the company (in the sense of its senior management) ought to have been aware of and what it ought to have done or not done in the circumstances.

Trade union movement

1.26   The Trades Union Congress (TUC) has also been a proponent for corporate failures needing to be the focus of greater sanctions in the quest to reduce accidents and in particular those that involve fatalities. To support their position they carried out a poll to obtain the views of the public. The report was produced under the title *TUC poll – British public urge crackdown on safety crimes*[1] which stated:

'People in Britain want to see more companies prosecuted for breaking health and safety laws and more health and safety inspectors to catch them, according to a poll conducted for the TUC ... will discuss the findings and press for 'Law enforcement and corporate accountability' ... Of those expressing a view in a poll of over 1,000 telephone interviews ... more than twice as many people said that they want to see more rather than fewer health and safety prosecutions (45% to 19%). Last year [2001] there were 376 deaths at work, 30% of which are likely to lead to an employer being prosecuted and in only 4 cases are manslaughter charges likely ... Even more people want to see extra safety inspectors. Overall, two thirds (66%) of those expressing a view said there are not enough inspectors. There are currently just 3000 workplace health and safety inspectors despite there being around 1 million injuries in workplaces last year.'

---

1 2002, Press Release, www.tuc.org.

1.27   The offence of corporate manslaughter has for many years been high on the agenda of the trade unions, not least since the great concern caused by the £50,000 fine imposed on the employers of student casual worker, Simon Jones. He died in April 1998 as a result of an accident on his first day in a job at Shoreham harbour, near Brighton. The employer company, which was acquitted of manslaughter by gross negligence, was found guilty only on safety offences relating to its duty of care. The judge described both the company's and the manager's attitude to safety as 'absolutely deplorable'.

1.28   One of the key issues raised was the question of imprisonment. Two distinct camps have evolved on this issue with those who demand custody for directors or their equivalent and those who claim that financial penalties are suitable and justifiable. There are those in the second group who determine that there is no need for new offences in that the HSWA 1974 is sufficient. The question of imprisonment is identified by d'Arcy[1] who states:

'jail the only answer ... Prison remains the only answer for serious safety offenders and accountability must start at the top ...'

The trade unions have set out their position and clearly place the lack of progress with the Government and submit a strong argument that if imprisonment is not an option then the proposed changes to health and safety law will be ineffective.

---

1 www.contractjournal .com.

1.29   Following the introduction of the Government's draft corporate manslaughter and corporate homicide bill (CMCH bill) the Rail, Maritime and Transport Union (RMT) commissioned Thompsons, the UK's largest firm of trade union solicitors, to produce a report on what practical differences the nsingING

Government's proposals on the CMCH bill would make.[1] The RMT, together with the rest of the Trade Union and Labour movement has consistently argued for new legislation on corporate manslaughter. However, the report produced by Thompsons Solicitors concluded that the Bill is a 'significant retreat' from the Government's original proposals.

1 *Corporate Manslaughter and Corporate Homicide Bill: Impact on major rail disaster cases*, Thompsons solicitors and RMT, November 2006, www.tuc.org.uk.

1.30 The Thompsons report dated November 2006 and commenting on the Bill before it was passed, identified that:

- The Government has stepped back from its position in 2000 which was the most progressive it has been on this issue. The present Bill represents a significant retreat from that position in a number of respects.

- The Government has performed a complete U-turn on two key issues. The Bill does not apply to unincorporated bodies such as partnerships, whatever their size. On individual liability, clause 16 expressly prevents this so that there is no personal liability for directors or senior managers under the Bill. Therefore, no person will be imprisoned under this legislation.

- There is a glaring loophole in the Bill in that companies can establish complex corporate structures using subsidiary companies to avoid any liability on the parent.

- The 'senior management' test will continue to cause difficulties and has already resulted in many companies pushing down health and safety matters to more junior managers to avoid liability under the Bill.

- Ultimately, the corporate manslaughter label is the only achievement the Government can claim. No new sanctions will apply to the new offence and it will be far harder to secure a conviction for corporate manslaughter than for the existing health and safety offences. The only real difference will be the label.

- On sanctions, it is clear that whilst prosecutions would now arise for corporate manslaughter, the sanctions would be no greater and indeed would be more restricted than under health and safety legislation.

- In respect of the railway disasters, from Southall in 1997 to Potters Bar in 2002, the Bill as currently drafted would make no difference in terms of sanctions.

1.31 The report identified a loophole in the Bill which would prevent parent companies from being prosecuted when a gross management failure in that company had caused death in one of their subsidiaries. It states:

'... this is because the Bill requires a civil duty of care and, under the current law, courts have not ruled that parent companies have a duty of care in relation to the activities of their subsidiaries. This is, therefore, a glaring loophole in the Bill in that companies can establish complex corporate structures using subsidiary companies to avoid any liability on the parent company.'

1.32 The senior management test would not solve the problems encountered with common law manslaughter prosecutions. Thompsons report states:

'... if the draft Bill were enacted as currently drafted there would be a gap in the law, where individuals in a company have contributed to the offence of corporate manslaughter but where there is not sufficient evidence to prove that they are guilty of individual gross negligence manslaughter ...'

The report continues:

'... just as the Government has taken the decision that when a company's gross management failing caused death it should be liable for a more serious offence than that available under health and safety legislation, so it should be possible to prosecute an individual who has been a secondary party to this gross management failing for a more serious offence also. We therefore recommend that secondary liability for corporate manslaughter should be included in the draft Bill. By analogy with the offence of causing death by dangerous driving the maximum term of imprisonment could be set at 14 years.'

1.33 The Thompsons report reminds us that when introducing the CMCH Bill, the then Home Secretary, John Reid stated:

'Basically, since we are considering a corporate offence, imprisonment will not be an option because individuals will not answer on behalf of any company or corporate organisation except in a legal capacity. Fines will be unlimited and one would expect substantial fines for the sort of offence that we are considering.'

He continued:

'The bill is limited, yet important. I do not claim that it will do everything everyone wants – that is why I say it is limited ... but I do claim that it is important in several different ways.'

1.34 Home Office Minister Gerry Sutcliffe clarified the situation when he stated:

'... concern that the [CMCH] Bill might not add anything to the existing health and safety legislation. For the families of those killed through the abject failure of organisations to meet their health and safety responsibilities, the Bill is far from pointless. It is important that culpable behaviour be properly labelled especially to the relatives of those who have died.'

As was pointed out by John Reid it was absolutely correct to state that the Bill was limited as the statement above is the only real difference that it is intended to make. However, the serious outcome of this would be that senior managers would be well advised by a good corporate lawyer that it would be reasonable to remove responsibility for all health and safety issues down to the lowest point, thereby avoiding any future prosecution for corporate manslaughter.

1.35   The Government makes it plain that:

> '... we see a significant problem with saying that a single person who can take responsibility for the organisation's failure can be and should be identified ... In our view it is not enough to move directly from the new CMCH bill to new individual accountability. That needs to start from current individual responsibility ...'

The question is that if secondary liability is not the answer, how is the question of board level responsibility addressed? The answer has moved from the Home Office to the Health and Safety Commission who are reviewing possible options.

1.36   The Thompsons report advises us that it will be much harder to secure a conviction for corporate manslaughter than it is presently to secure convictions under HSWA 1974. The report indicates that this appears to be the clear intention of government. The absence of individual liability, and without innovative sanctions such as corporate probation, the Act's only achievement is that identified by Home Office Minister, Gerry Sutcliffe, in that the company would be labelled as having been found guilty of corporate manslaughter. The directors would not be imprisoned or disqualified and the company would face the same sanctions as it does at present for health and safety offences, but with greater room to avoid conviction because of the defences available under the new law.

The employers

1.37   Employers are represented through bodies such as the Confederation of British Industry (CBI), the Institute of Directors (IoD) and a number of other professional associations and institutions. Any proposals for increased financial penalties will be focused on the management of an undertaking and will impact on businesses. There is also the question of individual custodial sentences for directors and senior management in manslaughter at work cases. Following the first Government draft Bill (published in a Home Office document in May 2000, *Reforming the Law on Involuntary Manslaughter: the Government's Proposals*) the CBI raised concerns about the proposed corporate killing offence and the CBI states[1]:

'Proposals for a new offence of Corporate Killing could leave companies defenceless because there are no clear tests of whether a firm is to blame ... The CBI argues that the proposals are unfair because firms could be convicted when they have no reasonable way of anticipating or reducing the risk. This would mean that a company could not cite the same defences available to an individual accused of a comparable crime ... The public needs reassurance that companies are accountable and the business community understands that ... If the law focuses responsibility on an individual, however senior, it runs the risk of others abdicating responsibility to the detriment of the team effort ... If the government goes ahead then it needs to listen to our concerns. We would need a further round of consultations to pin down appropriate tests of responsibility.'

1 CBI news release, www.cbi.org.uk

1.38   The CBI continued to raise concerns about the proposed law with regard to health and safety through an article in the Financial Times[1] which states:

'Government plans to make it easier to prosecute companies in the wake of disasters such as the Southall train crash are "unfair" and could "leave companies defenceless" ... The public needs reassurance that companies are accountable and the business community understands that ...but the tests for this new offence must be fair on companies. Under the present proposals they are not, and that could create unnecessary confusion and uncertainty.'

1 *CBI says corporate killing proposals 'unfair'*, Financial Times, 11 October 2000, p 3.

1.39   The IoD[1] also has concerns but appears to be more focused on who would be culpable:

'The Institute of Directors says this [new law of corporate manslaughter] would create scapegoats and a potential shortage of volunteers for boardroom posts with health and safety responsibilities.'

Concern about senior management and the proposed corporate killing law was the subject raised by Suzannah Thursfield,[2] director of safety and health at the Construction Confederation who stated:

'Gross negligence is an awfully difficult thing to prove. Providing that someone deliberately did something knowing that somebody could be killed will be very difficult. Nobody intentionally sets out to kill someone else.'

1 Eaglesham, J, *The companies accused of killing*, Financial Times, 22 April 2002.
2 d'Arcy, 1999, 2 Sept, www.contractjournal .com

1.40   With regard to the new offence of corporate manslaughter the CBI[1] has the view that existing health and safety law is adequate to address the issues targeted by the proposed legislation if implementation is properly resourced. They oppose the proposed formulation of the offence on the ground that it would add considerable uncertainty and unfairness to business operations. In particular it has suggested that the definition of conduct for which a company could be liable would mean that companies could be convicted when they had no reasonable way of anticipating or reducing the risk. They put forward the argument that any new offence should instead apply to behaviour that 'wilfully or recklessly disregards foreseeable risks' to employees or the general public.

---

1 www.cbi.org.uk.

1.41   The CBI has continued to lobby against the imposition of new individual liabilities for directors, arguing that:

> '... if the law focuses responsibility on an individual, however senior, it runs the risk of others abdicating responsibility to the detriment of the team effort.'

Initially, the CBI voiced concerns over the Government's proposals published in 2000, which removed the express exclusion of liability for individuals as secondary parties to the corporate offence which had been contained in the Law Commission's draft. They support the Government's announcement that it no longer intends that the new offence should target individual directors. However, the CBI also believes that if the new law is to be enacted then it should apply to Crown bodies.

1.42   The CBI position endorses high standards of corporate responsibility, but it was argued that the tests proposed by the Home Office in 2000 were unclear and unfair on business and on individual directors. The CBI pressed the point that if such an offence were introduced it should apply to all organisations including the Crown, in order to provide a level playing field for public/private partnerships and private finance initiatives. Any offence should be built on current risk management principles and forseeability. A suitable statutory defence should be included that distinguishes those that have done their best but have unfortunately not prevented a fatality from those that had a blatant disregard of the law. It should respect the collective responsibility for health and safety at the workplace. To provide business with greater certainty to assess liabilities the offence should be focused on employer/employee workplace issues.

1.43   The proposed offence of corporate manslaughter has its opponents among employers and employers' organisations who raise the question as to the need for it, as they consider that the current health and safety offences are sufficient and provide an adequate deterrent.

1.44   'The Law on Corporate Killing could be on the Wrong Track' was the headline in an article by Davidson in the *Daily Telegraph*:[1]

'Creating the crime of corporate killing is just a political reaction to appease a public outcry and can have no benefit to society.'

He continues his argument and states:

'If the link and evidence are strong enough to show a director knew what was going on, he can be prosecuted now. If there is not enough evidence, the company is prosecuted and the director suffers, there is a question of human rights ... the new process weakens the burden of proof for finding directors guilty, which cannot be right. The present law says that if the person responsible for the death can be identified and the evidence can show "he actually acted in a way that resulted in the death", he can be taken to court. It hardly ever happens. The reason is the difficulty in allocating blame, or "showing they knew what was going on". Trying to remove the responsibility from the manager, who is probably responsible to place it on someone who is remote and may have known little about it, is not justice. Such an increased pressure is hardly likely to encourage people to incorporate or to become directors. That is especially true of non executive directors who meet only monthly and are responsible that assets are looked after and procedures followed, but unlikely to know about detailed daily procedures though the law says they are equally responsible for the company's activities ... Fines are also a problem because they just hit the pockets of owners and shareholders though they are not to blame.'

---

1 Davidson, A, *Daily Telegraph*, May 2000.

1.45   Directors feel that they and their organisations could be exposed to a corporate manslaughter offence that occurs outside of their knowledge or consent. There may be suitable company procedures and guidance and there may be a system to ensure that individuals employed are competent. However, a deviation by an individual, particularly if working away from the organisation's principal place of work, could expose the organisation (and those who own or control it) to litigation. There is also an argument that responsible organisations employ safety professionals to manage health and safety issues, feeding the appropriate information in at board level and that therefore the responsibility lies with the health and safety professional and not with those on the board. It must be made very clear that the responsibility lies with those on the board or at senior management level, who have a significant role in the management of the organisation and not with the health and safety professional. The role of the safety professional is to provide advice and information to the decision makers who have to act appropriately. However, as will be seen throughout this book, the safety professional must be qualified and competent. There is further concern that if a director or someone of similar status is appointed to be responsible for health and safety, they could be used as a scapegoat in the event of legal proceedings against an organisation. A thorough and detailed investigation should expose the identity of the decision makers and determine their role in the incident. There is also concern about the proposition that directors could be disqualified from holding a management position; this is seen by some commentators as being a draconian measure. The answer is not straightforward but following a successful trial for corporate manslaughter, based upon management failure, disqualifying a director must remain an option.

1.46   At the time of writing the Institute of Directors and Health and Safety Commission have established a steering committee tasked with reviewing the current guidance on directors' duties and producing new updated guidance which will encompass the whole spectrum of companies, from small single director operations through to large multinational enterprises. The objective is to offer guidance to board members, both executive and non-executive, on their duties with regard to workplace health and safety. The guidance was launched in October 2007 (note, the author is a member of the steering group).

Health and Safety Commission

1.47   In an article in the *Guardian*[1] Bill Callaghan, Chairman of the Health and Safety Commission states:

'*Kill these deaths. Directors could soon be jailed over workplace fatalities.* But, says Bill Callaghan, chairman of the health and safety commission, employers should not fear the new law ... HSC supports the proposed corporate killing offence. We want the government to introduce it as soon as possible, and we believe that it should apply to all employers, including Crown bodies ... Before we start to talk about prosecuting for death at work however, I would like to draw attention to a much-overlooked fact: that prevention is better than prosecution. Therefore much of the HSC/E's efforts are directed at promoting behaviour that is likely to prevent fatalities happening ... Good health and safety is not about "bashing the bosses". We need consensus to drive progress – and this depends upon partnership and consultation between the enforcing authorities, employers and workers. In particular, the role of safety representatives is vital ... The HSC expects that the new Corporate Killing charge should provide a powerful deterrent to employers – and that its success should therefore be judged not by how many, but by how few ... Companies know that a Corporate Killing conviction would severely damage their reputation, and at a time when corporate image is becoming an increasingly important competitiveness issue ... Not every death at work is the result of a breach of health and safety law. But when it is, we expect the courts to impose high penalties. Our view is that the general level of fines for health and safety offences is still too low – and the Court of Appeal has said the same. We need the courts to recognise just how serious health and safety infringements are.'

1 *The Guardian G2*, 19 August 2002, p 3.

1.48   The article focused on the domain of health and safety control, the board and the need for culture changes that will adopt safe systems of work and continues:

> '... our message to Britain's bosses is that health and safety must be a board issue. Responsibility must start at the top, with every director sharing the challenge. We have published guidance on directors' responsibilities and this makes clear what we consider to be good practice. There is no excuse for ignorance ... The HSC has challenged Britain's leading 300 firms to include health and safety performance in their annual reports and set improvement targets as part of the national target to reduce fatal and minor injuries by a minimum of 10% by 2010. Many firms are already doing this – 60% of FTSE 100 companies include health and safety in their annual reports ... but what is the other 40% doing? We are asking that question, and so increasingly are the big investing institutions. They know that those companies that have high standards of health and safety are likely to have high standards of business performance. Quite simply, if you cannot manage health and safety, you cannot manage. The Corporate Killing offence is good news and no responsible employer should fear it.'

The message from the Commission is very clear and the HSC as the enabling arm of the Government confirms that there needs to be change. It again falls to government to give strategic direction to the regulators as well as sufficient resources to carry out the task, and establish the legal framework that will be effective.

Norton Rose

1.49   Norton Rose is a major international law firm with considerable experience of acting for clients in the transport, construction and energy sectors and advises companies on all aspects of their commercial activities and operational risks. After talking to many of its clients and listening to their concerns about the Government's corporate killing proposals, the firm decided to commission an independent research report to express the views of leading companies in these sectors. *The Norton Rose Report on Corporate Killing – Views from business* was published in 2004 (note: this was prior to the title change to Corporate Manslaughter in the new Act).

1.50   The research for the report was carried out between December 2003 and January 2004, through 105 telephone interviews. Respondents were drawn primarily from the transport, construction and energy sectors of industry. Interviews consisted of 16 questions and lasted approximately 15 minutes. In total, 55 senior management directors and 50 health and safety managers were interviewed giving a spread of opinion from director level to senior manager level. The results were analysed by level of seniority of respondent and industry sector type.

1.51   Interviewees were asked how well they understood the Government's corporate killing proposals. Most (80%) were well aware of the proposals, although only one-third had a full understanding of them and 55% had a rudimentary understanding. Where the respondent claimed only a rudimentary understanding, the interviewer then explained the Government's proposals to them as laid out by the Home Office in 2000. The survey base includes companies of a variety of size and type, of which two-thirds were publicly listed, and a quarter were private companies. Other organisations were divided between government and regulatory bodies, mutual societies and trade associations. In total, 30 of the organisations included in the survey are listed in the FTSE UK 350 Index and a further 12 are in the FTSE Global Sector Index.

1.52   The main findings of the report found the following:

- 60% of companies surveyed thought the Government's proposed corporate killing legislation was a political manoeuvre to satisfy public opinion. 10% were not sure and only 30% thought the legislation was motivated by a genuine desire to improve health and safety in the British workplace

- Two-thirds of respondents thought the proposals would have a negative impact on British business, increasing bureaucracy and costs and making companies more risk averse. 64% of respondents thought that introducing a new corporate killing charge would further the 'blame culture' already growing in industry. However, in economic terms, a majority of respondents did not think that the legislation would have an immediate impact on profitability (65%) or investment (66%)

- Most companies (59%) said their greatest professional fear about a corporate killing prosecution would be the impact on corporate reputation, compared to only 6% who mentioned unlimited fines. Respondents felt that being labelled a 'corporate killer' as the Home Office proposes, could even threaten business survival.

- A majority (59%) were not convinced that the proposed legislation would improve health and safety in the workplace. Most companies thought that the best way to effect meaningful improvement was by changing cultural attitudes from the top down, through better management and education. A significant minority (41%), however, did think that new legislation might improve safety standards through 'focusing minds' and raising the issue up the corporate agenda.

- Opinions were almost evenly divided as to the need for more legislation. However, most companies thought that the current legislation was not effective due to poor enforcement and were concerned that any new legislation would fall down on the same problem.

- A majority of respondents (68%) did not have confidence in the HSE's ability to carry out fair and effective investigations into corporate killing incidents based on previous experience of its approach. They felt the HSE was under-resourced, over-burdened and open to political pressure.

- The vast majority (79%) thought that one individual member of the company board should have overall responsibility for health and safety issues. Surprisingly, a small majority (55%) contrary to the Government's actual proposals believed that an individual director should be made personally responsible and criminally liable for failings within his or her organisation.

- General observations found that respondents from the transport industry, in particular the rail sector, were far more wary about the proposed corporate killing legislation than other sectors. More than any other sector, they felt that the legislation would force them to pull out of riskier lines of business and would impact upon profitability. The construction sector felt that they were doing as much as they possibly could to improve safety so were more sanguine about the government's corporate killing proposals.

1.53 In August 2005 Norton Rose produced a briefing which was submitted to the Home Office consultation team as part of the consultation process into the draft corporate manslaughter Bill. The briefing provided the opinions about the proposed new law and the impact on business that their clients provided. Norton Rose found that not all of the responses to the survey were negative. In fact one-third of the respondents considered that the proposed legislation promoted a genuine desire to improve safety and address the current difficulty in successfully prosecuting companies for manslaughter under existing laws. Some considered that the new legislation would lead to a review of existing health and safety procedures, but only a minority felt that safety would be improved by the legislation. The respondents were asked what needs to happen to improve safety in industry and about a third thought that a culture change is required from top to bottom along with better management and education. A slightly higher number thought that corporate manslaughter would not have any effect on their business as they were already doing as much as possible to improve safety. The majority of respondents stated that increased bureaucracy and costs would be the outcome from the new law with a focus on audit trails and the intensification of the existing 'blame culture'. 66% said that organisations would become risk averse and may well decline to undertake some types of work to avoid the possibility of a corporate manslaughter prosecution.

1.54 The Norton Rose survey identified one respondent who complained that:

> '... there was a decreasing public tolerance for risk and accidents of any type, and that the public perception of risk and the ways in which it can realistically be avoided had become severely distorted.'

Further, the report identified:

> 'Many respondents to the survey decried the growth of a "blame culture" in
> British industry, and the HSE's prosecution of individuals following the
> Hatfield disaster prompted one respondent to refer to "the safety industry"
> and express the view that "they are into headlines". On the subject of
> directors' liability, one industry respondent commented: "Someone should
> be personally liable for ensuring the correct procedures and audits are in
> place. But how can directors be criminally liable for operational accidents if
> someone breaks the rules?".'

The Centre for Corporate Accountability

1.55   The Centre for Corporate Accountability (CCA)[1] is a leading organisation promoting the strengthening of the law with regard to deaths at work. The
organisation was active in responding to the Government's latest draft Bill
before the passing of the Act and through their website David Bergman,
Director of the CCA said:

> 'There is a lot of detail that does need to be given careful consideration
> however; we have the following initial comments:
>
> … that there is a new test for determining whether or not an organisation can
> be prosecuted for corporate manslaughter which does not require the
> prosecution of an individual director or senior manager; that Crown bodies
> will be able to be prosecuted in principle for this offence – though we are
> concerned about certain exemptions; that the Government intends that police
> will be able to be prosecuted for this offence.'

---

1 www.corporateaccountability.org

1.56   The CCA has concerns that the offence will only apply to companies
and not unincorporated bodies such as unincorporated associations or partnerships. The view of the CCA is that the new offence should apply to all employing
organisations as the Government originally agreed in its consultation document
in 2000. Another concern raised is the fact that a jury must consider whether or
not senior managers 'sought to cause the organisation to profit from that failure'.
This evidence is extremely difficult to obtain and absence of evidence will be
used by organisations to show that their conduct was not grossly negligent."

1.57   A factor that has been a key issue throughout the years of debate and
consultation has been that of Crown immunity. A particular concern is the
prison service and the armed forces and the CCA remains unpersuaded that
there are legitimate reasons why management failures at a senior level within a
prison or within the armed forces (involving for example in training exercises in
Britain) which lead to a death should not be subject to a prosecution. There is

also the point that the new draft Bill only requires consideration of prosecution of the senior managers of an organisation rather than managers at all levels. This is different from the original test set out in the Law Commission recommendation in 1996.

1.58 The CCA are concerned that organisations could delegate their responsibilities down the management chain and thereby allow the organisation to escape manslaughter prosecution. Further, the new offence does not apply to British companies that cause death abroad. They are also aware that reforms to the offence of corporate manslaughter were always going to focus upon the conduct of the organisation rather than the individual. However, the Government has not come up with any alternative options to deal with the lack of accountability of company directors (which was an issue that the Government itself considered a concern in its original consultation document in 2000).

1.59 Research by the CCA reveals that only 11 company directors have ever been convicted of manslaughter following a work-related death. Five of the directors were sentenced to imprisonment, another five had a suspended sentence and one was given a community service order. The research also shows that in the two and a half years between April 2002 and November 2004, only 27 directors had been convicted for a health and safety offence brought by the HSE, of which eight involved deaths.

1.60 A Directors Duties bill has been tabled by Labour MP Stephen Hepburn, which is being strongly supported by the Transport and General Workers Union (TGWU) and Union of Construction Allied Trades and Technicians (UCATT) as well as safety organisations and charities including the CCA. David Bergman, Director of the CCA[1] stated:

'It is important to recognise, despite the large number of deaths and injuries, how little accountability there is for company directors. In the same period that 27 directors were convicted, over 1000 companies were found guilty of health and safety offences. It is the CCA's view that the absence of duties on directors makes it much more difficult for the Health and Safety Executive to identify what, in law, is expected that directors should know about health and safety in their company and what action they should be taking. As a result this makes it much more difficult to hold them to account for health and safety offences.'

He went on to say that:

'Although the Directors Duties bill will assist in making accountability easier, the primary purpose of the directors duties bill is to ensure that directors take the action that would both prevent deaths and injuries and ensure that they do not face criminal prosecution'

1 See www.corporateaccountability.org

1.61   In 2000 the Government supported introducing legislation to impose safety duties on directors, but the CCA has identified that the Government's preference now, is to support a 'voluntary' approach. The original Bill was based on a Ten Minute Rule Bill drafted by Ross Cranston QC and the CCA and is supported by the TGWU, UCATT, TUC, safety charities, bereaved families and safety campaign groups.

Disaster Action

1.62   Disaster Action, the umbrella organisation for members of family support groups, observes the common factor in all the disasters which have made headlines in recent years is that they were all preventable. Disaster Action[1] believes that insufficient steps are currently taken by companies to prevent such disasters because the consequences for companies and directors are not sufficiently serious. For example, Disaster Action states that directors currently have no specific legal obligations relating to the management of health and safety. In the case of fatalities, companies can easily avoid conviction unless specific criminal responsibility on the part of a director or senior manager can be pinpointed. Therefore, company directors know that only in the most unlikely circumstances will they or their companies face prosecution, however negligently they act, that any legal action taken will relate to a regulatory offence and that sentences will be minimal. It follows that the organisation believes that company directors will only stop putting lives at risk when they believe that they and their companies face the real possibility of criminal sanctions when their failure to manage causes death and injury.

---

1 www.disasteraction.org.uk

1.63   In its booklet entitled *The Case for Corporate Responsibility*, Disaster Action quotes the CBI as stating in relation to workplace death and injury:

> 'no one should be at peril unless there is clear evidence to place responsibility for the act resulting in injury or death upon the accused, but where there is such evidence then the full force of the law and penalties should be applied.'

1.64   There is a belief that, where corporate organisations fail in their duty of care and are grossly negligent or indifferent to safety, they should be subject to a workable process of law which imposes appropriate penalties. Deaths, serious injuries and disease resulting from intentional, reckless or grossly negligent conduct on the part of companies or directors should be treated as serious crimes of violence. There is a need for a system of investigation to detect and uncover corporate crimes, for the prosecution of companies and directors for appropriate offences and for the setting up of a sentencing regime that both punishes and rehabilitates.

1.65   Disaster Action advocates the following specific changes:

- a new test of liability (in line with the principles underlying the proposed new legislation) to determine whether companies have committed an offence involving the intentional, reckless or negligent causing of death, serious injuries or disease;

- legal safety duties imposed on directors;

- additional offences where a company negligently kills or seriously injures a person recklessly endangers life;

- a new sentencing regime where fines would reflect the seriousness of the offence and the wealth of the company involved;

- a requirement in certain circumstances for companies to publish (and include in their annual reports) details of offences committed by them and their directors;

- a related 'penalty points' system whereby a director accumulating a specified number of points will be disqualified from acting as a director.

Global influences

1.66   There is also another legal perspective to be considered and that involves corporate legal developments outside the EU. Countries such as Australia, Canada and the USA are reviewing workplace and corporate health and safety legal developments. It is acknowledged that the USA has been the focus of compensation claims for many years and that has had a dramatic impact on both business and individuals. The 'no win no fee' compensation culture has become part of life in the UK and that is already having an impact on businesses.

1.67   Canada and Australia, whose legal systems derive from those of the UK, are engaged in law reform as described by Wells[1] who states:

'There are moves also in Canada and Australia whose legal tradition is closer to our own, to introduce a more systems-based form of corporate liability which will allow the corporation to be held liable for that conduct if it can be proved that the practices or culture of the company encouraged or at least did not prohibit the offence complained of … in the Australian Criminal Code Act 1995, enacting Law Reform Commission proposals to extend and supplement the *Tesco v Nattrass* doctrine. It is envisaged that the standard principles the Code introduces will eventually extend beyond federal offences and apply to similar situations under state law … the idea of 'corporate culture' is specifically given legislative recognition. Where its culture encourages situations leading to offence the company will be responsible. 'Corporate culture' is defined as an attitude, policy, rule, course of conduct, or practice existing within the body corporate generally or in the part of the body corporate where the offence occurred.'

1 Wells, C, *Corporations and Criminal Responsibility*, Oxford University Press, 1993.

1.68   There are some important messages described above, with some key health and safety issues raised and identified with an overview of options. The global influence is highlighted at this point but developments are examined in Chapter 5 which examines the proposals and compares them with those of the UK, in particular with emphasis on corporate manslaughter legislation proposals.

European influences

1.69   The focus on health and safety law is not just a UK legal system issue; as a member of the EU there are European legal implications to be considered and adopted. This raises other and more complex issues such as the manner in which other countries administer and enforce health and safety. A number of commentators have addressed the European issues. Wells[1] makes constructive comments on the subject and states:

> 'In the particular field of corporate criminal liability, many individual European jurisdictions, despite their very different legal forms and systems are addressing the role of criminal law in relation to the corporate enterprise. The Council of Europe has recommended the promotion of corporate criminal liability and has spelled out principles to guide member states. Legal culture is more open-textured and open to influence from any number of sources than is often supposed.'

1 *Corporations & the Risk of Criminal Liability*, www.freedomtocare.org/page 166, 8 March 2002.

1.70   The European influence will evolve further and the future of health and safety incidents and enforcement is an unknown, but certainly not without complications. This is already seen where corporations have their corporate headquarters in other EU countries and are able to operate in the UK without redress to criminal legal process when incidents occur. Sengupta, writing in the *Independent*[1] stated:

> *'Loophole allows foreign firms to avoid safety fines.*
>
> Hundreds of companies and individuals were "named and shamed" yesterday after being convicted of health and safety crimes in a move described by watchdogs as a new and tough chapter in enforcement.

But the Health and Safety Executive (HSE) admitted a loophole in safety laws under which multinational firms based abroad and involved in some of the worst accidents in Britain have got away with refusing to pay the massive fines imposed on them.

The Government is negotiating with other European Union states to make payment of criminal fines enforceable for companies wherever they trade. The HSE acknowledges that even if this is achieved, British health and safety laws would still have difficulties with multinational corporations based abroad. It may be that if foreign companies are to operate in the UK some form of indemnity is provided to ensure legal liability cover is provided and fines could be recovered through British courts. At present there is no incentive for foreign companies to adopt UK health and safety systems, which could place UK business at a disadvantage.'

---

1 Sengupta, *The Independent*, 26 October 2000.

Summary

1.71   It will be seen that the whole subject of corporate manslaughter and individual gross negligence manslaughter has individuals, groups and organisations who have opposing views with the strongest arguing for the custodial option to be available in the UK. The fact is that where there are serious failings by the management of organisations then an effective sanction should be available. However, the judge and jury hearing and considering all the evidence should be allowed to make valid judgments and the issue should not be left to governments, lobby groups or other organisations to impose their views. That said, the judiciary must have balanced and effective laws by which to act and that should include a custodial option where appropriate and justified.

Chapter 2

Workplace Accidents and Disasters

Introduction

2.1 It is generally the large and dramatic disasters that gain the media headlines with a focus on loss of life, injuries and impact on commercial life. It is those cases from which the demand has come for the offence of corporate manslaughter to be introduced. The problem for prosecutors has been in identifying a 'controlling mind', or in other words selecting an individual who was personally responsible for a course of action that led to the death of a person or persons. The new offence of corporate manslaughter is based upon the failure of an organisation's senior managers to manage or organise the organisation's activities. The failures in the incidents below are all linked in varying degrees to management failure and by looking at the causes and outcomes of some of the incidents the failures become apparent.

The Piper Alpha disaster

2.2 In July 1988, the fire and explosions on the Piper Alpha platform, owned by Occidental, resulted in the world's worst offshore oil disaster, claiming 167 lives. At about 10.00 pm on 6 July 1988, an explosion occurred in the gas compression module on the Piper Alpha platform, 120 miles north east of Aberdeen. This initial explosion put the main control room and main power supplies out of action and caused extensive damage to hydrocarbon processing equipment. It was followed immediately by a large fire in the oil separation module, which gave rise to a massive plume of black smoke that engulfed the north end of the platform. This fire was fed by oil from the platform and a leak in the main oil line to the shore, to which the pipelines from two other platforms were connected.

2.3   At about 10.10 pm there was a second major explosion which caused a massive intensification of the fire. This was due to the rupture of the riser on the gas pipeline from one of the adjacent platforms. Ruptures of other risers further intensified the fire. The emergency systems failed. The platform structure collapsed as a result of the explosions. The east quarter's module lost its structural support and tipped to the west, crushing the west quarter's module, and then tipped northwards into the sea. Between 10:30 pm and 12:15 am the centre of the platform collapsed. The risers from the gas pipelines and the main oil pipeline were torn apart. The north side of the platform slowly collapsed until the additional accommodation module slipped into the water. There were 226 men on the platform at the time. The system for control in the event of an emergency was rendered almost entirely inoperative and smoke and flames outside the accommodation made evacuation by helicopter or lifeboat impossible. A number of personnel reached the sea by use of ropes and hoses or by jumping off the platform at various levels. 61 persons survived; 167 died.

2.4   The extent of death and injury resulting from the Piper Alpha disaster was of great concern to the offshore petroleum industry worldwide, and widespread reviews of safety equipment and emergency response were undertaken. In the UK, a public enquiry, undertaken by Lord Cullen, was immediately commissioned to establish the circumstances of the accident. One of the outcomes of the Cullen Report was the establishment of a discrete division within the Health & Safety Executive (HSE) which has responsibility for the regulating of the UK offshore oil and gas industry (see **2.5** below). At the time of the accident, the foundation of the HSE's regulating approach to the management of risk was based upon sector specific safety cases that were required for all fixed and mobile installations operating in the UK sector. Occidental, before the Piper Alpha disaster, was not a company with a good safety record and the company had narrowly escaped a disaster in 1984, which had required the mass evacuation of the same platform. In 1987, the company experienced a fatal incident. The company had clearly failed to learn from its mistakes and that was made clear by Lord Cullen whose Report concluded that there were 'significant flaws in Occidental's management of safety' and that 'senior management were too easily satisfied' and 'relied on the absence of any feedback of problems as indicating that all was well'. The facts that derived from the report indicate that, in the case of *Piper Alpha*, it was not a case of individual negligent workers, but of a corporation for which the importance of safety was relegated below that of profits. Numerous commentators argued that with the climate of profit before safety a Piper Alpha disaster was inevitable and could have occurred on many other North Sea platforms.

2.5   Prior to the incident, a sector-wide set of regulations and laws were applied to all platforms and were enforced by governmental inspection. This policy did not allow for customisation of safety regulations to a particular type of platform. Because of the numerous types of offshore platforms, this type of system was found to be inadequate for the North Sea production area. Subsequent to Piper Alpha, operators must produce a formal safety case to be approved by the regulatory body, the Offshore Safety Division of the HSE. In the formal safety case, the operator must have procedures in place to control risks to personnel and demonstrate that the current safety management is adequate. In addition to the formal safety case, a temporary refuge, typically, the accommodation unit, must exist and provide at least two hours of protection for the workers. Other factors include a Permit-to-Work-system, fire walls, deluge systems, safety training, auditing and risk assessment.

2.6   Occidental escaped enforcement action in the courts because the authorities concluded that there was insufficient evidence to proceed with a prosecution. This raises the question as to whether economic considerations to maintain business mean that a corporation is absolved from criminal legal repercussions. The other possibility is to pass the blame onto individuals. While no official prosecution was taken, a private criminal prosecution by victims' families was an option but could not be pursued because of the legal costs involved. Piper Alpha was the ultimate and most costly management failure in the UK offshore oil industry and one that changed the legislative structure of its regulation.

The Herald of Free Enterprise

2.7   The first of a line of disasters that proceeded to court for manslaughter prosecutions and failed focused the minds of the public on the very serious failings of the justice system. The case was against P&O European Ferries (Dover) Ltd. Here was a corporation prosecuted for its management failings, but failing to obtain a conviction. It was a case of the corporate entity placing the blame on junior employees and because of the inability to identify a controlling mind; the case was destined to fail. It was a case where the public saw a corporation fail to adopt safe practices and procedures and not be accountable at boardroom level. The public found that outcome unacceptable and through numerous lobby groups has placed pressure on government to change the law.

2.8   The findings of the subsequent report, known as the Sheen Report,[1] are reviewed below. The facts of this important case concerning corporate manslaughter are given and the failings of the corporate body drawn out. Under the offence of corporate killing, these are the fundamental boardroom issues that will need to be addressed by all undertakings.

---

1 Report of the Court No 8074, 1987, Department of Transport.

2.9   The *Herald of Free Enterprise* was built for the Dover-Calais passenger ferry run and incorporated very powerful engines, capable of rapid acceleration, to enable the crossing to be made at high speed. The concept of the vessel and her sister vessels was to be able to disembark their passengers and vehicles rapidly and then, without any delay, embark passengers and vehicles for the return voyage. This is of course done to ensure efficiency and cost benefit. On the Dover-Calais run, these ships were manned by an officers' complement of a master, two chief officers and a second officer. The officers were required to work a 12-hour shift on duty and have not less than 24 hours off duty. In reality each crew was on board the vessel for 24 hours and then had 48 hours ashore.

2.10   When the vessel was transferred to the Dover to Zeebrugge route the passage took 4½ hours, and because it is a longer journey than that of the Dover to Calais route, it gave the officers more time to relax. On this basis the company only employed a master and two deck officers, which they were quite entitled to do, providing that proper thought had been given to the organisation of the officers' duties and the safety of all those onboard. At Zeebrugge, the turn-round was different from the turn-round at Calais in four main respects. Only two deck officers were available, only one deck could be loaded at a time, it was frequently necessary to trim the ship by the head, and the bow doors could be closed at the berth. It was because of these differences that no real thought was given to the organisation of the duties of the officers, which meant that immediately loading was complete the Chief Officer considered himself under pressure to leave the loading deck to go to his harbour station on the bridge.

2.11   The report identified that there were three crews and five sets of officers for the manning of the *Herald* on this route, and that meant that the officers did not always have the same crew. This was a failing in the operating system because a competent superintendent, applying his mind to the organisation of the officers and crew, would have issued corporate adopted instructions, known within the company as Company Standing Orders, which would have been uniform for all the ships of one class. They would have covered all aspects of organisation, not only for the Calais run but also for the Zeebrugge run when the ship carried only two deck officers in addition to the master. This approach in management is fundamental; however, in this case, no company orders were issued. There were Ship's Standing Orders, which were in place in March 1987, but they serve to highlight that there was a lack of proper organisation.

2.12   On 6 March 1997 the *Herald of Free Enterprise*, under the command of Captain David Lewry sailed from Number 12 berth in the inner harbour at

Zeebrugge. The ship was manned by a crew of 80 hands and was laden with 81 cars, 47 freight vehicles and three other vehicles. Approximately 459 passengers had embarked for the voyage to Dover. There was prevailing good weather with a light easterly breeze and very little sea or swell. The *Herald* passed the outer mole at 18.24 hours and capsized about four minutes later. During the final moments the *Herald* turned rapidly to starboard and was prevented from sinking totally by reason that her port side rested on the bottom in shallow water. Water rapidly filled the ship below the surface level with the result that 150 passengers and 38 members of the crew lost their lives and many others were injured.

2.13 The immediate cause of the disaster occurred because the ship went to sea with her inner and outer bow doors open. The assistant bosun accepted that it was his duty to close the bow doors at the time of departure from Zeebrugge and that he failed to undertake this duty. He had opened the bow doors on arrival in Zeebrugge and was engaged in supervising members of the crew in maintenance and cleaning the ship until he was released from work by the bosun. He then went to his cabin, where he fell asleep and was not awakened by the call 'Harbour Stations', which was given over the tannoy address system. He remained asleep on his bunk until thrown out of it when the *Herald* began to capsize.

2.14 The full burden of the duty to ensure that his ship is in all respects ready for sea falls to the master. He is responsible for its safety and that of every person on board. On 6 March 1987, the master of the *Herald* took the ship to sea with the bow doors fully open, resulting in tragic consequences. He must accept personal responsibility for the loss of his ship. However, subsequent investigations highlighted a number of points of mitigation that were made on his behalf, of which there were three principal ones. First, the master merely followed a system, which was operated by all the masters of the *Herald* and was approved by the senior master of the ship. Secondly, the court was reminded that the 'Ship's Standing Orders' issued by the company made no reference, as they should have done, to opening and closing the bow and stern doors. Thirdly, before this disaster there had been no less than five occasions when one of the company's ships had proceeded to sea with either bow or stern doors open. The management knew about some of those incidents, but had not drawn them to the attention of the other masters. The master told the court that if he had been made aware of any of those incidents, he would have instituted a new system under which he would have required that the doors were closed.

2.15 This was clear evidence of a failure in the management system, where senior management knew or ought to have known that there was a potential hazard with a high severity risk outcome that could place both crew and passengers in an unsafe situation. This was exacerbated by the fact that one of the five masters who took it in turn to command the *Herald* was the senior master and one of the functions as senior master was to act as a co-ordinator between all the masters and officers of the ship, in order to achieve uniformity in the practices operated by the different crews.

2.16   From the facts surrounding the disaster it can be seen that the combined errors or omissions on the part of the master, the chief officer and the assistant bosun, and the failure of the senior master were the root cause. However, a full investigation into all the circumstances of the disaster determined that serious faults lay higher up in the company in that, for some unknown reason, the board of directors did not appreciate their responsibilities for the safe management of their ships. In fact all concerned in management, from the members of the board of directors down to junior superintendents were guilty of fault in that they must be regarded as sharing responsibility for the failure of management. In the Sheen report there is the now famous statement:-

> '... from top to bottom the body corporate was infected with the disease of sloppiness ... The failure on the part of the shore management to give proper and clear directions was a contributory cause of the disaster ...'

Based upon the evidence of the case, the Director of Public Prosecutions (DPP) instituted a corporate manslaughter prosecution. It was also considered that while the company was charged with manslaughter, any legal actions should reach every person, whatever their employment status and so two representatives of senior management, the assistant bosun, the bosun, the chief officer, and the two captains were charged with manslaughter.

The Marchioness

2.17   A case that evoked much publicity calling for a corporate manslaughter prosecution was the sinking of the *Marchioness*, a Thames cruiser, in August 1989. It raised the issue of public confidence as discussed in the Law Commission Report.[1] 'The loss of 51 lives was caused by the captain of the dredger *Bowbelle* not having a lookout. The vessel's owners were not prosecuted. The captain was charged with the offence of failing to keep a proper lookout under the Merchant Shipping Act 1988, s 32, but the case was dropped after two juries failed to agree. A private prosecution for manslaughter was then mounted against the owners; but the Divisional Court stated that the Director of Public prosecutions might take over the proceedings and discontinue them or if it was too late to discontinue offer no evidence. It was thought that public confidence in industry and in enforcement bodies suffered if the perpetrator appeared to escape prosecution or conviction on a technicality rather than having his culpability tested in court by the same standards as that court would apply to a private individual on a charge of manslaughter.' Neither the DPP or CPS progressed the case, therefore making it one of the focus cases seen by the public as the authorities failing to administer justice through the courts.

---

1 Law Commission Report, Legislating the Criminal Code: Involuntary Manslaughter, 1996.

2.18   The report into the *Marchioness* tragedy[1] was passed in March 2001 to the Director of Public Prosecution, David Calvert-Smith for review. The Deputy Prime Minister, John Prescott appointed the Right Hon Lord Justice Clarke to conduct the public enquiry into safety on the river Thames and the circumstances surrounding the sinking of the *Marchioness* pleasure cruiser. The report places responsibility on the skipper, the owners and the managers of the *Marchioness* and the Dredger *Bowbelle*.

1 *Thames Safety Inquiry: Final Report* (Cm 4558, HMSO, 2000).

2.19   The media reported at the time that there was criticism at there not being a public enquiry earlier as it might have been possible to take disciplinary action against Captain Douglas Henderson, master of the *Bowbelle*, under the Merchant Shipping Act 1988. It would have been unfair to take any action so long after the event because he was entitled to have any case brought against him within a *reasonable time*; after 11 years there was little prospect of a successful prosecution.

2.20   Corporate memory fails, as can be shown in the incident involving the *Princess Alice*,[1] a paddle steamer, launched in 1865 and built for pleasure cruising on the Thames. For 13 years she carried holidaymakers up and down the river, but the party came to a terrifying end on 3 September 1878. Returning at dusk from an excursion to the Thames estuary with around 750 passengers aboard, she was sliced in two by the *Bywell Castle,* an 890 ton collier steaming down river. The *Princess Alice* sank immediately and despite some heroic rescue attempts about 640 passengers and crew lost their lives. The Board of Trade held an inquiry and the owners of the two steamers brought legal actions against each other. There were accusations and counter-accusations, claims and counterclaims. What clearly emerged was the need for more stringent shipping regulations and a strict compliance with them.

1 Bond, J, 1996, *The Hazards of Life and All That.*

The Great Western Trains Disaster

2.21   The dramatic newspaper headlines of an article by J Twomey[1] declared, 'Judge attacks Government for failure to bring in law of corporate killing – No one can be tried over this carnage'. It was the opening of an article reporting on the corporate manslaughter trial of Great Western Trains. The judge launched a stinging attack on the Government as he threw out manslaughter charges against a railway company which had been accused of the deaths of seven passengers.

1 J Twomey, *Daily Express*, 3 July 1999.

2.22   The case of *Great Western Trains Ltd*[1] involved the 10.32am Swansea to London Paddington train, which was driven by Larry Harrison. The train, which was an Inter City 125, passed through a red signal at 125 mph and crashed into a freight train near Southall Station in West London. The train was fitted with two safety devices, which could have prevented the incident, but neither was working. As a result, the company was charged with corporate manslaughter and the train driver with individual manslaughter. It was anticipated that the managing director of GWT, Richard George, would be personally charged with manslaughter because of his responsibility to ensure that trains follow adequate safety procedures. The train driver had looked down to pack his bag and had therefore not seen the red signal. The case against him was dropped because it was said that the crash had left him psychologically unfit to face trial. The case for the Crown failed because it failed to identify a senior figure within GWT who was the *directing mind and will* and who failed to ensure the safety of the passengers.

---

1 *Attorney-General's Reference (No 2 of 1999)* [2000] QB 796.

2.23   This was a landmark case and focused on the prosecution of a large corporation, Great Western Trains Ltd for corporate manslaughter, which, as reported, was terminated by the Old Bailey judge, Mr Justice Scott Baker:[1]

> 'The Old Bailey judge rebuked ministers for failing to act on the recommendations of the Law Commission three years ago to introduce a new offence of corporate killing.'

The impact of this ruling for the future of corporate manslaughter prosecutions means that no large organisation can ever be prosecuted for manslaughter unless there is a radical change in the law. In his article, Twomey continued:

> 'Attorney General John Morris is to appeal against the findings ... The case against the company foundered on an age old principle ... For the prosecution to succeed, the Crown had to identify a senior figure within GWT who was the *directing mind and will,* and who failed to ensure the safety of the passengers.'

---

1 Twomey, J, *Daily Express*, 3 July 1999.

2.24   This again defines the basis of corporate manslaughter failings which was clarified by the judge who said:

> 'The only basis on which the prosecution may, in law, advance a case against Great Western Trains for manslaughter is by identifying some person within

the company whose gross negligence was that of Great Western Trains itself. The only candidate would be managing director Richard George, who was responsible for all matters of safety. In the absence of Mr George having procured, authorised or directed any tortuous act, he cannot be guilty of manslaughter. Consequently, neither can Great Western Trains ... were the law otherwise, a conviction would mark public abhorrence of a slipshod safety system leading to seven deaths and many injured victims.'

The impact of this ruling for the future of corporate manslaughter prosecutions means that no large organisation can ever be prosecuted for manslaughter unless there is a radical change in the law.

2.25   In addition to the charge of corporate manslaughter against Great Western Trains being dropped, the train driver, Larry Harrison walked free after the prosecution stated that the crash had left him psychologically unfit to face trial. He took early retirement and received a pension. In reviewing the case it was accepted that the train was faulty because the automatic warning and protection systems were not working and there was no second driver in the cab. However, he was the driver and was under a duty undertake his work task correctly and he failed to do so. The case would have lasted several weeks and Mr Harrison would have been unable to pay a fine and would probably have been unfit to serve a prison sentence. It could be argued that he was the victim of a corporate culture of failure.

Port Ramsgate case

2.26   In 1995 six people were killed and seven others seriously injured when a ferry walkway at the Port of Ramsgate collapsed. This was not a manslaughter case, and the company was prosecuted under health & safety legislation. The outcome of the trial was a record fine of £1.7 million. Two Swedish companies responsible for the design and construction of the walkway were fined £1 million, Lloyd's Register of Shipping £500,000 and Port Ramsgate Ltd £200,000. Mr Justice Clarke determined that the companies had been guilty of gross negligence and that the level of fines were in part to deliver a message to boardrooms of companies and the controlling minds of all organisations that the safety of the public is paramount. Port Ramsgate Ltd and the Swedish firms denied failing to ensure the safety of passengers, but were found guilty after a four week trial. Lloyd's Register of Shipping, which had issued a safety certificate, had pleaded guilty. The Swedish companies were tried and sentenced in their absence, not guilty pleas having been entered on their behalf. Fartygsentreprenader AB (FEAB) was fined £750,000 and Fartygskonstruktioner AB (FKAB) (who designed the walkway) was fined £250,000. In addition costs of £251,000 were awarded jointly against these two companies. Lloyds register was fined £500,000 plus costs and Port Ramsgate Ltd were fined a total of £100,000. As of this date the two Swedish companies have not paid either their fines or costs. This case raises the issue of liability with foreign companies operating in the UK who it appears can undertake work but not be liable for criminal offences.

Ladbroke Grove railway disaster

2.27 On 5 October 1999, a train passed a red signal at Ladbroke Grove and continued on for some 700 metres into the path of a high-speed train. As a result of the collision and the subsequent fires, 31 people died and 227 were taken to hospital.

2.28 An inquiry following the incident identified that there had been several incidents where drivers had crossed signal SN 109 at red. Mr David Franks, the Production Director of Thames Trains, informed the inquiry[1] that both the seventh and eighth occasions on which the signal was passed at danger (SPAD) had involved experienced drivers; in view of the failure of Railtrack to carry out remedial action, he stated:

'I insisted that Railtrack should accept that the primary cause of these SPADs was the signalling equipment itself. I accepted the drivers had some responsibility but this was not the root cause'.

1 Ladbroke Grove Rail Inquiry Part 2, Executive Summary by Lord Cullen.

2.29 In his report, Lord Cullen stated in the summary (at para 1.15):

'The evidence clearly demonstrated that the rail industry needs to develop the ability to behave as a learning organisation. I identify a number of areas of importance. Firstly, identifying unsafe acts and conditions and taking prompt steps to deal with them. Secondly, applying and disseminating the lessons of accidents and incidents (including near misses). Here the evidence showed the process was inhibited by the "blame culture", and the lack of a co-ordinated system for the collation of recommendations and ensuring that they were followed up. Thirdly, using risk assessment in order to drive improvements in safety. Fourthly, gaining benefit from the process of auditing. This has been less than fully effective. Fifthly, using data and analytical tools. The evidence shows there were weaknesses in the industry's use of these materials. Sixthly, training with particular reference to refresher courses, into which greater effort requires to be put'.

2.30 Further, at para 1.16, Lord Cullen states:

'Finally I direct attention to the desirability of the industry developing a culture in which there is a progressive movement from a situation where management make the rules and tell employees what to do, to a situation where individuals can contribute ideas and effort, while complying with the rules and procedures, through to a position where there is a committed, dedicated team approach, with a high degree of interdependency between teams and across company boundaries'.

2.31   To conform with Lord Cullen's recommendations to enable employees to contribute ideas and effort, local management teams can be formed to close out their own incidents and implement improvements and, on a regular basis, senior management can review the incidents and confirm their approval of the improvement measures taken by the local teams. A team from senior management with operational and engineering skills can be established to monitor trends and, having recognised a trend, may request line management to issue a series of measures to mitigate against further incidents.

2.32   Thames Trains was fined £2 million in December 2003 for two breaches of the Health and Safety at Work etc Act 1974 (HSWA 1974) for failing to protect its employees (s 2(1)) and the public (s 3(1)). Specifically, there were serious omissions in its driver-training programme. It took a further three years to bring Network Rail, which replaced Railtrack as the infrastructure controller in 2002, to trial.[1]

---

1 HSB No 358 May 2007.

2.33   The court heard that Railtrack had been warned five years before the collision that the signals were poorly laid out and that drivers had misinterpreted them on seven occasions since November 1995. Despite an internal inquiry, it did nothing. It was described by Philip Mott QC as a 'catalogue of failures' that 'started with the culture at the top of the body ... and affected staff at all levels of the organisation'.

2.34   Sentencing Network Rail on 30 March, Mr Justice Bean said that the crash had been the result of 'incompetent management and inadequate process'. The offence had been aggravated by the seriousness of the risk involved in the breach of duty, which was 'underlined by the disastrous consequences' and the persistence of its failures in the months before the crash. He fined Network Rail £4 million and ordered them to pay costs of £225,000 for safety failures.

Potters Bar railway disaster

2.35   In an article by Dipesh Gadher[1] the headlines stated: 'Rail Contractor to Escape Potters Bar Death Charges'. The Potters Bar railway crash happened in May 2002 after the last coach of a four-carriage train travelling from London to Cambridge derailed when passing over points at Potters Bar station in Hertfordshire. An HSE report earlier in 2003 stated that nuts were absent from the rear stretcher bar of the points and that the appropriate lock mechanism was worn out. This ruled out the likelihood of sabotage, which was a claim made by

Jarvis, the maintenance company, immediately after the derailment. The HSE report concluded that the poor condition of the points 'resulted from inappropriate adjustment and from insufficient maintenance'.

---

1 Gadher, D, *Sunday Times*, 24 August 2003.

2.36 The Sunday Times article revealed that executives at Jarvis, the company at the centre of the investigation into the rail crash, were expected to escape manslaughter charges. The reason given was that the police believed there was insufficient evidence for a criminal case against the engineering contractor despite an investigation lasting 15 months.

2.37 The final decision rested with the Crown Prosecution Service (CPS) where lawyers would have reviewed the evidence gathered and compiled by British Transport Police (BTP) investigators. This is said to have consisted of more than 1,300 statements as well as CCTV footage from station cameras which was sent to the FBI in America for analysis.

2.38 Jarvis, however, still faced the possibility of being brought to court for alleged breaches of health and safety laws. This meant that if the CPS decided not to proceed with manslaughter charges then the case could be taken up by the HSE which had been carrying out a parallel investigation. The families of those killed and injured wanted to pursue a damages claim against Jarvis and Railtrack, the company which managed Britain's rail infrastructure at the time of the tragedy. But they had been denied legal aid and were, at that time, unable to fund a case in the civil courts which could have forced the two firms to admit liability for the crash. The key argument was that even if the CPS was unable to bring manslaughter charges it did not mean that a case cannot be proven in a civil court that, on the balance of probabilities, Railtrack and Jarvis were to blame.

2.39 The article[1] raised the issue that Jarvis executives had provoked outrage when they raised the prospect of escaping serious criminal charges. Noel Broadbent, the company's director of compliance and standards, predicted the police would 'give up' soon. Paris Moayedi, Jarvis's chairman, also drew criticism by claiming that the HSE's findings had 'no concrete backing'. In an emotive confrontation between the two sides, Perdita Kark, whose father, Austen, former head of the BBC World Service, was killed and whose mother, the author Nina Bawden, was badly injured, was quoted as saying, 'This is absolute rubbish and it is deeply offensive'.

Any undertaking will want to defend itself against serious legal charges and adverse statements from the senior management will only inflame the public perception of a 'don't care' corporate culture.

---

1 Gadher, D, *Sunday Times*, 24 August 2003.

2.40   The outcome was that the senior managers accused of negligence following the Potters Bar rail crash that killed seven people were not charged with manslaughter offences. The CPS concluded that there was 'insufficient evidence' to pursue criminal charges against any individual or company, despite finding 'systemic failures' on the part of engineering firm Jarvis and Railtrack, now Network Rail. The CPS also uncovered considerable 'confusion' in the industry over who exactly was responsible for the maintenance of the track following a ten-month review of evidence provided by the British Transport Police. A three-year investigation by the Rail Safety and Standards Board into the causes of the Potters Bar crash demanded a review of the frequency of maintenance examinations. The investigators discovered a series of misalignments that had put points under greater stress than necessary. Jarvis has apologised for its role in the disaster. Railtrack had been wound up and a new public interest company, Network Rail, created with entirely new management. The question asked was what was to be gained by punishing the new company for the previous misdeeds in such a case. However, the HSE has continued to examine whether Jarvis or Network Rail should be charged under the HSWA 1974; if found guilty they would face unlimited fines. No individuals will be charged in connection with the crash.

Hatfield rail accident

2.41   In January 2001 the railways suffered another devastating blow when a train crashed at Hatfield and four people were killed. The accident investigation found that a defect in the line had been discovered in November 1999 by Balfour Beatty and reported to Railtrack soon after. In contravention of the rules no speed restrictions were imposed. A report identified that work to replace the track should have been conducted but was not completed because a machine that would have speeded up the process did not arrive. Management should have closed the line or imposed a speed restriction, but this was not done.

2.42   The British Transport police believed that there was sufficient evidence to bring a prosecution for corporate manslaughter. In addition they believed that there was sufficient evidence to charge individuals with manslaughter, including three from Railtrack and two from Balfour Beatty. For a prosecution to succeed the CPS would have needed to identify key executives who were negligent and *controlling minds* responsible for directing the will of the company. The police stated that they had such individuals. It was said that the evidence was in the form of documents which identified individuals in Railtrack and Balfour Beatty as having been warned about safety problems but who had failed in their duty. The CPS examined the evidence in order to identify the individuals that should be deemed to be the *controlling minds*, which has in the case of large companies proved to be an impossible task.

2.43 The CPS concluded that no board director would face prosecution. This meant that even with guilty knowledge, the *controlling minds* would not face trial for manslaughter or even lesser offences. Those who faced prosecution were further down the command chain, a situation that the law reformers have sought to remedy by having those at board level held accountable.

2.44 For breaching Health and Safety law Balfour Beatty was fined £10 million and Network Rail £3.5 million. Balfour Beatty appealed against the size of the fine; their lawyers argued that the fine was excessive and did not credit the company with pleading guilty.[1] The Court of Appeal Judges, Lord Phillips, the Lord Chief Justice, sitting with Mr Justice Nelson and Mr Justice Silber, upheld the appeal. The record £10 million fine imposed was reduced to £7.5 million by the Court of Appeal. The appeal judges stated:

> 'We consider there is scope for a reduction in the interests of proportionality which will still do justice to the applicable principles and, in particular, to the victims of the Hatfield disaster.'

Until the Hatfield case, the largest fine imposed in the English courts for health and safety failings was £2 million on Thames Trains following the 1999 Paddington rail crash. A more detailed review of the Hatfield prosecutions and the outcomes are described in Chapter 4.

---

1 Press Association, July 5, 2006.

Transco gas explosion, Scotland

2.45 A large gas explosion destroyed a house in Lanarkshire in 1999, claiming the lives of Andrew Findlay, 34, his wife Janette, 37, and their children, Stacey, 13, and Daryl, 11. It had been caused by a leak from a severely corroded gas main outside their home. It had been proposed that the company should be prosecuted on a charge of culpable homicide. It would have been the first 'corporate killing' trial in Scotland, but Transco persuaded appeal judges to dismiss the charge, which named no individual director or employee. The Crown was left only with a charge under the HSWA 1974 which, although not carrying the same condemnation as culpable homicide, also exposed Transco on conviction to an unlimited fine.

2.46 J Roberson[1] provides an insight into the background of the case by explaining that the Larkhall main was laid in 1973, but Transco's records were in such disarray that some sections were said to have been laid in the 1980s and some in the 1990s, and it was stated that stretches of the pipe were made of polyethylene and not ductile iron. For years before the blast, it had been known in the industry that ductile iron was susceptible to corrosion in certain soil types within ten years of being laid. There had been a number of explosions in England which highlighted the problem, and while Transco resolved to take proactive measures to address the risks, it failed to increase significantly the level of ductile iron replacement.

---

1 Roberson, J, *Scotsman*, 26 August 2005.

2.47   In another report[1] it was revealed that gas bosses had been warned seven years before the Findlay family died that the main gas pipe was too close to the homes on the street. A senior gas engineer highlighted the risk to the firm which later became Transco, after seeing plans for new homes in Larkhall in the early 1990s.

---

1 *Sunday Mail*, August 28, 2005.

2.48   Figures released revealed that the Transco chief executive, Roger Urwin saw his pay increase to £1.13 million from £1.05 million the year before. Urwin, 59, also had a £7.3 million pension fund. Transco were shamed by auditors in 2000, just a few months after the Larkhall tragedy. It emerged that they had underspent their agreed pipeline maintenance and replacement programme by £358 million over the previous two years to benefit shareholders.

2.49   Roberson, in his article, stated:

'... Transco showed a lack of grace when its spokesman declined to say sorry after being fined £15 million for breaching health and safety laws ... During the trial at the High Court in Edinburgh, the prosecutor suggested Transco had put profits before safety, the company had tried to put the blame on an internal pipe leak, something for which it was not responsible. Lord Carloway said that that attempt was "despite overwhelming evidence to the contrary, including the views of their own employees on site after the explosion". He added: "There was no evidence at all in this case that such an internal leak had occurred. That aspect of the defence by the company serves only to demonstrate that the corporate mind of Transco has little or no remorse for this tragedy which, they ought at least now to accept, was exclusively their own creation." '

2.50   He also highlighted that:

- The Lord Advocate, Colin Boyd QC, believed that Transco's failings had shown:

  'a complete and utter disregard for the safety of the public'

- The Advocate-Depute, Frank Mulholland, QC, in his closing speech to the jury, submitted that:

  'from 1988 until the Larkhall tragedy, Transco had replaced 'a derisory amount of ductile iron, far less than was required to deal with the problem."

Over several years, a number of gas escapes from the main had been reported by members of the public, but no steps had been taken to determine the extent of corrosion that had occurred or the likely rate of corrosion. Mr Mulholland said:

> 'The public trusted Transco to respond appropriately when they realised their mains were unsafe. They also trusted Transco to have accurate records of what they had in the ground. In this case, it is quite clear that this trust was misplaced. This was an accident waiting to happen.'

2.51   The trial also identified additional failings when Lord Carloway said:

> 'During the period up until the explosion at Larkhall, substantial sections of the public were exposed to significant danger from corroded and corroding ductile iron mains in close proximity to their homes and workplaces.'

He continued:

> 'Transco were well aware that sections might already be corroded and that this could cause a leak and result in a serious incident, potentially involving multiple fatalities ...'

It was of some note, said the judge:

> '... that in the mid-1990s there had been sharp staff cuts and other cost-saving exercises throughout the company. Billions were being spent on re-organising the structure of the company.'

Lord Carloway said:

> 'That aspect of the defence by the company serves only to demonstrate that the corporate mind of Transco has little or no remorse for this tragedy which they ought, at least now, to accept as exclusively their own creation ...'

2.52   The company had been doing pretty well, making £390 million after tax. The explosion in Larkhall ruffled no papers on the desk of the company's bookkeepers. Focusing corporate minds is what health and safety legislation is supposed to do. Lord Carloway has done his best to use this law by imposing a fine that is 15 times higher than anything awarded in Scotland before, and seven-and-a-half times the £2 million handed down to Thames Trains for the Ladbroke Grove rail disaster. Under the law, Lord Carloway could have set any penalty he liked. The death of the Findlays proves that the richer and more powerful you are, the less you need concern yourself with the law. Ruaridh Nicoll[1] reported:

> '... Transco showed a lack of grace when its spokesman declined to say sorry after being fined £15 million for breaching health and safety laws ... Part of National Grid, it is one of the major energy suppliers, so any confession would be tested to destruction by lawyers concerned about

further liability. Yet the judge's words at the end of this epic trial, in which he focused on Transco's attempt to slither away by blaming the Findlay's themselves, shows an apology is exactly what he wanted to see.'

---

1 Nicoll, R, *Observer*, 8 August 2005.

2.53   Transco had been charged with culpable homicide, the first company to face such a sanction in Scotland. Transco's lawyers argued that the whole company could not face such a charge. Lord Carloway disagreed, but was overturned on appeal. With only the health and safety charges remaining, Transco argued that the case was too complicated for a jury to understand and Lord Carloway dismissed that, too.

2.54   Transco tried to block Alastair McMurtrie from testifying during the trial. Mr McMurtrie, a chartered engineer who still works in the gas industry, made recommendations to his superiors that the houses being built on the Carlisle Road were too close to the gas main that supplied Larkhall. He said it would have cost just £20,000 to divert it away from the new houses and, under guidelines at the time, if the builders refused to pay, gas bosses should have picked up the costs. However, when the builders refused to pay, no further action was taken. Mr McMurtrie gave evidence early in the six-month trial. Transco lawyers continued to try to block his evidence. Having been asked by prosecutors whether he had recommended diverting the main, counsel for the defence leapt to his feet, demanding: 'Don't answer that.' But Mr McMurtrie had already said, 'Yes'. Lord Carloway allowed prosecutors to continue questioning him.

2.55   The BBC News[1] stated:

> 'Transco is no longer responsible for Scotland's gas supply network. The firm sold it earlier this year and it is now owned by Scotia Gas Networks, which is part of Scottish and Southern Energy. Transco's full statement said: "Transco has always deeply regretted the terrible tragedy at Larkhall in 1999, and we apologise for what happened. Our thoughts remain with the family and community affected by the explosion. We said at the time of the verdict that we were disappointed and this is still the case. However, we have decided not to appeal the verdict, in order that these proceedings can be brought to a close for all concerned. We are deeply sorry that this tragedy ever happened. Since 2000, we have worked closely with the HSE and Ofgem and invested nearly £2bn in our networks. Over the next five years, we have agreed a replacement programme that will involve the same amount again being spent. Whilst nothing we do or say can make amends for the terrible tragedy, safety remains our number one priority." '

The trial lasted six months and following a guilty verdict the judge fined the company £15 million.

---

1 www.bbc.co.uk, 8 September 2005.

BP Texas City disaster

2.56   A disaster that occurred outside of the UK had an impact on one of the largest household name companies in the country, BP. In this case BP was operating in the USA and was sited at the Texas City disaster which killed 15 people and injured 180. The reports that resulted from the investigation were damning against BP's senior management, in particular, Lord Browne the chief executive.

2.57   According to the US Chemical Safety Board (CSB), a series of situations evolved on the day of the explosion, 23 March 2005. It involved a 170-foot tower, known as a blowdown drum which was being refilled with liquid hydrocarbons following a maintenance shutdown. An employee, who was working the nightshift and had worked 12-hour shifts for 33 consecutive days, began filling the tower. However, inadequate notes were left for a day operator who took over the task at 6am, working his 29th consecutive day of duty. There were two managers, who were supposed to be overseeing events, but they had worked 37 and 31 days respectively and a supervisor had departed the site early to deal with a family medical emergency. The tower was overfilled with the result that some 7,600 gallons of unstable chemicals shot into the sky over a 107-second period, causing a geyser of some 7 metres. This in turn formed a cloud of flammable vapour over the refinery, which was ignited by a spark from a truck idling nearby.

2.58   Four workers who were filling the tank when it exploded were among the 15 people killed. Most of the others who died were in the administration accommodation which had been placed too close to the tower. In addition to those who died a further 180 people were injured, 70 vehicles were damaged and windows were shattered as far away as three-quarters of a mile.

2.59   Carolyn Merritt, chairwoman of the CSB,[1] a government-backed agency, identified that there was an 'iron-clad case' for pinning some of the responsibility on budget cuts and stated:

> 'Budget cuts had an impact on safety and that impact on safety had a causal relationship with what happened on March 23 … We have an iron-clad case for the impact of cost-cutting on safety … a series of "geyser-like releases" of flammable liquid similar to the one that caused the explosion had already occurred, but a culture of "complacency and disregard for the inherent danger of what was being done" existed at all levels of the company … The message that was communicated was that cost-cutting and maximising profits was the most important thing.'

1 Dan Milmo, *The Guardian*, 22 January 2007.

2.60   The report also states that there is evidence to suggest that the operators' fatigue degraded their judgment and problem-solving skills. This hindered their ability to determine that the tower was overfilling. This was combined with evidence that there were misleading readings from poorly maintained measurement equipment.

2.61   A key issue in the CSB report[1] identifies that the disaster was caused by organisational and safety deficiencies at all levels of the BP management. Cost cuts enforced by the company's London headquarters contributed to the disaster because it was said that senior management had ignored successive warnings that an accident was imminent.

---

1 Clark, Andrew, March 20, 2007, Guardian Unlimited.

2.62   BP endured serious criticism; in particular Lord Browne. As the chief executive and head of the BP board of directors he had not exercised effective safety oversight. One outcome was that Lord Browne brought forward his retirement.

2.63   BP headquarters stated:

> 'While we cannot change the past or repair all the damage this incident caused, we have worked diligently to provide fair compensation, without the need for lengthy court proceedings, to those who were injured and to the families of those who died.'

2.64   Among the key issues resulting from the report's findings was that following its merger with Amoco in 1999, BP ordered a 25% cut in costs. At Texas City, capital spending had already been reduced by 84% in eight years. The refinery's training budget was halved over the five years to 2004 from $2.8m to $1.4m and its 28 staff were cut to eight. The company relied heavily on cheaper computer-based training which focused on 'memorising facts' and box-ticking rather than troubleshooting. Because of a lack of attention to the subject, staff were given the impression that safety procedures were 'not strict instructions but outdated documents to be used as a guideline'.

2.65   To make matters worse in 2002, a senior BP executive in Houston warned that the ageing infrastructure at Texas City was 'in complete decline' and just five months before the disaster, an internal plant safety meeting included a slide warning: 'Texas City is not a safe place to work.'

2.66   The report identified the underlying causes as follows:

- Over the years, the working environment had eroded to one characterised by resistance to change, and lacking in trust, motivation, and a sense of purpose. Coupled with unclear expectations around supervisory and management behaviours this meant that rules were not consistently followed, rigour was lacking and individuals felt disempowered from suggesting or initiating improvements.

- Process safety, operations performance and systematic risk reduction priorities had not been set and consistently reinforced by management.

- Many changes in a complex organisation had led to the lack of clear accountabilities and poor communication, which together resulted in confusion in the workforce over roles and responsibilities.

- A poor level of hazard awareness and understanding of process safety on the site resulted in people accepting levels of risk that are considerably higher than comparable installations. One consequence was that temporary office trailers were placed within 150 feet of a blowdown stack which vented heavier than air hydrocarbons to the atmosphere without questioning the established industry practice.

- Given the poor vertical communication and performance management process, there was neither adequate early warning system of problems, nor any independent means of understanding the deteriorating standards in the plant.

- The underlying reasons for the behaviours and actions displayed during the incident are complex, and the team had spent much time trying to understand them.

It is not possible to review the report in detail but there is evidence that there was management failure within BP senior management leading to a major disaster. It must be said that BP strongly disagreed with some of the content of the Chemical Safety Board's report, particularly many of the findings and conclusions.

2.67   In context, if the accident occurred in the UK with the offence of corporate manslaughter and corporate homicide available the evidence in the Texas City report provides many of the ingredients for the prosecution of the company. In future, while senior management cannot be prosecuted, their actions will be under detailed scrutiny and will form a major part of the prosecution's case. If an individual's action amounts to gross negligence then that individual could be charged with manslaughter. The Crown will be required to prove there was gross breach of a relevant duty of care and that the way the defendant company's activities were managed by its senior managers was a 'substantial' element in the breach. Part of the case will focus on organisational charts, board and safety committee minutes, e-mails, internal memos and all other relevant communications. In addition a major element will be the question of safety and a jury will have to consider the attitudes, policies, systems or accepted practices within the organisation that were likely to have encouraged any such failure or to have produced tolerance of it. Therefore, the elements of a safety culture, or lack of it, will become a key issue at trial and it will be a matter for the defendant company to show that they had a positive, trusting and open business environment in place, with effective lines of communication between management and workforce.

Summary

2.68   From the cases above the reader will identify that there are numerous lessons to be learned. The concept of management failure is not clear-cut and defined but it is evident that those at the very top of an organisation set the standards by which the rest of the organisation will abide. If they fail to set effective standards then it could be argued that they have failed and they could be exposed to a case of corporate manslaughter.

Chapter 3

Corporate and Individual Manslaughter Cases

Introduction

3.1   There are demands from the public for the use of the law to charge corporations with manslaughter at work offences. However, there is also evidence that public opinion considers it wrong if all the blame is placed on a junior employee. If it is the directors who determine the operational philosophy as the *controlling minds* and have the most to gain from the corporation, then they should carry the overall responsibility.

3.2   The following cases are an example of small company manslaughter prosecution and show where custodial sentences have been awarded. In some cases the defendant actually spends time in prison, while in others the sentence is suspended. This means that the defendant does not go to prison and providing he does not offend during the period of the suspension he will not go to prison. The whole subject of manslaughter prosecution is fraught with problems. Many cases are seen to be similar, but one results in a manslaughter conviction while another has an outcome where there is a minimal fine.

3.3   For many years it had been thought that a corporation could not be guilty of manslaughter, because the law of homicide required the killing of a human being to be the outcome of an act by another human being. On this basis Justice Finlay in *Cory Bros Ltd* (1927) (see below) made the decision to quash an indictment against a company for manslaughter. It was clear that he found himself bound by earlier authorities, which he concluded, showed *quite clearly* that an indictment would not lie against a corporation for a case involving personal violence. This case was, however, decided before the principle of *identification* was developed.

Cory Bros Limited

3.4   The case of *Cory Bros Ltd*[1] was an interesting case in that it was a private prosecution brought by the deceased's brother through the South Wales Miners' Federation. The basis of the case involved the directors of a private mining company, who during the miners strike of 1926, erected a fence around a power house belonging to the company. It was intended to provide protection against pilfering by strikers and their families, but to make the fence totally effective it was electrified.

---

1 *R v Cory Bros Ltd* [1927] 1 KB 810; Law Commission 237 (1996).

3.5   The deceased was an unemployed miner, who was scavenging close to the fence when he fell against it and was electrocuted. The South Wales Miners' Federation determined that the company and three of its engineers had set a predetermined mantrap and supported the private prosecution against them for manslaughter. Committal proceedings against the company and the engineers were successful but the outcome was to determine that the law did not allow an indictment to lie against a corporation. The charges against the three individual engineers remained. They were prosecuted but were acquitted.

Northern Strip Mining (Construction) Co Ltd

3.6   It was to be some 38 years before another case of corporate man-slaughter was to reach the courts. During this time the attitudes of the courts changed and were highlighted in the case of *Northern Strip Mining Construc-*

tions Co Ltd. The case involved a welder-burner who was drowned when a railway bridge, which the company was demolishing, collapsed. Employees had been instructed to burn down sections of the bridge, starting in its middle. At trial the defendant company was acquitted on the facts of the case, but neither counsel nor the presiding judge appeared to have any doubt about the validity of the indictment; and the defence counsel seems to have concurred with those opinions. It was reported[1] that the judge argued that it was the prosecution's task to show that the defendant company, in the person of the managing director, was guilty of such a degree of negligence that it amounted to a reckless disregard for the life and limbs of his workmen. There does not seem to be any report of the argument or of the judge's reasons. It is the identification principle that has been the key factor to corporate manslaughter offences and the reason for failure to obtain convictions.

---

1 *Northern Strip Mining Constructions Co Ltd*, The Times 2, 4 and 5 February 1965.

OLL Ltd – Lyme Bay Canoe Tragedy – Peter Kite case

3.7   The most important case in the development of a corporate offence for manslaughter occurred with the first conviction in English legal history of a company for corporate manslaughter. The case is *R v OLL Ltd and Peter Bayliss Kite*,[1] heard in Winchester Crown Court, which was more commonly known as the *Lyme Bay canoe tragedy*. It is an interesting case in that it identifies management failure to ensure a safe activity, leading to a conviction for gross negligence manslaughter, when evidence showed that warnings about safety had been given.

---

1 *R v OLL Ltd* (1994) unreported.

3.8   The company, known as Active Learning and Leisure Limited and which operated as a leisure centre at St Alban's Centre in Lyme Regis, was charged with corporate manslaughter and as a result of the trial, convicted of that offence. The corporate structure was that Mr Kite was the managing director, and Mr Stoddart was the manager. Therefore the company was a one man operation so the *directing mind* was that of its managing director and the company's liability came from the *'directing mind'* having formed the *mens rea.* A company can only act and be criminally responsible through its officers or those in a position of real responsibility in conducting the company's affairs. In other words if it is proved that some person or persons who were the *controlling minds* of the company were themselves in the case guilty of manslaughter then the company is likewise guilty.

3.9   The outcome was that on 8 December 1994 Peter Kite was found guilty of individual manslaughter and jailed for three years. The case against the

Lyme Bay centre manager Joe Stoddart was dropped when the jury failed to reach a verdict. The company, OLL Limited, was convicted of corporate manslaughter and fined £60,000.

3.10   The incident involved a group of sixth form students from the Southway Comprehensive school in Plymouth who were participants in an activity holiday at the St Albans Challenge Centre at Lyme Regis. Canoeing was among the range of activities that were available to the students and, as part of the introduction to the activity, the party was given a half-hour basic instruction with canoes in the swimming pool. The following day members of the party decided which activities they wanted to do and eight pupils and one teacher decided to go canoeing. Two instructors, one male and one female, neither of whom were qualified to teach canoeing, accompanied this group of novices. Each participant was provided with a wetsuit and life jacket, but no foot or head wear. The day's activity plan was basic and involved paddling from Lyme Regis to Charmouth and back, a journey to be undertaken at sea.

3.11   At about 10.00 am the party set off and soon encountered problems. One of the students' canoes capsized and it required the male instructor to right the craft and help the student back into it. The teacher then capsized and required the male instructor to assist in recovery of the canoe and help the teacher back into the canoe. During this incident, the female instructor directed the others to *raft up* in a line so making a more controlled and stable group. However, the group was drifting out to sea and the wind had increased causing the waves to get bigger, all adding to the students' problems. They then became seasick which in turn caused distress, and added to the very evident concern as to their situation. While they did what they could to help one another, the problems developed rapidly with canoes capsizing and depositing the students in the cold water, clinging to the upturned craft.

3.12   The group was in serious trouble and because of a management failure, they had no method of raising the alarm. Nobody onshore was aware of any possible problems and so the hours passed with the youngsters in the water, cold, tired and distressed. In an act of desperation two students decided to swim to shore and as events unfolded were the last to be rescued. The male instructor and teacher were located some eight miles down the coast, having been in the sea for seven hours. The main group was rescued two and a half miles from the nearest coast. The final outcome was that four of the youngsters died as a result of the tragedy.

3.13   Mr Peter Kite, the managing director of Active Learning and Leisure Ltd, the operators of the centre, had failed to ensure the safety of the group. He had been notified in writing by previous employees of the failings in safety procedures and equipment. The ill-fated group had gone to sea, with very limited instruction, unqualified instructors, and no flares for alerting the coastguard, no emergency plan and no support boat. The students had not been taught how to work their life jackets; nor were they told to inflate them when they were in the water. The situation was compounded when the group failed to return, and the management delayed in alerting the rescue services.

3.14   The prosecution alleged that Kite, as the managing director of OLL Ltd, had the primary responsibility for devising, instituting, enforcing and maintaining an appropriate safety policy and was therefore responsible for the safety standards at the centre which were found to be deficient. By way of industry standards it was said that the defendants had breached guidelines issued by the British Canoe Union.

3.15   Reliance during the case was placed on a brochure published by OLL Ltd and it was submitted at the trial that the judge did not give the jury the guidance that they could expect in relation to the relevance of the brochure. The prosecution also relied on the letter written by Miss Cawthorne and Mr Retallick, previous instructors with OLL Ltd, and the facts of that letter are quoted in part:

> 'At present we are walking a very fine line between *getting away with it* and having a very serious incident ... We would also like to know why we do not get supplied with a first-aid kit and tow-line ... It's unsafe and not organised ... having seen your 1993 brochure and planned expansion, we think you should have a very careful look at your standards of safety, otherwise you might find yourselves trying to explain why someone's son or daughter, will not be coming home. Nobody wishes or wants that to happen, but it will sooner or later.'

3.16   It was Mr Kite's case, through his evidence, that he took that letter seriously, and had acted upon the contents. The report identifies that the letter was written in 1992 and, consequently, it might not provide very useful evidence as to the situation as it was in March 1993. In fact it could be argued that it would be very good evidence because if notice had been taken and the concerns actioned, then a safe system of working would have been in place. It was identified in the evidence that Mr Kite had made considerable efforts to comply with the complaints that were raised, and that substantial changes had taken place. It again could be argued that the changes were not suitable and sufficient, particularly based upon the evidence that convicted Mr Kite.

3.17   In addition to those matters the prosecution alleged that Mr Kite had failed to supervise Mr Stoddart which, as the *controlling mind* of the company, he was expected to do. Expert evidence was called by the prosecution, and a number of criticisms were made including, in particular, the lack of experience and suitability of Mr Mann and Miss Gardner as instructors to lead the canoeing expedition.

3.18   Mr Kite gave evidence on his own behalf and he stated the he was responsible for overall policy and money matters, but left the actual day-to-day operational running of the centre to the manager, Mr Stoddart. He went on to state that he had absolutely no knowledge that novices were taking part in sea activities, and was horrified when he heard that they were and that this accident had occurred. He further stated that he had immediately taken steps in relation to the Cawthorne letter and had fulfilled his duties in so far as he could in relation to safety precautions.

3.19 A crucial aspect to this case was the fact that Kite had personal knowledge of the safety failings which were referred to in court by Ognall J, who identified the letters sent to Mr Kite months before the tragedy by two competent instructors who had in fact left the centre because they were concerned about safety. The judge told Kite that it was obvious that what separated this case from others was the fact that warnings were given in cold clear terms as to the way he was operating and the potentially fatal consequences of failing to act. It was pointed out that those warnings became reality because of his complete failure to take action and that there was evidence that he was, in part, more interested in sales than safety.

3.20 On 8 December 1994, at Winchester Crown Court, after a trial lasting three weeks, Peter Kite was convicted by a majority verdict on four counts of manslaughter and sentenced to three years' imprisonment on each count concurrently.

3.21 There was never any suggestion that Mr Kite was directly responsible for what occurred on 22 March 1993 because he was not present, but it was his failure to provide a suitable health and safety system that rendered him guilty of the offence. When the judge had passed sentence on Mr Kite he stated that beyond doubt the matters were so serious that they demanded a sentence of immediate custody, and of some substance. While the fact that a term of imprisonment was imposed on Mr Kite as the *controlling mind* was not in question, what was in question, and the subject of the appeal, was whether in all the circumstances of the case, was a sentence of three years' imprisonment too long. It was recognised that court proceedings involving health and safety failings generally cause great difficulties because the court has to make a balanced judgment between two extreme positions. There is the situation when people have been killed through a workplace accident and in particular when the lives of young people have been lost. It is therefore, very natural for the families of the deceased to take the view that no sentence can be too long in the light of what has happened. The opposite situation is where there is an individual who has been convicted of serious offences, where he had no *criminal intent*, but will not readily understand why he has been sent to prison.

Peter Kite appeal

3.22   Peter Kite appealed against his sentence of three years' imprisonment for manslaughter, for his part in the *Lyme Bay* tragedy. Interesting issues were raised by the defence in respect to mitigation in manslaughter at work cases. His appeal was referred to the Court of Appeal.

3.23   With regard to the management failure it is important to define the charge that was laid which was one of manslaughter and that of unlawful killing which although there were nine people in the party, excluding centre staff, the charge was brought against only one person.

3.24   The details of the gross negligence case against Mr Kite were based on the absence of a safe system of operating at the centre, on failing to take notice of the letter from former employees, who made complaints about the absence of safety, and on his failure to adequately supervise the manager. The evidence raised the point that Kite was not directly responsible for the canoeing activities that formed the fatal incident, which was the allegation made by the prosecution against Stoddart, the manager, who was jointly charged with Kite. However, the jury disagreed, and the prosecution decided not to continue the case against Stoddart.

3.25   In the summing up in the Court of Appeal it was recognised that Mr Kite was aged 46 and a man of previously impeccable character. Any prison sentence imposed on a man in these circumstances is, of course, devastating to him. Nonetheless, the facts quite clearly demanded a substantial sentence. Taking those matters of a personal nature together with the facts as proved, the court was persuaded that the sentence imposed by the learned judge was too long. It was proposed to substitute for the sentence of three years' imprisonment one of two years' imprisonment on each count to run concurrently.

3.26   Criminal intent is an interesting issue in health and safety cases. The Health and Safety at Work etc Act 1974 (HSWA 1974) requires every employer to ensure the health and safety of those in his employment and those not in his employment but who could be affected by his activities. The Management of Health and Safety at Work Regulations 1992[1] define more explicitly the requirements of managing health and safety. If an individual or corporation disregards the prescribed legislation and Approved Codes of Practice (ACoPs), then it could be described as intentional and therefore be a criminal act, albeit not in the normal publicly accepted criminal context. It is the task of the court and in particular the jury to determine whether a particular case is one of gross negligence and that is what is often most difficult. In this case the jury came to the conclusion that Mr Kite's conduct was that of gross negligence and found that he was criminally liable, and he was convicted on the basis of his negligence.

---

1   SI 1992/2051.

Jackson Transport

3.27   Following the success of the Lyme Bay case Jackson Transport (Ossett) Limited was convicted in 1996 of corporate manslaughter and fined £22,000. Its director, Alan Jackson, was convicted of the individual manslaughter of one of his employees and jailed for 12 months and fined £1,500. The case centred on 21-year-old James Hodgson, an employee of the company, who died less than an hour after being splashed with a deadly chemical while cleaning the inside of a chemical tanker at Jackson Transport's base in West Ossett, Yorkshire. Mr Hodgson was carrying out the dangerous cleaning job protected only by a pair of overalls and a baseball cap. Special suits for protection against chemical risks were only provided to the tanker drivers of the vehicles and the protective suits that were available on the company's premises were in poor condition and there were no hats, visors or goggles.

3.28   The trial judge, Mr Gerald Coles QC, determined that if Alan Jackson did address the subject of safety clothing he failed to do so adequately. The fact that the deceased was not concerned to wear safety clothing made it all the more important that his employer should have made sure that he not only had it, but that he wore it. This is an important issue, in that not only does the employer have a duty to *provide* adequate and suitable personal protective equipment, he has to ensure that it is *used and used correctly*. In this case the judge found that Jackson was totally indifferent to his statutory duties in that: (i) he failed to address the issues of a system of safety; (ii) he failed to take precautions against inevitable disasters; and (iii) the failure to provide a safe system of work was only the last in a long catalogue of deficiencies.

3.29   Reporting on the case Jolliffe[1] provides details of the summing up of the case where the judge said:

> 'If you did address your mind to the subject of safety clothing you failed to do so adequately. The fact that the deceased was not concerned to wear safety clothing made it all the more important that you should have made sure that he not only had it, but that he wore it.'

He further stated:

> 'I'm afraid you were at most, totally indifferent to your statutory duties ... you failed to address your mind to any real system of safety and you failed

to take precautions against inevitable disasters ... the failure to provide a safe system of work was only the last in a long catalogue of deficiencies.'

Apart from the failings outlined by the judge in the lack of personal protective equipment (PPE), there were no trained first-aiders, nor was there first-aid equipment provided by the company. There were no procedures to ensure safe entry to the tank or rescue equipment for use in an emergency. It was ironic that the failings were made worse in that the company had drawn up a manual detailing safe methods of cleaning out tankers. That manual had been produced six years before Hodgson's death and had been put in a drawer and forgotten. However, the management had identified the hazards and associated risks and failed to implement a safe system of work.

---

1 Jolliffe, 'Director jailed for indifference that killed 21-year old worker', Safety Management, December 1996.

English Brothers

3.30   'Construction Company Guilty of Corporate Manslaughter', was the headline of a Health and Safety Executive (HSE) Press Notice.[1] English Brothers Ltd, a construction company, was convicted as a result of a prosecution brought by the Crown Prosecution Service (CPS). The fatality involved Bill Larkman who was employed as a gang foreman for the erection of an onion store on a farm, The Crofts, Newton, near Wisbech in Cambridgeshire. Mr Larkman was working on the roof in June 1999 when the accident occurred. Although there were no witnesses to the actual incident it was thought that he lost his footing when roofing material slipped causing him to fall more than eight metres to his death. The seriousness of the incident was enhanced because a HSE inspector had found Mr Larkman on another site working without the correct safety equipment. The matter was taken up with the company who agreed to remedy the problem, but they failed to take any action. This failure meant that the incident occurred not as an oversight but as a failure of management to take action. That failure amounted to gross negligence with the consequence of a manslaughter prosecution. Melvyn Hubbard, a director of the company was also charged with manslaughter, but after the company pleaded guilty to manslaughter, those charges were not proceeded with. The company was fined £25,000 for manslaughter. In addition there was a fine of £5,000 for an offence under HSWA 1974, s 3 for failing to ensure the health and safety of people not in its employment. The company was also ordered to pay prosecution costs of £12,500. The financial penalty against the company was said to have amounted to one year's profits for the organisation.

---

1 HSE Press Notice E140: 01, 3 August 2001.

3.31   The successes and failings of these cases highlight the fact that there are key elements that form the basis of establishing a manslaughter at work prosecution. Under the current homicide law it is doubtful if a successful case could be brought against a large corporation. The evidence shows that the directors of P&O European Ferries (Dover) Ltd had prior knowledge that the company fell short in its safety culture, failed to do anything about it and yet were not held liable under the law as it was at the time. In the case of Great Western Trains, Judge Scott Baker could not identify an individual *controlling mind* responsible for health and safety in the company. (See Chapter 2 for these cases.)

Denis Clothier

3.32   In October 2002, the company, Dennis Clothier and Sons, and one of its directors, Julian Clothier, were found guilty of the manslaughter of Stephen Hayfield.[1] He died in November 2000 when he was hit by a 20-tonne trailer which was owned by the company. The Court heard that the trailer became detached from a tractor because it was dangerously loaded and the hitch mechanism connecting the trailer to the tractor was 'badly worn'. Mr Clothier was responsible for the maintenance on the company's vehicles and he should have noticed the defect which was 'obvious to the naked eye'. The court heard farm worker Mr Burrows had been trying to tow the trailer loaded with straw and weighing the equivalent of two double-decker buses up a steep country lane. As the tractor struggled up the hill, the hitch mechanism connecting the tractor to the trailer failed under the strain. Mr Hayfield was in his car sheltering from the rain while on a fishing trip in the Mendip Hills and it is thought that he must have seen the trailer careering down the hill towards him and he decided to abandon his car. That decision to abandon his car cost him his life because he stumbled as he tried to escape and was struck by the trailer as it veered towards him.

In December 2002, Julian Clothier was sentenced to 240 hours' community service. However, his conviction for manslaughter was quashed by the Court of Appeal.

---

1 www.corporateaccountability.org

3.33   During a claim for compensation the High Court in London heard that Mr Hayfield led an active and normal life despite having slightly shorter than normal arms and fingers and one leg shorter than the other. There was a dispute over damages centred on the life expectancy and work potential of Mr Hayfield, who was a thalidomide victim. He had worked as an engraver and was a father of three. David Clarke J approved the award of £425,000 against the firm, which had admitted liability.

3.34   The family's solicitor, Andrea Risoli, said:

'It was disappointing ... that the family of Stephen Hayfield found themselves fighting a battle to prove that having a disability does not always preclude one from enjoying an active, normal life, from raising a family and contributing to society. If this result can go just a small way to changing the public misconception of thalidomide victims and other individuals under a disability, then Stephen will not have died in vain.'

Teglgaard Hardwood

3.35   Teglgaard Hardwood (UK) Ltd and one of its directors, John Horner, pleaded guilty to the manslaughter[1] of an 18-year-old labourer. Christopher Longrigg died when a nine-metre stack of timber fell on him on 26 April 2000 whilst he was working for the company at a shipyard in Hessle. Mr Horner was standing next to the teenager, who suffered massive head injuries and was killed instantly, when he was hit by the timber which had not been stacked properly. It had broken loose from its metal ties and collapsed like a toppling building.

[1] www.corporateaccountability.org

3.36   The court heard that the company had paid scant regard to even the most basic health and safety precautions and had not assessed the risks to employees. When sentencing, the judge commented on the 'callous indifference' of company director John Horner. He was given a 15-month prison sentence, suspended for two years, and his firm, Teglgaard Hardwood UK was fined £25,000.

Nationwide Heating Systems

3.37   Nationwide Heating Systems Ltd was found guilty of manslaughter[1] and Alan Mark, 45, the managing director was convicted of manslaughter and jailed for 12 months after Ben Pinkham, a young apprentice, was killed in a boatyard explosion. Mark had persuaded Princess Yachts that he was a suitable contractor to do the job of cleaning a resin storage tank, despite limited experience. His risk assessment did not mention acetone would be used to clean the tank.

1 www.corporateaccountability.org

3.38   Mr Pinkham, of Saltash, Cornwall, was working at the boat manufacturer's in Plymouth when the explosion occurred in February 2003. He was using a highly flammable solvent to clean a resin storage tank at the Princess

Yachts International yard but had not been warned about the dangers of using the chemical in a confined space. On the day of the incident he was suspended from a harness inside the tank and had knocked over a halogen light he was using. There was an explosion and smoke and flames came from the tank. He died in hospital six days after suffering 90% burns in the explosion.

3.39   The trial judge Steel J said:

> 'The life of a young man has been needlessly lost in a terrible way. This case must be viewed as a warning to all employers to pay rigorous and robust attention to matters of safety.'

Steel J continued:

> 'Princess Yachts had left quantities of acetone in open buckets with no warnings on them.'

Princess Yachts International, which had pleaded guilty at an earlier hearing to two health and safety offences, was fined £90,000 with £10,000 prosecution costs.

Easy Moss Products case

3.40   Following joint investigation by the HSE and the police, Roger Jackson, trading as Easy Moss, was charged with manslaughter following the death of an employee. John Speight had learning difficulties and was employed under a scheme for the disabled. He was helping to transfer waste into a skip by being lifted in an unsecured former platform luggage trolley by a forklift truck. The trolley fell off the forks, crushing his abdomen beneath the steel cage and he died several days later. Jackson pleaded not guilty to the health and safety charges but changed his plea to guilty during the trial. On 3 March 2000 Jackson was convicted of manslaughter and received a 12-month prison sentence. The judge was in no doubt that he should impose the sentence but suspended it for two years for fear that the business might fail, putting 18 people out of work. Jackson was fined £5,000 under HSWA 1974, s 2 and £5,000 under HSWA 1974, s 3 and ordered to pay £25,000 prosecution costs.

Harper Building Contractors Ltd

3.41   The managing director of Harper Building Contractors Ltd, a small construction company, was jailed for 16 months for the manslaughter of an employee.[1] Daryl Arnold was killed after falling through a roof light in an incident that would have been avoided had his employer followed simple HSE guidance. The incident occurred on 11 June 2003 during the removal and replacement of a warehouse roof. The work was being carried out by Harper Building Contractors Ltd. Arnold was working with other Harper employees on the roof when he stepped backwards onto a fragile roof light on an adjoining warehouse. The roof light gave way and he fell 6.75 metres onto the ground floor sustaining fatal head injuries. The company's sole director, Lee Harper, had not prepared a safe system of work before the work began. There were no safety precautions or equipment in place at the time of the incident and he failed to provide its workers with any health and safety training. Harper himself had no knowledge of health and safety rules, and Arnold had no previous experience of working on a roof.

McComb J said the company's standards 'fell far below' the level he would expect. The charges against the company remain on file because it is in liquidation.

---

1 www.hazards.org

Glen Hawkins

3.42   Glen Hawkins, a garage manager branded by the judge as a health and safety 'dinosaur', was sentenced to nine months' imprisonment for the manslaughter of an 18-year-old worker who died in a petrol explosion.[1] On the day of the accident, Murphy was helping his manager, Glen Hawkins, to empty a mixture of petrol and diesel from a dustbin into a waste-oil disposal tank on the forecourt. The incident occurred when fuel vapour was sucked into a flue pipe outlet from a gas boiler situated next to the tank. As a result, the vapour ignited, causing an explosion that engulfed Murphy in flames. Murphy suffered 60% burns and died of his injuries four days later. Glen Hawkins and his father Howard Hawkins, the owner of the garage, failed to put in place a safe system of work for handling and draining fuel. The fuel was drained close to a source of ignition, left overnight in an open dustbin, and emptied into a waste-oil tank allowing flammable vapour to accumulate and create an explosion risk. Glen Hawkins said that he was not present when the accident happened and had relied on his mechanics to carry out the work safely.

---

1 www.hazards.org

3.43   Judge Richard Hayward said:

'To say that you were complacent about health and safety is an understatement. You regarded health and safety as a tiresome intrusion into your business and a matter of common sense that you could leave to your mechanics. Being a dinosaur can sometimes be endearing, but not on health and safety matters.'

Glen Hawkins was jailed for nine months for the manslaughter of Lewis Murphy. Meanwhile, Howard Hawkins was fined £10,000 under HSWA 1974, s 2(1), and ordered to pay £15,000 costs.

3.44   Glen Hawkins was freed after the Court of Appeal ruled that a statement made by him should not have been admitted as evidence because it was prejudicial. Lord Justice Pill said that the statement was made to the police in the immediate aftermath of the accident, when Hawkins was in pain, under the influence of morphine and in a state of shock. He added that because of the time that Hawkins has already spent in prison, no retrial would be allowed.

Simon Jones

3.45   Simon Jones, a 25 year old student at Sussex University, was killed on 24 April 1998 within two hours of commencing a job at Shoreham docks, West Sussex. He was employed by a Dutch owned company Euromin, a stevedore company.[1] Jones was sent as casual labour to a job at the docks by an employment agency. He was tasked with attaching bags of cobblestones to hooks which had been welded to the inside of the open grab. The conventional method would have been to attach a hook to the crane but employees stated that the company was reluctant to change the crane from grab to hook and back again because it cost time and money. Jones received only a few minutes training and no health and safety briefing. As work progressed the crane driver pulled the wrong lever in the crane cab and the two-tonne grab closed, partially severing his head. The crane driver and Mr Martell, the manager of the company were arrested but released without charge. The CPS decided that there was insufficient evidence to prosecute for manslaughter, which resulted in a campaign to have that decision reversed. The Director of Public Prosecutions, David Calvert-Smith, ordered a judicial review which ruled that the CPS should reconsider its earlier decision not to prosecute. As a result of the review he announced on 19 December 2000 that there was sufficient evidence to charge Martell with manslaughter through gross negligence. After nearly three years summonses were issued against Richard Martell and Euromin.

---

1   The Independent, 1 April 1999.

3.46   The trial of Euromin Ltd and Richard Martell was held at the Old Bailey and on 29 November 2001 the company was found guilty of two breaches of the HSWA 1974. The company was ordered to pay fines of £50,000 and costs of £20,000. Richard Martell was cleared of manslaughter. The outcome increased calls for changes to the law in respect to manslaughter at work. David Calvert-Smith, QC said[1]:

> 'Employees like Simon Jones should be able to carry out their work in a safe environment free from the fear of death or serious injury'.

He confirmed the problems encountered with prosecuting companies with corporate manslaughter and called for immediate changes to the law.

---

1 *The Independent*, 20 December 2000.

Paul White prosecution

3.47   On 16 September 2005 Paul White was sentenced to 12 months in prison, a £30,000 fine and ordered to pay costs of £55,000 at Norwich Crown Court after admitting a charge of manslaughter.[1] The incident involved the company MW White Ltd, of Ketteringham. Mr White, the managing director, was charged with the offence following the death of his employee Kevin Arnup on 22 December 2003. Mr Arnup was a foreman at MW White Ltd's premises near Wymondham in Norfolk and died after being fatally injured by a 'paper hogger' machine. The HSE, supporting the police in the investigation, found bad working practices, and malfunctioning machinery. The machine which killed Kevin was malfunctioning because of a build-up of dirt inside it. It should have been fitted with an isolator to make it safe whilst members of staff were working on it, but this part was never fitted and so the paper shredder was essentially running with the cabinet open which then allowed dust and debris to build up inside, causing it to eventually malfunction. Sentencing White the judge said the safety breaches were 'chronic'. Norwich Crown Court heard that the machine started up as Mr Arnup was inside it trying to clear a blockage. There was no lock off on the 'paper hogger' and the emergency stop button did not work. Addressing White, Bell J said:

> 'It must have been obvious to you that if the hogger started up during the operation when anyone was in the chamber it was really inevitable they would have been killed'.

The failure was made worse because to have prevented this accident would have cost less than £100.

---

1 South Norfolk Advertiser, 17 June 2005.

Brian Dean Demolition and Civil Engineers

3.48   The Court of Appeal, in October 2002,[1] quashed the conviction of Brian Dean, the former owner of Brian Dean Demolition and Civil Engineers, who had been convicted in March of the manslaughter of two of his employees, Michael Redgate and his son Carl, who died in July 2000 when a kiln collapsed on top of them. The two men had been sent to demolish the disused kiln without proper instruction and with no previous experience of kiln demolition. The

Court of Appeal however, ruled that the judge had failed to give proper directions to the jury on issues relating to causation and on the defence case. The manslaughter conviction was substituted by a health and safety offence.

---

1 HSE Press Release EO97:02 May 2002.

Nightingale Cleaning Services and Industrial Cleaning Services

3.49   Norman Cliffe (who traded as Nightingale Cleaning Services) and Justin Amos (who traded as Industrial Cleaning Services) were acquitted of the manslaughter of Glenn Whalley and Anthony Redfern who died in October 2000. They were burnt to death whilst cleaning Holmes Place health club in Nottingham. The men had been using unsuitable chemicals and had not been made aware of the dangers they faced. They died after the industrial chemicals they were using ignited. The two men pleaded guilty to two health and safety offences and were fined £5,000 and £2,500 respectively. Simon Construction Ltd, the main contractors, was convicted of two health and safety offences and fined a total of £40,000.

Change of Style

3.50   On 4 August 2006, Michael Shaw, managing director of Change of Style stone-cutting company was convicted of gross negligence manslaughter following the death of one of his employees.[1] He originally denied the charge but changed his plea to that of guilty during the trial.

---

1 www.news.bbc.co.uk (2006).

3.51   The case involved David Bail, an employee who suffered massive head injuries in the accident at the factory on 13 May 2003, when he was caught in a stone-cutting machine and crushed. The automated machine, which cut stone for kitchen worktops, had light sensors around it that immediately stopped it when a continuous light beam was broken. It also had hinged guards which, if lowered when the machine was working, would break a circuit and stop it. However, when the machine had been installed in 2000 the safety devices had been bypassed to make the machine more efficient, because if it was stopped it had to start the programme again every time which cost time and money.

3.52   Mark Dennis QC, prosecuting, told the jury at Winchester Crown Court that Michael Shaw and his 25-year-old son, Gavin, a fellow director, were responsible for the death of Mr Bail because they put 'profits before safety'.

Shaw received a suspended two-year jail sentence which the judge said was his consideration of the consequences of a prison term on Shaw's other 25 employees. Shaw and his company were fined £70,000. Shaw's son and fellow director, Gavin Shaw, was fined £1,500 for one breach of health and safety legislation. He had earlier been cleared of a charge of manslaughter on the directions of the judge, due to the lack of evidence against him.

3.53   The CPS appealed against what was considered to be an 'unduly lenient' sentence for manslaughter. The original trial judge, in imposing the suspended sentence, took into account the fact that people would lose their jobs should Shaw be jailed. While the appeal judges agreed that this was a factor to be considered they held that it should not be a bar to sending someone guilty of such a serious offence to prison, and that the suspended sentence was 'unduly lenient', given the nature of the offence. They therefore jailed Michael Shaw for 15 months for the manslaughter of David Bail.

3.54   An article in Health and Safety Bulletin[1] identifies that the 'aggravating' factors in the Change of Style and Shaw prosecutions were that:

- the offences arose from Shaw's desire to put profit and productivity above safety;

- Shaw had displayed insufficient regard for safety, even though he had been warned by the company's safety consultants;

- the failures that led to the death were not an 'uncharacteristic exception'; the machines had been used in an unsafe and dangerous state for about five years;

- Shaw failed to admit his guilt immediately, meaning that the witnesses and Bail's family had to endure the ordeal of a trial.

- Shaw only changed his manslaughter plea after the jury had convicted him of the safety offences.

---

1 HSB, December, 2006, No 354.

3.55   Mitigating factors included:

- the HSE had served an improvement notice on Bavelloni, which was responsible for the installation and maintenance of the machine;

- Change of Style's losses since the incident of around £200,000 (its turnover for the year before the incident (2002/03) was £1.64 million);

- Shaw had cooperated with the HSE during the investigation and had taken steps to remedy deficiencies after they were drawn to his attention;

- Shaw's otherwise good character, display of 'some remorse', health problems since the death, contribution to the community, and the effects of any prison sentence on him, which were likely to be 'devastating'.

The CPS appealed, claiming that a suspended sentence was too lenient. The Court of Appeal agreed and, on 4 October 2006, imposed an immediate 15-month custodial sentence, stating that suspension lacked a 'deterrent effect' and was 'wrong in principle'.

The Daniel Dennis case

3.56 On the question of manslaughter at work it is not always straightforward as shown in the following case. At an inquest on 15 March 2005, a Coroners Court jury took less than ten minutes to reach a verdict of unlawful killing of Daniel Dennis who in 2003 fell through a skylight and died. It happened during his first week of work for the roofing company North Eastern Roofing when Dennis was sent up scaffolding on to the roof of a B&Q store in Cwmbran, Gwent during a re-cladding project.[1] However, at the time of the incident he had not received any safety training from his employers, nor had he been given training for working at heights, and he was not wearing a safety harness.

---

1 www.workplacelaw.net

3.57 Equally important was the fact that the skylight area had not been fenced off. The situation is further aggravated in that his father, Peter Dennis, had previously contacted the company and warned it that his son had not received any safety training and should not undertake any work at height.

3.58 Following the Coroners Court verdict the family made representations to the CPS to have a case brought in the criminal court; however, they were informed that gross negligence manslaughter charges would not be brought against anybody in the company.

A Judicial Review was pursued by the GMB union and Thompson's Solicitors in the High Court which was only the second time in legal history that the CPS has been brought to court in a workplace death case. This is a situation that exposes the CPS's lack of expertise in health and safety and gross negligence law and a lack of proactivity in investigating workplace death cases. It must also be remembered that the CPS are signatories of the workplace deaths protocol and have access to specialist investigators in the HSE.

3.59 The outcome was that the High Court decided that the case merited a judicial review on the basis that:

'The grounds in support of this claim are arguable. There is also a public interest in having full argument in a case such as this, where the inquest jury found there to have been unlawful killing but [the CPS] has decided not to prosecute anyone.'

The findings of the High Court ruled that the Crown Prosecution Service (CPS) should review its decision not to bring corporate manslaughter charges against the employer of Daniel Dennis. It concluded that the way in which the CPS interpreted the evidence, including describing the finding of the inquest jury as 'perverse' and its apparent lack of understanding of health and safety law, should be looked at again.

3.60 There is no case outcome readily available but it does show the problems of inter-agency agreements: if they are used a case may proceed but if they are not there are problems. It follows that for there to be successful prosecutions for corporate manslaughter, organisations must work closely together.

Mark Connolly & Roy Kennett

3.61 Four workers were killed on the West Coast Main Line on 15 February 2004[1] when one of two three-tonne flatbed trailers, 'grossly overloaded' with 16 tonnes of scrap rail, ran away from a work site at Scout Green in Cumbria. The trailer ran at up to 40 miles an hour for three miles before hitting the men at Tebay.

---

[1] HSB No 358 May 2007.

3.62 The trailers belonged to MAC Machinery Services, which was owned by Mark Connolly. Following the deaths the investigation found that Connolly had, for financial gain, deliberately dismantled the trailers' braking systems. He had done this 'rather than repair the damage caused to the trailers by his earlier incompetent operations on the railways'. As a direct result of his greed and deceit and the connivance of his employee, Roy Kennett, who was well aware that there were no working brakes and that Connolly had used forged certificates of competence for his staff, the four men died.

3.63 At Newcastle Crown Court on 17 March 2006, Holland J jailed Connolly for nine years and Kennett for two years on four counts of manslaughter each. The sentence was appealed on the basis that the convictions were unsafe because the judge had misdirected the jury on issues such as what constituted a grossly negligent breach of duty and the cause of the accident. On 1 March 2007 May LJ, sitting with Butterfield and King JJ, dismissed the appeals on the basis that when looking at the matter as a whole they were satisfied that the convictions were safe because of the 'chain of causation' between Connolly's actions and the incident. However, the Court of Appeal reduced the manslaughter sentence imposed by two years because it was considered that nine years was 'rather too great'.

Summary

3.64   This is a small selection of cases where there was a workplace manslaughter prosecution involving individuals. It will be seen that the organisations are small and the prosecution was able to focus on the failings of an individual. It may also be considered that even with these cases that there are inconsistencies in the prosecution, trial and outcomes. This further strengthens the need for the legal processes to be consistent and the corporate manslaughter offence should clarify the situation.

Chapter 4

Workplace Manslaughter – the Complexities

Introduction

4.1   A factor that has faced the authorities up until the introduction of the corporate manslaughter and corporate homicide law is the dividing line between whether a prosecution should be one for manslaughter or a Health and Safety at Work offence. It was accepted that there was a test for gross negligence but in the case of corporations it was not so simple, because a 'controlling mind' had to be identified. There have been a number of prosecutions involving large organisations which have all failed. What has been evident is that small organisations have been vulnerable to a corporate manslaughter prosecution and there has been an increase in the number of individual directors prosecuted for gross negligence manslaughter. The decision on which kind of offence to prosecute is based upon evidence and is dependent on the element of gross negligence combined with the prospect of a conviction and whether it is in the public interest. The fact is that with the new law in place, directors of small businesses will still be vulnerable to a manslaughter prosecution. However, larger organisations as a body corporate will be liable to the corporate manslaughter prosecution but directors will remain remote from the prospect of an individual manslaughter prosecution. Prior to the introduction of the new law there were four cases that were in the public eye and the objective of this chapter is to provide an overview with some key outcomes that provided the basis of either a prosecution for gross negligence manslaughter or an offence under the Health and Safety at Work etc Act 1974 (HSWA 1974).

4.2   It is important to note that discussions on any of the cases in this chapter are based on the information that is available through the public domain. The main focus is on the size of the organisation, the extent of their duty of care, senior management involvement and culpability and the complexity of prosecuting an individual. Each case emphasises the many factors that have to be taken into account and show that in the case of large organisations juries are less willing to convict a manager where those at the senior level were not involved in the fatal incident, even where there have been failings by senior management. The four cases are very different and whilst each may warrant a chapter in their own right, it is worth reviewing each case to provide a 'thumbnail sketch' of the implications and culpability of people with responsibilities at work with regard to health and safety.

The Gillian Beckingham case

4.3   The first case to be reviewed is that of Gillian Beckingham[1] who was the head of the design services group at Barrow Borough Council and was tried for seven counts of manslaughter. This followed the deaths of seven people from legionnaires' disease in July and August 2002. The cause of the deaths was through water droplets containing legionella bacteria that emanated from the heating system in a Council controlled arts centre, Forum 28.

1 *Northwest Evening Mail*, 13 April 2006.

4.4   It is very important to understand that the prosecution claimed[1] that in her management role Ms Beckingham had been responsible for the upkeep of the ageing air conditioning system at Forum 28 and months before the outbreak she allegedly cancelled the contract which was in place to ensure that the air conditioning system was maintained. Without such maintenance work the system was said to have provided 'an almost perfect breeding ground for the Legionella bacteria'. Water droplets laced with the bacteria showered people as they walked past the arts centre. Evidence from one survivor claimed that there was so much spray that they thought it was raining.

1 *The Independent*, 11 February 2004.

4.5   Various media sources claimed that as a result, some 500 people were admitted to hospital suffering from respiratory problems. Of these 179 contracted legionnaires' disease; seven people died and many of the survivors were left with continuing health problems.

4.6   The overall management failure lay with the council and, under the existing law at the time, the only organisations that could be prosecuted for corporate manslaughter were 'companies'. Local councils were established as 'corporate bodies' by the Local Government Act 1972, s 2, which meant that they could be treated just like any other company and could be charged with manslaughter under the same principles of liability. For a local council to have been prosecuted for corporate manslaughter charges there must first have been a gross negligence charge laid against an individual person and that individual had to be senior enough within the council to be deemed in law to be a 'controlling mind'. This meant that where there was sufficient evidence against an individual senior council officer, the council (as a corporate body) could have been charged with corporate manslaughter. It follows that if the individual was acquitted, the council would be acquitted; and if the individual were to be found guilty, so would the council. In this case the prosecution went ahead because it was considered that the council was culpable of manslaughter because Ms Beckingham was deemed to be 'so far up the chain of command'.

4.7   However, throughout the trial,[1] Ms Beckingham maintained that she was not responsible for the air conditioning system and in determining the 'controlling mind' test, Mr Justice Poole described Beckingham as 'a third-tier official' and said:

> 'No reasonable jury could conclude that Gillian Beckingham was the council's controlling mind.'

That statement then eliminated Barrow Borough Council, which owned Forum 28 and employed Beckingham, from the prospect of a corporate manslaughter conviction. Ms Beckingham still faced gross negligence manslaughter charges as an individual with management responsibilities.

---

1 *The Independent*, 11 February 2004.

4.8   As far as the prosecution was concerned Alistair Webster QC, prosecuting, told the jury[1] that the deaths were 'avoidable and unnecessary'. This statement was certainly correct and if the council had managed the risk, the resulting failures would have been negligible. He continued:

> 'It was an outbreak that could have been avoided by the exercise of a moderate amount of care. 'The person who was properly responsible for this human disaster was Gillian Beckingham, a qualified architect employed by Barrow Borough Council as head of design services.'

On the evidence that came out in court, the quote above was totally incorrect and the facts are discussed below. He further stated:

> 'Beckingham, 47, "failed to take any effective action" to prevent the tragedy. The significant cause of each death was Legionnaire's Disease caused by bacteria emitted from Forum 28, and that the outbreak was caused by gross negligence, negligence so gross that it was criminal, on the part of Gillian

Beckingham ... The measures normally taken to avoid the build-up of bacteria were well established and "far from rocket science" ... Beckingham, the head of Barrow's design services group, bore the principal responsibility for the outbreak ... Until she was instrumental in its cancellation, there had been a contract, which ensured that the necessary tests were carried out. She negotiated, after a gap of months, when this system was not covered by any maintenance contract at all, the new contract did not provide for any water treatment regime. Service engineers warned her as to the serious dangers brewing up. She failed to take any effective action and the tragedy unfolded ... Beckingham was by no means the only person who contributed to the outbreak. Barrow's health and safety systems were woefully inadequate and there were ineffective communications between the council and the company handling mechanical and electrical maintenance. Ultimately, however, Beckingham was at the centre of it all.'

---

1 *Northwest Evening Mail*, 28 April 2005.

4.9   The outcome of the first trial was that the jury, having deliberated for almost 23 hours over five days, failed to reach majority verdicts on the manslaughter charges. The jury did, however, convict Ms Beckingham of an offence under HSWA 1974, s 7. Following the collapse of the case the Crown Prosecution Service (CPS) decided that Ms Beckingham should face a retrial for the seven manslaughter charges.

4.10   Again based upon the revelations from witnesses and the defendant at the trial (which are not generally known), a number of the prosecution statements were incorrect. That means that there are vitally important issues which in the interest of justice, everybody who is employed at whatever level should know. I am indebted to Kathryn Gilbertson, a specialist health and safety solicitor and head of the defence team involved in the retrial for providing the following important facts.[1]

---

1 Greenwoods Solicitors LLP, Monkstone House, City Road, Peterborough, PE1 1JE.

4.11   It is correct to say that Gillian Beckingham was the Head of the Design Services team whose main function within the council was in the renovation of older buildings. She did not have any responsibility for or involvement with Forum 28, the building at the centre of the case. In the line management chain she reported to the Head of Development who in turn reported to the council's Chief Executive, Tom Campbell; she was, as previously described by the trial judge, a third-tier manager.

4.12   The facts are that Forum 28 had had a maintenance contract for the air conditioning system with a company (GS Hall), but the Arts Centre manager Neil Ward cancelled the contract and left the council the same day. Equally important, he did not officially divulge the information about the cancellation of the contract to anybody in the council. This meant that there was no maintenance contract in place. Mr Ward's assistant, Kevin Borthwick, the Technical Manager, was said to have known and reported the fact to Sue Jenkins, the Culture Services Manager, who had responsibility for the Forum 28 building. Sue Jenkins was a second-tier manager reporting to the CEO.

4.13   Sue Jenkins and Kevin Borthwick requested a meeting with Ms Beckingham who was told about the cancelled contract and asked if she could identify a number of organisations who could service a maintenance contract for Forum 28. It is very important to note that Ms Beckingham's only involvement was to provide the details of organisations that could be approached and asked to bid for the contract.

4.14   Sue Jenkins' department arranged for standard contract letters to be sent to the five companies. This involved Kevin Borthwick, who knew the Forum 28 building in some detail but was a lower tiered Council employee. Following delivery of bids for the contract an international company Interserve was selected. They were the most expensive but had provided details of their ability to undertake the task with competent staff, risk assessments, audits and health and safety compliance. Ms Beckingham was not involved in the evaluation and adoption of Interserve's services.

4.15   The contract ran for 18 months prior to the incident under the responsibility of Sue Jenkins and her department with day-to-day involvement of Kevin Borthwick who administered the invoices for work done. It became evident to Mr Borthwick that the contract was not being complied with and he raised the matter with Sue Jenkins. In fact Interserve had not undertaken any maintenance work at all, even though they invoiced for it. Jenkins and Borthwick approached a council Environmental Health Officer (EHO) with regard to determining the implications of the lack of maintenance work. They consulted the Health and Safety Executive's (HSE) guidance document L8 – *Legionnaires' disease – The control of legionella bacteria in water systems* – but neither Sue Jenkins, Kevin Borthwick nor the EHO understood the requirements of the document.

4.16   It was said that seven people died from Legionnaires' disease and Ms Beckingham was charged with seven counts of gross negligence manslaughter. In fact only five people died from Legionnaires' disease and two died from other medical conditions. This became known in the prosecution process and the original legal defence team did not seek to reduce the seven to five cases.

4.17   The evidence that has not generally been made known to the wider public but was addressed in court is a damning indictment on the legal system and in particular the investigating police force. Police officers who were in the public gallery of the court for the retrial were eventually excluded for the duration of the trial because of misbehaviour which was distracting the jury.

4.18   Mr Campbell, Barrow-in-Furness chief executive, admitted to the court that, before the outbreak, the council did not have a safety committee.[1] In

April 2001, a council safety officer post had been reduced to part-time and following the incident the full time post had been reinstated. Mr Campbell also told the court that he was not aware of the need for a specific Legionnaires' disease risk assessment. The judge criticised Barrow Borough Council, saying its failings were 'grave in the extreme'. It is very evident that the management failings in the council lay at the very top.

---

1 *Northwest Evening Mail*, 28 April 2005.

4.19   Ms Beckingham again faced trial by a new jury and on 31 July 2006 she was found *not guilty* of all counts of manslaughter but was found guilty of an offence under HSWA 1974, s 7. She was fined £15,000, which equated to half her salary. Her employer, Barrow Borough Council, was fined £125,000 and ordered to pay £90,000 costs for the s 3(1) offence. The judge stated that had it been a commercial organisation, the fine would have been at least £1 million but he had taken into account that the fine would be paid from public finances. This case emphasises the seriousness of the regulatory regime under which professionals now work.

4.20   Gillian Beckingham was found guilty under HSWA 1974, s 7, but what was her crime? She was asked when giving evidence if she could have done anything more. Although it was not her responsibility she implied that perhaps she could, following her identification of possible contractors, have contacted Sue Jenkins or Kevin Borthwick to enquire about the status of the contract and ongoing maintenance programme. She could perhaps have intervened in management that was not her responsibility. She did not do this (why would she?) but it appears that general statements were enough to make her guilty of the offence.

Comment

4.21   This is the classic case of an individual facing trial for manslaughter whilst the organisation and its senior officers are not affected. From the evidence above Ms Beckingham should not have been charged with manslaughter in the first place. In fact she should not been charged with any offence. Her only involvement was to identify organisations that could provide a maintenance service. Neither she nor her team had any responsibility for Forum 28.

4.22   It was evident that Ms Beckingham was a manager and not a 'controlling mind'. She had not had any specific health and safety training and there was not a full-time health and safety advisor to whom she could refer had she needed to, because senior management had in fact reduced the health and safety adviser's role to part-time.

4.23   An HSE report followed two public hearings in 2006 and makes the following points:

> 'The number of fateful coincidences involved was scarcely credible. Such basic failings should not have occurred and, sadly, these failures could have been easily prevented'.

The failures by Barrow Borough Council included:

- failing to carry out risk assessments;

- failing to commit sufficient resources to health and safety and to act on advice;

- a general lack of leadership and direction within the council;

- poor communication channels between the different levels of management;

- health and safety, in particular the risks from *Legionnella,* were not appropriately controlled;

- poor management of contractors.

It will be noted that many of the failings of the council are key elements of senior management not managing to an appropriate level. It would be expected that under the new law the council would have been subjected to a corporate manslaughter offence.

4.24   What happened to those involved?

- Tom Campbell, the CEO, who was ultimately responsible for the management within the council was not charged with any offence and is still in post.

- Sue Jenkins, Culture Services manager, responsible for Forum 28, the selection of a new contractor and the ongoing maintenance programme went off work with ill health and stress. She has not been charged with any offence.

- Kevin Borthwick was responsible for the day-to-day activities of the new contract. He identified that no maintenance had been done but was not charged with any offence.

- Gillian Beckingham, whose sole part in the entire event was to provide the names and addresses of contractors who could provide maintenance services for the air conditioning unit, was charged with seven counts of gross negligence manslaughter. She was found guilty under HSWA 1974, s 7 because, when asked if she could have done anything more she admitted that she could have made contact with Sue Jenkins or Kevin Borthwick to enquire about the status of the contract and ongoing maintenance programme.

- Finally, the contractor Interserve who failed to undertake its maintenance agreement obligations were not charged with any offence.

4.25   The prosecution case was flawed in the following key points:

- Beckingham had 'failed to take any effective action' to prevent the tragedy. But she did what she was asked and that was to provide details of potential contractors to undertake the maintenance programme.

- 'The outbreak was caused by gross negligence, negligence so gross that it was criminal, on the part of Gillian Beckingham'. Again there is no evidence to support this; only that others were responsible. The not guilty verdict clearly shows this.

- 'Until she was instrumental in its cancellation, there had been a contract which ensured that the necessary tests were carried out'. Wrong – Neil Ward cancelled the original maintenance contract.

4.26   Following this important case the implication for every manager is that if there is any involvement, no matter how small or obscure, with others in a decision-making process then you could find yourself liable if things go wrong. The message is simple: following an incident in which you are implicated, trust no one; if there is a fatal accident in the workplace and you are interviewed seek good professional advice and support from a solicitor with health and safety experience at the earliest opportunity. Your future and well-being could depend upon it.

The Morecambe Bay cockle pickers case

4.27   The second case to be reviewed is that of the cockler gangmaster Lin Liang Ren, 29 who following a trial for 21 counts of gross negligence manslaughter was found guilty and sentenced to 14 years' custody. He hired illegal immigrants as a cheap labour force to work on the known danger spot of Morcambe Bay. He ignored every aspect of safety and focused on making a profit. Forcing 21 cockle pickers to work at night with the tide coming in, he left them to drown. The authorities had been advised about illegal immigrant workers being exposed to danger.

4.28   The incident, on the night of 5–6 February 2004, involved a group of some 35 workers, mostly Chinese, who went out in the afternoon to the cockle banks on Morecambe Bay and were cut off by the tide after dark. The outcome was that 21 bodies were subsequently recovered, though it is believed that two other people died. Following the investigation into the deaths five people were prosecuted by the CPS.

4.29 The trial was held at Preston Crown Court in September 2005 and on 24 March 2006, Lin Liang Ren was found guilty of 21 counts of manslaughter, guilty of conspiracy to commit facilitation (a criminal offence of enabling illegal immigrants to work in this country) and guilty of conspiracy to pervert the course of justice; Zhao Xiao Qing was found guilty of conspiracy to commit facilitation and conspiracy to pervert the course of justice; Lin Mu Yong was found guilty of conspiracy to commit facilitation; David Anthony Eden Snr was found not guilty of conspiracy to commit facilitation; and David Anthony Eden Jnr was found not guilty of conspiracy to commit facilitation.

4.30 At the trial, when passing sentence, Mr Justice Henriques said:

> 'Lin Liang Ren had 'cynically and callously' exploited his countrymen and women and provided them with dreadful living conditions ... the gangmaster had been motivated by avarice and displayed little regard for the safety of the cocklers.'

Liang Ren had waited 50 minutes before alerting the authorities to the impending disaster.

4.31 The judge said: 'Had you even then decided to evacuate the beach, there might have been no loss of life' and that he had rarely heard a more 'contrived, deliberate and extended series of lies' from a defendant. The judge commented that Lin Liang Ren had told a series of 'spectacular lies' to the authorities in a bid to evade justice and displayed complete indifference to the fate of the victims. He had attempted to blame everyone but himself for the deaths of the illegal Chinese workers.

4.32 The judge sentenced Lin Liang Ren to 12 years for the manslaughter charges and six years for the facilitation charges, which he ordered should run concurrently. He then jailed Lin Liang Ren for a further two years for the charges of conspiracy to pervert the course of justice to run consecutively (14 years). Zhao Xiao Qing was sentenced for one count of facilitation and three counts of perverting the course of justice. Liverpool businessman David Eden and his son, also called David, ran a company selling cockles. They were cleared of breaching immigration law by employing illegal immigrants in connection with the tragedy. David Eden Jnr said they had no knowledge that the migrant workers did not have legal documentation.

4.33 It was reported that Lin Liang Ren was brought up in Fuqing City in south east China's Fujian province, his family owning a second house in the country. His father, Lin Xien Hua and mother Chen He Zhu ensured that Lin, his

brother and sister were well-educated. He qualified as an accountant and
became head of finance at Fuqing's Mo Chang Plastics Company, a firm that
employed 900 people. In 2000 Lin Liang Ren came to Britain and posed as a
student to gain a visa which was a cover which he kept up by paying £1,500 a
time to enrol in college courses in London and Manchester. It was Liverpool's
Chinatown which provided him the illegal manpower he needed to start his
business which required him to forge cockling permits and providing fake
national insurance numbers. He transported the workers between the sands and
the squalid overcrowded houses and flats he rented for them and while they
worked he either went back to the house he shared with his young girlfriend,
Zhao Xiao Qing, or used his red Mitsubishi sports car to drive into the city
centre to visit casinos. Following the tragedy, he tried to claim he was just an
ordinary worker and threatened serious consequences for anybody who said
otherwise.

4.34   Martin Hamer[1] reported that the Lancashire coastguard were directed
to the Morecambe Bay cockling area after the alarm had been raised. They
arrived at the scene but had no real information and so had no idea of what was
going on, nor could they identify how many people were on the sandbank. There
was a strong wind blowing, the tide was flooding and it was night time. Added to
the conditions, there is only a short period of time when there is access to be able
to walk along that beach because then it becomes marshland.

---

1 BBC News, North West, 2006.

4.35   It was a pitch black night and the coastguard operated with torches and
floodlights, but as they worked through the night the situation deteriorated such
that it was to become a body recovery operation and the decision was made to
stand down until first light. As soon as it was viable the operation continued and
the coastguards found the bodies laid out in a long line where the tide had left
them. The tide started to flood and the bodies had to be recovered quickly using
a tractor to speed up the process.

4.36   The bodies had no marks on them but had shed most of their clothes,
the conclusion being that the cocklers thought that by removing their clothes it
would be easier to swim to shore. However, because of the strong current they
did not make it. Because of the time of night and the tide everything was against
the coastguard during the rescue operation and against the cocklers, who were
neither prepared and nor should have been there.

4.37   The exploitation has been a political issue and as Morecambe and
Lunesdale Labour MP Geraldine Smith said, officials turned a blind eye to the
issue and the cocklers 'were a low priority so they were just left to wander
around'. She had previously alerted ministers to the number of illegal workers
in the town and feared further loss of life because a large number of cocklers had
returned to work in the bay. The court was shown an e-mail sent by the Home
Office in 2003 which said:

'The resource implications of arresting, interviewing and releasing such numbers are huge and simply not justifiable'.

4.38   The Home Office[1] has denied it could have done more to prevent the deaths of the 21 Chinese cockle pickers who drowned working illegally. Immigration Minister Tony McNulty said:

'I would say to those who say that, were the Home Office and the government more reactive, this appalling tragedy wouldn't have happened, I'm afraid life's not as simple as that … We deal with illegal working as much as we can and in full, but there are other factors, like the willingness of the illegal workers themselves to assist us and we're trying to deal with things like that as well.'

4.39   It was reported that more than 40 organisers of cockling made improvements to meet the guidelines, including: purchasing better vehicles; providing high visibility and protective clothing, waders, flares, mobile phones, tide timetables and compasses. Some also carry lifejackets, life rafts and dinghies etc. The Department for the Environment, Food and Rural Affairs sent HSE's guidelines to Sea Fisheries Committees around Britain and requested they distribute them to anyone regularly working cockle beds under their jurisdiction. Legislation setting up the gangmasters Licensing Authority was brought in after the deaths in Morecambe Bay. Its chairman, Paul Whitehouse, said the new regulations were much tougher:

'If you are not licensed and operating as a gangmaster you can be arrested and possibly go to prison for 10 years – that's just for not being licensed.'

4.40   Within the UK people-smuggling is big business and involves many different nationalities, working in different ways in different countries. Immigration enforcement raids are carried out in factories, restaurants, hotels and farmers' fields as part of ongoing operations against international organised immigration crime. It is said that there are some 250,000 Chinese people who are a part of British society, but nobody knows how many other people are in the country illegally. Migrant workers are defined as people who have come to the UK in the last five years to find or take up work, whether intending to stay permanently or not, and whether documented or not.

Comment

4.41   Of the four cases discussed in this chapter, this one is the most clear cut. The substantial evidence showed that the defendant was guilty of an act of financial gain, cover up, fraud and a total disregard for the lives of others. He and those who assisted him were culpable. The two British defendants, father and son, were found not guilty, a situation not based on racism as promoted by

81

some, but due no doubt to the lack of sufficient and suitable evidence that would secure a conviction. There had been warnings from local cocklers but these had not been heeded. In the circumstances it could be considered fair to pass some of the blame for the deaths onto the Government and government departments for their open door policy for the import of cheap labour.

The Jean Charles de Menezes shooting

4.42   The third case is that of the shooting of Jean Charles de Menezes by officers of the Metropolitan Police in an anti-terrorist operation. The operation went wrong and through a failure in communication the wrong man was shot and killed. The CPS decided that there were no manslaughter charges to be laid but prosecuted the Metropolitan Police under health and safety laws. The questions that have to be asked are that if someone is to be culpable, should it be the officers who pulled the trigger, the supervising officers in charge of the operation and/or the man at the top (the head of the Metropolitan Police), or should any individual or organisation be culpable under the 'special' circumstances.

Culpability for managing frontline anti-terrorist operations?

4.43   James Galbraith[1] writes:

'On July 22, 2005, a 27 year-old Brazilian electrician from Minas Gerais, Jean Charles de Menezes, left his flat, wearing jeans and a light denim jacket. He was on his way to a job, but not carrying any tools as they were already at his destination. He walked to the bus, caught the bus to the Stockwell underground station, walked into the station picking up a newspaper, passed through the turnstiles in the usual way, and then sprinted to catch a departing train. Once on board, he took a seat.

Presumably unbeknown to de Menezes, the apartment house in which he lived had figured (it was later said) in the address book of one of the July 21 bombers, who had been arrested. It was under surveillance. Mr de Menezes was followed on and off the bus to the underground by a surveillance team. Coordinating between several teams, they allowed him to enter the station, and then the train. When he took a seat one of the officers grabbed him and pinned his arms. Officers in plain clothes surrounded him, and in slow motion several of them fired their service weapons into his head. Witnesses, including one professional journalist, recalled hearing shot after shot, spaced many seconds apart, as they fled from the scene. Eight bullets hit de Menezes, seven of them in the head.

All this emerged from investigation but the initial story was quite different. According to those first reports from the police, de Menezes was a suspicious character. He was wearing a bulky coat on a hot day. He was carrying a bag. He jumped the turnstile. He refused to stop when ordered. Once in the train, he looked like a 'cornered fox.' He tripped and fell. Officers had reason to fear that he was a suicide bomber about to detonate his charge. They thus took the correct steps under the 'shoot-to-kill policy' that had been activated on July 7. Indeed they were heroes, endangering their own lives to protect the public in a situation of crisis.

Yet every detail of this original official story was false.'

1 James Galbraith, www.free.guardian.co.uk, 2006.

4.44   There are two distinctive camps: those who want to see individual officers face manslaughter prosecution for the killing and who consider the health and safety charge as an insult, and those who claim that the officers were honestly doing their duty and should not be prosecuted. Scotland Yard as a 'body corporate' stated that it was 'surprised and disappointed' and said that the health and safety charge would create uncertainty. The London police authority echoed that, and said the decision raised 'very difficult questions'.

4.45   As we are reminded by Martin Kettle[1] who in an article states:

'... the question of unintended manslaughter had become a major growth area in the law long before Met officers gunned down De Menezes in Stockwell in July 2005. Cases like the Marchioness river-boat tragedy, the Hatfield and Potters Bar train crashes and the like have thrust the issue of corporate manslaughter to the centre of the legal stage. It is 11 years since the Court of Appeal, in a case against British Steel arising from the death of a subcontractor, ruled that "It shall be the duty of every employer to conduct his undertaking in such a way as to ensure, so far as is reasonably practicable, that persons not in his employment who may be affected thereby are not thereby exposed to risks to their health or safety"...'

1 Martin Kettle, www.commentisfree.guardian.co.uk

4.46   The prosecution of the Metropolitan Police over De Menezes, where the killing was intentional, may be on the fringe of the involuntary manslaughter argument and the duty of care to non-employees laid down by the court of appeal applies to the police as it applies to any other employer. The HSWA 1974, ss 2 and 3 require defendants to show that they did everything 'reasonably practicable' to prevent the death.

4.47   An article[1] headlined 'How the Story Has Changed,' stated:

'The conduct of the surveillance officers made clear that they did not consider de Menezes to have been a terrorist threat. Otherwise, why follow him on and off a bus? Why allow him to enter the underground station? Why not approach him, or even kill him, in the open air where less damage would

83

be done if the bomb did turn out to be detonated by a 'dead man's switch' such as a hand grenade with the pin pulled?'

It was reported that the police themselves admitted they had not thought de Menezes was a risk and the official report confirms that the surveillance teams knew that de Menezes was not a threat. It states that there was no motive; that the entire episode was a tragedy of miscommunication, with orders to 'stop' de Menezes interpreted as orders to shoot him dead. Those orders were carried out by a firearms team said to have rushed belatedly onto the scene, unaware of what fellow-officers already knew.

---

1 *The Independent*, 26 July 2006,

4.48   James Galbraith[1] reviews the evidence and identifies that there were three possibilities, of which two can now be ruled out:

'i) The first is that the firearms officers acted on their own, without orders, against protocols. In that case, the killing alone would be enough to establish a crime. The manner of the deed and the identity of the officers are, as of now, undisputed. The unauthorized execution of a detained person might be manslaughter or even murder, depending on the conditions at the scene. Either way, it would have to be considered a very serious offence. But this possibility is out. No charges will be filed against the officers who executed Jean Charles de Menezes.

ii) A second possibility would place blame on the designated senior officer, Commander Cressida Dick who according to the Times, is still under internal investigation. But in what world can a police officer, on her own authority, order the execution of a person already detained? It is obvious that what is not permitted for the firearms officers, acting on their own, could not be permitted to their commander, acting on her own. Commander Dick could have acted only to invoke a protocol, previously established. The Guardian puts this precisely: "Commander Cressida Dick was designated as the officer who would decide whether the suspect was so dangerous that a 'shoot-to-kill' policy should apply."

iii) The remaining possibility is that the blame lies with the 'shoot-to-kill policy.' It is that superior authorities had previously established protocols, which could have been interpreted by firearms officers as demanding the summary execution, on orders, of a man already being pinned down. That is the possibility left open by the exculpation of the firearms officers. Their mistake, it is said, lay in misunderstanding certain words, which in their minds triggered an unintended, but otherwise legitimate order.'

The outcome is that the last option appears to be the official explanation for this incident.

---

1 *The Observer*, 21 August 2006.

4.49   Vikram Dodd[1] states that:

'The police shot dead Jean Charles de Menezes despite officers in charge of the operation intending that he should be arrested outside Stockwell tube station and taken into custody alive, new details of the official investigation show. The evidence it gathered went to the Crown Prosecution Service [CPS] which on Monday announced that no officer would be charged with the death of de Menezes, who was shot seven times in the head and once in the shoulder by two armed officers.

A letter from the CPS to his family shows the Independent Police Complaints Commission [IPCC] investigation found:

- Officers running the operation ordered that de Menezes be stopped from boarding the train and arrested;

- A firearms team was out of position and thus unable to detain him as ordered;

- A misunderstanding between commanding officers and firearms officers meant the order to arrest him was not 'made explicit' to the team rushing to the train to stop the suspect;

- When firearms officers arrived they mistakenly thought they had to shoot him because he was going to attack the underground train.

The CPS letter also reveals that the two officers who shot the Brazilian told investigators de Menezes was wearing a 'bulky jacket', when he was not. The marksmen also said they had shouted 'armed police' before firing, but no independent witness corroborated their assertions … The IPCC say it will not publish its report until after the prosecution of the Met Police is completed, which may not be until next year. The CPS says the officers who opened fire honestly believed the Brazilian was a terrorist. Even though they were wrong, the CPS contends there is not enough evidence to convince a jury that their error amounted to a criminal act … The order was given that de Menezes was to be stopped from getting on the train. Although officers in the control room intended that Jean Charles should be arrested outside the station, the firearms team were not in place to make such an arrest, nor was this intention made explicit to the firearms officers who were being sent down to the train.'

---

1 *Guardian,* 22 July 2006.

4.50   Vikram Dodd further states:

'In its letter the CPS gives the most graphic details to date of the last moments inside the tube carriage before de Menezes was shot: Both [firearms officers] refer to de Menezes getting up and advancing towards them with his hands down by his side before he was tackled by a surveillance officer and forced back into the seat. The firearms officers then shot him. I [CPS] had to consider whether the prosecution could argue that the restraint meant that no bomb could be detonated and that the firearms officers' actions were unlawful ... However I must bear in mind that this happened in a matter of seconds and there is some independent evidence that supports the officers' accounts that they feared Jean Charles might detonate a bomb. A witness sitting opposite Jean Charles said: "I got the impression that he was reaching to the left-hand side of his trouser waistband." '

4.51   Following the incident senior police officers were called to account and provided a response to the public including the family. Stewart Tendler[1] stated that:

'Sir Ian [Blair] returned from a family holiday abroad after the CPS issued a warning last week that the announcement on charges is due today. As Commissioner of the Metropolitan Police he has to receive formally any summons from the CPS that would be answerable at a Central London Magistrates court. Police sources were forecasting yesterday that police would not challenge a decision to prosecute under the Health and Safety Act 1974 but that there would be a 'vigorous defence' that would include putting the death of Mr de Menezes in the context of events that day. Police marksmen fired seven shots into the Brazilian electrician's head on July 22 as he was held on the floor of a Tube train after being followed and mistakenly identified as one of four would-be bombers who had targeted the transport system the previous day. Scotland Yard is also waiting for more information from the Independent Police Complaints Commission, which investigated the shooting, because police expect that some of the 11 officers will face disciplinary charges for misconduct. The IPCC also has to decide what action should be taken over the alteration of a Special Branch surveillance log after the shooting that was changed to suggest that there were doubts that Mr de Menezes was the suspected terrorist.'

---

1 *Times*, 17 July 2006.

Comment

4.52   Whilst we consider the options of workplace manslaughter or health and safety at work offences with regard to the police or security services there are some factors that must be addressed. At the time of the incident and at the time of writing the UK is at war. Not an open global conflict such as those of the two world wars but a war of terror. There are no uniformed armies to engage and whilst the IRA and other elements of the Irish terrorist actions were not in a face to face conflict they did not intentionally blow themselves up with their own bombs. They would generally place a bomb and then deliver a telephone warning which allowed the emergency services time to evacuate. This is a critical factor and must remove such operations from the general duty of care that police officers must extend to members of the public.

4.53   The current war is against an unidentifiable enemy who will and do go to extreme lengths to undertake their terrorist activities. They strap explosives to their bodies or carry them in a holdall and enter a crowded place and then detonate the device with the intention of creating maximum deaths. The only method of dealing with such tactics is to physically immobilise the terrorist and then neutralise. In such circumstances the 'rule book' term 'stop armed police' cannot be adopted. It follows that in every war or conflict there are innocent victims both from the direct action of the terrorists and those combating such actions. The Metropolitan Police did not seek this war but have had it thrust upon them and they, with restricted resources, have to fight the war on behalf of the British public. This means that this case cannot be readily compared with the range of workplace deaths reviewed elsewhere in this book involving a diverse range of incidents all involving management failure.

4.54   Having established that this particular case is part of a terrorist war it means that a wide and diverse range of intelligence is gathered and has to be evaluated often very quickly (unlike in a commercial operation where an evaluation of options can be discussed and decided at board level). The police command centre has to evaluate all the available data in order to make decisions which are those of defending the British public against terrorist action. The people on the ground are provided with information who, in turn, provide information in a potential critical and volatile environment. The officers on the ground are trained to use and are equipped with weapons that kill (there is already the intention to cause harm). Under normal policing situations the officers would identify themselves as being armed police officers and call upon the individual[s] to surrender (in the current terrorist situation this would allow the terrorist to detonate the device).

4.55   The duty of care is:

(a)   HSWA 1974, s 2: a duty for the Metropolitan Police to take care of its employees, its officers (albeit armed) going about their business;

(b)   HSWA 1974, s 3: a duty of the Metropolitan Police to take care of those not in its employ (this would be the normal approach for the police).

4.56   The prospect of a workplace manslaughter or HSWA 1974 case against (a) senior officers or (b) officers on the ground has to be considered in the light of the following:

•   In managing a 'terrorist' situation there are no clear defined rules as would be expected in a commercial operation. In such a situation the hazard is such that if risk is assessed against the requirements of the

HSWA 1974 no officer could be committed to anti-terrorist operations. Senior management is intentionally directing an employee to face a situation where there could be an outcome of death or serious injury.

- For officers on the ground the 'terrorist' situation is an extreme hazard (in fact it is a kill or be killed situation) and the risk control measures will include suitable and sufficient equipment, training and knowledge of the potential situation, as well as the capability of taking direct action (eg to kill an individual[s]) which is not a situation that corporations are exposed to.

- The 'terrorist' situation and the HSWA 1974, s 3 requirements are incompatible. This raises serious operational issues. The prospect of a prosecution, particularly under the corporate manslaughter law, may well affect the operational capability of officers in dealing with a terrorist threat. If the police body and/or individual officers can face prosecution for acting prior to an incident, the option will be to let the terrorist act be carried out and only deal with the outcome.

4.57   The family of de Menezes lost a High Court[1] bid on 14 December 2006 to hold the individual officers accountable. The CPS had decided in July 2006 that no officer involved in the operation should face charges. Instead London's Metropolitan Police as a whole is being prosecuted on health and safety charges.

---

1 Michael Holden, Reuters, 14 December 2006, 'De Menezes family lose court bid'.

4.58   The family's lawyers argued at the High Court that the failure to prosecute police for murder amounted to a breach of Art 2 of the European Convention on Human Rights covering the right to life. In dismissing the challenge, Richards LJ said the decision by the director of public prosecutions not to prosecute was a 'reasonable one'. The family of de Menezes criticised the ruling and de Menezes' cousin Patricia da Silva Armani said: 'We believe the judges came to the wrong decision … We will continue fighting for justice until someone is held responsible for my cousin's murder'. The family will appeal to the Lords.

4.59   This whole case, serious and tragic though it is, must fall outside of gross negligence manslaughter for the organisation and the officers involved. However, on 1 November 2007 the Metropolitan Police was found guilty of a single charge under HSWA 1974, s 3 which requires an employer to ensure the safety of a person not in their employ. The penalty was a fine of £175,000 with £385,000 in court costs.[1]

It is important to note that in the context of this book it is not possible to examine this case in the detail that it requires but some points are included. The prosecution alleged that the police operation to follow and stop 27-year-old de

Menezes who lived in the same south London block of flats as the terror suspect Hussein Osman was carried out 'so badly that the public were needlessly put at risk'.

The judge called the case a 'corporate failure, not an individual failure'. He further stated that 'This was very much an isolated breach brought about by quite extraordinary circumstances. One person died and many others were placed in potential danger.'

During the trial, the jury heard that a surveillance officer was 'relieving himself' just as De Menezes left his home for the last time, and this meant that an opportunity to identify him was missed. To complicate matters, a specialist firearms unit, SO19 – since renamed CO19 – has been called to detain suspects but had not arrived.

One special branch officer told the jury he believed the delay was 'totally unacceptable' given that specialist units were told they were needed at 5am but had not been in position until 9.30am. That meant surveillance officers were told by superiors in Gold command to wait for the specialists to arrive in the mistaken belief that they would be in place before de Menezes entered Stockwell station.

Commanders twice changed their minds about who should move in on the suspect, the court was told. CCTV footage played to the court showed de Menezes walking down an escalator to the platform. Moments later, firearms officers arrived and shot him.

Crucial to the case was evidence concerning whether the police's shoot tot kill command, a codeword 'Kratos', was ever given. Ms Dick, who has since been promoted, said she had only issued a command to 'stop' de Menezes, implying a 'conventional challenge' by armed officers. The prosecution sought to portray the police operations room as chaotic.

Ronald Thwaites QC, defending, claimed that de Menezes had been killed because he acted in an 'aggressive and threatening manner' when challenged by police. He claimed the Brazilian could have failed to comply with officers because he thought he had drugs in his pocket (the court heard traces of cocaine were found in his urine) or because he had a forged stamp in his passport. In contrast Clare Montgomery, proscuting, told the court de Menezes had been acting no differently to 'hundreds of others' when he was gunned down.

In a highly unusual move, the judge, Mr Justice Henriques, allowed the jury to insert a rider, or caveat, into the verdict stating that Cressida Dick, the commander in charge of the operation of the day, should not be held personally culpable for the events.

Whilst the police must be accountable for their actions it could be argued that the successful prosecution under the HSWA 1974 may harm the security of the UK and put millions of members of the public at risk. The balance is such that we may have to accept the loss of one unfortunate individual against the loss of possibly hundreds of lives if a device is used.

---

1 See James Stureke, Guardian Unlimited, 2 November 2007, www.guardian.co.uk.

The Hatfield train crash

4.60   The fourth and final case considered here involves the train crash at Hatfield in January 2001 where four people were killed. The accident investigation found that a defect in the line had been discovered in November 1999 by Balfour Beatty and reported to Railtrack soon after. In contravention of the rules no speed restrictions were imposed. A report identified that work to replace the track should have been conducted but was not completed because a machine that would have speeded up the process did not arrive. Management should have closed the line or imposed a speed restriction, but this was not done. Five rail executives from Railtrack and Balfour Beatty were charged with manslaughter and Balfour Beatty was charged with corporate manslaughter. No board director faced prosecution even though they were aware of the critical situation.

4.61   The manslaughter charges against the five rail executives were dismissed when the trial judge ordered the jury to find the executives not guilty of manslaughter. The trial proceeded on the health and safety charges that were also made against all of the defendants.

4.62   Mackay J[1] told jurors:

> 'It is not open to you to convict any of the six defendants on charges of manslaughter. The trial will proceed on the health and safety charges faced by all the defendants.'

One very important aspect was that the judge said he could not give reasons for his decision. He told the jury:

> 'I must ask you to accept my ruling, which does not affect one way or the other the important decisions you will have to make when considering verdicts on the health and safety counts.'

Corporate manslaughter charges against Balfour Beatty, the engineering firm were also dismissed.

---

1 Tran, M, Guardian Unlimited, 14 July 2005.

90

4.63   The incident occurred when the London to Leeds train derailed at 115mph near Hatfield on 17 October 2000, after a stretch of defective track shattered. The prosecution claimed that faulty rails identified 21 months before the crash were left unrepaired and that more than 200 defects had been found on the 43 miles of line from Kings Cross. There were many other dangerous decisions made, mainly to cut costs and boost profits. The prosecution maintained that in the totality of the indictment the company was guilty and that the crash was a disaster waiting to happen which should have been avoided. Balfour Beatty admitted that between 14 December 1999 and 18 October 2000, the company failed to conduct the safe maintenance of the line to ensure passengers were not exposed to health and safety risks. It was said that there was no one single cause of the derailment but all the causes were significant when aggregated with failures on the part of others. The company admitted that they neither acted on reports of track defects at the crash site nor ensured that the reports were acted upon.

4.64   In November 2000 Gerald Corbett, the former Railtrack chief executive, admitted that the track was in an appalling and totally unacceptable condition and that there should have been a speed restriction. He further stated that there were a multitude of other things that should have happened but did not happen. He told the Commons Transport Select Committee that Railtrack and Balfour Beatty failed.

4.65   It is important to note that despite the admissions by Mr Corbett, who resigned after the tragedy, he did not face prosecution and in fact no board director faced prosecution. This meant that even with guilty knowledge, the *controlling minds* did not face trial for manslaughter or even lesser offences. Those who were prosecuted were managers further down the command chain.

4.66   At trial Richard Lissak QC[1] for the prosecution stated:

'… there were more than 200 maintenance defects over a 43-mile stretch of track north of London's King's Cross station. Eight months before the derailment, the rail was identified as needing replacement "urgently". A new rail sat alongside the track waiting for installation for at least five months before the crash took place.'

Timothy Langdale QC said:[2]

'Sean Fugill, a manager for Railtrack at the time of the October 2000 crash, had never been told, and had no reason to suspect, that inspections and patrols of the track were not taking place as they should [he] had he ever been aware that the rail which led to the crash had become a safety risk. The court was told that Mr Fugill was responsible for 1,400 miles of track. He was an honest, conscientious man, not disposed to be careless or negligent. The question was, how could he act if it was not brought to his attention? He was not the sort of man to gamble with safety. It was explained that it was not Mr Fugill's duty to patrol track to see how the contractor, Balfour Beatty was doing.'

---

1 Clark, A, *The Guardian*, 1 February, 2005.
2 Ibid.

4.67   Edmund Lawson QC, counsel for another Railtrack manager, Alistair Cook, told the court[1] that his client was 'wholly unaware and was never informed of serious defects'. The court was told that he [Cook] did not know until after the crash, that trackside inspection was being conducted with crass incompetence or that there had been a failure of those on the ground to identify and classify potentially dangerous defects.

---

1 Clark, A, *The Guardian*, 1 February, 2005.

4.68   The court was also told that Railtrack track engineer Keith Lea, was not guilty of gross negligence in his handling of Balfour Beatty's plan to deal with the backlog of defects on the southern end of the east coast mainline. It was said that:[1]

'Two senior engineers from Balfour Beatty had gone to see him to say that additional manpower and resources were being injected into the area to reduce the backlog. It was said that Lea had no reason to question the professionalism of the two men or the integrity of the recovery plan which had been worked out. The two men were qualified engineers, speaking with the authority of Balfour Beatty behind them.'

---

1 Clarke, A, *The Guardian*, 1 February 2005.

4.69   It was explained to the court that as part of the privatisation the engineering expertise which had resided in British Rail should be carried over into the contractors. The broken rail which caused the accident was described by health and safety experts as containing one of the worst cases of fatigue they had ever seen. Yet no speed restriction had been imposed in the area.

4.70   Mark Milner reporting in the *Guardian*,[1] said that at the opening of the trial, prosecutors said the Hatfield crash was a disaster waiting to happen but which should have been avoided. Mr Richard Lissack QC said there had been a 'cavalier approach to the safety of those in trains'. But he said:

'I regard Balfour Beatty as one of the worst examples of sustained industrial negligence in a high risk industry I have seen. Over three-quarters of a million passengers would have been put at risk by passing over this area. Both companies fell below appropriate standards. Balfour Beatty's failure lay at the top of the scale.'

However, Balfour Beatty's counsel, Ronald Thwaites QC, rejected allegations that the company was 'indifferent' to safety or had neglected its obligations.

---

1 15 July, 2005.

4.71   Jonathan Goldberg QC,[1] for the five men, Alistair Cook, Sean Fugill and Keith Lea from Railtrack, and Tony Walker and Nick Jeffries from Balfour Beatty, told the jury at the opening of the trial that it would be unfair to make the men scapegoats and said:

> 'They were honourable men doing their duty. These five men worked in an underfunded, under-invested railway industry which had been neglected by governments for over 40 years and which had recently undergone a botched and unworkable privatisation.'

A view was expressed that:

> 'People will see this as another example of the failure of the existing corporate manslaughter law to secure a conviction. It will increase the pressure for reform, which is already very considerable.'

---

1 As reported by Mark Milner, *The Guardian*, 15 July, 2005.

4.72   A very important newspaper report stated:

> 'Ten days after the October 17 2000 crash in which four people died, the prime minister was pressuring Railtrack bosses into changing emergency safety measures to try to get services back to normal quickly ... Railtrack raised speed restrictions because the risk had been 'syndicated with the prime minister', according to a diary entry by David Ventry, Railtrack's head of track ...'

The court heard an extract, which read:

> 'On the morning of October 27 Gerald Corbett [Railtrack's former chief executive], Richard Middleton [Railtrack's commercial director] had had a breakfast meeting with Tony Blair, the prime minister ... He told them that the network must return to normal quickly ... I [Mr Ventry] was asked into Gerald Corbett's office at 9.30am on October 27 and told that I had applied the right action [in imposing speed restrictions] but pressure had been applied by the prime minister'

Quoting Mr Corbett, the entry read:

> 'The risk has been syndicated with the prime minister and I will now accept a higher level of risk.'

Asked what he thought this meant, Mr Ventry told the court:

'It was clear to me that we must increase speeds and accept a lower level of safety.'

---

1 Milner, M, *The Guardian,* 15 July, 2005.

4.73   A month later Richard Middleton, effectively acting as Railtrack head following Mr Corbett's resignation, had a further meeting with Mr Blair. Mr Ventry's diary for 28 November 2000 read: 'Told of pressure to increase speed.' Later, it was decided that speed limits were to increase from 20 mph to up to 60 mph. Of the demands made by the government, Mr Ventry told the court:

'I was uncomfortable with the pressure. I thought it was inappropriate.'

4.74   Richard Lissack QC for the prosecution stated that there were more than 200 maintenance defects over a 43-mile stretch of track north of London's King's Cross station. Eight months before the derailment, the rail was identified as needing replacement 'urgently'. A new rail sat alongside the track waiting for installation for at least five months before the crash took place. Mr Lissack revealed that senior executives from the two companies met six months before the crash to discuss the poor state of the east coast mainline. At the meeting he said Railtrack granted a 'general derogation' to Balfour Beatty which waived usual maintenance deadlines because of a vast backlog of repairs. It was agreed by the men that the clock which measured time for carrying out outdated repairs would be turned back to zero. This was 'a flagrant breach of standards' which was outside the contractual obligations of both companies.

Comment

4.75   This is an interesting case in that from the evidence available it was a situation where the senior management of a private company were manipulated by the direct involvement of the Prime Minister. No member of the Board was prosecuted and the blame was placed on managers who were charged with manslaughter. The evidence shows that the trial was stopped and the judge was unable to tell the jury why. From what we have learned of the Prime Minister's input, he would have to have been called to court to give evidence. Senior managers knew of the dangerous conditions of the rails, they told the Prime Minister. He appears to have put undue pressure on the managers to keep the trains running. There was no possibility of a corporate manslaughter prosecution or gross negligence manslaughter prosecution of senior managers because of the law at the time. The jury would not have convicted the managers on the basis of the senior management and Prime Minister's interface. Under the terms of the new law the company could be charged with corporate manslaughter but if there is to be influence imposed by the Prime Minister or indeed other senior members of the Government there will not be a successful prosecution.

Summary

4.76   These are four very different cases, each with their own particular complications, reflecting the diverse range of cases that can be expected. With the new law in place it will be easier to prosecute companies for corporate manslaughter or corporate homicide. However, defences will be complex and with large organisations there may well be political influence. The one fact that will remain is that the directors of small businesses and sole traders will remain open to individual charges of manslaughter, whilst their counterparts in large organisations will still remain remote from individual prosecution for manslaughter.

Chapter 5

Corporate Manslaughter Outside the UK

Introduction

5.1   In the previous chapters the focus has been on workplace manslaughter in the UK but it is worth briefly examining the situation outside the UK legal system. The principal countries that are involved in changing their corporate killing or manslaughter laws include Australia, Canada, the USA and some European countries. This is part of a focus on corporate crime for health and safety failures. It is a topic that is discussed in the media as being introduced and those countries that are developing corporate manslaughter offences and strengthening existing health and safety legislation are being closely monitored.

5.2   It is important to note that as in the UK there is constant review and draft proposals in other countries and therefore, information quickly becomes outdated. This evidence is supported within *Corporate Liability: Work Related Deaths and Criminal Prosecutions*:[1]

> 'The issue of corporate criminal ability has been a concern not only in the UK, but also in other jurisdictions worldwide. Death resulting from accidents at work, and which have been caused by the failure of corporations to ensure safe working conditions and practices, is the subject of increased scrutiny by legislators.'

---

1 Forlin, G, Appleby, et al, *Corporate Liability: Work Related Deaths and Criminal Prosecutions*, Lexis Nexis UK, 2003, now published by Tottel Publishing Ltd.

5.3   Corporate criminal law for workplace offences is the focus of legislative reform and the subject of much debate on what penalties should be available to the courts. In fact literature on the subject focuses on the punishment element with two very distinct factions, those who want a manslaughter element with imprisonment as an option and those who do not. It a subject raised by Wells who states:[1]

> 'What about corporate penalties? Again, there are indications from other jurisdictions that this is an issue being taken seriously. It is trite to note that a company cannot be imprisoned. A combination of a fine and the incarceration of directors may be the most effective punishment. Fines are not the only option for the company itself. Corporate probation is used in the United States in addition to or as an alternative to fines. The maximum fine per offence was increased in 1984 to US$500,000 (half-million dollars) but the really significant changes came with the federal sentencing guidelines introduced in 1991, making companies vulnerable to extensive deterrent penalties.'

---

1 Wells, C, *Corporations & the Risk of Criminal Liability*, www.freedomtocare.org p 166 (2002).

Europe

5.4   There is a loophole in safety laws under which multinational firms based abroad and involved in some of the worst accidents in Britain have, by default, got away with refusing to pay the massive fines imposed on them. Examples include two prominent incidents involving non UK companies; while they did not involve manslaughter they do raise serious questions about liability. The first involved two Swedish companies who were contractors involved in the walkway collapse at a port in Ramsgate, Kent, in which six people died and seven were injured. They were fined but have not paid any of the £1.25m in fines and costs. Two British companies, Port Ramsgate Ltd and Lloyd's Register of Shipping, which were also convicted, had to pay their penalties of £1.7m. The Swedish firms, Fartysentreprenader AB and Fartysgskonstruktinor, of the Mattson Group, did not attend the court.

5.5   The second case involved an Austrian company, Geoconsultants, which was convicted following the collapse of a tunnel at Heathrow, west of London, in October 1994, and has not paid any of the £500,000 in fines and costs despite losing its appeal against conviction, while Balfour Beatty paid its fine of £1.2m. The UK Government is negotiating with other EU states to make payment of criminal fines enforceable for companies wherever they trade, but it is acknowledged that there will still be difficulties with multinational corporations based abroad.

5.6   This poses a serious and growing problem and it may be that if foreign companies are to operate in the UK some form of indemnity to ensure legal liability cover should be provided so that fines can be recovered through the UK courts. At present there is no incentive for foreign companies to adopt UK health and safety systems, which could have the effect of placing UK business at a disadvantage.

5.7   Europe itself poses an interesting view on health and safety law, crime and punishment in that the principal focus is on insurance as opposed to authority regulation. This is further portrayed in a system of defined compensation and rehabilitation programmes as opposed to enforcement, prosecution and civil claims for compensation. European civil code countries, where non-human liability under penal law has been historically unacceptable, have enacted a raft of administrative penalties for corporate wrongs. France has had corporate criminal liability since March 1994 with rules that apply not only to corporate entities but also to other entities such as trade unions and local authorities. Portugal, Spain, Norway, Finland and Denmark have all incorporated criminal punishments against culpable corporations under their new or revised penal codes.

5.8   The obtaining of a full and clear picture of corporate health and safety crime in European countries is according to Jacqui Welham[1] (who researched the subject) a difficult task in that there is a variance in the method and type of statistical gathering. This is further hindered in that not all countries make information and statistical data available, but there is evidence that it is getting better. From the data that is available it can be ascertained that penalty options include:

*   Austria: Fine, non-accidental injury or negligent homicide; tribunal's sentence: imprisonment or fine.

*   Belgium: Prison sentence or fine. If judge decides not to prosecute an administrative fine is imposed on employers.

*   Germany: Enterprises are made to pay penalties for failure to comply with legislation.

*   Ireland: Average fine £5,000. Maximum on summary conviction £1,500; unlimited on indictment, maximum to date £15,000.

*   Spain: Financial penalties and administrative fines.

*   Sweden: Fines – only two cases of imprisonment in last 27 years.

---

1 Welham, J, *European Health and Safety Law – Transposition and Harmonisation*, LLM Thesis, University of East Anglia, 2002.

5.9   European countries place emphasis on rehabilitation, to return people to work as opposed to making civil compensation claims. Austria, Belgium,

Finland, France, Germany, Ireland, Italy, Luxembourg, Netherlands, Spain and Sweden have workplace insurance compensation schemes. There was no data for Greece or Portugal and both Spain and Ireland have civil claim options.

Italy

5.10   Two examples of prosecution for manslaughter at work offences in Italy are identified. The first occurred in the mid 1970s when two owners of a dye factory in Turin,[1] were sentenced to six years in prison after 13 workers died of bladder cancer. This was caused by their chemical exposure and the outcome was manslaughter charges. Two other directors were sentenced to three and four years respectively and the company doctor was sentenced to four and a half years. The second case was more recent and more serious and occurred in 1996. A court in Turin jailed the nine owner managers of the Societa Italiana Amianto, an asbestos factory, for terms of between seven months and eight years and ordered them to pay compensation totalling $12million. The company bosses had been found guilty of murdering 32 workers and of causing the occupational disease suffered by 11 more who were still alive. It is interesting to note the use of the word murder. In comparison, the UK sees self-employed and director/ owners of small business facing very limited custodial sentences. This is in contrast with large undertakings where no senior representative has been imprisoned unlike the asbestos case sited above.

---

1 Risk 69–31, Trade Union Congress e-bulletin, August 2002.

Italian Civil Aviation Disaster

5.11   An Italian judge said that an out-of-service ground radar unit at a Milan airport and confusion in the control tower were key factors in the 2001 crash of an SAS airliner and a small aircraft that killed 118 people. Judge Nicola Clivio made his comments in July 2005[1] in a 200-page document explaining his reasons for convicting four people and acquitting three others in March in the trial for Italy's worst civil aviation disaster. Judges in Italy are required to give a written explanation after they issue a ruling. Three of those convicted in March were employees of Italy's air traffic control agency, ENAV, and one was an official at Milan's Linate airport, where the crash occurred. Clivio wrote that those convicted were responsible for the inefficiency of the air traffic control unit and for leaving the airport's ground radar out of service. Clivio wrote that all those involved had the certainty that the ground radar was indispensable in the environmental conditions in which Linate was operating.

---

1 www.news.bbc.co.uk/2/hi/europe/4348077.stm – 37k – Supplemental Result.

5.12   The crash occurred on 8 October 2001 when a corporate jet and a Scandinavian Airlines System airliner bound for Copenhagen collided in the morning fog on the Linate tarmac. The collision killed 110 people on the SAS MD-87 jetliner, four people on the Cessna business jet and four ground crew. The victims included Italians, Danes, Swedes, Finns, Norwegians, a Romanian, a Briton, an American and a South African. While the clearance given by the control tower to the planes involved was the main human error behind the crash, lack of organisation at the traffic control unit played a 'decisive role'.

5.13   The four people convicted in the crash were sentenced to prison terms of up to four years and four months for multiple manslaughter charges. Also convicted in a separate trial in 2006 were four other people, including the controller on duty the morning of the crash and a former chief executive officer of ENAV.

Germany

5.14   In the UK, there has been a series of failures to prosecute senior corporate officers in the litany of rail disasters. This imbalance is further exemplified in a German case[1] where an example of manslaughter at work in Germany is portrayed by the following case:

> 'Two German rail managers and an engineer are in court accused of responsibility for the country's worst post-war rail disaster. The three men are blamed for the deaths of 101 people who were killed when a high-speed train smashed into a bridge near the town of Eschede in June 1998. The two high ranking Deutsche Bahn officials and the engineer went before the court ... charged with manslaughter and causing bodily harm through negligence ...'

The outcome of the case is not known, but clearly the German courts have a legal system that readily allows for the prosecution for manslaughter in a large undertaking where negligence is the focus of the charges.

---

1 Risk 69–31, Trade Union Congress e-bulletin, August 2002.

France

5.15   In France there is evidence that there have been changes in health and safety law following an explosion at a chemical factory in Toulouse.[1] The explosion killed 30 people and 2,500 others were injured. Four months after the disaster the French cabinet was said to be examining a package of new laws aimed at reducing the risk of industrial accidents. A media report provides a brief insight into both sides of what will probably be an ongoing debate, the government producing laws that will not be onerous on industry and the 'other side' who will claim the laws do not go far enough. Whatever the outcome, it must be presumed that the pending laws will strengthen health and safety regulations with serious corporate failings falling within a manslaughter offence.

---

1 www,bbc.co.uk/1/hi/world/Europe/1817986.stm

Mont Blanc Tunnel Fire

5.16   A French judge[1] pronounced ten defendants and three companies guilty of manslaughter in connection with the Mont Blanc tunnel fire that killed 39 people in 1999. The verdict came after a three-month trial at Bonneville Criminal Court in the French Alps. Civil servants, security advisers and the Mayor of Chamonix were among the defendants whose failure to prepare for a fire, or take effective action when one broke out, was condemned by judges.

---

1 www.english.peopledaily.com

5.17   The 16 defendants on trial were mainly individuals and companies that oversaw the tunnel and its security. They faced questions about a shortage of security equipment, the lack of security preparedness exercises before the fire and a mishap with the ventilation system that appeared to fan the fire rather than put it out. The prosecutor said expert testimony had cast substantial doubt on whether the company could be held responsible.

5.18   The court ordered a four-month suspended sentence for the driver of the Volvo truck, Gilbert Degrave of Belgium, who was transporting flour and margarine when his vehicle caught fire. He was convicted of manslaughter. Investigators said the truck caught fire after an external heat source, possibly a cigarette, came in contact with the truck's air filter. Shortly after the incident, Mr. Degrave said he had been alerted to the fire as oncoming vehicles flashed their headlights about halfway through the tunnel. After he stopped and checked underneath the truck, it exploded in a ball of fire. The court was told that the nearest smoke detector was broken, that radio frequencies were incompatible with those used by French emergency services and that Italian authorities pumped air into the tunnel instead of extracting the smoke.

5.19   About 20 tractor-trailers and 11 cars were destroyed in the fire. French investigators said a two-way ventilation duct apparently left in the wrong position by Italian authorities may have fed the fire, blowing cold air into the tunnel instead of sucking smoke out. The 11-kilometre passage, inaugurated in 1965, was closed for more than three years to be rebuilt and fitted with safety improvements. The fire was one of the worst road disasters in European history. The six-month trial followed a 4½-year investigation into the 24 March 1999 inferno. The court acquitted Swedish bus and truck maker Volvo in the deaths. Investigators said they found defects in Volvo FH12 trucks, the model involved in the fire, but the prosecutor said expert testimony had cast substantial doubt on whether the company could be held responsible. The blaze burned for two days while firefighters tried to reach victims and vehicles trapped inside the tunnel under Western Europe's highest peak. Families of the victims said they were satisfied with the sentencing, which for many defendants was heavier than what the prosecutor requested.

5.20   The heaviest sentence went to Gerard Roncoli, the French head of security at the tunnel. He was given a six-month jail term with an additional 24-month suspended sentence. State Prosecutor Vincent Le Pannerer had requested a 30-month suspended term for Mr Roncoli, saying it was his job to run the tunnel and his fault that safety measures had failed. He was also fined £8,300 for what the president of the court called an 'avoidable catastrophe'. Remy Chardon, former president of the French tunnel operator ATMB, was given a two-year suspended jail term and an $18,000 (US) fine, while Michel Charlet, mayor of the nearby town of Chamonix, got a six-month suspended term and a $1,800 fine. Six other people, including the tunnel's Italian security chief, were handed suspended terms and fines. Three companies, the French and Italian firms that operated the tunnel received fines of up to $180,000. Two other people were acquitted of manslaughter charges along with Volvo.

Finland

5.21   On 31 May 2006 a Finnish district court found a lorry driver guilty of 23 counts of negligent manslaughter and handed him a three-month suspended sentence.[1] The driver was behind the wheel of the lorry whose cargo of 700kg paper rolls tore into a coach in March 2004, killing 23 people and injuring 15. The court also ordered haulage firm Transpoint to pay a 10,000-euro corporate fine for an occupational safety crime. However, the court rejected relatives' demands that Transpoint pay compensation for suffering, saying there had been no intentional or aggravated negligence. The court added that the driver had maintained excessive speed considering the circumstances and that overload had contributed to him losing control of the vehicle.

1 Unidentified Source.

Canada

5.22   In Canada the Occupational Health and Safety Act allows those convicted where there is a death at work to be imprisoned. While custody is not a common option, it is available and it is used. A case that explores the custody option and a possible trend to provide more custody cases is summarised under the title *Jailhouse blues – The punishment to fit the crime, but will it deter others?*[1]:

'On June 1, 2000, Michael Peetz, a former supervisor of New Sun Cookies, was sentenced to 20 days in jail for violations of the Occupational Health and Safety Act related to the fatal injury of a worker. This is just the third time that a supervisor has been jailed for a conviction under the act.

This case raises important issues about the role of jail term penalties, the most effective means of encouraging compliance with health and safety legislation, and whether this case indicates a trend on the part of the Ministry of Labour to seek more jail terms.

On February 11, 1999, David Ellis, of Burlington, was removing cookie dough from an industrial ribbon mixer when the mixer became activated. Ellis was drawn into the mixer by the rotating blades and struck his head on the edge of the mixer. He died of head injuries six days later. The incident occurred on Ellis' second day on the job. He was only eighteen years old at the time of the incident.

The employer, 1169711 Ontario Inc., operating as New Sun Cookies, an Oakville cookie manufacturer, was charged with violations of the act. The employer pleaded guilty to failing to ensure that the exposed moving parts of the mixer were guarded contrary to section 24 of the Regulation for Industrial Establishments and section 25(I)(a) of the act.

At the time of the guilty plea, Peetz was no longer a supervisor at the company. Richard Hates, supervisor at the time of the plea, also pleaded guilty to one count each of failing to ensure that the exposed moving parts of the mixer were guarded contrary to section 24 of the Regulation for Industrial Establishments and section 27(I)(a) of the act. The two individuals accused were co-owners of the company at the time of the incident.

The company was fined $62,500 and Peetz was sentenced to 20 days in jail. Bales was fined $7,500. The penalties were levied by Justice John Takach of the Ontario Court of Justice in Oakville. It was the third time in Ontario a jail term has been ordered for violations of the act. Jail terms were ordered for individuals in unrelated matters in 1993 and in 1988.'

1 Keith, N, *Accident prevention*, October, 2000.

5.23   The case above was heard in Ontario, but that is not the only province in Canada to employ custody as a sentence for health and safety offences. A case heard in British Columbia showed that custody was used under the province's Industrial Health and Safety Regulations. The case is summarised under the title *What's happening elsewhere*:[1]

'Ontario is not the only jurisdiction in Canada seeking jail terms for individuals who contravene health and safety laws.

On February 16, 2000, in Port Alberni provincial court (British Columbia), Maurice Ricard, a supervisor at Vantastic Holdings Ltd., pled guilty to two charges of violating the province's *Industrial Health and Safety Regulations*. He was sentenced to 45 days in a jail per count, to be served concurrently. This is the first time a BC court has imposed jail sentence for a violation of the regulations. Vantastic Holdings also pled guilty to two charges and was fined $15,000, which it has two months to pay to the Workers' Compensation Board. In addition, Vantastic must submit a report to the board outlining the maintenance schedule and condition of all its mobile equipment.

This prosecution arose from a June 13, l996 accident in which a young worker was killed on his first day on the job while riding in a fully loaded five-tonne tuck. The vehicle lost its airbrakes on a steep logging road. The operator of the truck, Maurice Ricard, was neither trained nor licensed to operate an airbrake-equipped vehicle.'

The evidence shows that in Canada there already exists the option to use custody for workplace prosecutions. However, there still remains the situation where there is a need for a corporate manslaughter offence.

---

1 Keith, N, *Accident prevention*, October, 2000.

The Westray Case

5.24   Westray[1] was an underground coalmine in Stellarton, near New Glasgow, Pictou County, Nova Scotia, Canada, that blew up on 9 May 1992 instantaneously killing all 26 people working in the mine. Westray was a corporation wholly owned by Curragh Resources, a company controlled by Clifford Frame and based in Ontario. The disaster resulted in a Public Enquiry, which began public hearings in May 1995. Clifford Frame, the CEO of Curragh Resources and Marvin Pelley, vice president of Curragh Resources and president of Westray refused to cooperate with the enquiry. The management used every legal avenue to avoid being subpoenaed to give evidence. Gerald Phillips, the Westray mine manager, and Roger Parry, the underground manager also refused to take part in the enquiry and left Nova Scotia despite facing criminal charges. There can be little doubt as to why there is a prolonged campaign to change the corporate manslaughter laws, as the existing legal structure is totally inadequate.

---

1 www.uswa.ca/eng/hse/bkg468_2.htm

5.25   In an article *Bureaucrats, bosses blamed for mine deaths* Hamilton[1] examines the Westray case:

'Westray inquiry cites "incompetence, mismanagement, bureaucratic bungling, deceit, ruthlessness, cover-up, apathy". A deadly mix of corporate ruthlessness and regulatory incompetence made the Westray coal mine "an accident waiting to happen" before an explosion killed 26 men, a provincial inquiry has found. "It is a story of incompetence, of mismanagement, of bureaucratic bungling, of deceit, of ruthlessness, of cover up, of apathy, of expediency and of cynical indifference," Nova Scotia Supreme Court Justice Peter Richard wrote in his long-awaited report ...

[Judge Richard concluded]... the explosion that ripped through the underground mine on May 9, 1992 was entirely preventable', subtitling his 750-page report *A Predictable Path to Disaster*. He had harsh words for the mine's managers and executives, the provincial bureaucrats charged with enforcing safety regulations and the politicians who blindly supported the risky venture ... Former Nova Scotia premier Donald Cameron and senior officials of the mine developer, Curragh Resources Inc., had blamed the explosion on miners who tampered with methane monitors. Judge Richard acknowledged that miners were guilty of "many dangerous and foolhardy practices" in the days leading up to the explosion. But he stressed that they were reacting to management pressure for increased production. In the end, it wasn't the tampering that caused the explosion but "a sad litany" of problems, including poor design, inadequate ventilation and non-existent safety training ... an unfathomable disregard for workers' safety, condemning the "cavalier attitude" of mine management and the "hands-off" approach of provincial regulators. He concludes that primary responsibility for safety at Westray lay with the mine's management.'

---

1 Hamilton, Graeme, Bureaucats, *Bosses blamed for mine deaths*, Ottawa Citizen, Tuesday 2 December 1997.

5.26   Westray management, starting with the chief executive officer (Clifford Frame):

'was required by law, by good business practice and by good conscience to design and operate the Westray mine safely, "... driven by production concerns, the company failed to properly train its workers and ignored warning signs". The report concludes that management was well aware that coal-dust accumulations and methane levels underground were hazardous ... management at Westray displayed a certain disdain for safety and appeared to regard safety-conscious workers as the wimps in the organization ... Faced with overwhelming evidence that Westray was unsafe, provincial Department of labour mine inspectors reacted with "apathy and complaisance," ... the "unacceptable performance" of Mr. McLean and his superior, Claude White. He recommends the two men who remain employed in the Labour Department's occupational health and safety division, "be removed from any function relating to safety inspection or regulation." ... Judge Richard concludes that the controversial mining project went ahead thanks to the "unwavering support" of the provincial government and the deep pockets of the federal and provincial governments, which together committed a total of more than $100 million.'

5.27 The legal system in Canada has introduced corporate probation, which came about as a result of the Westray Mine Disaster. The prosecution of the company failed because of the need to identify a controlling mind or directing mind, similar to problems faced in similar UK prosecutions. This led to all party support for a new bill which had similar objectives to the UK Corporate Manslaughter and Corporate Homicide legislation. Unlike the UK the Canadian legal system reviewed alternative sentencing options. The result was that new Canadian law created a criminal code duty on 'every one who undertakes, or has the authority, to direct how another person does work or performs a task … to take reasonable steps to prevent bodily harm to that person, or any other person, arising from that work or task'. The outcome is that Canadian law provides for probation orders which could be useful in directly influencing the future conduct of organisations convicted of offences.

5.28 Among the optional probation conditions available are:

- making restitution;

- establishing policies, standards, and procedures to reduce the likelihood of subsequent offences (however, the court must first consider whether it would be more appropriate for another regulatory body to supervise the development of implementation of such policies, standards and procedures);

- communication of those policies, standards, and procedures to its representatives;

- reporting to the court on the implementation of those policies, standards and procedures;

- identifying the senior officer responsible for compliance with those policies, standards and procedures;

- providing, in the manner specified by the court, the following information to the public, (i) the offence of which the organisation was convicted, (ii) the sentence imposed, and (iii) any measures taken by the organisation to reduce the likelihood of its committing further offences, and (iv) complying with any other reasonable conditions considered desirable by the court in preventing subsequent offences by the organisation or to remedy the harm caused by the offence.

The United States of America

5.29 The USA has diverse homicide laws whereby murder and manslaughter are determined in degrees. This allows the prosecutor flexibility when identifying potential charges against corporations or individuals and means that in certain circumstances charges of murder can be applied in workplace fatal incidents.

5.30 In debating the subject of corporate or workplace crime and punishment, there is concern that issues identified ten years ago have not changed and it is said that corporate negligence still remains unchecked. It is the focus of an article under the heading *Corporate Crime and Punishment*[1] that states:

> 'Corporate carnage and crime runs rampant. That was the central argument of an editorial published at the beginning of the decade. Sadly, almost nothing has changed. The close of the decade marks yet another 10 years of largely unrestrained corporate criminality and violence. Nor has corporate criminal enforcement advanced noticeably … Russell Mokhiber's report in this issue on the top 100 corporate criminals of the 1990s illustrates at least four critical components of the problem.

> First, corporate crime is pervasive. The most serious acts of corporate criminality, which are measured by size of resulting fine, involve many of the largest and most well established companies in the United States and the world. (Mokhiber's review only covers US prosecutions.) Companies with familiar names like Alcoa, Borden, Bristol-Myers Squibb, Chevron, Eastman Kodak, Exxon, General Electric, Hyundai, IBM, Mitsubishi, Royal Caribbean and Tyson Foods were among the decade's leading corporate criminals.

> Second, criminal prosecutions are not done for "technical" violations of the law, but generally for intentional or reckless acts. Many of the top 100 cases involve premeditated, planned and consciously designed criminal acts.

> Third, financial penalties for corporate crime are far too small to deter wrongdoers. When Kodak was hit with a $1 million fine for a chemical spill, one neighbouring resident correctly said, 'It's equivalent to you or I getting a jaywalking incident.' With perhaps an arguable exception in the case of cartels and overt price-fixing, it is generally the case that corporate crime pays.

> Fourth, criminal prosecutions are infrequent compared to the massive number of regulatory violations; and too many acts of corporate wrongdoing are improperly considered civil violations under the law, or are defined as legal altogether. No example makes the point more clearly than the tobacco industry's escape from criminal prosecution, despite its well documented record of concealing health risks and the addictive properties of smoking, manipulating cigarette ingredients to promote addiction, and marketing to children …'

---

1 *Corporate Crime and punishment*, Multinational Monitor, June 1990.

5.31 There was dissatisfaction with the outcomes and the article goes on to identify changes that should be adopted which are more aggressive and creative as corporate criminal sanctions and include:

'... Equity fines: The payment of fines not in cash, but stock, a penalty that diminishes the value of already issued stock and garners shareholder attention;

Probation: Placing companies under the continuing surveillance of a court-appointed supervisor, with strong sanctions-issuing powers for repeat violations;

Revocation of subsidies and privileges: Taking away government-granted tax and other subsidies, or denying government-granted privileges for corporate offenders; and

Adverse publicity: Requiring corporate criminals to advertise their criminal convictions, an antidote to the image-enhancing advertisements ...'

In addition to the ultimate sanction of imprisonment there are serious reviews of possible options to punish and deter corporate failures. Until there are effective sanctions available to the courts and the will of those courts to deliver substantive penalties there will continue to be a disregard for the safety of those at work.

5.32 The National Institute of Occupational Safety and Health (NIOSH) reports that homicide is the second leading cause of death in the workplace. Murder is the number one killer of women and the third leading cause of death for men, after motor vehicle accidents and machine-related fatalities. Annually, robberies account for the greatest number of workplace deaths, followed by business disputes, personal conflicts, and law enforcement line-of-duty deaths. The large majority of workplace homicides are committed by firearms.

5.33 Workplace violence costs American businesses over $4 billion annually, including lost work time, hiring and retraining of new employees, decreased productivity, increased insurance premiums, increased employee medical benefits payouts, increased security costs, bad publicity and lost business, and expensive litigation costs. The average cost of a single workplace violence incident was $250,000 in the mid-1990s.

5.34 According to Bureau of Justice statistics and other studies, the riskiest occupations for all different forms of physical injury are recreational workers, bartenders, liquor store salespersons, taxicab drivers, retail sales clerks, food service workers, police officers, parking attendants, auto mechanics, security guards, social workers, grocery store and jewellery store cashiers, bus drivers, firefighters, and service station attendants. Service and sales workers have the most work-related homicides, especially if they work alone and/or at night, followed by executives, administrators, and managers. Non-lethal violence can also take the form of sabotage against company or personal property, as well as bullying, intimidation, sexual harassment, stalking, and domestic violence spillover.

5.35   Organisations who ignore the requirement for a safe place and systems of work leave individuals liable in the courts. One case was reported in an article entitled 'Cheese plant faces charges in death – Man died after slipping off greasy pallet in 1995':[1]

> 'A cheese factory faces criminal charges in connection with the death of an employee who fell into a grinder while cutting large blocks of cheese and loading them into the machine. A criminal complaint alleges that Mid-America Dairymen Inc., which has since become Dairy Farmers of America Inc., caused the death by knowingly creating and maintaining dangerous working conditions. The company has been charged with third-degree murder, second-degree manslaughter and wilful violation of employer duty. The charges result from an incident Oct. 25, 1995, when Jeffrey Steffenhagen, 33, was killed.
>
> Steffenhagen fell from a greasy pallet when a cutter broke while he was cutting cheese with his back to the grinder, according to the complaint. Safeguards for the grinding machine were not in place, despite the concerns of several employees ...'

---

1 www.uphere.com/news/stories/news-981111-211410.

5.36   The case highlights the point that in the case of a workplace death where a dangerous situation was created, the charges included murder and manslaughter to varying degrees. The outcome of the case is not known; however; the next example (which is not referenced) shows that the level of custodial sentence for a serious injury caused through the workplace can provide a deterrent factor.

> 'In 1999 a United States employer was jailed for 17 years for knowingly endangering an employee's life. Allan Elias, owner of Evergreen Resources,[1] an Idaho industrial chemical reprocessing plant, was also ordered to pay US$ 5.9 million in restitution to the employee, Scott Dominguez, and his family. Dominguez suffered severe brain damage after being ordered to clean out the sludge at the bottom of a storage tank that contained cyanide and phosphoric acid. Company boss Elias provided neither safety training nor equipment for staff. Speaking at the sentencing, Judge B Lynn Winmill said, "The sentence adequately reflects the danger Mr Elias posed to the community and to one individual in particular. I hope it will deter Elias and others similarly situated individuals in the future".'

---

1 www.vthc.org.au/anthonycarrick/overseas.

5.37 It is very useful to undertake a comparison at this point between the Elias case above and that of Jackson in the UK. Jackson Transport (Ossett) Limited[1] was convicted in 1996 of corporate manslaughter and fined £22,000.00. Its director Alan Jackson was convicted of individual manslaughter of one of his employees and jailed for 12 months and fined £1,500. The case centred on 21-year old James Hodgson, an employee of the company who died less than an hour after being splashed with a deadly chemical while cleaning the inside of a chemical tanker at Jackson Transport's base in West Ossett, Yorkshire.

---

1 Jollife, G, *Safety Management*, December 1996. see **3.27**.

5.38 In another case, a US company boss was found guilty of double homicide after the deaths of two employees.[1]

'Brent Weidman, the former president of Far West Water and Sewer Company, was found guilty by a jury of two counts of negligent homicide and two counts of endangerment in the deaths in 2001 of 26-year-old James Gamble and 62-year-old Gary Lanser. A sentencing hearing is expected to take place next week. The two men were killed in a confined space incident while working on an underground sewage tank. Gamble entered the tank to remove a plug that was blocking a line into the tank. He was overcome by hydrogen sulphide fumes when a pump that ran raw sewage into the tank from a different line was turned on. Lanser died trying to save Gamble. The air in the tank had not been tested on the day of the incident, the workers had not been properly trained and the required safety and rescue procedures were not followed. Last year, Arizona prosecutors Christina Fitzpatrick and Mark Horlings convinced a jury to find Far West guilty on five of the six felony charges filed against it. In January, a Yuma judge imposed $1.77 million (£960,000) in criminal fines against the company.'

---

1 Source unidentified.

5.39 It is worthy of note that the outcomes of the first two cases above, one in the USA and the other in the UK, both involved workplace inexperienced young men who were placed into confined areas containing toxic chemicals. Neither had been provided with safety training or personal protective equipment with the result that one died and the other suffered brain damage. The comparison is made that in the USA there was a custodial sentence of 17 years whilst in the UK it was 12 months. In the USA the compensation amounted to almost $6 million while in the UK there would have been a civil claim. There are no details of any settlement but it would not have reflected the level of payment made in the USA. It is also important that while Hodgson died, Dominguez was alive, albeit with a severe disability.

5.40 Russell Mokhiber[1] states that there is strong precedent for a criminal homicide investigation into the Sago mine disaster that killed 12 miners. The focus should be on the company that owned the mine and its executives. The Sago Mine is located in Upshur County, West Virginia. Mokhiber states in a letter to the County prosecutor:

> 'It is clear to that the corporate owners and executives of the Sago Mine are deserving of your attention … You are the only person with authority in West Virginia to bring a homicide prosecution. And there is strong – although little noticed – precedent for a homicide prosecution of a corporation and its executives in a worker death case.'

1 Mokhiber, R, *Corporate Crime Reporter*, January 9, 2006.

5.41   As part of his evidence, Mokhiber provided press reports documenting how over 23 months beginning in February 2004, two dozen miners were hurt in a string of accidents at the mine, some of them caused by rock chunks falling from the mine ceiling. The evidence also showed that federal safety inspectors executed the mine with 273 citations which equates to an average of one every two and a half days. In 1990, the SA Healy company of Milwaukee, Wisconsin was convicted of reckless homicide in connection with an underground explosion of methane gas that killed three workers.

5.42   Mokhiber explained that:

> '… the corporate owners of the Sago mine in Upshur County sent a group of workers into the mine. The owners of that mine knew the mine was unsafe and they knew that they could get away with running an unsafe mine, because the federal regulators have been effectively defanged.'

He continued:

> '… Twelve human beings are dead and one has been seriously injured. The 12 miners died at the hands of a corporation that operated an unsafe mine. The case reeks of recklessness. It is clear that federal regulators have not taken their responsibility seriously … you should investigate the Sago mine deaths with an eye toward a homicide prosecution. Federal regulators have been neutered. The Justice Department cannot bring a homicide prosecution in this case, even if they wanted to. It is up to you to fill the void and investigate and prosecute those responsible for this disaster.'

This clearly shows that the subject of corporate manslaughter is a growing issue around the world.

Australia

5.43   In Australia, the movement to introduce a corporate manslaughter offence made strong headway in the state of Victoria. It came with pressure to introduce the toughest industrial manslaughter laws in the country. The Victorian Trades Hall Council issued a press release about the Bill which states:[1]

' ... *Crimes (Industrial Manslaughter) Bill* allows the aggregate conduct of any number of employees, agents or officers of the company to be taken into account in determining guilt. The common law crime of manslaughter under the *Crimes Health and Safety at Work* can only look at the conduct of an identified individual, thus making it almost impossible to get a conviction, particularly when looking at the conduct of a large company ...'

1 www.vthc.org.au/anthonycarrick/overseas

5.44   The focus and pressure for a new law gathered pace and was the subject of a report, which saw the imminent introduction of a Bill. The Department of Justice, Victoria, Crimes Industrial Manslaughter Bill, will have an impact on business with regards to failures in health and safety. This was clarified by Dunlop, Chief Executive Officer of the Australian Institute of Company Directors who has identified in a report that directors, officers and senior managers potentially face liability in three areas, which are:[1]

'1)   Corporate manslaughter and negligently causing serious injury: liability under proposed section 14B (*5 years imprisonment and $180,000 fine or 2 years maximum prison term or $120, 000 fine respectively*); or

2)   The Occupational Health and Safety Act (Vic) 1985: liability under section 52A, for breach of the section 21 employer's duty (*$120,000 fine or 12 month prison term maximum*)

3)   Manslaughter pursuant to the Crimes Act (Vic) 1958: the EI acknowledges that the proposed new offences will co-exist with existing Crimes Act offences.'

1 www.companydirectors.com.au/posub/tdojvcimb

5.45   Concern has been raised that senior officers are subjected to too many offences, that the new offence is unnecessary and is deemed confusing and onerous on directors, senior managers and corporations. The report continues:

'Pursuant to section 14B of the proposed draft Bill, in circumstances where it is proved that a body corporate had committed an offence of either industrial manslaughter or negligently causing serious injury, a senior officer (as defined in sub-section 5 of 14B) will also be guilty of an indictable offence and liable to penalties, if that senior officer was:

●   organisationally responsible for the conduct or part of the conduct (presumably of the body corporate); and

- contributed to the commission of the offence of the body corporate; and

- knew or ought to have known that as a consequence of their conduct there was a substantial risk that the body corporate would engage in the conduct that involved a high risk of death or serious injury; and

- whose conduct involved a great falling short of the standard of care that a reasonable officer would exercise.'

5.46   The report identifies that one of the elements to be proved by the prosecution to link liability to directors, officers and senior managers:

'… is at best unclear and at worst, because it is vague, could operate unfairly to attach liability to a director or senior manager. It is of considerable concern that aggregated conduct (which has been justified on the basis of the difficulty in prosecuting corporations in the past) is likely to be relied upon either directly or indirectly in establishing liability against directors, officers and senior managers … That conduct is the aggregated conduct of any number of employees (whose conduct is not regulated by the proposed draft Bill) agents, directors, officers or senior managers. There is no justification for this aggregated conduct to be used against individuals.'

If the proposed changes are adopted, a senior officer of a corporation is faced with the burden of defending three separate offences, each with its own particular elements. This potentially creates a situation where it is unclear by what standards a senior officer would be judged.

5.47   In brief, the proposed draft Bill, if passed, would result in directors, officers and senior managers being subject to three separate and different regulatory regimes. Such over-regulation will result in confusion and unjustified hardship, not only for company directors but also, potentially, for persons who are not in positions of control over corporations. Moreover, there are sufficient avenues of prosecution against directors and officers under existing crimes and occupational health and safety legislation. There is no reason for the imposition of criminal liability on directors and officers based on the aggregated conduct of employees whose own conduct is not regulated by the proposed Bill.'

5.48   Although there were political promises of support to deliver the Bill, those promises failed to materialise and a political change of direction meant that the proposed Bill for Industrial Manslaughter failed to be enacted. Commentary deploring the action followed, but there is little evidence as to any sound reasoning as to why it was not forthcoming.[1]

'The Victorian Government has backed down on its promise to introduce controversial industrial manslaughter legislation despite a November landslide win that could guarantee the Upper House reforms it said were needed to push the laws through parliament ... the government said one of its key election commitments was to introduce the toughest OHS regime in the country by introducing the new crime of industrial manslaughter ... Victorian Government spokesperson ... sufficient to modify existing laws.'

1 www.companydirectors.com.au/posub/tdojvcimb.

5.49   The effects are far-reaching for the negative outcome shows that the political aspect is untrustworthy and there was never an accepted intention to support workplace health and safety. The situation is highlighted in another news item after the failure to introduce the Bill, which identifies the following issues:[1]

'A 17 per cent rise in Victorian workplace fatalities demands a policy reversal from the State opposition on the recently defeated Crimes Workplace (Deaths and Serious Injuries) Bill ... The State Opposition and Victorian employer groups based their earlier rejection of the Bill on the fact that workplace fatalities had been in steady decline since the introduction of the Occupational Safety Act in 1985 ... Australia has an extremely poor workplace fatality record in comparison to other industrialised countries. For every 70 workers killed in Australia, 53 are killed in the United States and 14 are killed in the United Kingdom.'

1 www.asuvic.org/asuvic_news.

5.50   In terms of law Australia runs a federal system of government with six separate 'states' and 'territories' which means that there are two parallel systems of criminal law. The federal criminal justice system is based on a very limited number of offences which are generally regulatory or common law.

5.51   Every year in Queensland, between 60 and 100 people die in workplace incidents and in 2000, the Queensland Government published a discussion paper proposing a new offence of 'dangerous Industrial Conduct (Causing Death or Grievous Bodily Harm)'.[1]

1 www.asuvic.org/asuvic_news.

5.52   Under the existing Criminal Code, there are a number of offences that a company or individual could be prosecuted for in relation to a work-related death or serious injury. These are:

'●   Manslaughter – this is defined as any unlawful killing that does not constitute murder and can be committed by criminal negligence which means that in such cases, it is sufficient if the prosecution shows that the act which caused the death was done by the accused person consciously and voluntarily, without any intention of causing death or grievous bodily

115

harm but in circumstances which involved such a great falling short of the standard of care which a reasonable person would have exercised and which involved such a high risk that death or grievous bodily harm would follow that the doing of the act merited criminal punishment'.

- Grievous bodily harm – involves criminal negligence resulting in grievous bodily harm and provides that any person who unlawfully does grievous bodily harm to another is guilty of a crime and is liable to imprisonment for 14 years.

- Negligent acts causing harm – provides that any person who unlawfully does any act or omits to do any act which it is the person's duty to do, by which act or omission bodily harm is actually caused to any person, is guilty of a misdemeanour, and is liable to imprisonment for two years.'

5.53   The Western Australian Government conducted a review of its safety legislation and a report issued in February 2003 contained 107 recommendations. One of them proposed that the Western Australian Government enact legislation to hold corporations and senior officers of corporations accountable for fatal workplace accidents.

5.54   The Tasmania Law Reform Institute has identified that Tasmanian law already allowed corporations to be found guilty of criminal offences. However, difficulties arose because crimes such as manslaughter or grievous bodily harm had evolved to deal with the actions of individuals. The problem is the same as all other countries in that manslaughter requires a homicide, which is defined as 'the killing of a human being by another', and that excludes organisations. This means that modern corporate decision-making made it hard to attribute actions and a state of mind to the head of the company. It is noted that the Tasmanian Chamber of Commerce and Industry rejected the Institute's recommendations, saying existing state law already covered the area comprehensively where companies face steep fines and potential loss of corporate reputation.

South Africa

5.55   South Africa has the Corporate Manslaughter Act and from limited information available it appears that it is being adopted as shown in the following cases. The legal battle between Metrorail and a Cape Town commuter group[1] came to a head in 2006. The Rail Commuter Action group has laid criminal charges against Metrorail under the Corporate Manslaughter Act. The defendants, Metrorail says crime on trains has decreased but the Rail Commuter Action group does not believe the situation has improved, and said it receives daily reports of crime and violence against commuters.

---

1 Unidentified source.

5.56   In the meantime the community police forum and the police from Elsies River in the Western Cape have launched their own campaign on train commuter safety and the community police forum handed out safety tips to commuters. The outcome is that some commuters said it is now safer to use trains in Cape Town following the introduction last year of 400 railway police members on trains and security staff on platforms.

Summary

5.57   When examining corporate manslaughter under its many titles there is no simple crossover for comparison as each country has a legal system that has evolved to suit its own requirements and a major factor is a country's workplace culture. This means that what is acceptable in one country may not be so in another. There are also factors such as compensation, remedial actions, rehabilitation and the degree of criminalisation for workplace incidents and injuries.

5.58   One thing that seems to provide a common thread is a need for some form of corporate manslaughter offence with a focus on holding senior management responsible for failures, particularly where there has been a death. Many of those where a corporate manslaughter offence is in debate or review are watching the UK and when the Corporate Manslaughter Act is fully adopted, it can be anticipated that there will be increased activity outside of the UK.

Part 2

Corporate Manslaughter and Corporate Homicide

Chapter 6

The Law Commission's Original Proposal

Introduction

6.1   The Law Commission produced a report in 1996[1] which outlined the proposal for new offences of reckless killing, killing by gross carelessness and corporate killing. It was a report with an accompanying draft Bill which was produced as a result of detailed consultations and research, covering a wide and diverse range of organisations, businesses and industries. It examined the failures of the existing law and reached a positive conclusion with the proposed offences.

1 The Law Commission, *Legislating the Criminal Code: Involuntary Manslaughter*, Law Commission No 237, HMSO, 1996.

6.2   It was four years later in 2000 when the Government produced *Reforming the Law on Involuntary Manslaughter: the Government's Proposals*.[1] This provided a draft Bill which was based upon the Law Commission's proposals. However, there was to be another five years and much debate before the Government produced a modified draft Corporate Manslaughter Bill (2005)[2] accompanied by another consultation period. A key element in the 2005 draft was the change in the title from 'Corporate Killing' to 'Corporate Manslaughter'. The more dramatic title of corporate killing was removed as well as the proposed individual offences which had been in the original Law Commission proposal and the Government's first draft Bill.

1 *Reforming the Law on Involuntary Manslaughter: the Government's Proposals*, The Home Office, 2000.
2 *Corporate Manslaughter: The Government's Draft Bill for Reform*, The Home Office, 2005.

Corporate offences

The original proposal

6.3   The concept of the original offence has been changed considerably and in this chapter some of the more far-reaching elements that have now been excluded are identified. The intention of the original proposed offence was to deal with deaths at work where there had been a management failure of such a serious nature that it warranted a charge of corporate killing. The proposed offence was developed strictly for the *undertaking* and not for individuals. If it was considered that there were individuals who could be identified as being at fault, they could be charged with either reckless killing or killing by gross carelessness. This meant that there would be no need to have been a controlling or directing mind, as under the current law of manslaughter because the offence would be one of management failure. It was anticipated that cases of individual failure would be from management, probably, but not exclusively, at board level.

6.4   Responsibility for the investigation and prosecution of the original corporate offence was anticipated to lie with the Health and Safety Executive (HSE) and other enforcing authorities. However, the report identified that there would need to be close co-operation with the police, as they would retain the authority to prosecute the individual offences. Clearly if there were corporate and individual prosecutions it would have been expedient to progress all matters together, and that would have involved a joint prosecution with the police and Crown Prosecution Service (CPS) in conjunction with the HSE or other regulatory body.

6.5   It was evident that the Law Commission's original proposal for corporate killing and the individual offences far exceeded in terms of seriousness an offence under the Health and Safety at Work etc Act 1974 (HSWA 1974) and it was the degree of seriousness resulting from a management failure that would have to be decided. The decision would be aided by the outcome of an accident investigation which would determine whether an *undertaking* would be charged with the offence of corporate killing. The original title of the offence was expected to have an added impact on the public's perception of the gravity of the offence and was intended to be clearly in the league of current law of manslaughter. The key element of the proposed offence was that the *undertaking* could be held liable and there would no longer have to be any individual identified as a 'controlling mind', which had been the problem under the existing law.

6.6   Under the original proposal, the offence would only have been prosecuted in the Crown or High Court and the penalty for an *undertaking* would have been an unlimited fine. Prosecution costs would have been claimed and awarded in addition to the fine. The court could also have ordered remedial actions that could have serious implications for an *undertaking*, particularly if an organisation was not financially sound. It further focused on the option that directors and senior officers could face disqualification from holding management positions. The courts could have taken the view that the management of an undertaking that failed to ensure safe practices and did not have the financial resources or management competencies available, should not be operating its business in any event. The implications for all *undertakings* and those who manage them were potentially serious with far-reaching consequences.

Undertakings

6.7   It was originally proposed that the law of corporate killing should encompass a diverse range of enterprises and it was intended to describe them as *undertakings* to conform with the meaning within the HSWA 1974, ss 2(1) and 3(1). Although an *undertaking* is not specifically defined in the HSWA 1974, the HSE have relied on the definition provided in the Local Employment Act 1960 where it is described as any 'trade or business or other activity providing employment'. This definition avoids many of the inconsistencies that would have occurred if the offence were applied to corporations but not to other similar bodies.

6.8   Clearly, the use of the word *undertaking* greatly broadened the scope of the original proposed offence. It would have encompassed the range of bodies that had previously not been classified as corporations, including schools, hospital trusts, partnerships and charities, as well as one or two person businesses such as self-employed gas fitters. In effect the offence would have applied to all employing organisations. The Law Commission sought to encompass all organisations whether incorporated or not and to use the collective term *undertakings*. However the new Act will only apply to *incorporated* companies.

The new offence

6.9   The new offence of corporate manslaughter has evolved to exclude reckless killing and killing by gross carelessness. The other change is that the offence of corporate manslaughter will be investigated by the police and prosecuted by the CPS. The HSE or local authority will assist with expert support in matters of health and safety. In addition it will apply to corporations and not to the wider context of 'undertakings'.

Individual offences

6.10   The original draft Bill produced by the Law Commission and the draft Bill in 2000 identified individual offences of reckless killing and killing by gross carelessness. However, the individual offences were totally excluded from the 2005 Corporate Manslaughter Bill.

Reckless killing

6.11   The offence of reckless killing would only have applied to incidents that occurred within the jurisdiction of the English and Welsh courts. Scotland was expected to make its own arrangements to align with the proposed offences.

6.12   The offence was to be one of homicide and was considered so serious that it fell just below that of murder. An individual found guilty of this offence could have faced life imprisonment. The key element of the proposed offence was that of continuing to act recklessly regardless of the outcome, despite knowing that there was a risk of death to another at work; that is, where an individual conducted themselves in such a way as to disregard risks that it would warrant a charge of reckless killing. This meant that for there to have been a failure there would have to have been an individual acting in some capacity either within an undertaking or as a self-employed person. In an undertaking the individual would probably, but not exclusively, be at board or senior management level and in either situation there would have been a death either at work or due to work activities.

6.13   It would have been a matter for the prosecution to prove beyond all reasonable doubt that a person was aware of the risks, in other words that they had the knowledge and understanding of the potential outcome. It would be the conduct of that person that would be identified as being the cause of the death or serious injury. It is impossible to provide a definition of serious injury and it would have been for the jury to determine, having heard all of the facts and circumstances surrounding the incident causing the death.

Penalty

6.14   The maximum penalty that was proposed for an individual convicted of reckless killing would have been life imprisonment. This was to reflect the seriousness of the offence which meant that the case would only have been heard in the Crown Court.

Killing by gross carelessness

6.15   The offence of killing by gross carelessness was also to be a serious crime but fell short of the most serious act of reckless killing. The distinction was to have been the degree of fault that distinguished between the two offences. The basis of the fault was that with reckless killing there would have been an act with full knowledge of the risk and failure to take action, while with killing by gross carelessness there would have been a failure to appreciate the consequences of an action.

6.16 It would have to have been proved beyond all reasonable doubt that a person's conduct caused the death of another. In other words, the conduct of a person would have caused the death and that would be obvious to a reasonable person in the same position. The word 'obvious" in this context means 'immediately apparent', 'striking' or 'glaring'. A person could not have been blamed for failing to notice a risk if it would not have been obvious to a reasonable person in his place. The use of *obvious* as opposed to *foreseeable* was in the defendant's favour. It followed that the person must have been capable of appreciating the risk at the time in question, and that the conduct of the person falls far below what could have been reasonably expected in the circumstances. An objective of the definitions within the offence was to avoid reliance on the concepts of negligence and duty of care, which have caused much concern to the courts over the years.

6.17 The second part of the proposed offence was that it was unreasonable for a person with knowledge of the facts to take a risk, having regard to the circumstances as they were known or believed to be. It would have needed to be proven that an individual was fully aware of the risks and potential outcome and, even with that information, allowed the situation to continue. In addition to being aware of risk, it would have been the element of conduct that was the cause. Following on from the awareness and conduct is the unreasonableness of the action and whether the conduct was *intended* to cause injury. The injury caused forms the basis of an offence. However, the proposed offence of killing by gross carelessness has not been included in the new Act.

Penalty

6.18 The maximum penalty that was proposed for an individual upon conviction for killing by gross carelessness would have been 10 to 15 years in prison. This meant that a case could only have been heard in the Crown Court. For a person found guilty of killing by gross carelessness the judge would have to have examined the mitigation submitted by the defence which would have been used in an effort to obtain the lowest possible custodial sentence. This would have included such details as the individual's antecedents with particular regard to health and safety, and their management status within an *undertaking*. This should have identified whether the individual had been in a position of authority and had been the recipient of the subject of formal enforcement notices, letters of condemnation, written or verbal warnings, any of which were focused on poor health and safety management or breaches of the appropriate legislation. Other factors would focus on whether there had been full co-operation by the individual with the investigating officers. The court would need to have considered the failures that had been a root cause of the incident and balanced them against any direct action or failure on the part of other senior managers.

Transmission of disease and corporate killing

6.19 It was originally proposed that a management failure in an *undertaking* which led to liability for the transmission of a disease which in turn led to death would be an offence. The liability could have arisen if a management failure was *a* cause; rather than the *sole* cause of death. It would have been necessary to show that the management's conduct had fallen far below what could be expected of an *undertaking* in the circumstances.

6.20 The transmission of disease is more complex than the general acceptance of the corporate killing offence and would have focused on those who recklessly or through gross carelessness passed on a disease that resulted in death. The *undertaking* would not have been liable where the transmission of a disease occurred directly between one individual and another unless the person who transmitted the disease owed the person to whom it was passed a professional duty of care. This was an important aspect and it would have been necessary to define the circumstances in which the transmission of disease could have been covered by the new offences.

6.21 An example provided in the Law Commission report described situations where the offence could have been used. One is where a baker sold pies that he knew were infected and which might cause death. This could have involved a corporate killing offence for the *undertaking*, but also an individual offence for the individual concerned. Another would be where someone contaminated food for blackmail purposes and a victim subsequently died. A further example was where a patient was infected with a disease due to the obvious recklessness or gross negligence of a health care worker. In this situation there was a duty of care, and the offence could have encompassed the *undertaking* as well as an individual. It would have been imperative that those undertakings where some form of disease could have been transmitted should have had effective safeguards in place. Staff would have to be aware of the potential risks, be competent and have sufficient knowledge and equipment to carry out their duties without risk to others.

Avoidance of responsibility

6.22 The Law Commission also proposed that there would not be scope for avoidance measures by unscrupulous *undertakings* or directors and that enforcement action would be applied to act as a real deterrent, even in large *undertakings* and within groups of *undertakings*. It would not have been possible for the holding organisation to have attempted to evade possible liability on a charge of corporate killing through the establishment of subsidiaries, who would carry on the group's riskier business and could most readily give rise to charges of corporate killing. A subsidiary *undertaking* within a large group of *undertakings* might have had insufficient assets to pay a large fine, and in such cases, liability could be transferred to its parent company. It was deemed important that group structures could not be used as a mechanism for evasion.

6.23 Directors of an *undertaking*, or of parent *undertakings*, would not have been able to evade fines or compensation orders, or otherwise frustrate corporate killing proceedings, by dissolving the *undertaking* or by deliberately making it insolvent. The court would have had the power to ensure that criminal proceedings in relation to corporate killing could have continued through to completion notwithstanding the formal insolvency of the *undertaking*.

6.24 One of the most controversial aspects of the Law Commission's proposal would have been the ability to allow for the assets of *undertakings* to be frozen pending the outcome of the trial. This would have been similar to the charging and restraint orders used under the drug trafficking offence legislation. In the case of a potential corporate killing prosecution, the prosecuting authority may have been able to take some form of action to freeze certain company assets before criminal proceedings were started. The objective would have been to prevent the directors or shadow directors of the *undertaking* transferring assets in the knowledge that it had been involved in a death that might give rise to a corporate killing charge. If this had been allowed to occur then the directors could have created a financial situation resulting in a much reduced fine.

6.25 The problem with this concept was that it is a fundamental principle of English law, also contained in the European Convention on Human Rights, that a person (including a legal person) is innocent until proven guilty. The court could more readily use such powers where a plea of guilty had been entered where there would be some knowledge of what the likely penalty was and therefore could freeze that portion of the assets. However, for the proposed offence of corporate killing to have been effective and encompass all *undertakings,* there would have to have been no legal loopholes and senior management would have been held culpable for any avoidance activities.

6.26 It will be seen that comparing what had been proposed by the Law Commission to what made it into the statute books varies a great deal in a number of key and important areas. One is the removal of individual liability as originally proposed, leaving only the option for a gross negligence prosecution where there is suitable and sufficient evidence. The other key change is from undertakings to corporations which has had the effect of excluding a wide and diverse range of organisations. However, it is argued that in unincorporated organisations individuals are already liable for individual offences as they are not shielded from exposure through a corporate body.

Chapter 7

Gross Negligence Manslaughter

Introduction

7.1 It is not the intention to describe in detail the criminal law of homicide which encompasses murder and manslaughter, but to provide an overview of the key elements and their status in the current criminal law. With regard to health and safety the offences are regulatory but where the degree of negligence has been so serious it goes beyond a regulatory situation and moves to the higher level of manslaughter. It will be seen that for an offence of manslaughter one individual has to do an act that causes the death of another. This means that when a company is in the course of its business the law requires an individual to be identified as being grossly negligent. In a large organisation that is generally impossible to do; individuals in small organisations can more readily be identified.

Homicide

7.2 The constituents of homicide are adequately described by Smith[1] as follows:

'The *actus reus* of murder and manslaughter is generally the same. It is the unlawful killing of any person "under the Queens Peace", the death following within a year and a day. It must be proved that the defendant caused the death of the deceased person. At common law homicide was committed only if the death occurred within a year and a day of the act of causing death. That rule was abolished by the Law Reform (Year and a Day Rule) Act 1996. If an act can be shown to be the cause of death, it may now be murder, or any other homicide offence, or suicide, however much time has elapsed between the act and the death. The Act, however, requires the consent of the Attorney General to the prosecution of any person for murder, manslaughter, infanticide, or any other offence of which the element is causing a person's death, or aiding and abetting suicide, (i) where the injury alleged to have caused the death was sustained more than three years before the death occurred or (ii) where the accused has previously been convicted of an offence committed in circumstances alleged to be connected with the death.'

---

1   Smith, JC, *Smith and Hogan, Criminal Law*, (9th edn) Butterworths.

Manslaughter

7.3   Manslaughter is described by Smith as a complex crime of no less than five varieties. It covers three cases where the defendant kills with the fault required for murder but, because of the presence of a particular extenuating circumstance recognised by law, the offence is reduced to manslaughter. These cases are traditionally known as *voluntary manslaughter*. The other cases are *involuntary manslaughter* and consist of homicides committed with a fault element less than that required for murder but recognised by the common law as sufficient to find liability for homicide. It should be emphasised that there is only one offence. Whether the defendant is convicted of the voluntary or involuntary variety, he is convicted simply of manslaughter. A life sentence is mandatory for murder but for manslaughter the maximum is life but with no minimum. It is an offence which may be committed with a wide variety of culpability and sometimes may be properly dealt with by a fine or a conditional or absolute discharge. The law might be summarised as follows:[1]

'A person is guilty of manslaughter where:

(a)   he kills or is a party to the killing of another with the fault required for murder but he acted:

   (i)   under diminished responsibility (Homicide Act 1957 s 2)

   (ii)   under provocation (Homicide Act 1957 s 3)

   (iii)   in pursuance of a suicide pact (Homicide Act 1957 s 4)

(b)   he is not guilty of murder by reason only of the fact that, because of voluntary intoxication, he lacked the fault required;

or

(c)   he kills another:

    (i)   by an unlawful and dangerous act; or

    (ii)   being (a) grossly negligent as to death or (b) reckless (in the Cunningham sense) as to the death or serious harm; or, possibly; (c) grossly negligent as to serious bodily harm or (d) reckless as to any bodily harm.'

---

1 Smith, JC *Smith and Hogan, Criminal Law*, (9th edn) Butterworths.

7.4   The case of *R v Cunningham*[1] concerned a charge brought under s 23 of the Offences Against the Person Act 1861, which makes it an offence 'unlawfully and maliciously' to administer etc to any person any poison or other noxious thing so as to endanger life or inflict grievous harm. The facts of the case involved Cunningham stealing a gas meter and its contents from the cellar of a house, during which a gas pipe was fractured causing coal gas to escape. This percolated through the cellar wall to the adjoining house and entered a bedroom, with the result that Mrs. Wade, who was asleep, inhaled a considerable quantity of the gas, with the result that her life was endangered. Cunningham's conviction was quashed because of the misdirection of the trial judge as to the meaning of 'maliciously' in s 22 of the Act.

---

1 [1957] 2 QB 396. See Smith, J.C. *Smith and Hogan, Criminal Law*, (9th edn) Butterworths.

7.5   Kenny[1] states:

'in any statutory definition of a crime, "malice" must he taken not in the old vague sense of wickedness in general but as requiring either (1) an actual intention to do the particular *kind* of harm that in fact was done or (2) recklessness as to whether such harm should occur or not (i.e. the accused has foreseen that the particular kind of harm might be done, and yet has gone on to take the risk of it). It is neither limited to, nor does it indeed require any, ill-will towards the person injured.'

The court held that the jury should have been left to decide whether, even if the appellant did not intend the injury to Mrs Wade, *he* foresaw that the removal of the gas meter might cause injury to someone but nevertheless removed it.

---

1 Kenny, Professor CS *Outlines of Criminal Law*, (1st edn, 1902), set out in the 6th edn (1952) p 86.

Voluntary and involuntary manslaughter

7.6   Where there has been a death, but the key element of intent is missing, the offence is reduced to that of manslaughter. There are two categories of manslaughter: voluntary and involuntary manslaughter. In the case of voluntary manslaughter the defendant has the *mens rea* and *actus reus* for murder but there are circumstances that offered some form of excuse for his conduct. On this basis, murder can be reduced to manslaughter on the grounds of provocation or diminished responsibility. These two manslaughter options are not offences in themselves but form a partial defence to murder. Involuntary manslaughter is unlawful homicide, but the *mens rea* for murder is not present. This is further divided into unlawful act manslaughter and manslaughter by gross negligence or recklessness. Unlawful act manslaughter is determined by an unlawful act as identified in *R v Church*[1] where a reasonable person would realise that it created a risk of injury, and death results. The defendant need not foresee the risk of death, nor need it be reasonably foreseeable.

---

1 [1965] 2 All ER 72.

7.7   The case involved Church who according to his account of events, took a woman, Mrs Nott, to his van for sexual purposes. He was unable to satisfy her and she reproached him and slapped his face. They had a fight and he knocked her out. He tried unsuccessfully for about half an hour to wake her, panicked, dragged her out of the van and put her in the river. Mrs Nott was drowned.

7.8   At the trial, for the first time, Church said that he thought she was dead when he put her in the water. The judge directed the jury that if Nott was in fact alive when thrown into the river, whether the appellant knew it or not, that was manslaughter; the jury convicted him of manslaughter.

Gross negligence manslaughter

7.9   Manslaughter by gross negligence occurs where there is an act or omission of negligence that goes beyond the civil law concept of negligence. The act or omission would be so extreme that criminal liability would be the outcome. The determination of the degree of negligence is a matter of legal process through the courts. It will be a matter for the jury to determine the degree of negligence to identify that there was gross negligence. The law was somewhat radically altered by the House of Lords judgment in *Adomako*.[1]

---

1 *R v Adomako* [1994] 3 All ER 79; [1995] 1 AC 171.

7.10   This was the case where Adomako was assisting as anaesthetist in charge during an eye operation. During the operation, the endotracheal tube carrying oxygen from the ventilator to the patient became disconnected. Adomako failed to notice the disconnection and some six minutes later the patient suffered a cardiac arrest from which, despite efforts at resuscitation, he died. At no stage did Adomako check the integrity of the equipment. The case against him was that he had been grossly negligent in failing to notice or respond appropriately to obvious signs that a disconnection had occurred and that the patient had ceased to breathe. The defence conceded at trial that the doctor had been negligent but denied that this negligence was so bad it should be deemed criminal.

7.11   In *Adomako*, Lord Macky LC ruled that the test for gross negligence:

> '... in my opinion the ordinary principles of the law of negligence apply to ascertain whether or not the defendant had been in breach of a duty of care towards the victim who has died. If such breach of duty is established the next question is whether that breach of duty caused the death of a victim. If so the Jury must go on to consider whether that breach of duty should be characterised as gross negligence and therefore as a crime ... The Jury will have to consider whether the extent to which the defendant's conduct departed from the proper standard of care incumbent upon him, involving as it must have done, a risk of death (to the deceased) was such that it should be judged criminal.'

The judge, appreciating the difficulty such a test postulated, went on to say:

> 'It is true that to a certain extent this involves an element of circularity, but in this branch of the law I do not believe that it is fatal to its being correct as a test of law for conduct must depart from accepted standards to be characterised as criminal. This is necessarily a question of degree and an attempt to specify that degree more clearly is I think likely to achieve only a spurious precision.'

7.12   It is important to note that being a director does not, on its own, give rise to a duty of care to those injured or killed by the company's activities under current law. The usual tests of foreseeability, proximity and reasonableness apply in determining whether such a duty arises.

7.13   Following the House of Lords decision in *R v Adomako*, the *actus reus*, or elements of the offence, of gross negligence manslaughter are that:

- the defendant owed a duty of care to the deceased;

- a breach of that duty was a substantial cause of death;

- the breach was so grossly negligent that the defendant can be deemed to have had such disregard for the life of the deceased that it should be seen as criminal and deserving of punishment by the state.

7.14   In the same case, the court went on to consider what might be considered to be a grossly negligent act. These included:

- an indifference to an obvious risk of injury to health;

- actual foresight of the risk coupled with the determination nevertheless to run it;

- actual foresight of the risk together with an intention to avoid it but involving such a high degree of negligence in the attempted avoidance as the jury considered justified conviction.

7.15   A charge of gross negligence has numerous factors to be considered and in a landmark decision, given on 5 October 2004, the Court of Appeal in *R v Misra and Srivastava*[1] was asked to consider if this offence is compatible with the European Convention on Human Rights (ECHR). It was argued by the defendants that the offence of gross negligence manslaughter breached art 7 of the European Convention on Human Rights as it was too uncertain. Article 7(1) states:

> 'No one shall be held guilty of any criminal offence on account of any act or omission which did not constitute a criminal offence under national or international law at the time when it was committed.'

---

1 *R v Misra; R v Srivastava* [2004] EWCA Crim 2375.

7.16   The defendants were doctors in charge of the post-operative care of the patient who had had surgery to repair a tendon in the knee. The outcome was that the patient became infected with staphylococcus aureus and died because the doctors failed to diagnose or treat it. Both doctors were charged with gross negligence manslaughter and convicted on the basis that they had failed to spot the signs of the condition and, as a consequence, did not treat it.

7.17   The defendants' lawyers argued that gross negligence manslaughter was an offence that lacked clarity and so was not compatible with art 7 of the ECHR. They argued that, in effect, the jury was being asked to consider whether any negligence found on the part of the defendants was so bad it was grossly negligent, and then to consider if it should be classed as a criminal offence. The Court of Appeal rejected this argument. What the law required was not for the jury to consider whether the conduct of the defendant should be a crime but whether the conduct was grossly negligent and consequently criminal. The Law Commission's paper *Involuntary manslaughter* (Law Com No 237) was relied on in support of this argument. The paper had identified that the current test was circular and this circularity led to uncertainty. On this point the paper concluded:

> 'It is possible that the law in this area failed to meet the standard of certainty required by the European Convention on Human Rights.'

7.18   The Court of Appeal held that the elements of the offence of gross negligence manslaughter were made clear in *Adomako* in that:

- a duty of care was owed;

- that duty had been broken;

- the breach of the duty of care amounted to gross negligence; and

- the negligence was a substantial cause of the death of the victim.

7.19   With regard to risk it is shown in *Adomako* and subsequent cases that the risk must relate to death. It is not enough to show that there was risk of bodily injury or injury to health. This means that the elements of gross negligence manslaughter are clear and there was no breach of art 7 of the ECHR.

Guilty act and guilty mind

7.20   A person cannot ordinarily be found guilty of a serious criminal offence unless two elements are present: the *actus reus* or guilty act and the *mens rea* or guilty mind. A wrongful act on its own therefore cannot usually be criminal unless the wrongful state of mind required for that offence is also present. The *mens rea* for murder is malice aforethought, and that term has been made clearer through a House of Lords decision in the case of *R v Moloney*.[1] The case involved a soldier who became involved in a heated discussion with his stepfather about guns. The stepfather goaded him that he would not dare to fire a live bullet. At that point Moloney fired a loaded gun at him and killed him. The case focused on the definition of malice aforethought and the House of Lords determined that nothing less than the intention to kill or cause grievous bodily harm would constitute malice aforethought.

---

1 *R v Moloney* [1985] 1 All ER 1025, HL.

7.21   The first element is called the *actus reus* of the crime. This is the guilty act or in some cases the failure to act, for instance the failure to comply with positive duties imposed by certain legislation. This is the part of the offence that is not concerned with the mental state of the person committing the crime.

7.22   Secondly, the *mens rea* of the crime must be established. This is the 'mental' or 'fault' element of the crime and varies with each crime. The *mens rea* can include intent, recklessness or gross negligence, each of which is tested by different criteria. The difficulty in establishing the *mens rea* in an offence committed by a corporation is discussed below.

7.23   Criminal law requires, in most cases, that for an offence to be committed both the *mens rea* and *actus reus* must exist at the same time or be sufficiently linked so as to create a chain of causation, but there are also offences of strict liability where only the *actus reus* is required and where there is no need to show any level of guilty intent.

7.24   The *actus reus* and *mens rea* of a corporation are raised by Clarkson[1] who states:

> 'The criminal law was developed as a mechanism for responding to individual wrongdoing. Individuals can be held responsible and blamed for their actions. Stigmatic punishment can be used to mark the appropriate degree of censure. Particularly when dealing with crimes involving *mens rea*, such individualistic notions of responsibility do not naturally encompass artificial organisations and could only be applied by humanising companies in the sense of breaking them down, metaphorically, into their underlying human components to see if there was an individual within the company who had committed the actus reus of a crime with the appropriate mens rea. This individual must be sufficiently important in the corporate structure to be said to represent the company's directing mind and will, and for his or her acts to be identified with the company itself; in such circumstances could be directly criminally liable (as well as the individual). This identification doctrine became established and the main route to the imposition of corporate liability, at least for crimes involving proof of *mens rea*.'

---

1 Clarkson, CMV, *Kicking Corporate Bodies and Damning Their Souls*, The Modern Law Review, 1996.

Culpable homicide

7.25   Culpable homicide in Scotland is the term which covers a number of different types of criminal homicide, roughly equivalent to manslaughter in other legal jurisdictions. The concepts are similar in that they both encompass cases where death is caused by improper conduct and where the guilt is less than murder. To convict anybody of a common law criminal offence (i e not one created by statute), it is necessary to demonstrate not only that their conduct fell below a certain standard of behaviour, but also to consider what they were thinking at the time. To achieve that intent, knowledge and recklessness are all different standards used to define what state of mind will make a harmful act a criminal one (as opposed to simple carelessness or accident). The mental element required for culpable homicide during the course of a lawful act was given by Lord Justice-Clerk Aitchison[1] who stated:

> 'The difficulty that the case presents is whether there was evidence that the appellant was guilty of criminal negligence in the sense in which we use that expression. At one time the rule of law was that any blame was sufficient, where death resulted, to justify a verdict of guilty of culpable homicide. Unfortunately, this law has to some extent been modified by decisions of the Court, and it is now necessary to show gross, or wicked, or criminal

negligence, something amounting, or at any rate analogous, to a criminal indifference to consequences, before a jury can find culpable homicide proved.'

---

1 Lord Justice-Clerk Aitchison, 1936, *Paton v His Majesty's Advocate.*

7.26   An outcome from the Transco appeal that it is not necessary to prove that the defendent owed a 'duty of care' (as is required in the English law of manslaughter). This was explained by Lord Osborne[1] who stated in his ruling that:

'From my consideration of the nature of the common law crime of involuntary culpable homicide, it appears to me to follow that civil common law duties of care, or civil statutory duties of care, can play no direct part in the assessment of guilt, except to the extent that their existence may serve to demonstrate the particular area of responsibility which an individual may carry.'

It is necessary to prove a particular state of mind on the part of the defendant rather than just assessing the conduct of the defendant against an objective standard.

---

1 See www.corporateaccountability.org

7.27   Lord Osborne stated further:

'… where there is an issue of involuntary culpable homicide, the resolution of the issue depends, not upon some objective assessment of the conduct of the perpetrator alone, but upon an assessment of "his state of mind at the time of the accident", in other words, an enquiry into whether he possessed the necessary criminal intent at the material time, namely a "complete disregard of potential dangers and of the consequences of his [conduct]".'

7.28   And Lord Hamilton[1] stated:

'… in my view, that under the law of Scotland the mental element (mens rea) is and remains a necessary and significant element in the crime of ("lawful act") culpable homicide. That element may, of course, be proved in various ways, including proof by inference from external facts. But it is, in my view, erroneous to suppose that the actual state of mind of a person accused of culpable homicide of this kind can be ignored and guilt or innocence determined solely on the basis of proof that the conduct in question fell below an objectively set standard.'

---

1 See www.corporateaccountability.org

7.29   In England it is not necessary to prove a particular state of mind (although it can be taken into account) and therefore, it is more difficult to prove that an individual has committed the offence of culpable homicide than that of manslaughter in England. With the introduction of the new law of corporate homicide court cases will highlight any disparities between the English and Scots law principles.

Manslaughter at work

7.30   Until the offence of corporate manslaughter and corporate homicide was introduced, there has not been an offence in law for corporate manslaughter and it is a term that has evolved. It occurs where those at the highest level of the organisation are grossly negligent and while they are charged with manslaughter, they are considered to be the embodiment of the organisation and therefore the offence constitutes corporate manslaughter. This is described[1] as being where there has to have been gross negligence on behalf of individual defendants who could be *identified* with the company and who are deemed to be the *controlling mind* who would themselves be guilty of manslaughter. In some cases it may be employees who are killed while in others it is members of the public. All have the common thread that there have been serious failings in the management of health and safety. The Health and Safety at Work Act 1974 (HSWA 1974) determines that it is the duty of the employer, in other words the board of directors of a company, to ensure the health and safety of those who are employed as well as those who are not employed but affected by their activities.

---

[1] Law Commission Report No 237.

7.31   To meet these obligations in their most basic form, corporations must provide a health and safety policy outlining the company's standards and objectives with regard to health and safety. That policy must be adopted and signed by the most senior person of the company. Even if this has been done, the argument is made that directors do not have 'hands on' control of the company and therefore cannot reasonably be liable for any failings within the company. For example it could be argued that the managing director of P & O European Ferries, who at the time of the *Herald of Free Enterprise* disaster was not aboard the vessel could not be liable for it, even though he knew the vessel sailed with the bow door open and that the request for warning lights on the bridge had been declined. On the other hand in the cases of Kyte and the Lyme Bay Canoe Tragedy and Jackson and Jackson Transport it was found that being directors they were operating in a 'hands on' manner and they had first hand knowledge of the situation. It followed that because of the closeness they were reckless in that they did nothing to eliminate or reduce the risks to employees and those not employed, but affected by the activities of the business.

7.32   This means that small *one man* type companies can be held accountable whilst, in large corporations, the *controlling minds* of the company can hide behind the remoteness of their positions. This is the case even though they may have had knowledge of failings of safety within their organisations. Therefore, because there has been no specific offence of corporate manslaughter it has proved difficult, if not impossible, to identify an individual within a large corporation with direct responsibility for the management of health and safety.

7.33 The case for corporate culpability is made by Clarkson[1] who states:

> 'The Law Commission's proposed general test for the offence of killing by gross carelessness can easily be applied to companies. The issue would be whether the risks would have been obvious to a reasonable *corporation* in that position and whether the *corporation* had the capacity to appreciate the risks. Of course, this latter requirement that the company have the capacity to appreciate risks will be of little significance in practice because a company, by definition, will necessarily have this capacity if the risks are obvious. However, it is important, if corporate killings are to be condemned appropriately, that liability be limited not only to those cases where the company's conduct fell far below what could reasonably be expected, but also to cases where the risks would have been obvious to other companies in the same situation. Application of the same test to both individuals and companies will serve to emphasise that corporate offences are not *'poor cousins'* of crimes committed by individuals ... The Council of Europe has proposed that whenever a company's activities or those of its employees lead to a prohibited harm, the company should be *prima facie* liable; the evidential burden would then switch to the company itself to prove that it had a safe system that could not be faulted.'

---

1 Clarkson, CMV *Kicking Corporate Bodies and Damning Their Souls*, The Modern Law Review, 1996.

Prosecutions of individuals for manslaughter

7.34 Prosecutions of individuals for manslaughter at or due to work have been far more successful. The reason is simply that an 'individual' can easily be identified. Whilst the number of cases of individuals prosecuted for manslaughter at or due to work are increasing, emphasis has often been placed upon specific groups such as gas fitters and landlords, the latter cutting corners to get a cheap job, particularly in low cost student accommodation. There are an increasing number of cases where individuals, albeit as directors, have been found guilty and received custodial sentences. It will be noted that in a number of cases the term of imprisonment was suspended for a defined period, generally two years. What this means is that the defendant does not get punished for the crime at the time sentence is passed; however, if that defendant commits another offence of any description the original offence can be punished as well as any sanction for the new offence.

Breach of the duty of care

7.35   To determine a breach of the duty of care, the ordinary civil law of negligence is applied. The question is whether the accused in acting, or omitting to act, has failed to reach the standard of a reasonable person. If there has been a breach of duty of care by the accused, it must also be established that the breach directly caused the death. If a breach of the duty of care by the accused has occurred, and it is established that death of the deceased was caused by that breach, it is necessary to establish whether the breach was so great as to be classified a gross negligence. The main consideration is the extent to which the accused's conduct departed from the standard expected of any reasonable person in that position.

7.36   An employer owes a duty to take reasonable care for the safety of its employees and a number of cases outline the legal determinations to show the extent of the duty. However, this is becoming increasingly complicated with the changes in the labour market and, in particular, the growth in the numbers of workers such as the self-employed, agency workers and those on fixed-term contracts when set against the decline in number of those workers legally classified as employees. With the work practice changes, the law is increasingly recognising duties of care owed to those subject to another's control, regardless of whether they are its employees or not.

7.37   The law deems that an employee is someone who works under a contract of service, which is in contrast to a contractor who works under a contract for service. The type of contract is relevant but not decisive and the legal test is based on the factual relationship between the parties. The definition of 'employment' between the various areas of law has become particularly apparent in the authorities in the field of those involved in health and safety at work.

7.38   There are a number of cases that show the extent of the duty of care and they include the case of *Paris v Stepney Borough Council*[1] which is one of a special duty of care where a one-eyed garage worker became completely blinded after a chip of metal entered his good eye. Along with others working in the vehicle repair department, no protective equipment had been given to Mr Paris. Following the accident Mr Paris successfully claimed damages for his injury but this was overturned on appeal. Mr Paris then appealed to the House of Lords. The House of Lords held that where an employer is aware that an employee has a disability which, although it does not increase the risk of an accident occurring, does increase the risk of serious injury, special precautions should be taken if the employer is to fulfil its duty to take reasonable care for the safety of that employee. It was found that Stepney Borough Council owed a special duty of care to Mr Paris and had been negligent in failing to supply goggles to him, even though such equipment was not given to other employees.

Lord Oaksey in *Paris v Stepney Borough Council* stated that the duty was 'to take reasonable care for his servants' safety in all the circumstances of the case'.

1   [1950]1 All ER 42.

7.39   In *Wilsons and Clyde Coal v English* the House of Lords articulated the principle underlying those earlier authorities, rejecting a narrow basis for liability. Lord Wright[1] said:

> 'The whole course of authority consistently recognises a duty which rests on the employer, and which is personal to the employer, to take reasonable care for the safety of his workmen, whether the employer be an individual, a firm or a company, and whether or not the employer takes any share in the conduct of the operations.'

1   [1938] AC 57 at 84.

7.40   Lord Keith[1] in *Cavanagh v Ulster Weaving Co Ltd* said:

> 'The ruling principle is that an employer is bound to take reasonable care for the safety of his workmen, and all other rules and formulas must be taken subject to this principle.'

1   [1960] AC 154.

7.41   In *McDermid v Nash Dredging & Reclamation Co Ltd*[1] the House of Lords made it clear that the duty is not merely to devise a safe system but to put it into and maintain it in operation. A tug captain employed by an associated company, which also owned the tug, who was in charge of the operation, arranged a system of waiting for a signal from the claimant deckhand that the mooring lines had been cast off before the tug moved away from the dredger to which it had been made fast. The captain failed to wait for the signal, the line the claimant was releasing injured him and the House of Lords held the employers were liable. The captain was the man in charge on behalf of the employers and had failed to put into operation his own system. His negligence could not be dismissed as the 'casual' negligence of an employee (for which the employers would not have been responsible as he belonged to another company). The reasons for this are not entirely clear. Lord Brandon said:

> 'The negligence of [the captain] was not casual but central. It involved abandoning the safe system of work which he had devised and operating in its place a manifestly unsafe system.'

1   [1987] 1 AC 906.

7.42   If the employer delegates performance of this duty to another, the employer remains liable if the duty is breached since the duty itself is non-delegable. It is not sufficient for the employer merely to select a competent person to perform the duty. Parker LJ[1] in *Davie v New Merton Board Mills* states:

'The duty owed by a master to his servant at common law can he stated in general terms as a duty to take reasonable care for the safety of his servants if the master delegates ... the performance of that duty to another he remains liable for the failure of that other to exercise reasonable care this principle holds good whether the person employed [i e employed to carry out the duty] by the master is a servant, a full-time agent or an independent contractor.'

1 [1958] 1 QB 21.

7.43   In the House of Lords, Lord Tucker[1] said:

'... the employer may delegate the performance of his obligations in this sphere to someone who is more properly described as a contractor than a servant, but this does not affect the liability of the employer, he will be just as much liable for his negligence as for that of his servant. Such a contractor is entrusted by the employer with the performance of the employers' personal duty.'

1 *Davie v New Merton Board Mills* [1959] AC 604.

7.44   The duty for an employer to protect employees is shown in the case *Thompson and Other v Smiths Shiprepairers (North Shields) Limited*[1] where a number of men employed in the shipyards from about the 1940s to the 1970s suffered impaired hearing. The employers knew about the noise levels but no official guidance on the problem was available until 1963, and no protective equipment was provided until the 1970s. In 1980 and 1981, actions were brought against the employers for hearing damage due to negligence by the employers throughout this time. The High Court held that an appropriate test should be used to establish the date from which the behaviour of the employer could be considered to be negligent. The test was determined to be what would have been done by a reasonable and prudent employer, in terms of what such an employer would or should have known about the issue of ear protection and noise levels at the time and in line with common practice in the industry. Using this test, the employer was held to be negligent only from 1963. Damages could only be recovered from this time, when the failure to provide protection against noise levels became a breach of the employers' duty of care. In this case, therefore, the claimants could only recover a portion of their loss, determined from 1963 onwards and taking into account the uncertainties involved in making such an apportionment.

1 [1984] QB 405.

7.45   The case of *Qualcast (Wolverhampton) Ltd v Haynes*[1] provided for a higher duty of care expected of an experienced employee and involved a 38 year old who had been a moulder all his working life was casting moulding boxes. The ladle of molten metal which he was holding slipped, and some of the metal splashed onto his left foot when he was wearing ordinary leather boots. The employers had a stock of protective spats and of reinforced boots at a price, but they never recommended the claimant wear them. At the county court, judgment was given to the claimant, subject to 75% contributory negligence, as the employer was bound to urge the use of the protective equipment. However, on appeal, Lord Denning stated that:

> '... he knew all there was to know, without being told; and he voluntarily decided to wear his own boots, which he had bought for the purpose ... this workman, after he recovered from the injury went back to work and did the same as before. He never wore spats. If the warning given by the accident made no difference, we may safely infer that no advice beforehand would have had any effect.'

He lost the appeal because he was experienced and should have guarded against the danger.

---

1 [1959] 2 All ER 38.

7.46   Safety of third parties was focused on the case of *R v Associated Octel Co Ltd*[1] and involved the defendant company who engaged some contractors to carry out repairs of a tank during a shutdown period. A permit-to-work was issued by the defendant but it proved to be inadequate and was not monitored. A contractor took a flammable liquid into the tank to clean the inner surface. However, a flash fire developed and the contractor was seriously burned. Following a successfully prosecution Octel appealed first to the Court of Appeal, who upheld the conviction and then to the House of Lords. The Lords held that if an employer engages a contractor who works on his or her premises then the employer, subject to reasonable practicability, must ensure the contractor's health and safety. The House of Lords appeal was concerned with the definition of the term 'undertaking', which effectively includes any work carried out on the employer's premises.

---

1 [1994] 4 All ER 1051.

7.47   Another case that involves the safety of third parties is that of *R v Swan Hunter Shipbuilders Ltd*[1] where the employer had a duty to provide information and instruction to ensure, so far as was reasonably practicable, the health and safety at work of his own employees also extends to providing such information and instruction to employees of a subcontractor, where necessary. The case involved a fire which broke out on board a ship which was under construction by Swan Hunter Ltd. The fire was intense because the atmosphere inside the vessel had become oxygen enriched and eight men were killed. The oxygen had escaped from a hose left by an employee of a firm of subcontractors. Swan Hunter Ltd had distributed a book of rules to their own employees for the safe use of oxygen equipment, but this was not distributed to subcontractors' employees, except on request. Swan Hunter Ltd were prosecuted under the HSWA 1974 for failing to provide a safe system of work. The trial judge ruled that the Act imposed a duty to inform or instruct employees other than Swan Hunter's own with regard to all relevant safety matters. Swan Hunter Ltd appealed. The Court of Appeal dismissed the appeal and upheld the trial judge's ruling. If, to ensure a safe system of work for an employer's own employees, it was necessary to provide persons other than his employees with information and instruction as to potential dangers, then he was under a duty to provide such information and instruction, so far as was reasonably practicable.

---

1 [1982] 1 All ER 264.

Summary

7.48   With the new corporate manslaughter and corporate homicide law on the statute book, individuals who are grossly negligent whether they are a director of a large or small company should be exposed to possible prosecution for manslaughter. However, it will be easier to prosecute the director of a small organisation and with careful structuring directors of large organisations will be able to avoid individual prosecution.

Chapter 8

The Corporate Manslaughter and Corporate Homicide Act 2007

Schedule 1: list of Government Departments etc	8.52
Schedule 2: Minor and consequential amendments	8.53

Introduction

8.1 The reader will quickly see that the Corporate Manslaughter and Corporate Homicide Act bears little resemblance to the draft Corporate Killing Bill originally proposed by the Law Commission or the preceding draft Government Bills. There is already concern with the fact that there is no individual liability in the new law which has been a key issue from the first inception of a corporate killing offence. The argument has been and remains that for the law to be effective those at a senior level, generally considered to be the directors or equivalent in an organisation, must be answerable as individuals for their management failings. If that is not to be the case (and with the new legislation it is not), then the law that has taken so long to get onto the statute books may be considered to be ineffective.

8.2 The new offence is called corporate manslaughter in England and Wales and corporate homicide in Scotland. It had originally been proposed to use the title of corporate killing. Scotland was proposing to have its own legislation which would include individual offences that were outside of the English remit and it was evident that the two laws needed to be compatible. The Government decided to encompass both sectors into one legislative package.

8.3 The offences of corporate manslaughter and corporate homicide have been developed from the main elements of the current common law offence of gross negligence manslaughter in England, Wales and Northern Ireland. It makes corporations and a range of Crown bodies liable for the way in which their activities are run by senior managers, rather than focusing on the failings and guilt of any particular individual. The offence is committed when an organisation owes a duty to take reasonable care for a person's safety, but the way in which its activities have been managed or organised by senior managers is a substantial element in an incident and a gross breach of the duty which causes the person's death.

Section 1: The offence

8.4 '(1) An organisation to which this section applies is guilty of an offence if the way in which any of its activities are managed or organised—

    (a)   causes a person's death, and

    (b)   amounts to a gross breach of a relevant duty of care owed by the organisation to the deceased.

(2)   The organisations to which this section applies are—

    (a)   a corporation;

    (b)   a department or other body listed in Schedule 1;

    (c)   a police force (as defined in section 12(1));

    (d)   a partnership, or trade union or employers' association, that is an employer.

(3)   An organisation is guilty of an offence under this section only if the way in which its activities are managed or organised by its senior management is a substantial element in the breach referred to in subsection (1).

(4)   For the purposes of this Act—

    (a)   "relevant duty of care" has the meaning given by section 2, read with sections 3 to 7;

    (b)   a breach of a duty of care by an organisation is a "gross" breach if the conduct alleged to amount to a breach of that duty falls far below what can reasonably be expected of the organisation in the circumstances;

    (c)   "senior management", in relation to an organisation, means the persons who play significant roles in:

        (i)   the making of decisions about how the whole or a substantial part of its activities are to be managed or organised, or

        (ii)   the actual managing or organising of the whole or a substantial part of those activities.

(5)   The offence under this section is called—

    (a)   corporate manslaughter, in so far as it is an offence under the law of England and Wales or Northern Ireland;

    (b)   corporate homicide, in so far as it is an offence under the law of Scotland.

(6)   An organisation that is guilty of corporate manslaughter or corporate homicide is liable on conviction on indictment to a fine.

(7)   The offence of corporate homicide is indictable only in the High Court of Justiciary.'

Comment

8.5   The 'senior management' aspect of the offence places culpability on a corporation in a different way from the previous test for corporate liability for gross negligence manslaughter. It focuses on the way in which an organisation's senior managers manage or organise the organisation's activities rather than focusing on questions of individual culpability. This adopts the general approach recommended by the Law Commission in its 1996 report: that liability should lie in the system of work that the organisation has developed for conducting a particular activity. This means that management's conduct can be considered collectively as well as individually. There must be a duty of care and the breach of duty must have been gross to have caused the victim's death. The test for the offence is to determine whether the act that constitutes the failure falls far below what could reasonably have been expected of the organisation in the circumstances.

This clearly places responsibility at board level or its equivalent. In smaller organisations it would be the directors. Following a workplace fatality the investigation will examine in detail the actions of senior management. If it is identified that there are failures in the way an organisation's senior managers managed or organised an activity which warrant a corporate offence, then the senior managers would be under the spotlight. If the investigation finds that senior management failure amounts to a (gross) breach of the duty of care owed by the organisation to the victim, then individual senior managers could face prosecution.

Health and safety is a board, directors' or equivalent responsibility and as such, those holding such posts will collectively make decisions about the whole or a substantial part of the organisation's activities. However, like the captain of a ship or aircraft, the chairman, managing director or CEO is the most senior person and as such carries the ultimate responsibility. That responsibility cannot be delegated to another such as a director responsible for health and safety or professional health and safety advisor.

Whilst there are no individual offences within the corporate manslaughter and corporate homicide legislation the link between senior management, the decision making process and the managing or organising aspects could expose individuals to a possible gross negligence manslaughter offence or one under the Health and Safety at Work etc Act 1974 (HSWA 1974).

Section 2: Meaning of 'relevant duty of care'

8.6 '(1) A "relevant duty of care", in relation to an organisation, means any of the following duties owed by it under the law of negligence—

    (a) a duty owed to its employees or to other persons working for the organisation or performing services for it;

    (b) a duty owed as occupier of premises;

(c)   a duty owed in connection with:

      (i)   the supply by the organisation of goods or services (whether for consideration or not),

      (ii)   the carrying on by the organisation of any construction or maintenance operations,

      (iii)   the carrying on by the organisation of any other activity on a commercial basis, or

      (iv)   the use or keeping by the organisation of any plant, vehicle or other thing.

(d)   a duty owed to a person who, by reason of being a person within subsection (2), is someone for whose safety the organisation is responsible.

(2)   A person is within this subsection if—

    (a)   he is detained at a custodial institution or in a custody area at a court or police station;

    (b)   he is detained at a removal centre or short-term holding facility;

    (c)   he is being transported in a vehicle, or being held in any premises, in pursuance of prison escort arrangements or immigration escort arrangements;

    (d)   he is living in secure accommodation in which he has been placed;

    (e)   he is a detained patient.

(3)   Subsection (1) is subject to sections 3 to 7.

(4)   A reference in subsection (1) to a duty owed under the law of negligence includes a reference to a duty that would be owed under the law of negligence but for any statutory provision under which liability is imposed in place of liability under that law.

(5)   For the purposes of this Act, whether a particular organisation owes a duty of care to a particular individual is a question of law. The judge must make any findings of fact necessary to decide that question.

(6)   For the purposes of this Act there is to be disregarded—

    (a)   any rule of the common law that has the effect of preventing a duty of care from being owed by one person to another by reason of the fact that they are jointly engaged in unlawful conduct;

    (b)   any such rule that has the effect of preventing a duty of care from being owed to a person by reason of his acceptance of a risk of harm.

(7)   In this section—

"construction or maintenance operations" means operations of any of the following descriptions—

(a)   construction, installation, alteration, extension, improvement, repair, maintenance, decoration, cleaning, demolition or dismantling of—

    (i)   any building or structure,

    (ii)   anything else that forms, or is to form, part of the land, or

    (iii) any plant, vehicle or other thing;

(b)   operations that form an integral part of, or are preparatory to, or are for rendering complete, any operations within paragraph (a);

"custodial institution" means a prison, a young offender institution, a secure training centre, a young offenders institution, a young offenders centre, a juvenile justice centre or a remand centre;

"detained patient" means—

(a)   a person who is detained in any premises under—

    (i)   Part 2 or 3 of the Mental Health Act 1983 ("the 1983 Act"), or

    (ii)   Part 2 or 3 of the Mental Health (Northern Ireland) Order 1986 ("the 1986 Order");

(b)   a person who (otherwise than by reason of being detained as mentioned in paragraph (a)) is deemed to be in legal custody by—

    (i)   section 137 of the 1983 Act,

    (ii)   Article 131 of the 1986 Order, or

    (iii) article 11 of the Mental Health (Care and Treatment) (Scotland) Act 2003 (Consequential Provisions) Order 2005;

(c)   a person who is detained in any premises, or is otherwise in custody, under the Mental Health (Care and Treatment) (Scotland) Act 2003 or Part 6 of the Criminal Procedure (Scotland) Act 1995 or who is detained in a hospital under section 200 of that Act of 1995;

"immigration escort arrangements" means arrangements made under section 156 of the Immigration and Asylum Act 1999;

"the law of negligence" includes:

(a)   in relation to England and Wales, the Occupiers' Liability Act 1957, the Defective Premises Act 1972 and the Occupiers' Liability Act 1984;

(b)   in relation to Scotland, the Occupiers' Liability (Scotland) Act 1960;

(c)   in relation to Northern Ireland, the Occupiers' Liability Act (Northern Ireland) 1957, the Defective Premises (Northern Ireland) Order 1975, the Occupiers' Liability (Northern Ireland) Order 1987 and the Defective Premises (Landlord's Liability) Act (Northern Ireland) 2001;

"prison escort arrangements" means arrangements made under section 80 of the Criminal Justice Act 1991 or under section 102 or 118 of the Criminal Justice and Public Order Act 1994;

"removal centre" and "short-term holding facility" have the meaning given by section 147 of the Immigration and Asylum Act 1999;

"secure accommodation" means accommodation, not consisting of or forming part of a custodial institution, provided for the purpose of restricting the liberty of persons under the age of 18.'

Comment

8.7   Corporate manslaughter and corporate homicide only applies where an organisation owed a duty of care to the victim under the law of negligence, which is the case with the offence of gross negligence manslaughter. The duties of care are those owed by an employer to his employees where they have to provide safe systems of work and as an occupier of buildings and land to people in or on, or potentially affected by, the property. It also includes activities such as the duty owed by transport companies to their passengers.

The existence of a 'duty of care' in a particular case is a matter of law and that will be for a judge to decide. Because a judge will be deciding whether the circumstances of the case give rise to a duty of care, they will have to make certain determinations of fact that are usually for the jury to decide. The reason for this is because of complexities that can arise, such as when considering whether a corporation owes a duty of care as employer, the judge will need to decide whether the victim was an employee of the corporation.

Whilst the duty of care extends to employees through the provision of a safe system of work there may be duties of care to others. This could include contractors or volunteers whose work the organisation is able to manage, even though they are not directly employed by it. As the occupier of premises an organisation may well have responsibilities to ensure that buildings they occupy are kept in a safe condition and premises includes land, buildings and moveable structures. Organisations that supply goods or services have duties of care to their customers, as do transport providers and in the case of retailers their duty extends to the safety of their products. The duty of care extends to the supply of services by the public sector such as NHS bodies providing medical treatment.

It is important to note that the offence of corporate manslaughter and corporate homicide does not impose new duties of care where these are not currently required but where such duties are required, a breach could result in a prosecution. Senior managers must determine the extent of their duty of care for their organisation and ensure that there are suitable and sufficient safeguards in place to manage risks of harm to everybody who could be affected by the organisation's activities.

Section 3: Public policy decisions, exclusively public functions and statutory inspections

8.8 '(1)   Any duty of care owed by a public authority in respect of a decision as to matters of public policy (including in particular the allocation of public resources or the weighing of competing public interests) is not a "relevant duty of care".

(2)   Any duty of care owed in respect of things done in the exercise of an exclusively public function is not a "relevant duty of care" unless it falls within section 2(1)(a), (b) or (d).

(3)   Any duty of care owed by a public authority in respect of inspections carried out in the exercise of a statutory function is not a "relevant duty of care" unless it falls within section 2(1)(a) or (b).

(4) In this section—

"exclusively public function" means a function that falls within the prerogative of the Crown or is, by its nature, exercisable only with authority conferred—

(a)   by the exercise of that prerogative, or

(b)   by or under a statutory provision;

"public authority" has the same meaning as in section 6 of the Human Rights Act 1998 (disregarding subsections (3)(a) and (4) of that section);

"statutory function" means a function conferred by or under a statutory provision;

"statutory provision" means provision contained in, or in an instrument made under, any Act, any Act of the Scottish Parliament or any Northern Ireland legislation.'

Comment

8.9   Some duty of care decisions taken by public bodies where negligence is claimed are not subject to examination in the courts where they involve decisions involving competing public priorities or other questions of public policy. This could include such situations as where decisions made by Primary Care Trusts about the funding of particular treatments, or whether the Department of Health owed a duty of care to issue interim advice about the safety of a particular drug, mean that deaths alleged to have been caused by such decisions will not come within the scope of the corporate manslaughter and corporate homicide offence.

An organisation will not be liable for a breach of any duty of care owed in respect of things done in the exercise of 'exclusively public functions', unless the organisation owes the duty in its capacity as an employer or as an occupier of premises. This is not confined to Crown or other public bodies but also excludes any organisation (public or otherwise) performing that particular type of function. 'Exclusively public functions' are defined by the Home Office as functions falling within the prerogative of the Crown (for example, where the Government provides services in a civil emergency) and types of activity that by their nature cannot be independently performed by private bodies.

This does not affect questions of individual liability, and prosecutions for gross negligence manslaughter and other offences will remain possible against individuals performing these functions who are themselves culpable. The management of these functions will continue to be subject to other forms of accountability such as independent investigations, public inquiries and the accountability of Ministers through Parliament.

Organisations carrying out statutory inspections will not be liable, unless the organisation owes a duty of care in its capacity as an employer or as an occupier of premises. This would include regulatory activities that are carried out to ensure compliance with statutory standards: for example, inspection activities by the health and safety enforcing authorities. These bodies would not normally owe duties of care in respect of such activities as the activities are not performed commercially and do not amount to the supply of services.

Public authorities are defined by reference to the Human Rights Act 1998 and include core public bodies such as Government departments and local government bodies, as well as any other body some of whose functions are of a public nature.

Section 4: Military activities

8.10 '(1) Any duty of care owed by the Ministry of Defence in respect of—

> (a) operations within subsection (2),
>
> (b) activities carried on in preparation for, or directly in support of, such operations, or
>
> (c) training of a hazardous nature, or training carried out in a hazardous way, which it is considered needs to be carried out, or carried out in that way, in order to improve or maintain the effectiveness of the armed forces with respect to such operations, is not a "relevant duty of care".

> (2) The operations within this subsection are operations, including peacekeeping operations and operations for dealing with terrorism, civil unrest or serious public disorder, in which members of the armed forces come under attack or face the threat of attack or violent resistance.

> (3) Any duty of care owed by the Ministry of Defence in respect of activities carried on by members of the special forces is not a "relevant duty of care".

> (4) In this section "the special forces" means those units of the armed forces the maintenance of whose capabilities is the responsibility of the Director of Special Forces or which are for the time being subject to the operational command of that Director.'

Comment

8.11 Some aspects of military activities are exempt in respect of all categories of duty of care such as the conduct, preparation and support of military operations as well as other hazardous and unpredictable circumstances, including peacekeeping operations and operations dealing with terrorism or serious public disorder.

With regard to the law of negligence the military authorities rarely owe a duty of care in such circumstances and the exemption extends both to training exercises that simulate these sorts of operations and to the activities of the special-forces. However, there is a duty of care for general day-to-day military activities including basic and other elements of training which are therefore not exempt from the offence.

Section 5: Policing and law enforcement

8.12 '(1)   Any duty of care owed by a public authority in respect of—

    (a)   operations within subsection (2),

    (b)   activities carried on in preparation for, or directly in support of, such operations, or

    (c)   training of a hazardous nature, or training carried out in a hazardous way, which it is considered needs to be carried out, or carried out in that way, in order to improve or maintain the effectiveness of officers or employees of the public authority with respect to such operations, is not a "relevant duty of care".

  (2)   Operations are within this subsection if—

    (a)   they are operations for dealing with terrorism, civil unrest or serious disorder;

    (b)   they involve the carrying on of policing or law enforcement activities;

    (c)   officers or employees of the public authority in question come under attack or face the threat of attack or violent resistance, in the course of the operations.

  (3)   Any duty of care owed by a public authority in respect of other policing or law enforcement activities is not a "relevant duty of care" unless it falls within section 2(1)(a), (b) or (d).

  (4)   In this section "policing or law-enforcement activities" includes—

    (a)   activities carried on in the exercise of functions that are:

      (i)   functions of police forces, or

      (ii)   functions of the same or a similar nature exercisable by public authorities other than police forces;

    (b)   activities carried on in the exercise of functions of constables employed by a public authority;

    (c)   activities carried on in the exercise of functions exercisable under Chapter 4 of Part 2 of the Serious Organised Crime and Police Act 2005 (protection of witnesses and other persons);

    (d)   activities carried on to enforce any provision contained in or made under the Immigration Acts.'

Comment

8.13   Law enforcement bodies will have regard to the conduct, preparation and support of operations dealing with terrorism, civil unrest or serious public disorder. This means that the policing of violent disorder where the police come under attack or the threat of attack will not invoke a liability on the part of the employer and so with regard to the corporate manslaughter or corporate homicide law, the employers are exempt from the offence.

This extends to training exercises that simulate these sorts of operations. Other activities that are not covered by the offence include decisions about and responses to emergency calls, the manner in which particular police operations are conducted, the way in which law enforcement and other coercive powers are exercised, measures taken to protect witnesses and the arrest and detention of suspects.

The exemption from corporate manslaughter or corporate homicide is not confined to police forces but it extends to other bodies operating similar law enforcement activities. This would include the activities of Her Majesty's Revenue and Customs when conducting investigations. It also extends to the enforcement of immigration law, which would cover circumstances where, for example, the immigration authorities are taking action to arrest, detain or deport an immigration offender. It is important to note that none of the actions exempt individuals from investigation or prosecution for individual offences because the corporate manslaughter or corporate homicide offence does not include individual liability.

Section 6: Emergency services

8.14 '(1)   Any duty of care owed by an organisation within subsection (2) in respect of the way in which it responds to emergency circumstances (or circumstances believed to be emergency circumstances) is not a "relevant duty of care" unless it falls within section 2(1)(a) or (b).

(2)   The organisations within this subsection are—

(a)   a fire and rescue authority in England and Wales;

(b)   a fire and rescue authority or joint fire and rescue board in Scotland;

(c)   the Northern Ireland Fire and Rescue Service Board;

(d)   any other organisation providing a service of responding to emergency circumstances either—

(i)   in pursuance of arrangements made with an organisation within paragraph (a), (b) or (c), or

     (ii)   (if not in pursuance of such arrangements) otherwise than on a commercial basis;

(e)   a relevant NHS body;

(f)   an organisation providing ambulance services in pursuance of arrangements—

     (i)   made by, or at the request of, a relevant NHS body, or

     (ii)   made with the Secretary of State or with the Welsh Ministers;

(g)   an organisation providing services for the transport of organs, blood, equipment or personnel in pursuance of arrangements of the kind mentioned in paragraph (f);

(h)   an organisation providing a rescue service;

(i)   the armed forces.

(3)   For the purposes of subsection (1), the way in which an organisation responds to emergency circumstances does not include the way in which—

    (a)   medical treatment is carried out, or

    (b)   decisions within subsection (4) are made.

(4)   The decisions within this subsection are decisions as to the carrying out of medical treatment, other than decisions as to the order in which persons are to be given such treatment.

(5)   Any duty of care owed in respect of the carrying out, or attempted carrying out, of a rescue operation at sea in emergency circumstances is not a "relevant duty of care" unless it falls within section 2(1)(a) or (b).

(6)   Any duty of care owed in respect of action taken—

    (a)   in order to comply with a direction under Schedule 3A to the Merchant Shipping Act 1995 (safety directions), or

    (b)   by virtue of paragraph 4 of that Schedule (action in lieu of direction), is not a "relevant duty of care" unless it falls within section 2(1)(a) or (b).

(7)   In this section—

"emergency circumstances" means circumstances that are present or imminent and—

    (a)   are causing, or are likely to cause, serious harm or a worsening of such harm, or

    (b)   are likely to cause the death of a person;

"medical treatment" includes any treatment or procedure of a medical or similar nature;

"relevant NHS body" means—

(a) a Strategic Health Authority, Primary Care Trust, NHS trust, Special Health Authority or NHS foundation trust in England;

(b) a Local Health Board, NHS trust or Special Health Authority in Wales;

(c) a Health Board or Special Health Board in Scotland, or the Common Services Agency for the Scottish Health Service;

(d) a Health and Social Services trust or Health and Social Services Board in Northern Ireland;

"serious harm" means—

(a) serious injury to or the serious illness (including mental illness) of a person;

(b) serious harm to the environment (including the life and health of plants and animals);

(c) serious harm to any building or other property.

(8) A reference in this section to emergency circumstances includes a reference to circumstances that are believed to be emergency circumstances.'

Comment

8.15   The offence does not apply to the emergency services when responding to emergencies. Prosecutions under the new offence are excluded in such matters as the timeliness in responding to an emergency, the level of response and the effectiveness of the way in which the emergency is tackled. Generally, public bodies such as fire authorities and the Coastguard do not owe duties of care in this respect and therefore would not be culpable under the new offence. However, it does include the responsibilities that the authorities owe in providing safe systems of work for their employees or to ensure the safety of their premises and maintaining vehicles in a safe condition.

This means that the liability for the new offence is to ensure emergency service providers have a consistent approach in respect of their responsibilities. They have to provide safe working conditions for employees and in respect of their premises, vehicles and equipment.

Organisations that are exempt from the corporate manslaughter and corporate homicide offence include:

- fire and rescue authorities in the UK;

- other bodies who employ firefighters;

- NHS bodies and those providing ambulance services or the transport of organs or blood under contract to such a body;

- bodies such as the Coastguard and Royal National Lifeboat Institution;

- the armed forces (who may be responding to emergency circumstances in respect of their own activities or providing assistance to civil authorities responding to an emergency).

It is important to note that the organisations are only precluded from the new offence when responding to an emergency, defined in terms of circumstances that are life-threatening or threatening to cause serious injury or illness or harm to the environment or buildings or other property.

Section 7: Child protection and probation functions

8.16 '(1) A duty of care to which this section applies is not a "relevant duty of care" unless it falls within section 2(1)(a), (b) or (d).

(2) This section applies to any duty of care that a local authority or other public authority owes in respect of the exercise by it of functions conferred by or under—

  (a) the Children Act 1989,

  (b) Part 2 of the Children (Scotland) Act 1995, or

  (c) Parts 5 and 6 of the Children (Northern Ireland) Order 1995, so far as relating to the protection of children from harm.

(3) This section also applies to any duty of care that a local probation board or other public authority owes in respect of the exercise by it of functions conferred by or under—

  (a) Chapter 1 of Part 1 of the Criminal Justice and Court Services Act 2000,

  (b) section 27 of the Social Work (Scotland) Act 1968, or

  (c) Article 4 of the Probation Board (Northern Ireland) Order 1982.'

Comment

8.17   There is existing legislation that imposes a number of functions and duties on local authorities to safeguard the welfare of children. These include the protection of a child from being harmed and as such include the power to take a child into care.

Corporate manslaughter or corporate homicide does not apply in relation to the taking of action or the failure to action those powers nor does the offence apply in relation to the responsibilities of probation boards (or other equivalent public authorities) to supervise offenders or provide accommodation in approved premises.

Further, it is doubted whether such bodies would owe a duty of care should a person be killed in connection with those activities such as where a child was not identified by the authorities as being at risk and taken into care but was subsequently fatally injured.

This means that local authorities and probation services will be covered by the offence in respect of ensuring the safety of their employees or the safety of the premises they occupy but does not apply in relation to the manner in which they exercise various statutory functions.

Section 8: Factors for jury

8.18 '(1)   This section applies where—

    (a)   it is established that an organisation owed a relevant duty of care to a person, and

    (b)   it falls to the jury to decide whether there was a gross breach of that duty.

  (2)   The jury must consider whether the evidence shows that the organisation failed to comply with any health and safety legislation that relates to the alleged breach, and if so—

    (a)   how serious that failure was;

    (b)   how much of a risk of death it posed.

  (3)   The jury may also—

    (a)   consider the extent to which the evidence shows that there were attitudes, policies, systems or accepted practices within the organisation that were likely to have encouraged any such failure as is mentioned in subsection (2), or to have produced tolerance of it;

(b)   have regard to any health and safety guidance that relates to the alleged breach.

(4)   This section does not prevent the jury from having regard to any other matters they consider relevant.

(5)   In this section "health and safety guidance" means any code, guidance, manual or similar publication that is concerned with health and safety matters and is made or issued (under a statutory provision or otherwise) by an authority responsible for the enforcement of any health and safety legislation.'

Comment

8.19   The jury is a very important part of the legal process and as such there are a number of factors that a jury will have to consider in determining whether there has been a breach that will make an organisation culpable. They will have to consider whether the conduct that constitutes the management failure fell far below what could reasonably have been expected and whether the breach of duty involved in the senior management failure was gross. To assist them the existing common law offence of gross negligence manslaughter should address the question as to whether the conduct was so negligent as to be criminal.

The jury will have to consider the organisation's obligations under health and safety legislation and to what extent it was in breach of these and the risk to life that is involved. In addition the jury will have to consider the wider context in which these health and safety breaches occurred, including the overall culture with regard to health and safety within the organisation. This would include factors such as senior management attitudes and the acceptance of breaches of health and safety issues.

To assist in the consideration of breaches of health and safety requirements, juries may also consider guidance such as ACoP's and other industry guidance to identify how those requirements should have been adopted. Whilst guidance does not provide authoritative requirements it does provide objectives that have to be met and how that can be achieved. This means that where breaches of relevant health and safety duties are established, such guidance may assist a jury in considering how serious the failing was.

Juries are allowed to reach verdicts on health and safety charges where the offender has also been convicted of manslaughter. This can mean a verdict on any secondary participation by individuals in the health and safety offences.

Section 9: Power to order breach etc to be remedied

8.20 '(1)   A court before which an organisation is convicted of corporate manslaughter or corporate homicide may make an order (a "remedial order") requiring the organisation to take specified steps to remedy—

    (a)   the breach mentioned in section 1(1) ("the relevant breach");

    (b)   any matter that appears to the court to have resulted from the relevant breach and to have been a cause of the death;

    (c)   any deficiency, as regards health and safety matters, in the organisation's policies, systems or practices of which the relevant breach appears to the court to be an indication.

(2)   A remedial order may be made only on an application by the prosecution specifying the terms of the proposed order. Any such order must be on such terms (whether those proposed or others) as the court considers appropriate having regard to any representations made, and any evidence adduced, in relation to that matter by the prosecution or on behalf of the organisation.

(3)   Before making an application for a remedial order the prosecution must consult such enforcement authority or authorities as it considers appropriate having regard to the nature of the relevant breach.

(4)   A remedial order—

    (a)   must specify a period within which the steps referred to in subsection (1) are to be taken;

    (b)   may require the organisation to supply to an enforcement authority consulted under subsection (3), within a specified period, evidence that those steps have been taken. A period specified under this subsection may be extended or further extended by order of the court on an application made before the end of that period or extended period.

(5)   An organisation that fails to comply with a remedial order is guilty of an offence, and liable on conviction on indictment to a fine.'

Comment

8.21   The health and safety regulating authorities have powers through prohibition and improvement notices to require an organisation to take remedial action. In addition the courts now have the power to order an organisation convicted of a corporate manslaughter or corporate homicide offence to take steps to remedy the management failure that led to the death and to remedy any consequence of the management failure, if it appeared to the court to have been a cause of death.

This can be explained as being where the management failure related to inadequate risk assessment and monitoring procedures, the consequence of which was inadequate safety precautions resulting in death. In this situation the court would be able to order the convicted organisation to improve both the management of risk and the resulting safety precautions. However, because of the time delay in getting the case into court relevant remedial steps would generally have been taken by the organisation immediately following the fatality. This would have been achieved through enforcement actions taken by the regulating authority.

There may be situations where an organisation appeals a notice and is successful but the enforcing authorities are not satisfied and make an application to the court for a remedial order. Also it is possible that during the course of the trial evidence is revealed that identifies the need for remedial action. In either situation, the application will be made by the prosecution, who must set out the proposed terms of the order. The convicted organisation will then have an opportunity to make representations to the court about the order. The judge will then make a decision and where appropriate make an order. The order must specify how long the organisation has to comply with the required steps; however, the period may be extended on application. A failure to comply with a remedial order is an indictable offence for which the sanction will be an unlimited fine.

Section 10: Power to order conviction etc to be publicised

8.22 '(1) A court before which an organisation is convicted of corporate manslaughter or corporate homicide may make an order (a "publicity order") requiring the organisation to publicise in a specified manner:

    (a) the fact that it has been convicted of the offence;

    (b) specified particulars of the offence;

    (c) the amount of any fine imposed;

    (d) the terms of any remedial order made.

  (2) In deciding on the terms of a publicity order that it is proposing to make, the court must—

    (a) ascertain the views of such enforcement authority or authorities (if any) as it considers appropriate, and

     (b)   have regard to any representations made by the prosecution or on behalf of the organisation.

(3)   A publicity order—

     (a)   must specify a period within which the requirements referred to in subsection (1) are to be complied with;

     (b)   may require the organisation to supply to any enforcement authority whose views have been ascertained under subsection (2), within a specified period, evidence that those requirements have been complied with.

(4)   An organisation that fails to comply with a publicity order is guilty of an offence, and liable on conviction on indictment to a fine.'

Comment

8.23   Courts will now be able to make a publicity order requiring a convicted organisation to publicise its conviction for manslaughter; details of the offence; the amount of the fine; and the terms of any remedial order. In drawing up the publicity order the court must ascertain the view of the enforcing authority and have regard to representations made by the prosecution and the offender.

The consequences of not complying with a court remedial order following a conviction for manslaughter are an unlimited fine in the Crown Court. The Health and Safety Executive (HSE) will ensure that convicted organisations comply with the order's safe practices. Courts can also require an organisation to provide evidence of compliance to an enforcement authority.

Section 11: Application to Crown bodies

8.24'(1)   An organisation that is a servant or agent of the Crown is not immune from prosecution under this Act for that reason.

(2)   For the purposes of this Act—

     (a)   a department or other body listed in Schedule 1, or

     (b)   a corporation that is a servant or agent of the Crown, is to be treated as owing whatever duties of care it would owe if it were a corporation that was not a servant or agent of the Crown.

(3)   For the purposes of section 2—

     (a)   a person who is—

        (i)   employed by or under the Crown for the purposes of a department or other body listed in Schedule 1, or

        (ii)   employed by a person whose staff constitute a body listed in that Schedule, is to be treated as employed by that department or body;

    (b)   any premises occupied for the purposes of—

        (i)   a department or other body listed in Schedule 1, or

        (ii)   a person whose staff constitute a body listed in that Schedule, are to be treated as occupied by that department or body.

(4)   For the purposes of sections 2 to 7 anything done purportedly by a department or other body listed in Schedule 1, although in law by the Crown or by the holder of a particular office, is to be treated as done by the department or other body itself.

(5)   Subsections (3)(a)(i), (3)(b)(i) and (4) apply in relation to a Northern Ireland department as they apply in relation to a department or other body listed in Schedule 1.'

Comment

8.25   Corporate manslaughter and corporate homicide applies to Crown bodies that are either bodies corporate or are listed in Sch 1. This means that the immunity that generally prohibits the prosecution of the Crown does not apply for the purposes of the new offence.

The Crown's liability with regard to the law of negligence is governed by the Crown Proceedings Act 1947 which makes the Crown liable as an employer or occupier where there is a personal duty of care to the victim. However, many of the activities and functions carried out by government departments and other Crown bodies are in law performed by the Crown rather than that body. This can be clarified in that civil servants in government departments are employed by the Crown rather than the department for which they work.

It follows that conduct relevant to the offence might legally be attributable to the Crown rather than the body concerned and the employer's duty of care. Therefore, the duty may technically be considered to be owed by the Crown rather than by the relevant department and it is important to ensure that the activities and functions of government departments and other Crown bodies can properly be attributed to the relevant body.

Section 12: Application to armed forces

8.26 '(1) In this Act "the armed forces" means any of the naval, military or air forces of the Crown raised under the law of the United Kingdom.

(2) For the purposes of section 2 a person who is a member of the armed forces is to be treated as employed by the Ministry of Defence.

(3) A reference in this Act to members of the armed forces includes a reference to—

(a) members of the reserve forces (within the meaning given by section 1(2) of the Reserve Forces Act 1996) when in service or undertaking training or duties;

(b) persons serving on Her Majesty's vessels (within the meaning given by section 132(1) of the Naval Discipline Act 1957).

Comment

8.27 The armed forces includes all naval, military or air forces and includes reserve forces all of which are employed by the Ministry of Defence. A wide range of operational military activities will be considered to be exclusively public functions and so exempt from the offence. The exemption applies to the conduct, preparation and support of military operations as well as other hazardous and unpredictable circumstances, including peacekeeping operations and operations dealing with terrorism or serious public disorder. In addition, the exemption extends to training exercises that simulate these sorts of operations and to the activities of the special forces. However, that exemption does not relate to an organisation's duties as employer or occupier.

Section 13: Application to police forces

8.28 '(1) In this Act "police force" means—

(a) a police force within the meaning of—

(i) the Police Act 1996, or

(ii) the Police (Scotland) Act 1967;

(b) the Police Service of Northern Ireland;

(c) the Police Service of Northern Ireland Reserve;

(d) the British Transport Police Force;

(e) the Civil Nuclear Constabulary;

(f)   the Ministry of Defence Police.

(2)   For the purposes of this Act a police force is to be treated as owing whatever duties of care it would owe if it were a body corporate.

(3)   For the purposes of section 2—

> (a)   a member of a police force is to be treated as employed by that force;
>
> (b)   a special constable appointed for a police area in England and Wales is to be treated as employed by the police force maintained by the police authority for that area;
>
> (c)   a special constable appointed for a police force mentioned in paragraph (d) or (f) of subsection (1) is to be treated as employed by that force;
>
> (d)   a police cadet undergoing training with a view to becoming a member of a police force mentioned in paragraph (a) or (d) of subsection (1) is to be treated as employed by that force;
>
> (e)   a police trainee appointed under section 39 of the Police (Northern Ireland) Act 2000 or a police cadet appointed under section 42 of that Act is to be treated as employed by the Police Service of Northern Ireland;
>
> (f)   a police reserve trainee appointed under section 40 of that Act is to be treated as employed by the Police Service of Northern Ireland Reserve;
>
> (g)   a member of a police force seconded to the Serious Organised Crime Agency or the National Policing Improvement Agency to serve as a member of its staff is to be treated as employed by that Agency.

(4)   A reference in subsection (3) to a member of a police force is to be read, in the case of a force mentioned in paragraph (a)(ii) of subsection (1), as a reference to a constable of that force.

(5)   For the purposes of section 2 any premises occupied for the purposes of a police force are to be treated as occupied by that force.

(6)   For the purposes of sections 2 to 7 anything that would be regarded as done by a police force if the force were a body corporate is to be so regarded.

(7)   Where—

> (a)   by virtue of subsection (3) a person is treated for the purposes of this Act as employed by a police force, and
>
> (b)   by virtue of any other statutory provision (whenever made) he is, or is treated as, employed by another organisation, the person is to be treated for those purposes as employed by both the force and the other organisation.'

Comment

8.29   Police force includes all police officers including special constables, police cadets or police trainees and are employees of the relevant police force. As police forces are not incorporated bodies, similar issues arise for the application of the offence to them as with Crown bodies.

This means that police officers are to be treated as the employees of the police force for which they work and are therefore owed the employer's duty of care by the force. There is also a similar provision in relation to special constables and police cadets, police trainees in Northern Ireland and police officers seconded to the Serious Organised Crime Agency or National Policing Improvement Agency.

Police authorities, which are bodies corporate under the Police Act 1996 or the Police (Scotland) Act 1967 are subjected to the offence as with any other corporate body.

Section 14: Application to partnerships

8.30 '(1)   For the purposes of this Act a partnership is to be treated as owing whatever duties of care it would owe if it were a body corporate.

(2)   Proceedings for an offence under this Act alleged to have been committed by a partnership are to be brought in the name of the partnership (and not in that of any of its members).

(3)   A fine imposed on a partnership on its conviction of an offence under this Act is to be paid out of the funds of the partnership.

(4)   This section does not apply to a partnership that is a legal person under the law by which it is governed.'

Comment

8.31   The Act includes large partnerships and bodies such as trade unions and employers' associations 'that already have a quasi-corporate status under statute' and that are themselves employers. Prosecutions will be brought against the body (i e not its members) and fines will similarly be paid out of the body's funds.

Section 15: Procedure, evidence and sentencing

8.32'(1)   Any statutory provision (whenever made) about criminal proceedings applies, subject to any prescribed adaptations or modifications, in relation to proceedings under this Act against—

  (a)   a department or other body listed in Schedule 1;

  (b)   a police force;

  (c)   a partnership;

  (d)   a trade union; or

  (e)   an employers' association that is not a corporation as it applies in relation to proceedings against a corporation.

(2)   In this section—

"prescribed" means prescribed by an order made by the Secretary of State;

"provision about criminal proceedings" includes—

  (a)   provision about procedure in or in connection with criminal proceedings;

  (b)   provision about evidence in such proceedings;

  (c)   provision about sentencing, or otherwise dealing with, persons convicted of offences;

"statutory" means contained in, or in an instrument made under, any Act or any Northern Ireland legislation.

(3)   A reference in this section to proceedings is to proceedings in England and Wales or Northern Ireland.

(4) An order under this section is subject to negative resolution procedure.'

Section 16: Transfer of functions

8.33'(1)   This section applies where—

  (a)   a person's death has occurred, or is alleged to have occurred, in connection with the carrying out of functions by a relevant public organisation, and

  (b)   subsequently there is a transfer of those functions, with the result that they are still carried out but no longer by that organisation.

(2)   In this section "relevant public organisation" means—

    (a)   a department or other body listed in Schedule 1;

    (b)   a corporation that is a servant or agent of the Crown;

    (c)   a police force.

(3)   Any proceedings instituted against a relevant public organisation after the transfer for an offence under this Act in respect of the person's death are to be instituted against—

    (a)   the relevant public organisation, if any, by which the functions mentioned in subsection (1) are currently carried out;

    (b)   if no such organisation currently carries out the functions, the relevant public organisation by which the functions were last carried out.

This is subject to subsection (4)

(4)   If an order made by the Secretary of State so provides in relation to a particular transfer of functions, the proceedings referred to in subsection (3) may be instituted, or (if they have already been instituted) may be continued, against—

    (a)   the organisation mentioned in subsection (1), or

    (b)   such relevant public organisation (other than the one mentioned in subsection (1) or the one mentioned in subsection (3)(a) or (b)) as may be specified in the order.

(5)   If the transfer occurs while proceedings for an offence under this Act in respect of the person's death are in progress against a relevant public organisation, the proceedings are to be continued against—

    (a)   the relevant public organisation, if any, by which the functions mentioned in subsection (1) are carried out as a result of the transfer;

    (b)   if as a result of the transfer no such organisation carries out the functions, the same organisation as before.

This is subject to subsection (6).

(6)   If an order made by the Secretary of State so provides in relation to a particular transfer of functions, the proceedings referred to in subsection (5) may be continued against—

    (a)   the organisation mentioned in subsection (1), or

    (b)   such relevant public organisation (other than the one mentioned in subsection (1) or the one mentioned in subsection (5)(a) or (b)) as may be specified in the order.

(7)   An order under subsection (4) or (6) is subject to negative resolution procedure.'

Comment

8.34   This section makes provision for cases where functions have been transferred between (or out of) Government departments or other bodies listed in Sch 1, incorporated Crown bodies or police forces. This means that prosecutions will be commenced, or continued, against the body that *currently* has responsibility for the relevant function. But if the function is transferred out of the public sector entirely, proceedings will be against the body by which the function was last carried out.

The Crown's overall liability for proceedings if a function is transferred to a non-Crown body (for example, if a function were privatised) will remain with the Crown body that previously carried out the function. In some circumstances such as where a function transfers between government departments but there is no corresponding transfer of personnel, it might be more appropriate for the department responsible at the time of the fatality to retain liability. There is provision for the Secretary of State to make an order specifying that liability rest with a different body.

Section 17: DPP's consent required for proceedings

8.35

'Proceedings for an offence of corporate manslaughter—

(a)   may not be instituted in England and Wales without the consent of the Director of Public Prosecutions;

(b)   may not be instituted in Northern Ireland without the consent of the Director of Public Prosecutions for Northern Ireland.'

Comment

8.36   The consent of the Director of Public Prosecutions (or DPP for Northern Ireland in the case of that jurisdiction) is needed for proceedings to be instituted. In Scotland all proceedings on indictment are instigated by the Lord Advocate and so there is no need for a consent mechanism.

All prosecutions need to pass a test to determine that the evidence is such that there is a realistic prospect of conviction and that a prosecution will be in the public interest. While the latter test will usually be met, it would not be in anyone's interest to proceed with a prosecution where there is insufficient evidence. Failure would mean that the organisation's reputation would be tarnished unfairly, and the family's expectations would be unfairly raised.

Section 18: No individual liability

8.37 '(1)   An individual cannot be guilty of aiding, abetting, counselling or procuring the commission of an offence of corporate manslaughter.

(2)   An individual cannot be guilty of aiding, abetting, counselling or procuring, or being art and part in, the commission of an offence of corporate homicide.'

Comment

8.38   The offence sets out a means of attributing certain failures within an organisation to the body itself for the purposes of prosecuting it for manslaughter. It therefore only applies to organisations and does not apply to individuals, be they directors or anyone else within an organisation. Individuals who assist or encourage the commission of an offence can also be convicted of an offence where they have aided, abetted, counselled or procured it or, in Scotland, are guilty art and part. This is known as secondary liability: the person is guilty of the offence itself, but not as the primary offender.

Section 19: Convictions under this Act and under health and safety legislation

8.39 '(1)   Where in the same proceedings there is—

(a)   a charge of corporate manslaughter or corporate homicide arising out of a particular set of circumstances, and

(b)   a charge against the same defendant of a health and safety offence arising out of some or all of those circumstances, the jury may, if the interests of justice so require, be invited to return a verdict on each charge.

(2)   An organisation that has been convicted of corporate manslaughter or corporate homicide arising out of a particular set of circumstances may, if the interests of justice so require, be charged with a health and safety offence arising out of some or all of those circumstances.

(3)   In this section "health and safety offence" means an offence under any health and safety legislation.'

Section 20: Abolition of liability of corporations for manslaughter at common law

Comment

8.40   The common law offence of gross negligence manslaughter is abolished in its application to corporations and in any application it has to other organisations to which s 1 applies.

Section 21: Power to extend section 1 to other organisations

8.41 '(1)   The Secretary of State may by order amend section 1 so as to extend the categories of organisation to which that section applies.

(2)   An order under this section may make any amendment to this Act that is incidental or supplemental to, or consequential on, an amendment made by virtue of subsection (1).

(3)   An order under this section is subject to affirmative resolution procedure.'

Section 22: Power to amend Schedule 1

8.42 '(1)   The Secretary of State may amend Schedule 1 by order.

(2)   A statutory instrument containing an order under this section is subject to affirmative resolution procedure, unless the only amendments to Schedule 1 that it makes are amendments within subsection (3). In that case the instrument is subject to negative resolution procedure.

(3)   An amendment is within this subsection if—

(a)   it is consequential on a department or other body listed in Schedule 1 changing its name,

(b)   in the case of an amendment adding a department or other body to Schedule 1, it is consequential on the transfer to the department or other body of functions all of which were previously exercisable by one or more organisations to which section 1 applies, or

(c)   in the case of an amendment removing a department or other body from Schedule 1, it is consequential on—

(i)   the abolition of the department or other body, or

(ii)   the transfer of all the functions of the department or other body to one or more organisations to which section 1 applies.'

Comment

8.43   There is a procedure for amending Sch 1. This includes changes to the name of a particular department, as well as the addition of a department (if the reason for adding it is that it will have functions all of which were previously exercisable by another organisation to which the offence applies) or deletion of a department (for the same reasons).

Section 23: Power to extend section 2(2)

8.44 '(1)   The Secretary of State may by order amend section 2(2) to make it include any category of person (not already included) who—

    (a)   is required by virtue of a statutory provision to remain or reside on particular premises, or

    (b)   is otherwise subject to a restriction of his liberty.

    (2)   An order under this section may make any amendment to this Act that is incidental or supplemental to, or consequential on, an amendment made by virtue of subsection (1).

    (3)   An order under this section is subject to affirmative resolution procedure.'

Section 24: Orders

8.45 '(1)   A power of the Secretary of State to make an order under this Act is exercisable by statutory instrument.

    (2)   Where an order under this Act is subject to "negative resolution procedure" the statutory instrument containing the order is subject to annulment in pursuance of a resolution of either House of Parliament.

    (3)   Where an order under this Act is subject to "affirmative resolution procedure" the order may not be made unless a draft has been laid before, and approved by a resolution of, each House of Parliament.

    (4)   An order under this Act—

    (a)   may make different provision for different purposes;

    (b)   may make transitional or saving provision.'

Section 25 – Interpretation

8.46

'In this Act:

"armed forces" has the meaning given by section 12(1);

"corporation" does not include a corporation sole but includes any body corporate wherever incorporated;

"employee" means an individual who works under a contract of employment or apprenticeship (whether express or implied and, if express, whether oral or in writing), and related expressions are to be construed accordingly; see also sections 11(3)(a), 12(2) and 13(3) (which apply for the purposes of section 2);

"employers' association" has the meaning given by section 122 of the Trade Union and Labour Relations (Consolidation) Act 1992 or Article 4 of the Industrial Relations (Northern Ireland) Order 1992;

"enforcement authority" means an authority responsible for the enforcement of any health and safety legislation;

"health and safety legislation" means any statutory provision dealing with health and safety matters, including in particular provision contained in the Health and Safety at Work etc. Act 1974 or the Health and Safety at Work (Northern Ireland) Order 1978;

"member", in relation to the armed forces, is to be read in accordance with section 12(3);

"partnership" means—

    (a)   a partnership within the Partnership Act 1890, or

    (b)   a limited partnership registered under the Limited Partnerships Act 1907, or a firm or entity of a similar character formed under the law of a country or territory outside the United Kingdom;

"police force" has the meaning given by section 13(1);

"premises" includes land, buildings and moveable structures;

"public authority" has the same meaning as in section 6 of the Human Rights Act 1998 (disregarding subsections (3)(a) and (4) of that section);

"publicity order" means an order under section 10(1);

"remedial order" means an order under section 9(1);

"statutory provision", except in section 15, means provision contained in, or in an instrument made under, any Act, any Act of the Scottish Parliament or any Northern Ireland legislation;

"trade union" has the meaning given by section 1 of the Trade Union and Labour Relations (Consolidation) Act 1992 or Article 3 of the Industrial Relations (Northern Ireland) Order 1992.

Section 26: Minor and consequential amendments

8.47 'Schedule 2 (minor and consequential amendments) has effect.'

Section 27: Commencement and savings

8.48 '(1)   The preceding provisions of this Act come into force in accordance with provision made by order by the Secretary of State.

(2)   An order bringing into force paragraph (d) of section 2(1) is subject to affirmative resolution procedure.

(3)   Section 1 does not apply in relation to anything done or omitted before the commencement of that section.

(4)   Section 20 does not affect any liability, investigation, legal proceeding or penalty for or in respect of an offence committed wholly or partly before the commencement of that section.

(5)   For the purposes of subsection (4) an offence is committed wholly or partly before the commencement of section 20 if any of the conduct or events alleged to constitute the offence occurred before that commencement.'

Section 28: Extent and territorial application

8.49 '(1)   Subject to subsection (2), this Act extends to England and Wales, Scotland and Northern Ireland.

(2)   An amendment made by this Act extends to the same part or parts of the United Kingdom as the provision to which it relates.

(3)   Section 1 applies if the harm resulting in death is sustained in the United Kingdom or—

   (a)   within the seaward limits of the territorial sea adjacent to the United Kingdom;

    (b)   on a ship registered under Part 2 of the Merchant Shipping Act 1995;

    (c)   on a British-controlled aircraft as defined in section 92 of the Civil Aviation Act 1982;

    (d)   on a British-controlled hovercraft within the meaning of that section as applied in relation to hovercraft by virtue of provision made under the Hovercraft Act 1968;

    (e)   in any place to which an Order in Council under section 10(1) of the Petroleum Act 1998 applies (criminal jurisdiction in relation to offshore activities).

(4)   For the purposes of subsection (3)(b) to (d) harm sustained on a ship, aircraft or hovercraft includes harm sustained by a person who—

    (a)   is then no longer on board the ship, aircraft or hovercraft in consequence of the wrecking of it or of some other mishap affecting it or occurring on it, and

    (b)   sustains the harm in consequence of that event.'

Comment

8.50   The offence of corporate manslaughter and corporate homicide extends to the whole of the UK. Under s 10 of the Offences Against the Person Act 1861, English courts have jurisdiction in a case of homicide if the injury causing death is inflicted in England and Wales, or in a place where the English courts have jurisdiction (such as on a British ship), even if the death occurs elsewhere. The Act makes similar provision to this (but on a UK basis reflecting the application of the new offence across the UK), providing for jurisdiction if the harm causing death is sustained in the UK or other locations where criminal jurisdiction currently extends. The offence will still apply if the harm resulting in death is sustained as a result of an incident involving a British ship (or aircraft or hovercraft), but the victim is not on board when he suffers that harm: for example, if a grave safety failing resulted in a ship being wrecked and the passengers being killed by drowning.

Section 29: Short title

8.51

'This Act may be cited as the Corporate Manslaughter and Corporate Homicide Act 2007.'

Schedule 1: List of Government Departments etc

8.52   The departments listed are as follows: Assets Recovery Agency, Attorney General's Office, Cabinet Office, Central Office of Information, Crown Office and Procurator Fiscal Service, Crown Prosecution Service, Department for Communities and Local Government, Department for Constitutional Affairs (including the Scotland Office and, the Wales Office), Department for Culture, Media and Sport, Department for Education and Skills, Department for Environment, Food and Rural Affairs, Department for International Development, Department for Transport, Department for Work and Pensions, Department of Health, Department of Trade and Industry, Export Credits Guarantee Department, Foreign and Commonwealth Office, Forestry Commission, General Register Office for Scotland, Government Actuary's Department, Her Majesty's Land Registry, Her Majesty's Revenue and Customs, Her Majesty's Treasury, Home Office, Ministry of Defence, National Archives, National Archives of Scotland, National Audit Office, National Savings and Investments, National School of Government, Northern Ireland Audit Office' Northern Ireland Court Service, Northern Ireland Office, Office for National Statistics, Office of the Deputy Prime Minister, Office of Her Majesty's Chief Inspector of Education and Training in Wales, Ordnance Survey, Privy Council Office, Public Prosecution Service for Northern Ireland, Registers of Scotland Executive Agency, Revenue and Customs Prosecutions Office, Royal Mint, Scottish Executive, Serious Fraud Office, Treasury Solicitor's Department, UK Trade and Investment and the Welsh Assembly Government.

Schedule 2 Minor and consequential amendments

8.53'1 (1) The Coroners Act 1988 is amended as follows.

   (2)   In the following provisions, after "manslaughter" there is inserted ", corporate manslaughter"—

      (a)   section 11(6) (no finding of guilt at coroner's inquest) (twice);

      (b)   subsection (1)(a)(i) of section 16 (adjournment of inquest in event of criminal proceedings);

      (c)   subsections (1)(a) and (2)(a) of section 17 (coroner to be informed of result of criminal proceedings).

   (3)   In section 35(1) (interpretation), after the definition of "Greater London" there is inserted—

   ""person", in relation to an offence of corporate manslaughter, includes organisation;".

Criminal Justice Act 2003 (c. 44)

2 In Schedule 4 to the Criminal Justice Act 2003 (qualifying offences for purposes of section 62), after paragraph 4 there is inserted—

"*Corporate manslaughter*

4A An offence under section 1 of the Corporate Manslaughter and Corporate Homicide Act 2007."

3 (1) Schedule 5 to that Act (qualifying offences for purposes of Part 10) is amended as follows.

(2)   After paragraph 4 there is inserted—

"*Corporate manslaughter*

4A An offence under section 1 of the Corporate Manslaughter and Corporate Homicide Act 2007."

(3)   After paragraph 33 there is inserted—

"*Corporate manslaughter*

33A An offence under section 1 of the Corporate Manslaughter and Corporate Homicide Act 2007."

Criminal Justice (Northern Ireland) Order 2004

4 In Schedule 2 to the Criminal Justice (Northern Ireland) Order 2004 (qualifying offences for purposes of Article 21), after paragraph 4 there is Inserted—

"*Corporate manslaughter*

4A An offence under section 1 of the Corporate Manslaughter and Corporate Homicide Act 2007." '

Chapter 9

Enforcement and Fines

Introduction

9.1   It could be argued that if the current regime of fines and use of imprisonment were effective, the level of workplace incidents would have reduced instead of remaining a cause for concern. A response could be that there needs to be a review and radical change in the legal process and punishment options available to the courts. The introduction of the Government's Revitalising Health and Safety Programme was seen as a way ahead but there appears to be a reluctance to introduce a punishment and sanctions package as an option of ensuring compliance with health and safety legislation. However, public pressure is focused on change and the Government, although reluctantly, has laid the proposals for change which are summarised by Wood:[1]

> 'In the most radical overhaul of health and safety law in the past two decades, the government is proposing legislation that could see company directors facing fines, imprisonment and disqualification if one of their employees dies as a result of an accident at work. It will also widen the remit of responsibility to include those who provide strategic leadership and oversight, such as directors, as well as senior managers on boards who set a firm's policy on health and safety at work.'

Two companies have received substantial fines: one of £15 million and one of £10 million, which in the overall context of corporate profits will not have been excessive. Some commentators are suggesting that it is the shareholders who are paying for the failings of the directors and that the directors should be held accountable.

Individual offences

9.2   Offences for individuals including directors, managers, employees and others already exist within the HSWA 1974. Under the Act, a 'section 36 offence' is where there is the fault of another person, while s 37 is a corporate offence for directors, company secretaries and managers. Section 7 is used for individuals. These three offences cover a wide and diverse range of people who owe a duty of care to others with sanctions available when they fail in that duty.

9.3   The three individual offences are not regularly used because, particularly in the case of s 37, it is difficult to prove the offence. However, there have been an increasing number of successfully prosecuted cases and relevant details of case examples are provided below. This provides a background to the offences and the focus of individual liability.

HSWA 1974, s 36

9.4   Section 36 (offences due to fault of other persons) provides as follows:

'Where the commission by any person of an offence under any of the relevant statutory provisions (a) is due to (b) the act or default (c) of some other person (d) that other person shall be guilty of the offence, and a person may be charged with and convicted of the offence, by virtue of this subsection whether or not proceedings are taken against the first mentioned person.'

HSWA 1974, s 37

9.5   The Health and Safety Executive (HSE) and local authority enforcement officers can prosecute directors and senior company officers under HSWA 1974, s 37 (offences by bodies corporate), which provides as follows:

'Where an offence under any of the relevant statutory provisions (a) committed by a body corporate is proved to have been committed with the consent or connivance (b) of, or to have been attributable to any neglect on the part of, any director, manager, secretary or other similar officer (c) of the body corporate or a person who was purporting to act in any such capacity, he as well as the body corporate shall be guilty of that offence and shall be liable to be proceeded against and punished accordingly.'

It must first be established that the company committed an offence by breaching a duty imposed by the 1974 Act itself. It will then be necessary to show that the director 'consented' or 'connived' in the offence committed by the company, or that the corporate offence resulted from 'any neglect' on his or her part. It has to be established that a director consents to the commission of an offence when he or she is well aware of what is going on and agrees to it. It will be necessary to show that this agreement involved some positive action, which could be verbal, in writing or a gesture. It is important to note that the latter may offer difficulty in establishing proof to a level that would secure a conviction.

9.6   It can be considered that a director 'connives' in an offence when he is well aware of what is going on and whilst not actively encouraging what happens, allows it to continue and does nothing to stop the activity. As far as gathering evidence is concerned it should be easier to prove 'connivance' in that it has to be shown that the director was aware of the 'offence' and did nothing to stop it.

9.7   There is a need to prove 'neglect' on the part of a company officer who has a 'duty' to do whatever it is alleged he failed to do. However, the absence of *legal* duties does not preclude action as there is interpretation that shows neglect can also refer to the breach of *non-legal* duties.

HSWA 1974, s 7

9.8   Employees can be prosecuted under HSWA 1974, s 7 as they have a duty to take reasonable care for the health and safety of themselves and others who may be affected by their acts or omissions at work. It provides as follows:

'It shall be the duty of every employee while at work- (a) to take reasonable care for the health and safety of himself and of other persons who may be affected by his acts or omissions at work; and (b) as regards any duty or requirement imposed upon his employer or any other person by or under any of the relevant statutory provisions, to co-operate with him so far as is necessary to enable that duty or requirement to be performed or complied with.'

This offence provides for the prosecution of an employee who knowingly undertakes an unsafe action and as a result another is harmed. An employee who through an act of horseplay or skylarking while at work causes another to be injured could be prosecuted. Any employee who, provided with safety equipment, refuses to wear or use the equipment or abide by safety procedures could be liable for prosecution. In addition to the HSWA 1974, the Management of Health and Safety at Work Regulations 1999 (SI 1999/3242) impose additional duties on employees to report dangerous situations or shortcomings to the employer in matters of health and safety. It is often seen that the corporate body is prosecuted as having the ultimate general duty of care, with HSWA 1974, s 7 charges against an individual being for specific acts or omissions.

Section 37 case law

9.9   The following cases provide a background to the offences and the focus of individual liability showing the package of offences and the penalties that have resulted from successful prosecutions under HSWA 1974, s 37.

Fresha Bakeries

9.10   'Leicester Bakers Ordered to Pay £628,000 after Double Deaths in Oven', stated the headlines of an HSE Press release.[1] In the case of Harvestime Ltd, Fresha Bakeries, two directors and a manager were fined a total of £373,000 plus costs of £255,000 as a result of the death of two employees at their factory in Leicester on 16 May 1998. The two men had been sent into a giant oven to retrieve a broken part, using a slow moving conveyor belt to enter the oven where the temperature was more than 100 degrees and died as a result.

---

1 HSE Press Release July 2001.

9.11   Fresha Bakeries were prosecuted under s 2 of the HSWA 1974 because they failed to provide a safe system of work. Harvestime were prosecuted under the same offence. Both companies were prosecuted under s 3 of the Act for failing to ensure that persons not in their employ were not exposed to danger. For these offences the companies were fined a total of £350,000. Dennis Masters, the chief engineer and employee of Fresha Bakeries, was prosecuted under s 7 and fined £2,000. Brian Jones, an employee, was also prosecuted under s 7 and fined £1,000. John Bridson, managing director of Harvestime Ltd, was prosecuted under HSWA 1974, s 37 and fined £10,000. He was also prosecuted under s 37 and fined £10,000 as managing director of Fresha Bakeries Ltd, so being fined £20,000 in total. The costs were divided into £250,000 awarded against the companies and £5,000 against John Bridson.

The Post Office

9.12   The Post Office[1] case provides a good example of a director being prosecuted but with no evidence offered. The incident was not fatal, and the penalty was minimal in the event of serious injuries.

On 13 July 2001, the Post Office Royal Mail appeared in Birmingham Magistrates' Court being prosecuted by the HSE under HSWA 1974, s 3 for failing to ensure, so far as was reasonably practicable, that persons not in their employment were not exposed to risks to their safety. The managing director of Post Office Property Holdings, Crenville Collins, also appeared, having been charged under s 37 of the Act in that, allegedly, an offence by a corporate body was committed with his consent or connivance or was attributable to some neglect on his part. The prosecution was as a result of an incident where a roofing contractor fell through a fragile roof light at the Post Office Road Transport Workshop in Birmingham, suffering serious injuries. The Post Office was fined £2,500. No evidence was offered on the charge against Mr Collins.

---

1 www.cwu.org/about/health_safety_prosecution

JM Enterprises of Wetherby Ltd

9.13   The case of JM Enterprises of Wetherby[1] is an important case as it involves the prosecution of individuals on a number of offences and established a precedent for the enforcing authorities. The directors, Nigel Jackson and John Mather of JM Enterprises (JME) of Wetherby Ltd, a firework manufacturer, were fined for health and safety breaches. Firework display organiser, Mick Mason, died in a massive explosion after he took four boxes of condemned Turbo 3 Rocket fireworks from the company to burn in his kiln. Mr Mason lit the kiln, resulting in a massive explosion, which blew the upper door of the kiln 85 metres away causing his death.

---

1 HSE Press Release, September 2001.

9.14   The rockets had been declared unsafe by trading standards officers. They contained barium nitrate, sulphur and aluminium powder, which is referred to as 'flash composition', meaning that it is a high-energy, rapidly burning composition that can explode violently. A company employee who had no formal training had, because of a lack of knowledge, passed the broken up, volatile fireworks to Mr Mason. The fireworks were so unstable they could have exploded while being transported.

9.15   A parallel investigation identified that JME was an importer and supplier of fireworks, which involved large-scale importation of unclassified fireworks, which is illegal. Investigations showed that of 22 shipments, some 43% of fireworks imported in these consignments were unclassified. The HSE placed prohibition notices on the company to prevent transportation and supply of unclassified fireworks. The directors and a manager acting on behalf of the company breached the notices. Mr Mather had, prior to the notices being issued, supplied fireworks to a wholesaler. Because the directors and managers had close control over the activities of the company, the individuals were prosecuted.

9.16 There were two serious charges:

1 The directors (Jackson and Mather) pleaded guilty to a breach of a prohibition notice through consent or contrivance when they supplied unclassified fireworks to a wholesaler.

2 Jackson and Mather admitted breach of a prohibition notice through their neglect in that they transported an unclassified X-O-Set to Newcastle airport. Mather had intended to take the firework on board a plane to Poland. They both claimed to believe that the rocket was a dummy and contained no explosives. The rocket, which was in fact 'live', was discovered by security at Newcastle airport.

It is the first time that individual directors have been convicted for s 37 offences without the company being convicted of the same offence. The company (which was in receivership) and three individuals pleaded guilty to 24 offences. It is important to note that the HSE did not seek an order to disqualify either Mather or Jackson from acting as directors and both men are still employed in the firework industry in the UK. This case was important and the precedent is quoted:[1]

'The HSE prosecuted the directors and manager under the section 37 of the Health and Safety at Work etc Act 1974 because of the close control that they exercised over the company ... Until the JME case, the interpretation of section 37(1) has always been that to secure a section 37(1) conviction of a director, the company has first to be convicted of a parallel offence. But this case also saw the HSE secure four convictions of one director and two of the other four offences for which the company had not been convicted. This has not happened before.'

A very important aspect of the case was the breach of a notice, which as opposed to the s 37 offence, carries the possibility of imprisonment.

'The directors appear fortunate to have avoided imprisonment and disqualification. Mather and Jackson were convicted respectively of four and three breaches of prohibition notices; such offence is one of the few under the Health and Safety at Work etc Act 1974 that can result in imprisonment, accounting for three of the five prison sentences issued under the Act. One of the charges said that the notice had been contravened with the consent or connivance of Mr Jackson and Mr Mather. (All the other charges cited neglect.) The judge said he had considered a custodial sentence, but he felt that the offence that had involved consent or connivance – as opposed to the less serious neglect – concerned a risk that was insufficiently severe to merit prison.'

9.17   The case was successful to the degree that it set new guidelines for future cases. The downside must be the failure to obtain a custodial sentence, as it diminishes the weight and seriousness of a notice. The authorities use prohibition notices to stop an act that could result in serious injury or death. There is a right of appeal, which in this case did not appear to be an option taken. Therefore, the breach was a serious and calculated act but as the directors were not disqualified it weakened the success of the case.

Section 7 case law

Lincoln City Council v Helmrich[1]

9.18   Following the fatal electrocution of a 17 year old employee, the health and safety manager of a former national restaurant chain, Fatty Arbuckles, was found guilty under HSWA 1974, s 7(a) and fined £3,000 with £3,000 costs.

---

1 [2002] EWHC 1241.

9.19   Lincoln Magistrates' Court found that the health and saftey manager, Mr Helmrich (who pleaded not guilty), had failed to take reasonable care in his role as a manager. The case involved Mark Thorne, who was fatally electrocuted by a plate warmer while he was deck scrubbing a wet floor in August 1998 at Fatty Arbuckles' Lincoln branch. Mr Helmrich did not appeal against the conviction. The prosecution followed an inquest in 2000 which reached a verdict of unlawful killing.

9.20   Mr Helmrich was responsible for food safety and health and safety across 58 restaurants. He had been in post for a year and had made six visits to the Lincoln restaurant before the accident. The court heard that the plate warmer's cable had been incompetently repaired and that its plug had been wrongly wired. The plate warmer had been giving minor electric shocks for two months before the accident but there was an inadequate system for the maintenance of electrical equipment. According to the prosecution, Mr Helmrich had decided to prioritise food safety in his role, at the expense of health and safety. No documented health and safety risk assessment had been made across the chain and Mr Helmrich failed to act consistently, in response to warnings from other authorities. The prosecution did not set out to prove that Mr Helmrich's conduct caused the death, but maintained that it had put the employee's safety at risk, along with that of others.

9.21   District Judge Friel at Lincoln Magistrates' Court commented:

'This was a case of misjudgement rather than malice and you have become somewhat of a scapegoat for the failings of the company, I cannot deal with you on the basis that you caused his death but you did make the events more likely.'

It had been suggested that in an environment of highly publicised food hygiene scares, Mr Helmrich had devoted more effort in this area than in health and safety. The company had a history of breaches at its 50–60 branches long before Mr Helmrich's employment, and it was noted:

> 'It was not his job as risk manager to act as legal adviser to the company, his role was to get risk management procedures in place'

The company, Fatty Arbuckles, would also have been prosecuted if it had not gone into receivership in July 1999. Mr Helmrich's two professional bodies, the Chartered Institute of Environmental Health and the Institution of Occupational Safety and Health were informed of the details of the prosecution.

Prosecution of Mr Helmrich

9.22   The case for the prosecution of Mr Helmrich is important and is examined in more detail. A major investigation followed the fatality with a view to prosecuting Fatty Arbuckles for corporate manslaughter. During this process several managers, including Mr Helmrich, were interviewed under caution. Mr Helmrich went to the interview with the company solicitor and co-operated in answering the questions put to him. When Fatty Arbuckles went into receivership he was made redundant like everyone else.

9.23   A prosecution case such as this involves an emotional element for the person concerned (in this case it was over a four-year period) in respect of his employment and professional standing as well as the effect on his family.

Initial failings

9.24

- Mr Helmrich did some things which made it more likely that he would be prosecuted.

- He went to the interview which was under caution with the company solicitor.

- He was not under arrest and could leave the interview at any time and was entitled to decline to attend at all.

- Much of the prosecution case against him was based upon admissions made by him in the interview.

- There was a delay until he sought legal representation for himself.

- He was unaware that the company's insurance policy provided for him to have independent legal representation.

Key developments

9.25

- A couple of years after the fatal incident Mr Helmrich was called as a witness at the inquest. He attended the Coroner's inquest without legal representation.

- Some months later he received a letter telling him he was to be personally prosecuted under the HSWA 1974.

- No one else was to be prosecuted. Not the company, the directors, the restaurant manager, the chef in the kitchen where the incident occurred, the employee who wrongly wired the plug, nor the electrical contractor who attended to the appliance.

- He was on his own, the scapegoat, left 'carrying the can'.

His failings

9.26

- His contact with senior management was informal and few records were kept.

- The prosecution alleged he made decisions which, although not seriously wrong, could have been addressed more appropriately when reviewed with the benefit of hindsight.

- He was challenged on things he had not done. For example, why had he not given a written instruction to the company's employees not to attempt to wire an electrical plug?

Avoiding the situation

9.27   Mr Helmrich would have benefited from the following advice:

- Make sure you never end up in this position.

- Look at your job description and identify what you agreed to carry responsibility for.

- If your workload is excessive you need to inform management in writing.

- If you do not have the technical skill or experience to cover some aspect of your job inform management that you need training and/or guidance or external professional support.

- If you have identified a number of action points from risk assessments prioritise importance and action.

- There needs to be a visible involvement by managers to determine the priorities of the risk assessments to be adopted by the person with responsibility.

- If there is an investigation by the police or an enforcement agency such as the HSE, obtain legal advice for yourself at the earliest possible stage.

- Ensure you go to a specialist who understands safety, health and management issues.

- Workers directly involved in the incident are at risk, as are managers and, in some circumstances, directors.

9.28   It is very evident that Mr Helmrich did not have an objective job description and that his main function was focused on the food safety aspect as opposed to health and safety matters. If he was unable to cope with the workload he should have documented this to senior management, then undertaken an audit to assess the situation and draw up priorities. Part of the audit process would have determined if there was a safety management system upon which to establish a plan of action; it would also have identified whether he had the appropriate competences for the workscope. If he did not, then he could have submitted an action plan requesting external support and/or equipment. Throughout this period of communication he should have followed up in writing any face-to-face meetings, and e-mail or telephone conversations. In this way he would have transferred responsibility back to senior management for them to take action. Whilst it may be cumbersome to maintain a written procedure it does provide evidence in the event that something goes wrong.

Imprisonment and director's disqualification

9.29   In addition to the ss 36, 37 and 7 offences there are in some instances the options of disqualifying directors and imposing custodial sentences. Under current law the highest sanction that is available to the courts for certain health and safety offences is imprisonment. Throughout the years of the HSWA being in place, there has been a reluctance to commit an individual to prison as workplace incidents have been viewed as civil matters, where compensation is seen as the principal legal outcome. There is a change in public acceptance and the demand for imprisonment is being viewed as a viable punishment for workplace wrongdoers.

9.30   Imprisonment was the outcome in a case reported by Prior[1] who states:

> 'Britain's first building boss found guilty of manslaughter is behind bars this week starting an 18-month stretch. The sentence will send shockwaves through the industry, as courts get tough with health and safety offenders. Brian Dean, 60, from Stoke-on-Trent, was jailed last week after being found guilty by jury of the manslaughter of Michael and Carl Redgate. The father-and-son team died when a tunnel kiln they were demolishing collapsed in July 2000, burying them under tonnes of rubble. Sentencing Dean, Judge John Shand said: 'You took on this job of demolishing a tunnel kiln when you were out of your depth. The risk of the kiln collapsing was a risk you understood and you did not warn the Redgates of this risk. Two deaths followed from this case. The least sentence I can pass is 18-months.''

The article continues to provide the views of the Construction Confederation and states:

> 'Construction Confederation health and safety director Suzannah Nichol said: "If this doesn't make them stand up and take notice then they don't deserve to be in the industry. The 18-month sentence shows that courts can and will find directors responsible for their actions. Jailing directors has always been talked about, but this makes it a reality." Construction union leaders welcomed the sentence, which they believe will boost safety standards.'

---

1 Prior, G, Construction News, May 2002.

9.31   The failure to comply with a statutory notice is a serious disregard of health and safety law and has to be dealt with by the courts in a like manner. The seriousness is heightened when there is a failure to act upon advice provided. This leaves no defence and the sanction needs to reflect the displeasure of the legal system for such disregard as described in an article:[1]

> 'A self-employed building developer was sentenced to four months in jail after a court heard that he failed to comply with the requirements of an improvement notice issued by the Health and Safety Executive (HSE) ... The court heard that HSE inspectors had visited the site during June and July 1998, and advised Majeed that he needed to install edge protection to prevent workers falling from heights. The Inspectors also identified the need for Majeed to provide adequate welfare facilities for his workers – including running water. However, during a follow-up visit in November 1998, the inspectors found that no action had been taken to deal with the problems they had identified. In addition, they found that the protective fencing at the front and rear of the building had been removed. This meant that members of the public could easily gain access to the building and be exposed to risk.'

---

1 Safety Management, December 1999.

9.32   As a result, HSE inspectors issued an improvement notice requiring Majeed to install adequate fencing at the site by 20 December 1998. The inspectors visited the site again on 22 December 1998 to check that the improvement notice had been complied with. Although they found that some of the windows in the building had been boarded up, there was still no adequate protective fencing around the site. The inspectors also found that Majeed had failed to install suitable edge protection, which they had recommended during their earlier visits. As a result, they issued a prohibition notice requiring all work at height to be stopped until appropriate edge protection had been installed.

9.33   The court heard that Majeed had been fined for previous breaches of health and safety law during 1994. This included failure to comply with four prohibition notices and several breaches of building regulations. Majeed was sentenced to four months in jail under HSWA 1974, s 33(1) for failing to comply with the requirements of an improvement notice.

9.34   The previous record with breaches of notices and regulations exacerbates the seriousness of the offence in the above case. It does show a poor culture with regard to health and safety and in such cases, a prison sentence would probably be the only viable option.

9.35   The courts do have the option to disqualify directors although it is rarely used. Generally a director found guilty of a s 37 offence is fined. The disqualification of directors was an option that was considered as a penalty for the Law Commission's proposed new offence of corporate killing. A news item stated:[1]

'*Company director disqualified after employee accident*

A man has been disqualified from being a company director for five years, after one of his employees was severely injured by an unguarded machine ... an emergency call had been made at the premises of *Rainham Waste Recycling Ltd* in Essex. An employee, Ali Taofiq, was caught in the prop shaft driving a wood-chipping machine, and was only freed when his left arm came off. His neck was broken, paralysing him from the chest down and preventing movement in his right hand ... The decision was taken to prosecute the Managing Director, Tony O'Sullivan, personally, because the firm was small enough for him "to know exactly what was going on" in the factory. Section 37 of the Health and Safety at Work Act 1974 enables prosecution of an individual whose consent, connivance or neglect has allowed an offence to be committed.

O'Sullivan and Rainham Waste pleaded guilty to breaching Regulation 11(1) of the Provision and Use of Work Equipment Regulations 1992 by failing to guard dangerous machinery. On 24 September Snaresbrook Crown Court fined O'Sullivan £5,000 and his company £25,000 with costs of £4,000.

The Company Directors Disqualification Act 1986 was used to disqualify O'Sullivan. This Act was intended to crack down on fraud, but the H.S.E has used it eight times for safety offences. Hodges hoped the case "gives a clear message to directors that ultimately they are responsible for health and safety and can be held personally liable".'

1 Health and Safety, November 1998 'Company Director Disqualified after Employee Accident'.

9.36 One of the most serious criminal acts is perverting the course of justice and those found guilty inevitably receive a custodial sentence. An example is described in an article[1] which stated:

'Director convicted for cold and calculated attempt to pervert the course of justice: A property developer accused of covering up the cause of a fatal accident in a cold and calculated attempt to pervert the course of justice was sentenced to three months in prison and ordered to pay a fine of £12,000 ... Harper was given the jail sentence as a result of a police prosecution for attempting to pervert the course of justice. He was also fined £12,000 and his company JK Investments £20,000 for breaches of the Health and Safety at Work Act ... JK Investments was converting the Royal Hotel in Union Street, Dundee to flats when the accident occurred ... John Stupart was killed instantly after a gate, which had not been properly fastened to a hoist came loose and fell 40 feet, smashing Stupart's skull as he walked below.'

Harper, who pleaded not guilty to all of the charges laid against him and his company, accused police and HSE officials of lying to frame him. Defending Harper and JK Investments Ray Small QC told the court that Harper was not involved in the day-to-day running of the company and said that "Harper will carry the burden of what happened for the rest of his life." JK Investments Limited was ordered to pay £12,500 under Section 2(1) of the Health and Safety at Work Act (HSWA), £5,000 under section 3(1), and £2,500 under section 42(1) of the Construction (Lifting Operations) Regulations 1961. The firm was found not guilty of an offence under Section 37(1) of HSWA. Harper was ordered to pay £12,000 – the largest fine ever given to a director of a construction company in a Scottish court – under section 37(1) of HSWA. Costs are not awarded in Scottish court.'

1 Safety Management, February 1997.

9.37 Throughout the examples described above, there are a number of options available for prosecution of individuals for health and safety offences as well as other associated offences. They range from financial penalties, to disqualification from holding office, to imprisonment. It may be argued that the offences are used too infrequently and that there is too much reliance on the more global offences under the HSWA 1974. Due to the activities of such organisations as the TUC and the Centre for Corporate Accountability there is a sea change in particular with s 37, where there is a focus on more prosecutions.

Legal considerations

9.38   A major factor arising from prosecutions of undertakings is that of consistency in the numerous courts and the level of information about the undertaking that had been provided. The cases of *R v Howe & Son (Engineers) Ltd* and *R v Friskies Petcare (UK) Ltd* have been identified as providing the basis for consideration by the court when determining the level of fines to be imposed. The cases are summarised below.

Howe & Son Ltd[1]

9.39   Problems that have occurred with health and safety prosecutions have been the lack of consistency in case preparation and presentation as well as the courts' determination as to the level of penalties to impose. This has resulted in a variance throughout the country and from case to case, with some cases involving loss of life receiving fines lower than cases where there had been no loss of life. The situation changed when Howe & Son pleaded guilty on 10 November 1997 at Bristol Crown Court to four offences and was fined: £40,000 for a breach of HSWA 1974, s 2(1) for failing to ensure the safety of its employees as far as was reasonably practicable; £2,000 under reg 4(2) of the Electricity at Work Regulations 1989 (SI 1989/635) (EAW 1989) for failing to maintain an electric cable to a machine; £2,000 under reg 3 of the Management of Health and Safety at Work Regulations 1992 (SI 1992/2051) for failing to make a suitable and sufficient risk assessment; and £4,000 under the EAW 1989 for failing to ensure that means were provided to protect the electrical system supplying the machine from excess current. This amounted to a fine of £48,000. In addition the defendants were ordered to pay £7,500 costs.

---

1 *R v Howe & Son (Engineers) Ltd* [1999] 2 Cr App R (S) 37.

9.40   The case involved Giles Smith, aged 20, who was electrocuted on 13 August 1996 while cleaning Howe & Son's factory, which had been shut down for the purpose. The cleaning process involved water that was collected by an electric vacuum machine, which had been bought second-hand at an auction in 1995. The investigation found that the cable to the machine became trapped between one of its wheels and the floor, damaging the cable and making the machine live. Smith, who was holding the machine, was unable to let it go until the power was turned off. He was taken to hospital, where he was certified dead.

Aggravating/mitigating factors

9.41   The Court of Appeal set out the criteria for identifying mitigating and aggravating factors that judges should take into account when fixing the level of a fine. The court found that the trial judge had given insufficient weight to the company's financial position when sentencing, and addressed the situation by reducing the fine from £48,000 to £15,000.

9.42   The Court of Appeal established its sentencing on the following criteria:

> 'The objective of prosecutions for health and safety offences in the work-place is to achieve a safe environment for those who work there and for other members of the public who may be affected. A fine needs to be large enough to bring that message home where the defendant is a company not only to those who manage it but also to its shareholders ... fines should not be so large as to imperil the earnings of employees or create a risk of bank-ruptcy ... there might be cases where the offences are so serious that the defendant ought not to be in business ... it is impossible to lay down any tariff or to say that the fine should bear any specific relationship to the turnover or net profit of the defendant ...'

The Court split the 'relevant factors' that judges and magistrates should con-sider when setting a fine into three categories – criteria, other matters, and mitigating and aggravating factors.

The criteria categories include the following:

(a)   *Failure* – 'In assessing the gravity of the breach, it is often helpful to look at how far short of the right standard the defendant fell in failing to meet the 'reasonably practicable' test.'

(b)   *Death* – 'It is often a matter of chance whether death or serious injury results from even a serious breach. Generally where death is the conse-quence of a criminal act, it is regarded as an aggravating feature of the offence. The penalty should reflect public disquiet at the unnecessary loss of life.'

(c)   *Profit* –'A deliberate breach of health and safety legislation with a view to profit seriously aggravates the offence'. The court stated: 'Financial profit can often be made at the expense of [protecting] employees and the public'.

(d)   *Size* – Although this will affect the level of the fine, the Court of Appeal emphasised that: 'the standard of care imposed by the legislation is the same regardless of the size of the company ... The size of a company and its financial strength or weakness cannot affect the degree of care that is required in matters of safety. That said, how individual companies dis-charge their duties depends on the circumstances'.

9.43   It was identified that there may be other matters that may affect the sentence and these include:

> 'The degree of risk and extent of the danger created by the offence; the extent of the breach whether the failure was an isolated incident or continued over a period; and importantly, the defendant's resources and the effect of the fine on its business.'

In addition, the court identified particular aggravating and mitigating features:

1   *aggravating* factors include:

    (a)   a failure to heed warnings; and

    (b)   where the defendant has deliberately profited financially from a failure to take necessary health and safety steps or run a risk to save money;

2   *mitigating* factors include:

    (a)   prompt admission of responsibility and a timely plea of guilt;

    (b)   steps to remedy deficiencies after they are drawn to the defendant's attention; and

    (c)   a good safety record.

9.44   The first factor involves the aggravating features, which in this case included:

- it was not a one-off failure but a failure over many months;

- the case was very serious, involving four fatalities; and

- there was a failure to recognise the significance of, and deal with, previous adverse events.

To counter the aggravating aspects of the case, the mitigating features included:

- the companies had pleaded guilty at the earliest opportunity; and

- they had co-operated with the HSE to ensure that the problems had been rectified.

The Friskies judgment

9.45   When preparing a case for prosecution the regulating authorities carry out a 'Friskies' assessment to identify the aggravating and mitigating features of the defendant and submit the information as part of the prosecution bundle. This will provide the court with important information to aid them when determining the sentence. The case that brought about this change in procedure was *R v Friskies Petcare (UK) Ltd*.[1]

---

1   [2000] Cr App R (S) 401.

9.46   The company was fined £600,000 at Isleworth Crown Court after the electrocution of an employee in a meat silo at their factory at Southall, West London. Bryan Wilkins was repairing a metal ribbon stirrer at the bottom of the silo. He was arc welding in a confined, damp conductive environment in the silo when he was electrocuted while changing welding electrodes. The company pleaded guilty to breach of HSWA 1974, s 2 and the Management of Health & Safety at Work Regulations 1992, reg 3 for failing to ensure, so far as was reasonably practicable, the safety of employees, including Bryan Wilkins, whilst arc welding in metal meat silos. They also pleaded guilty to reg 3 of the Management of Health & Safety at Work Regulations 1992 for failing to make a suitable and sufficient assessment of the risks to which their employees, including Bryan Wilkins, were exposed whilst arc welding in metal meat silos for the purpose of identifying the measures needed to comply with the relevant statutory requirements. The company appealed against the level of fine.

9.47   The fine was reduced to £250,000 by the Court of Appeal in March 2000. This decision was made on the grounds that the trial judge had incorrectly included an 'aggravating' factor after he had erroneously found that the company had put profit before safety. It is considered that a deliberate breach of health and safety legislation with a view to profit seriously aggravates the offence. The court stated that 'financial profit can often be made at the expense of protecting employees and the public'. It was not disputed in court when the company claimed that there was no evidence of cost cutting for financial gain. The Court of Appeal judgment reinforced the sentencing criteria established in *Howe*, and identified that fines of £500,000 and above tend to be reserved for those cases where a major public disaster occurs. It can be anticipated that fines for corporate killing offences will be at the highest level. The court also provided guidance to the HSE and defendants about how they should prepare and present mitigating and aggravating factors to the trial court which would allow all factors to be considered. It was found that the Crown Court had made an error in finding the existence of the aggravating feature – profit – which meant that the fine of £600,000 took into account a factor that it should not have.

Aggravating/mitigating factors

9.48   The court found that the *aggravating* factors were:

* the death of Mr Wilkins;
* the position of the switch for turning off the current should anything go wrong, which was too inaccessible;
* the fact that the breaches had been going on for some time;
* none of the employees had had their attention drawn to HSE guidance on welding;

- the firm had conducted no assessment of the risk involved in repairing ribbon stirrers in situ;

- the incident represented a serious and obvious breach of duty.

The *mitigating* factors for the company were;

- a prompt admission and plea of guilty;

- a good health and safety record over the years;

- the steps the company had taken since the incident to improve safety, all of which had been taken with the approval of, and confirmation by, the HSE and which now agreed that Friskies had 'a high level of commitment to safety'.

9.49   The Court of Appeal also took into account the financial position of the company, which it described as a very substantial business with a considerable turnover, generating pre-tax profits at the relevant time of some £40 million. The court reduced the fine from £600,000 to £250,000. However, it refused to allow Friskies costs from central funds.

9.50   Observers may consider that the company took steps after the incident to improve safety and submitted this as mitigation as opposed to adopting safety procedures before the incident. It may also be considered that the fine was reduced to too low a level when balanced against the company's profit and original fine. Further, the offence was committed over a considerable period of time. It may also be argued that some undertakings put profit at the top of their operating activities, and there was no difference in this case because it was only luck that there had not been an accident earlier.

9.51   The considerations above are important factors for legal debate, but the *Friskies* judgment does focus the minds of the regulating authorities when investigating an incident and preparing the case for trial before the courts. This will be an equally important aspect when preparing a case for a corporate killing offence prosecution. This case should also serve as a warning to all undertakings to place health and safety at the top of the management agenda because the fine, prosecution costs, defence legal costs and remedial action costs show that it would have been more financially effective to adopt safety management procedures in the first place.

R v Janway Davies – HSWA 1974, s 40

9.52   A major milestone in health and safety law was attained when three Appeal judges ruled on an appeal between David Janway Davies and the HSE.[1] The appeal was in respect of HSWA 1974, s 40 and the court had to consider whether a reversal of the burden of proof provision in a statute creating offences is compatible with the presumption of innocence enshrined in art 6(2) of the European Convention on Human Rights. The statute in question is HSWA 1974. The combined effect of ss 3(1) and 33(1) of the Act make it an offence for an employer to fail to discharge:

> '... the duty to conduct his undertaking in such a way as to ensure, so far as is reasonably practicable, that persons not in his employment who may be affected thereby are not thereby exposed to risks to their health or safety'.

---

1 *R v Janway Davies* (2003) IRLR 17, CA.

9.53   Section 40 provides that in any proceedings for an offence:

> '... consisting of a failure to comply with a duty ... to do something ... so far as is reasonably practicable ... it shall be for the accused to prove ... that it was not reasonably practicable to do more than was in fact done to satisfy the duty'.

Davies ran a plant hire firm from a yard and workshop near Neath where he had three employees and employed three self-employed subcontractors, one of whom was Mr Gardner. On 25 January 2000, Gardner returned to the yard at about 3.30 pm and asked Davies if there was any further work for him to do. At the time, Davies was in the workshop working on a Volvo dumper truck when he told Gardner that he should go home and then shouted to an employee, Mr Ralph, who was in the yard, to bring a JCB down into the workshop and park it tight up to the dumper. Ralph, complying with the instruction, reversed the JCB with its lights flashing down into the open workshop. It was as he approached the truck that he had to retract the machine's rear arm which left him with very little visibility to the rear. Ralph did not see Gardner, who was then crushed between the two vehicles, sustaining fatal injuries. Davies had resumed working in the cab of the truck, and some time before the accident he noticed that Gardner had not left the workshop, but he did not see the accident itself.

9.54   Davies was convicted of an offence under HSWA 1974 in Swansea Crown Court on 7 September 2001. He was fined £15,000 and ordered to pay costs of £22,544. At the close of the prosecution case, the judge (Judge Price QC) ruled that HSWA 1974, s 40 was compatible with the ECHR and therefore directed the jury that there was a legal (persuasive) burden on Davies to prove (on the balance of probability) that it was not reasonably practicable for him to do more than he had in fact done. Davies based his appeal on this point, contending that s 40 is only compatible if it imposes an evidential burden. This appeal was of great importance because it could affect prosecutions for a number of offences under the Act and there were conflicting decisions at Crown Court level.

9.55   The court concluded that the imposition of a legal burden of proof under s 40 of the Act is justified, necessary and proportionate for the reasons set out below which take account of the various points:

'First the Act is regulatory and its purpose is to protect the health and safety of those affected by the activities referred to in sections 2 to 6. The need for such regulation is amply demonstrated by the statistics with which we have been supplied. These show that fatal injuries reported to the UK enforcing authorities by industry are running at an average of about 700 a year and non-fatal major injuries at nearly 200,000 a year. Following a survey in 1995/96 the Office of Statistics put the financial costs of accidents at work in the UK at between £14.5 and £18.1 billion. The Act's purpose is therefore both social and economic.'

The court continued:

'The reversal of the burden of proof takes into account the fact that duty holders are persons who have chosen to engage in work or commercial activity (probably for gain) and are in charge of it. They are not, therefore, unengaged or disinterested members of the public and in choosing to operate in a regulated sphere of activity they must be taken to have accepted the regulatory controls that go with it. This regulatory regime imposes a continuing duty to ensure a state of affairs, a safety standard. Where the enforcing authority can show that this has not been achieved it is not unjustifiable or unfair to ask the duty holder who has either created or is in control of the risk to show that it was not reasonably practicable for him to have done more than he did to prevent or avoid it … Before any question of reverse onus arises the prosecution must prove that the defendant owes the duty (in the case of section 3 to the person affected by the conduct of his undertaking) and that the safety standard (in the case of section 3 exposure to risk to health or safety) has been breached. Proof of these matters is not a formality … There may be real issues about whether the defendant owes the relevant duty or whether in fact the safety standard has been breached, for example, where the cause of an accident is unknown or debatable. But once the prosecution have proved these matters the defence has to be raised and established by the defendant. The defence itself is flexible because it does not restrict the way in which the defendant can show that he has done what is reasonably practicable'.

9.56   Clarity was given with regard to the application of reverse onus and the judgment identified:

'The reverse onus only applies to breach of the duties laid down by sections 2 to 6 of the Act. It does not apply to section 7, so there is no reverse onus of proof where it is alleged that an employee has breached his duty. The same applies to section 37 where a company's officers may be convicted if the company has committed an offence and they are proved to have consented, connived or contributed to it by neglect. This suggests that

Parliament must have considered when a reverse onus was justified and when it was not. Due regard must be paid to its choice.'

9.57   The defence is a critical issue and the judgment addressed the issue through the following statement:

'The facts relied on in support of the defence should not be difficult to prove because they will be within the knowledge of the defendant. Whether the defendant should have done more will be judged objectively. If all the defendant had to do was raise the defence to require the prosecution to disprove it, the focus of the statutory scheme would be changed. The trial would become focused on what it was the enforcing authority was saying should have been done rather than on what the defendant had done or ought to have done which is what Parliament intended. In complicated, and therefore potentially the most serious, cases the prosecution might face considerable difficulties in assuming this burden of proof where the only relevant expertise was with the defendant or even its state of the art supplier or licensor abroad. In such cases, therefore, enforcement might become impossible if the defendant only had an evidential burden'.

9.58   The court in its concluding decisions stated:

'Last but not least the defendant in cases where the reverse burden of proof applies does not face imprisonment. The offence involves failure to comply with an objective standard. The consequences of such failure may be newsworthy in some cases but the moral obloquy is not the same as that involved in truly criminal offences. The statistics we have been provided with show that only about 15% of those prosecuted under sections 2 to 6 of the Act are individuals. The rest are companies. For these reasons we think the judge reached the right conclusion in this case. The reverse legal burden of proof contained in section 40 of the Act is compatible with the ECHR. The appellant's conviction on this basis was not therefore unsafe.'

The importance of this judgment is equal to that of the *Howe* and *Friskies* judgments for both the prosecution and defendants in health and safety prosecutions.

9.59   Those having read the details of the three cases will know that there are considerations within the legal system that clarify some fundamental situations upon which any court can set basic principles. This aids the prosecution in its preparation of the case and makes the position clear for the defence. It also sets the scene for both the magistrates and judge upon which they can make sound decisions.

Chapter 10

The Legal Systems, Processes and Enforcement Agencies

Introduction

10.1   As a member of the European Union the focus is not just a UK legal system issue, but there are European legal implications to be considered and adopted. This raises other and more complex issues such as the manner in which other countries administer and enforce health and safety. A number of commentators have addressed the European issues. Wells[1] makes constructive comments on the subject and states:

> 'In the particular field of corporate criminal liability, many individual European jurisdictions, despite their very different legal forms and systems are addressing the role of criminal law in relation to the corporate enterprise. The Council of Europe has recommended the promotion of corporate

criminal liability and has spelled out principles to guide member states. Legal culture is more open-textured and open to influence from any number of sources than is often supposed.'

---

1   Wells, C, *Corporations and Criminal Responsibility* (Oxford University Press, 2001).

10.2   The European influence will evolve further and the future of health and safety incidents and enforcement is an unknown, but certainly not without complications. This is already seen where corporations have their corporate headquarters in other EU countries and are able to operate in the UK without redress to criminal legal process when incidents occur. Sengupta[1] states:

'*Loophole allows foreign firms to avoid safety fines.*

Hundreds of companies and individuals were "named and shamed" yesterday after being convicted of health and safety crimes in a move described by watchdogs as a new and tough chapter in enforcement. But the Health and Safety Executive (HSE) admitted a loophole in safety laws under which multinational firms based abroad and involved in some of the worst accidents in Britain have got away with refusing to pay the massive fines imposed on them ... The Government is negotiating with other European Union states to make payment of criminal fines enforceable for companies wherever they trade. The HSE acknowledges that even if this is achieved, British health and safety laws would still have difficulties with multinational corporations based abroad.'

It is limited evidence but highlights a growing problem. It may be that if foreign companies are to operate in the UK some form of indemnity should be provided to ensure legal liability cover is provided and fines could be recovered through British courts. It would appear that at present there is no incentive for foreign companies to adopt UK health and safety systems, which could place UK businesses at a disadvantage.

---

1   Sengupta, K, *Independent*, 26 October, 2000.

10.3   The EU introduces Directives, leaving each country to develop national regulations that fulfil the objectives which govern the framework for health and safety legislation. While the European Court of Justice (ECJ) is the ultimate court for European jurisdiction, each nation's legal system provides the day-to-day judicial process for the particular country. It is the responsibility of each country to have a legal system that will allow for accidents to be investigated and prosecutions initiated, enabling breaches of health and safety legislation to be enforced.

10.4   The legal system in England and Wales differs from that of Scotland, but the regulating agencies enforce the same legislation. It will be seen that a number of regulating agencies are involved in the legal process and it is imperative that these agencies co-operate with each other. To aid this process the Health and Safety Executive (HSE), police and Crown Prosecution Service (CPS) have a protocol that allows for the evaluation of a case to ensure that the appropriate enforcement is taken. The purpose of this chapter is to provide a broad overview of the legal structures and organisations that undertake the legal process and the key enforcement options that are available.

The European Union

10.5   Significant changes to health and safety legislation occurred as a result of the UK signing the Treaty of Rome in 1973 and the Maastricht Treaty in 1992, which binds the UK to European law. EU Directives provide a framework for occupational health and safety issues. The Directives require member states to create legislation and guidance on the topics and to enforce compliance. The objective is that every member state, working from the same template, should produce legislation within that member state's constitution that is broadly consistent with other member states. If there is a considerable disparity between member states' interpretation of the framework requirements, then the subsequent legislation and enforcement can create a socio-economic imbalance, which in turn can have a major impact on industry and business.

The Treaty of Rome

10.6   The Treaty of Rome was signed in 1957 by the six founding states, France, West Germany, Italy, Belgium, The Netherlands and Luxembourg. It was in 1973 that the UK, Ireland and Denmark signed. Greece joined in 1981, Spain and Portugal in 1992 with Austria, Finland and Sweden joining in 1995. Since then other countries have joined: Bulgaria, Cyprus, Czech Republic, Estonia, Hungary, Latvia, Lithuania, Malta, Poland, Romania, Slovakia and Slovenia. The foundation of the Treaty is to create economic harmonisation; In the health and safety field, if one country was to economise on health and safety matters it would be to the disadvantage of those who have addressed the issues. There is the added factor of the *social dimension* where there are positive steps being taken to increase the level of protection provided to workers from accidents and ill health at work. Article 118 of the Treaty stated that there was to be harmony in the laws relating to employment, labour law and working conditions, basic and advanced training and protection against occupational accidents and diseases. The outcome is that the effect of EU law on domestic law is increasing.

European health and safety law

10.7   As described, the Treaty of Rome is the supreme law for all European member states with the supreme policy making body being the Council of

Ministers, comprising a minister from each member state who attends each meeting. Support to the meetings is provided through the Committee of Permanent Representatives (COREPER). The European Commission has the task of initiating and drafting proposals for approval by the Council and mediates between states. It also monitors the observation of EU rules and has the power to refer a member state to the ECJ if there are failings. The European Parliament is made up of members (MEPs) elected directly from each member state; it can offer opinions on the Council of Ministers' proposals by submitting questions and can as a sanction, dismiss the Commission on a vote of censure. The ECJ gives rulings on the interpretation of European law (see **10.9** below). Based in Spain, the European Health and Safety Agency has the objectives of improving health and safety at work by imparting health and safety information and providing technical, scientific and economic information to member states.

EU Directives

10.8   The system for adopting a Directive under Article 118A of the Treaty of Rome is known as the *co-operation procedure* and must be adopted by the member states. The Commission submits proposals to the Council of Ministers. The European Parliament and the Economic and Social Committee are consulted for opinions to be offered. The Commission can amend the proposals, but are not obliged to do so. They are then submitted to the Labour and Social Affairs Council, a committee within the Council of Ministers. A review is undertaken and a majority vote option adopted. It is then reconsidered by the European Parliament which can approve the proposal, propose further amendments or reject them. If the outcome is the latter option then adoption is made by the Council of Ministers on a unanimous vote. Once a Directive has been passed by the Council of Ministers it is binding on the member states and identifies the results that have to be achieved.

The European Court of Justice

10.9   The jurisdiction of the ECJ is established under s 3 of the European Communities Act 1972 and decisions of this court are binding in matters of Community law on all courts up to and including the House of Lords. The court sits in Luxembourg and is formed of 27 judges and eight advocate generals who are appointed for six years. The role of the court is to give rulings on interpretation of European law, from either a reference provided by the Commission, a request from the courts of a member state or as a result of a claim brought by an individual person or corporation of a member state. Once the court has made a ruling the matter is returned to the member state courts to enforce compliance.

The Human Rights Act 1998

10.10   The Human Rights Act 1998 is one of the most important developments in the English legal system in recent times. Many of our existing laws, practices and procedures are already compatible with the European Convention on Human Rights. The Convention seeks to establish a fair balance between the demands of the general interest of the community and the protection of human rights. The Convention evolved as a result of the atrocities of the Second World War as a way of ensuring that such an event could not occur again.

10.11   The Convention comprises 18 Articles, which include the right to life, the right to a fair trial, no punishment without law and the right to liberty and security. It is a principal point that everyone charged with a criminal offence shall be presumed innocent until proved guilty according to the law. It follows that everyone is entitled to a fair public hearing within a reasonable time by an independent and impartial tribunal established by law and the judgment is pronounced publicly. The Act brings much of the Convention into domestic law, enabling people to use it in the UK courts as opposed to taking their case to the Court of Human Rights in Strasbourg.

Acts of Parliament

10.12   Acts of Parliament form the basis of law in the UK and are often the enabling Acts for developing more specific regulations. An example is the Health and Safety at Work etc Act 1974 (HSWA 1974) which forms the foundation of health and safety legislation in the UK. A range of industry specific and more general regulations supports this Act. An Act is introduced as a Bill into the Houses of Parliament. It receives a formal first reading where the House will hold a debate on the general concept of the proposed legislation. At this point a vote may be held on a proposal to give the Bill a second reading. If it is successful, the Bill is then sent to a committee where the content is considered in detail and amendments can be made. Having progressed to this stage, the Bill is produced in a report to the full House where amendments are considered. The final stage is the third reading of the Bill before it is passed to the House of Lords where a similar procedure is adopted. When both Houses have passed the Bill, it is presented to the Queen for Royal Assent, which is an automatic approval.

The House of Lords

10.13   The House of Lords is the highest Court in the UK. The House will normally sit with five members. Once a decision is made by the House of Lords on a point of law it will bind all lower courts until the House gives a different ruling, or until a decision is changed by an Act of Parliament. Precedence is given under the European Communities Act 1972, s 3(1) where decisions in this court are binding in matters of community law on all courts up to and including the House of Lords.

The legal process

10.14   There are two legal processes that affect health and safety: criminal law and civil law. While they are administered by separate courts, the same case can be heard in both courts, which means that a civil case generally follows a successful criminal prosecution. For a case to be taken through the civil courts there does not have to have been a criminal prosecution and it does not follow that where a company is found not guilty in criminal proceedings that there will not be a civil liability. In this respect the burden of proof differs: the criminal court requires guilt *beyond reasonable doubt* while the civil court works on the *balance of probabilities*. A civil court cannot send anybody to prison or impose a fine or other punishment, while a criminal court can. There are differences in the legal processes in England and Wales and those of Scotland, although the burden of proof and evidence is the same. The court structure is shown in **Figure 1**.

Criminal proceedings

10.15   Criminal offences are where there has been an offence against the state, which means in the case of health and safety offences, a breach of a statutory duty. The prosecution will be undertaken by the Crown as represented by a Health and Safety Inspector, a local authority Environmental Health Officer or a solicitor and barrister who may be appointed to undertake the prosecution on their behalf. There are three types of criminal offence. Those that are summary only are heard in the magistrates' court. Cases that are indictable only will be heard in the Crown Court. The third type is those cases which are triable either way; that includes most health and safety at work offences and these can be heard in either the magistrates' court or the Crown Court. Every case will initially be heard in a magistrates' court (see **10.16** below). Fines in the lower court are limited to maximum levels and with the more serious offences, the cases can be sent to the Crown Court to be heard before a judge and jury. These offences are punishable by an unlimited fine and in some cases imprisonment is available. There is a right of appeal to a higher criminal court. The main focus of criminal prosecutions is the employer's liability of a duty of care and the prosecution would have to prove a failing or negligence beyond all reasonable doubt.

Figure 1: Hierarchy of the courts

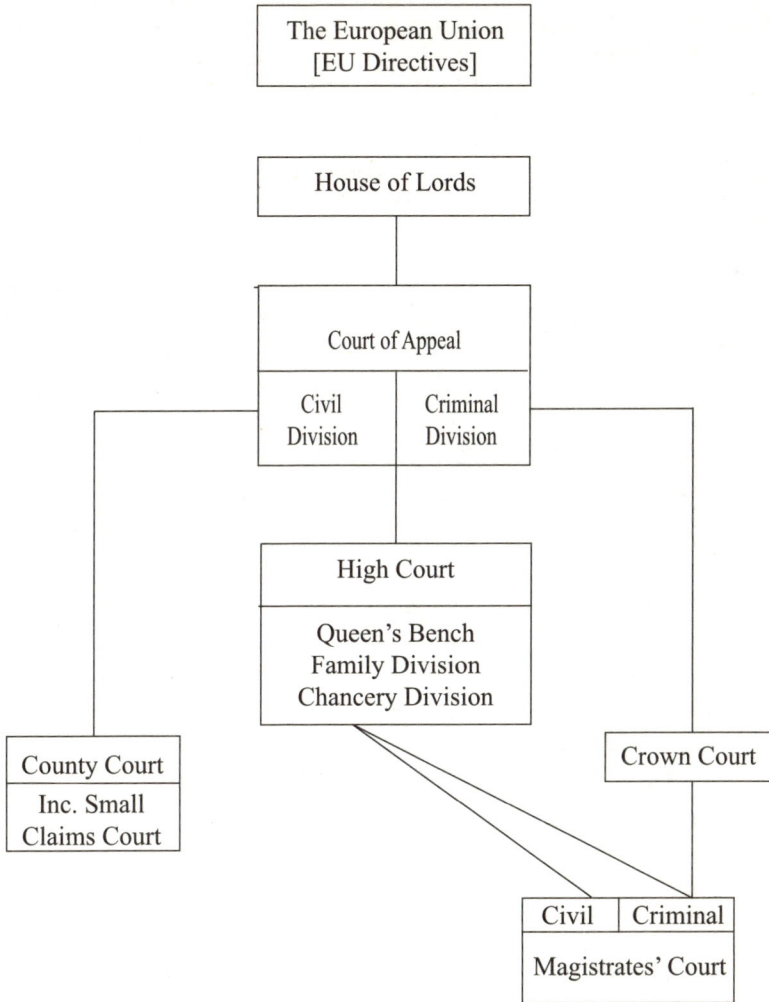

```
        ┌─────────────────────────┐
        │   The European Union    │
        │    [EU Directives]      │
        └─────────────────────────┘

        ┌─────────────────────────┐
        │     House of Lords      │
        └─────────────────────────┘

        ┌─────────────────────────┐
        │     Court of Appeal     │
        ├────────────┬────────────┤
        │   Civil    │  Criminal  │
        │  Division  │  Division  │
        └────────────┴────────────┘

        ┌─────────────────────────┐
        │       High Court        │
        ├─────────────────────────┤
        │     Queen's Bench       │
        │     Family Division     │
        │    Chancery Division    │
        └─────────────────────────┘

┌──────────────┐          ┌──────────────┐
│ County Court │          │ Crown Court  │
│  Inc. Small  │          └──────────────┘
│ Claims Court │
└──────────────┘
                  ┌──────────────────────┐
                  │  Civil  │  Criminal  │
                  ├──────────────────────┤
                  │   Magistrates' Court │
                  └──────────────────────┘
```

The magistrates' court

10.16   Magistrates are not lawyers but are trained and assessed for competence to national standards. In the magistrates' court there may be a bench of three lay magistrates; the Chairman is the only one who will speak in court. A court clerk who is either a solicitor or barrister supports them. The clerk is not part of the decision-making process but advises the magistrates on matters of law. Alternatively, there may be a single justice known as a district judge, who is a solicitor or barrister (formerly known as a stipendiary magistrate), who will also have a court clerk in the court. Every health and safety at work criminal prosecution will be heard initially in the magistrates' court where the magistrates, having heard brief details of the case, make the decision as to which court is the most appropriate. If the magistrates consider that the case is so serious that their powers of punishment are insufficient or if it is a complex case then they can decline jurisdiction and send it to the Crown Court for trial. The prosecution may also make a strong argument as to the seriousness of the case and request that it is sent to trial in the Crown Court. The defendant may also seek trial by judge and jury in the Crown Court. See **Figure 2**.

10.17   The following information is drawn from the Magistrates' Association guidelines[1] for the fining of companies for health and safety offences and is used by magistrates when hearing health and safety cases.

> 'In recent years the public has become increasingly concerned about ... the protection of employees' health and safety at work. There have been a number of high profile incidents sometimes involving death ... These concerns have been reflected in the greatly increased maximum fines for related offences. Defendants in such cases are frequently companies and sometimes multi-national companies with huge annual turnovers. We need to be reminded of the *Magistrates' Court Sentencing Guidelines* advice that our aim should be for any fine to have equal impact on rich or poor. This is true of companies as well as individuals ... health and safety offences to be encountered in the magistrates' court include ... matters relating to the protection of the employee in the workplace.'

For magistrates considering a health and safety case one of the first questions to be asked is whether the seriousness of the offence is such that the sentencing powers of magistrates are inadequate. If the court is prepared to hear the case then the general procedure adopted in the *Magistrates' Court Sentencing Guidelines* should be followed. After an initial consideration of the seriousness of the offence, an appropriate type of penalty should be considered. The penalty in these cases is usually a fine. The offences are 'non-violent' but can cause or risk death, serious injury or ill health and usually have no continuing threat to persons because the regulator will have used enforcement powers to prevent any such threat. They are often committed in situations where the defendant company has failed to devote proper resources to prevent a breach of the law, which means that a financial penalty would usually be the appropriate response.

---

1   www.sentencing-guidelines.gov.uk/guidance/other/magistrates

---

10.18   As in the sentencing guidelines, having heard the evidence and considered the seriousness of the offence and an appropriate form of penalty, the court considers those factors which could aggravate or mitigate the offence. The factors that are deemed to aggravate the seriousness of the offence include:

fFigure 2: The Magistrates' court

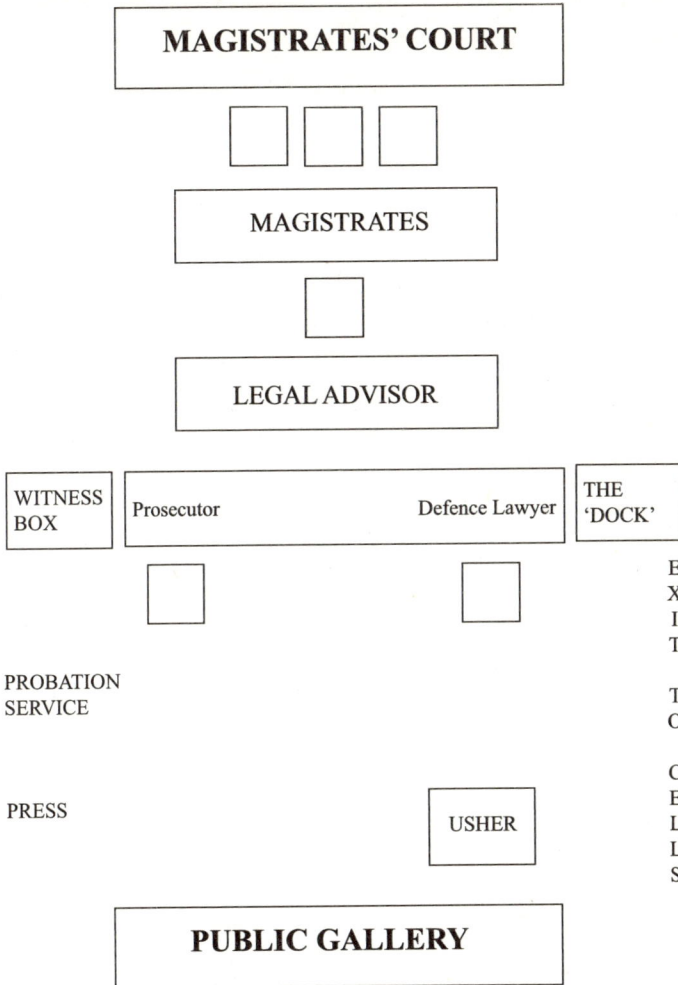

```
+------------------------------------------+
|         MAGISTRATES' COURT               |
+------------------------------------------+

      +----+  +----+  +----+
      |    |  |    |  |    |
      +----+  +----+  +----+

   +-------------------------------+
   |          MAGISTRATES          |
   +-------------------------------+

              +------+
              |      |
              +------+

   +-------------------------------+
   |        LEGAL ADVISOR          |
   +-------------------------------+
```

WITNESS BOX	Prosecutor Defence Lawyer	THE 'DOCK'

```
        +------+              +------+         E
        |      |              |      |         X
        +------+              +------+         I
                                              T

   PROBATION                                  T
   SERVICE                                    O

                                              C
   PRESS                 +--------+           E
                         | USHER  |           L
                         +--------+           L
                                              S
```

```
   +--------------------------------------+
   |          PUBLIC GALLERY              |
   +--------------------------------------+
```

- a deliberate or reckless breach of the law rather than carelessness;
- action or lack of action prompted by financial motives – profit or cost saving;
- disregarding warnings from a regulatory authority or the workforce;
- an awareness of the specific risks likely to arise from action taken;
- lack of co-operation with a regulatory authority;

- serious extent of damage resulting from offence (but lack of actual damage offence merely technical; it is still serious if there is risk);

- previous offences of a similar nature;

- death or serious injury or ill health of humans has been a consequence of the offence;

- other lawful activities interfered with.

10.19   The factors that may provide some mitigation:

- the offender's minor role with little personal responsibility;

- genuine lack of awareness or understanding of specific regulations;

- an isolated lapse.

There may also be some offender mitigation:

- prompt reporting;

- ready co-operation with regulatory authority;

- good previous record;

- timely plea of guilt.

Sometimes in a case much more damage has occurred than could have been reasonably anticipated. Any sentence should give weight to the evidence and reflect the culpability of the offender.

10.20   A fine is considered to be the form of penalty which is usually appropriate for both companies and individuals for these offences. The normal principles of the Criminal Justice Act 1991 should apply and the seriousness of the offence and the financial circumstances of the defendant should be taken into account. The level of fine should reflect the extent to which the defendant's behaviour has fallen below the required standard. High culpability should be matched by a high fine even though actual damage turned out to be less than might reasonably have been anticipated.

10.21   The level of the fine should reflect any economic gain from the offence resulting from failure to take precautions. It has been said that a deliberate failure to take the necessary precautions can be a form of stealing commercial advantage from law-abiding competitors. In all cases with corporate offenders the company's financial circumstances must be carefully considered. No single measure of ability to pay can apply in all cases. Turnover, profitability and liquidity should all be considered. It is not usual for an expert accountant to be available in summary cases.

10.22   If a company does not produce its accounts the court can assume that the company can pay whatever fine the court imposes. In most cases it is hard to imagine a company failing to provide such information, although with large known companies of national or international standing this may not be a necessary requirement. Where necessary the payment of fines can be spread over a longer period than the usual 12 months, if payment in full would be unduly burdensome on say, a smaller company.

10.23   A fine suited to the circumstances of a small local company would make no impact at all on a multinational corporation with a huge turnover. The fine imposed on any company should be substantial enough to have a real economic impact, which together with attendant bad publicity would pressure both management and shareholders to tighten their regulatory compliance. Such fines on large companies might often be beyond the summary fines limit and in such circumstances the case should be transferred to the Crown Court for trial or sentence. Where the court does not transfer the case of a larger company to the higher court, magistrates should look to a starting point near the maximum fine level then consider aggravating and mitigating factors.

10.24   Care should be taken to ensure that fines imposed on smaller companies are not beyond their capability to pay. The court might not wish the payment of the fine to result in the company not being able to pay for improved procedures or cause the company to go into liquidation or make its employees redundant.

10.25   Whilst fines will be the usual outcome in proceedings of this sort, other sentencing options may be available:

- a discharge will rarely be appropriate;
- compensation should be considered if there is a specific victim who has suffered injury, loss or damage. You should give reasons if you decide not to make a compensation order. The current limit is £5,000 per offence, although substantial civil claims are often pending in such cases;
- the legislation provides for the possibility of directors and senior managers appearing before the courts, and custodial sentences are available in specific instances. The courts have power to disqualify directors under the Company Directors Disqualification Act 1986. This is particularly important in health and safety enforcement, and breach of an order is itself a criminal offence carrying a term of imprisonment of up to two years.

10.26   The prosecution will normally claim the costs of investigation and presentation in court. These may be substantial, and can incorporate time and activity expended on investigation and remedial activities. Therefore where possible the enforcing authorities' costs should be fully recouped from the offender. However, the order for costs should not be disproportionate to the level of the fine imposed. The court should fix the level of the fine first, then consider awarding compensation, and then determine the costs. If the total sum exceeds the defendant's means, the order for costs should be reduced rather than the fine. Compensation should take priority over both the fine and costs.

10.27   It should be noted that this information will change in line with developments in the criminal justice systems. In the case of corporate manslaughter cases the first hearing in court will be in a magistrates' court to be committed to the crown court.

The Crown Court

10.28   The Crown Court hears indictable offences which can only be heard in the higher court (such as murder, manslaughter and rape) as well as those cases of a serious nature where the prosecution or defendant elects to have the case heard before a judge and jury. In the Crown Court, HSWA 1974 offences are punishable by unlimited fine and there are eight offences that carry additional punishments of a term of imprisonment. There have been several instances where custodial and suspended prison sentences have been imposed. A HSWA 1974 case heard in the magistrates' court can, upon hearing all the evidence and with a guilty verdict, be sent to the Crown Court for sentence. An appeal against conviction and/or sentence in the Crown Court is referred to the Court of Appeal. The Crown Court sits with a single judge and a jury of 12, selected from members of the public. England and Wales retains the formal dress code of wigs and gowns, both for the judge and the Queens Counsel's (QCs) and barristers who prosecute and defend cases. The QCs (sometimes referred to as *silks*), are appointed by the Lord Chancellor and are the senior members of the Bar. Both sides will present their case to the jury; the prosecution has the task of providing evidence that will prove their case beyond all reasonable doubt. The defence task is to counter that evidence to put sufficient doubt in the jury's mind. At the end of the prosecution and defence cases, counsel for each side will sum up, highlighting the salient points of the case that provide evidence for guilt or innocence. The judge then sums up the case to the jury and focuses on the points of law involved, before sending them out to determine their verdict. The jury retires to a room equipped with copies of all the evidence, including any exhibits that have been taken into court. This will also include photographs, videotapes, drawings and statements. They remain in the room until they reach a verdict on which they all agree. When they reach that point they re-enter the court and the person appointed as foreman of the jury announces the verdict. It the jury cannot reach a unanimous verdict, a majority verdict of 10 to 2 may be accepted for a guilty verdict. Following a guilty verdict the judge will hear representations from the defendants as to the financial standing of the company before imposing a financial penalty, and if appropriate in the case, committing individuals to prison. See **Figure 3**.

Figure 3: The Crown court

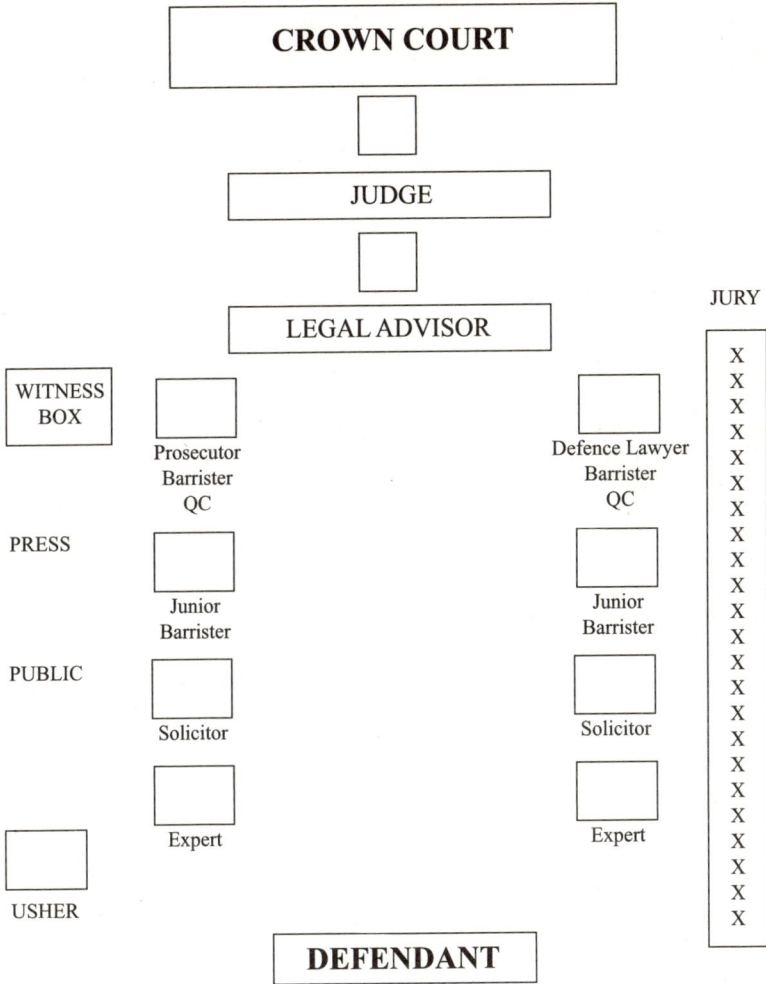

CROWN COURT

JUDGE

LEGAL ADVISOR

WITNESS BOX

Prosecutor
Barrister
QC

PRESS

Junior
Barrister

PUBLIC

Solicitor

Expert

USHER

Defence Lawyer
Barrister
QC

Junior
Barrister

Solicitor

Expert

JURY
X X X X X X X X X X X X X X X X X X X X X X X X

DEFENDANT

The County Court – civil proceedings

10.29 Under civil law, employers have a duty to their employees to provide a reasonable standard of care. If a person is injured at work and considers that the employer has been at fault, then they can take the employer to court and sue for damages. This means that the focus of the civil court is to determine if there is a case for damages to be made and if so, the value of such compensation. Unlike the criminal court where the outcome of cases is determined beyond all reasonable doubt, the civil hearing is judged upon the balance of probabilities, which is a lower burden of proof. Cases are heard before a single judge with the provision for a trial involving a jury of eight persons. The vast majority of civil cases are settled out of court, where an offer of compensation is made to the claimant. There may be numerous offers and rejections before settlement and in the case of claims that are dealt with outside of the courtroom, the claimant will also seek his legal costs. Often these settlements are made on the *steps of the court* where the defendants attempt to keep the level of compensation as low as possible. Even though an agreement can be reached over the level of compensation a corporation may not accept liability for the accident.

The Scottish legal system

10.30   In England and Wales an appointed health and safety inspector investigates an accident and prepares a prosecution report. The inspector or an appointed legal representative will take the case through the courts. In Scotland the inspector investigates the accident and prepares a report, which is submitted to the office of the Procurator Fiscal, who will then undertake an investigation and prepare a prosecution for trial in the Sheriff's Court.

10.31   There are no magistrates' courts in Scotland and so the Sheriff's court combines the functions of the Crown Court and magistrates' courts in England and Wales. Criminal prosecutions may be tried in the Sheriff's court, either on indictment before a Sheriff and jury or as a summary case before a Sheriff sitting alone. In Scotland there are no coroner's courts and inquests as such are not held. The Fatal Accident and Sudden Death (Scotland) Act 1976 requires that the Procurator Fiscal for a district will investigate the circumstances and apply to the Sheriff for the holding of an inquiry into a death. The death must have arisen as a result of an accident in Scotland while the deceased was at work either as an employee or self employed. The only exception is that an enquiry does not need to be held in cases where criminal proceedings have been concluded against any person in respect of the death, or the Lord Advocate is satisfied that the circumstances of a death arising from any accident have been sufficiently established.

10.32   At the Fatal Accident Investigation (FAI) hearing before the Sheriff, the Procurator Fiscal leads the evidence for the Crown. The conclusions of the inquiry will determine where and when the death and any accident resulting in death took place and the cause of death.

In line with England and Wales, Scotland now has Corporate Homicide legislation.

The Health and Safety Commission (HSC)

10.33   The responsibility for health and safety within government is with the Department of Work and Pensions. The head of this department is the Secretary of State, with a seat in the Cabinet, assisted by a number of junior ministers, one of whom has delegated responsibility for health, safety and welfare.

10.34   The Health and Safety Commission (HSC) was formed under HSWA 1974 with responsibility for the administration of the law on occupational health and safety. The corporate role of the HSC is to protect the health, safety and welfare of people at work, and to safeguard members of the public who may be exposed to risks from the way work is carried out. To undertake this work the Commission will propose new or update existing laws and standards, undertake research, as well as provide information and advice. The HSC comprises a Chairman appointed by the Secretary of State and not less than six and not more than nine members. At the time of writing the HSC comprises nine members. In the process of the selection of members, the Chairman must consult with various interested parties such as organisations representing employers, trade unions, local authorities and others representing health, safety and welfare. The Commission also appoints the Director General of the Health and Safety Executive (HSE). A prime role of the Commission is to make regulations and provide consent for the issue of HSC Codes of Practice. The HSE and local authorities are the HSC's regulating authorities and have the statutory responsibility for enforcing health and safety law. In addition local authorities enforce health and safety law in some kinds of workplaces such as distribution, retail, office, leisure and catering.

The Health and Safety Executive (HSE)

10.35   The Health and Safety Executive (HSE) was established as a result of the introduction into law of the HSWA 1974. It is headed by a Director General appointed by the Health and Safety Commission and approved by the Secretary of State. The HSE's headquarters is in London with a major centre in Bootle, Merseyside and other regional offices located throughout the UK.

10.36   There are 14 directorates and other departments forming the basic corporate structure. The HSE has to develop and introduce the policies of the Health and Safety Commission, and has policy units to undertake this work. Nearly half of the HSE's staff are in the Field Operations Directorate (FOD) and the Employment Medical Advisory Service (EMAS). Other key Directorates include the Nuclear Safety Directorate; Hazardous Installations Directorate and the Railways Directorate. Because of the diverse nature of the industries (other than those identified above) that fall within the scope of the HSWA 1974 there is a requirement for industrial specialisations to support operational inspectors. This is achieved through National Interest Groups (NIGs) with specialisation in metals and minerals, construction, services, agriculture and wood, fibres and polymers, engineering, utilities, customer services, safety issues and occupational health. The Health and Safety Laboratory provides valuable technical and specialist support to investigations, but it is the operational inspectors who are in the front line providing advice, undertaking inspections, investigating accidents and incidents as well as carrying out enforcement actions.

Local authority environmental health departments

10.37   Local authorities (LAs) have responsibilities for the enforcement of health and safety in certain activities, and are located within either District or Borough Councils in England or Wales or Islands or District Councils in Scotland.

10.38   There is the potential for overlapping between the HSE and LAs and there are qualified divisions in types of organisations, industry and activities. There is a link between the HSE and LAs through the Local Authority Unit (LAU). The unit is located at the HSE headquarters in London, and there are LA liaison officers within the HSE Regional Offices. This is to ensure co-operation and support to LAs and provide a go-between in cases of potential overlap. The local authority officials have a variety of titles such as enforcement officers; however, the most common title is the Environment Health Officer (EHO) who will generally be a member of the Chartered Institute of Environmental Health (CIEH). The EHO has a wide range of duties including food safety and hygiene as well as health and safety. The powers of EHOs are the same as those of an HSE inspector.

10.39   A local authority is able to transfer authority to the HSE (and the HSE may transfer authority to a LA). There has to be agreement by both parties and this will generally only be done if the primary activity being carried out at premises is specialised and the LA does not have appropriate expertise available. The other option is that a transfer will generally only apply if there is a substantial change of activity from one normally enforced by the LA to one enforced by the HSE. There is no option for self-inspection by an authority, and so the HSE will inspect local authority controlled premises and the LA will inspect HSE premises.

Police

10.40   In the event of a death at work or caused by a workplace activity the police have to be notified and will begin an investigation. They will take possession of any relevant documentation and equipment and will take statements from witnesses. At this point in time the police will be gathering evidence as to cause of death on behalf of the coroner. The HSE or the local Environmental Health department will also have to be notified and they will co-operate with the police in undertaking a joint investigation. The police will look for evidence of an unlawful act such as negligence, violence or arson that caused the death and advise the coroner of their findings. The health and safety inspectors will seek to identify the cause of the accident and if health and safety legislation has been breached. Once the police determine that there is no unlawful action or the level of negligence was not sufficient to consider manslaughter then they will cease their investigation. It will be left to the HSE or LA to undertake a full investigation under the HSWA 1974 and associated regulations. If in the course of the investigation the HSE or LA discover evidence that identifies that there may have been an action of such a serious nature that there may be a case of gross negligence, then the case can be referred back to the police. The HSE or LA will co-operate with the investigation as they have workplace and safety management systems knowledge and expertise, which the police do not. The Protocol for Liaison is described in detail at **10.62** below and provides additional information. If after an initial review the police consider that there is evidence, they will notify the coroner who will postpone the inquest and the CPS will be notified of the police findings. A review of the evidence will be undertaken and if the CPS is satisfied that there is a case for further investigation then they will direct the police to investigate. The HSE or LA inspectors will work with the police in the investigation. An investigation report is submitted to the CPS which then decides whether there is a case to answer or not. If there is a case to answer, the CPS will initiate the prosecution; if not the case is transferred back to the HSE or LA for those bodies to proceed with appropriate action and the police take no further action.

Crown Prosecution Service (CPS)

10.41   The Crown Prosecution Service (CPS) is a government department which prosecutes people in England and Wales who have been charged by the police with a criminal offence. They are completely independent of the police although they work closely with them.

10.42   The head of the CPS is the Director of Public Prosecutions (DPP). The DPP is supervised by the Attorney General who is the minister responsible to Parliament for the conduct of most criminal prosecutions.

10.43   The role of the CPS involves four main functions:

● advising the police on possible prosecutions;

● reviewing prosecutions started by the police to ensure that the right defendants are prosecuted on the right charges;

● preparing cases for court;

● prosecuting cases at the magistrates' court and instructing counsel to prosecute in the Crown Court and higher courts.

Once the police have investigated a crime they pass the papers to a Crown Prosecutor. The case will be examined to decide whether or not to go ahead with the case. The prosecutor's decision is based on the tests set out in the Code for Crown Prosecutors. The tests are focused upon two principal points:

10.44

• Is there enough evidence?

• Is it in the *public interest* to prosecute?

A case has to pass these tests before progress can be made to continue to a prosecution. The prosecutor also has to determine if there is sufficient evidence to provide a *realistic prospect of conviction*. If there is not sufficient evidence then the prosecutor can refer back to the police to look at the evidence for the case again. If there is still insufficient evidence then the case will not progress to court.

10.45   Even with enough evidence the prosecutor will consider if it is *in the public interest* to proceed. This will include the seriousness of the offence, the interests of the victim's family and friends and the need to send a *message* to industry/business.

When the prosecutor considers that there is sufficient evidence and is in the *public interest* the case continues to prosecution in court. Throughout this process HSE inspectors will have an advisory role and in some cases the CPS may include charges under the HSWA 1974 or associated regulations in addition to manslaughter charges.

Coroners

10.46   The coroner is generally a lawyer who is responsible for investigating deaths that occur in a number of situations. Among those that may be relevant are where the cause of death is not known or is uncertain or the death was violent or unnatural or occurred under suspicious circumstances. Another consideration is where a doctor did not attend the deceased during the last illness or the doctor treating the deceased had not seen him or her either after death or within 14 days before death. The coroner may arrange for a post mortem examination of the body. The consent of the relatives is not needed, but they are entitled to be represented at the examination by a doctor. In certain circumstances the coroner can direct the death to be further investigated, and can revert the case to the CPS for a police investigation.

10.47   Under the Coroners Rules 1984, r 57 the coroner is required to supply to any 'properly interested person, on application and on payment of the prescribed fee, a copy of any depositions taken at any inquest, of any report of a post mortem examination or special examination, of any notes of evidence, or any document put in evidence at an inquest.' The coroner may also permit such a person to inspect such documents free of charge.

10.48   Prior to the inquest most dealings are with the coroner's officers, who may be former or serving police officers who investigate on behalf of the coroner. In workplace accidents the coroner will obtain a report from the inspector on the who, how, where and when of the case. The inspector can be called to give evidence and if there is equipment involved an expert may be called to give evidence to assist the court.

10.49   The coroner normally has a jury where the death was caused by an accident, poisoning or disease, notice of which is required to be given under any Act to a government department, to an inspector or other officer of a government department or an inspector appointed under the HSWA 1974, s 19. Further, where the death occurred in 'circumstances, the continuation or possible recurrence of which is prejudicial to the health and safety of the public' or any section of the public, as was the case in *R v Poplar Coroner, ex-parte Chaudry*,[1] a jury must sit.

---

1   Times, 20 October 1992.

10.50   It is not the role of the coroner's court to apportion blame and the way individual coroners go about their investigations and conduct their inquests varies widely, as there is no formal structured format. Having heard the evidence a verdict is returned. The common verdicts are of accidental death or death by misadventure, which are materially the same. If a verdict of unlawful killing is reached then the coroner will refer the case to the police for further investigation. The coroner may, under the Coroner's Rules 1984, r 43, announce at the inquest that he is reporting the matter to the HSE with recommendations for action to prevent the recurrence of similar fatalities. A report is then forwarded to the HSE for action.

Enforcement actions

10.51   The enforcing authorities have a number of enforcement options available to them and have the support of the law to ensure that they are complied with. The options include an Improvement Notice (IN), a Prohibition Notice (PN) and prosecution. It is a policy of health and safety inspectors to ensure compliance with health and safety legislation by giving advice and using persuasion rather than resorting to the courts. The majority of prosecutions are taken in the magistrates' court where there is a maximum fine limit for each offence and if found guilty there will be prosecution costs to pay as well as the person's legal costs for going to court. Pleading guilty reduces court costs and reduces the size of the fine. More serious cases will be sent to the Crown Court for trial where fines are unlimited and costs increase to make it an expensive process. Imprisonment is also a possibility if found guilty.

Improvement Notice (IN)

10.52   An inspector can issue an IN if they are of the opinion that a person has contravened one or more statutory provisions (or in other words, there has been a breach of the HSWA 1974 or regulations), and is likely to repeat the contravention. If an inspector issues an IN, the recipient of the notice will have to comply with the requirements specified in the notice which will be time bound; the time for compliance being set by the enforcement officer has to be complied with or there can be an appeal. At the time of issuing a notice, the recipient will be informed of the appeal procedure, which is a formal process. The appeal is held before an Employment Tribunal who will hear and consider the inspector's reasons for the notice and the objections of the person who is appealing before making a ruling. This does mean that the recipient will have to prepare a reasoned objection as to why they should not have to comply with the notice. The process is generally informal compared with the courtroom environment. If the appeal is against the imposition of an IN the lodging of an appeal will automatically suspend the operation of the notice until the appeal is dealt with.

10.53   An example of the appeals process is shown in the Employment Tribunal case[1] involving Belhaven Brewery Co Ltd who was served with an IN requiring that a safety screen with an interlocking device be fitted around a kegging plant. The interlocking device would cut off the power and compressed air supply to the plant when a screen door was opened. As was its right, the company appealed against the notice, arguing that a far cheaper safety screen could be fitted which would still meet statutory requirements. Further, the company argued that the staff were sufficiently intelligent to ensure that the screen was kept in place whilst the machinery was operating and there would be a high level of management supervision. The case against the company was based upon the judgment of Mr McClean of HM Inspectorate of Factories. The inspector disagreed and maintained that irrespective of the staff's level of intelligence and the degree of supervision, only a system with an interlocking device could be secure and comply with the relevant legislation. The employment tribunal considered that failure to fit a system with an interlocking device would be a contravention of the Factories Act. Further, it was considered reasonably practicable for the company to fit the interlocking device. The reason for this view was because the risk associated with not fitting the device was not insignificant in relation to the sacrifice involved in fitting it. The tribunal held that the IN was to stand without modification and to be complied with.

The case clearly shows that a suitable safety device was available that integrated a fail safe system and that even though the workforce may be intelligent and there may be management supervision the two factors were not sufficient to provide a suitable safeguard to equal that of the interlocked guard.

---

[1] *Belhaven Brewery Co Ltd v A McLean (HM Inspector of Factories)* [1975] IRLR 370.

Prohibition Notice (PN)

10.54   If an inspector is in the opinion that activities are being carried out or are likely to be carried out which would mean there is risk of serious injury to any person, then the inspector can stop the activity by issuing a PN which has immediate effect. The inspector will provide details as to what has to be done to comply with the notice. In the case of a PN the inspector has only to be of the opinion that there is a risk of serious personal injury. The notice can be appealed against and placed before an employment tribunal; an application can be made for the notice to be lifted pending the hearing of the appeal. Such matters of appeal are dealt with as a matter of urgency. However, it must be borne in mind that if an inspector has issued a notice and stopped an activity because of safety issues, it is anticipated that there are good grounds for that action so caution needs to be exercised by the recipient in continuing work and pursuing an appeal.

10.55   An example of the appeals process is shown in the High Court, Queen's Bench Division[1] where Readmans, a cash and carry store, was using shopping trolleys which had a seat for babies or toddlers. There were a number of incidents in which it was alleged that trolleys had tipped forward due to the weight of children carried in them. As a result, Leeds City Environmental Health Inspector served a PN stating that the use of the trolleys to carry children involved *a risk of serious personal injury* and contravened the HSWA 1974, s 3. Readmans appealed to an employment tribunal, which held that the company had not put forward any convincing evidence as to why the PN should be lifted.

---

1   *Readmans Ltd and Another v Leeds City Council* [1992] COD 419.

10.56   The judge held that the tribunal had misdirected itself by not considering the correct burden of proof. He determined that it was for the inspector to establish, on the balance of probabilities, that there was a risk of serious personal injury and to make out a prima-facie case that there had been a breach of the 1974 Act. If this was established, the burden then shifted to Readmans to show, again on a balance of probabilities, that they had ensured, so far as was reasonably practicable, that visitors to Readmans' cash and carry were not exposed to those risks. In this regard, the judge stated that Readmans:

'… do not have to guarantee absolute safety, if such a thing is achievable, nor do they have to show that they have done what is practicable, that is to say, all that is physically possible. What they would have to establish is that they have done what is reasonably practicable to ensure that such risks as exist are avoided.'

The burden of proof rests with the company to establish that all reasonably practicable steps have been taken in the circumstances. In this case, evidence was presented concerning the facts that no other LAs had moved to impose PNs on the relevant trolleys, even though the trolleys were in wide use. Whilst such evidence may assist the company in certain circumstances, it is unlikely that a failure of one local authority to enforce relevant laws would demonstrate that no risk exists or that all reasonable practicable steps have been taken.

Appeals to employment tribunal

10.57   When a notice is issued there will be important information on the reverse or as a separate page and the recipient will be advised of their right of appeal to an Industrial Tribunal and given an explanatory leaflet for *Appellants and Respondents titled Appeals to Industrial Tribunals Concerning Improvement or Prohibition Notices under the Health and Safety at Work etc: Act 1974*. The leaflet explains the appeal procedure and how to lodge an appeal; where and within what period an appeal may be brought; that an appeal may be brought on any grounds; and that action required by a notice is suspended while an appeal is pending. The procedures and rights outlined above provide ways for those making the appeal to have their views heard if they are not happy with the inspector's action. If these procedures have not been followed, the appellant can take up the matter with the inspector's line manager.

Prosecutions in England and Wales

10.58   In England and Wales the decision to proceed with a prosecution case is a matter for the enforcing authority and there are tests that must be taken into account in the decision process. These are the evidential test and the relevant public interest factors that are described by the DPP in the *Code for Crown Prosecutors*. No prosecutions may proceed unless the prosecutor finds there is sufficient evidence to provide a realistic prospect of conviction and decides that prosecution would be in the public interest. The HSC considers that there is a public interest factor if any of the following issues apply:

- death was a result of a breach of the legislation;

- the gravity of an alleged offence, taken together with the seriousness of any actual or potential harm, or the general record and approach of the offender warrants it;

- there has been a reckless disregard of health and safety requirements;

- there have been repeated breaches which give rise to significant risks, or persistent and significant poor compliance;

- work has been carried out without, or in serious non-compliance with, an appropriate licence or safety case;

- a duty holder's standard of managing health and safety is found to be far below what is required by health and safety law and to be giving rise to significant risks;

- there has been a failure to comply with an improvement or prohibition notice; or there has been a repetition of a breach that was subject to a formal caution;

- false information has been supplied wilfully, or there has been an intent to deceive, in relation to a matter which gives rise to significant risk;

- inspectors have been intentionally obstructed in the lawful course of their duties.

10.59   There will also be consideration in the public interest to prosecute where:

- it is appropriate in the circumstances as a way to draw general attention to the need for compliance with the law and the maintenance of standards required by law, and conviction may deter others from similar failures to comply with the law;

- a breach which gives rise to significant risk has continued despite relevant warnings from employees, or their representatives, or from others affected by a work activity.

Prosecutions in Scotland

10.60   In Scotland it is the Procurator Fiscal who decides whether to bring a prosecution. The same standards apply in respect to there being sufficient evidence and that prosecution is in the public interest.

Prosecution of individuals

10.61   Individuals can and are prosecuted for health and safety offences. This can include directors, managers and supervisory staff where they have played a role in a breach, or the offence was committed with their consent or connivance or been negligent by their actions. Charges can be made under HSWA 1974 or health and safety regulations. There is also the option for the courts to disqualify directors under the Company Directors Disqualification Act 1986.[1]

---

1   Enforcement Policy Statement, Health and Safety Executive, HSC 15 01/02.

Protocol for Liaison

10.62   As part of the developing process to ensure effective investigation and legal process of accidents involving a death at work, the HSE, the Association of Chief Police Officers (ACPO), the CPS, the British Transport Police (BTP) and the Local Government Association (LGA) have drawn up a joint protocol.[1] The protocol is effective in England and Wales where the HSE is the enforcing authority for health and safety legislation. The objective of the protocol is to draw the organisations together where there has been a death at work to determine if there is evidence that there may be a case of individual or corporate manslaughter.

---

1   *Work Related Deaths, a Protocol for Liaison*, MISC491, HSE.

10.63   The five signatories to the protocol have different roles and responsibilities where there has been a work related death. The HSE and local government functions include enforcement within the scope of the HSWA 1974, but they cannot investigate or prosecute for general criminal offences, including manslaughter.

10.64   The police investigate criminal offences and that includes deaths at work. In this situation they are gathering evidence relating to manslaughter; they do not have the expertise to investigate work related deaths in detail; but the HSE provides assistance. If it is considered that there may have been a criminal offence committed the CPS will consider the evidence (which can be provided by the police alone or a combined police and HSE/LA report) and decide if there is sufficient evidence to provide a realistic prospect of conviction and if it is in the public interest to proceed.

10.65   The key points of the Protocol are:

- The HSE, LAs, police, BTP and CPS will establish effective mechanisms for liaison.

- The HSE and LAs will investigate under the HSWA 1974 and pass information suggesting possible manslaughter offences to the police or CPS.

- The police will conduct an investigation where there is an indication of possible manslaughter.

- The decision concerning prosecution will be made based on a sound investigation of the circumstances surrounding work-related deaths. The CPS, HSE/LA and police will make it without undue delay.

- The protocol has been signed up to and is public information.

The investigation process

10.66   In the event of a death at work the police are notified, as are the HSE/LA. A police detective of supervisory rank should attend the scene. At this point the liaison between the police and HSE/LA will commence with a joint investigation. That initial investigation will identify whether there is a need for a police involvement or whether it is an HSE/LA investigation. If the police decide that a charge of manslaughter or other serious offences cannot be justified, the investigation and forthcoming prosecution will be undertaken by the HSE/LA. Should the police in liaison with the HSE/LA decide that there might be a case to answer, then they will investigate for gross negligence or recklessness by either a company or an individual. In this situation the HSE/LA will provide technical support to the police and continue to investigate for offences under HSWA 1974.

10.67   When the investigations are completed a report is produced and provided to the CPS with recommendations for prosecution for manslaughter or other serious offences. The final decision of whether to prosecute and with what charges will be made by the HSE, LA, police, BTP and CPS in consultation. Where there are additional offences under the HSWA 1974 the HSE/LA and CPS will consider the initiation of joint proceedings.

10.68   To ensure that the protocol is working and effective a two-tier management system has been established. The first is where the HSE, LA, police, BTP and CPS have formed a national liaison committee, which meets at least once a year and will deal with high level issues. The second tier involves local liaison officers from each of the three groups and they meet on a regular basis to discuss the day-to-day working of the protocol.

Bereaved families

10.69   An inspector from the HSE or LA investigating a fatal accident provides advice and information to bereaved families and provides a leaflet that explains what the HSE/LA does following a fatal accident. This information is separate from that which may be given if there is an investigation for more serious incidents where the police are the lead authority; they have family liaison officers who are trained in providing information and support. Others may be involved such as the coroner's office, solicitor or other advice organisations.

Chapter 11

Penalty Options for Health and Safety Offences

Introduction	11.1
Fines	11.2
Alternatives to fines	11.10
NHS injury at work costs	11.36

Introduction

11.1   The sanction outcomes from a corporate manslaughter prosecution will be restricted to a fine. However, where individuals are identified as having failed in their management role there needs to be a range of penalty options available, whether it follows a corporate manslaughter offence or health and safety offences. There are opposing views on the options. On one side there are calls for putting directors on trial and having custodial penalties available for a wide range of health and safety offences. On the other side it is argued that it is wrong to criminalise corporations and directors to the degree that is current practice. The problem lies with the fact that accidents, many of a serious nature, are not reducing in number and in the subsequent trials or enquiries it has been found that there have been failings at senior management level. Senior management should be accountable by having effective systems in place and effective management of their implementation.

Fines

11.2   The Health and Safety at Work Etc Act 1974 (HSWA 1974) applies to all employees, apart from domestic servants in private households. There are problems with the Act, which is basically a criminal statute with determined penalties for breaches. It does not allow for compensation claims. Until recently the majority of cases brought under the Act were dealt with in the magistrates' court, with the result that there have been limited authoritative interpretations and few legal decisions from the higher courts. The financial penalties arising from the lower courts are restricted to a maximum of £20,000 for certain sections of the Act. Fines imposed by the regulations made under the Act are subject to a maximum of £5,000. However, cases that are referred to the Crown Court are subject to unlimited fines.

Financial penalties for health and safety offences

Offence	Summary Conviction (Magistrates' Court)	On indictment (Crown Court)
Failure to discharge a duty under ss 2–6	£20,000	Unlimited fine
Contravening ss 7–9	£5,000	Unlimited fine
Contravening health and safety regulations	£5,000	Unlimited fine
Contravening any requirement made by regulations relating to investigations or inquiries made by the Commission, etc under s 14, or obstructing anyone exercising his powers	£5,000	–
Contravening any requirement under s 20 (powers of inspectors)	£5,000	–
Contravening any requirement under s 25 (power of the inspector to seize and render harmless articles or substances likely to cause imminent danger)	£5,000	Unlimited fine
Preventing a person appearing before an inspector or from answering questions under s 20(2) (examinations and investigations)	£5,000	–
Contravening a requirement or prohibition imposed by an improvement notice	£20,000 and/or 6 months' imprisonment	Unlimited fine and/or 2 years' imprisonment
Contravening a requirement or prohibition imposed by a prohibition notice	£20,000 and/or 6 months' imprisonment	Unlimited fine and/or 2 years' imprisonment
Intentionally obstructing an inspector	£5,000	Unlimited fine
Contravening a notice served by the Commission under s 27(1) requiring information	£5,000	Unlimited fine

Using or disclosing information in contravention of s 27(4) (disclosure by the Crown or certain Government agencies of information to the Commission or Executive	£5,000	Unlimited fine and/or 2 years imprisonment
Making a false or reckless statement in purported compliance with a statutory provision, or for the purpose of obtaining the issuance of a document under any statutory provision.	£5,000	Unlimited fine
Intentionally making false entry in any register, book or other document required to be kept, or to making use of such entry, knowing it to be false	£5,000	Unlimited fine
With intent to deceive, using a document issued under a relevant statutory provision	£5,000	Unlimited fine
Pretending to be an inspector	£5,000	–
Failing to comply with an order of the court under s 42 (order to remedy)	£20,000 and/or 6 months' imprisonment	Unlimited fine and/or 2 years' imprisonment
Acting without a licence which is necessary under a relevant statutory provision	£5,000	Unlimited fine and/or 2 years' imprisonment
Contravening the terms of such a licence	£5,000	Unlimited fine and/or 2 years' imprisonment
Acquiring, using or possessing explosives contrary to the relevant provisions	£5,000	Unlimited fine and/or 2 years' imprisonment
Breach of regulations made for the purpose of Offshore Safety Act 1992, s 1(1)	£20,000	Unlimited fine and/or 2 years' imprisonment.

11.3   Fines are the most commonplace option for organisations and individuals that are found guilty of health and safety offences. Companies will often argue that to be subjected to a heavy fine and costs will have a detrimental effect on the shareholders and employees. This was experienced by the author when prosecuting a case for health and safety breaches: the defendants pleaded not guilty at the initial hearings, opting for trial in the magistrates' court. Prior to the trial date they changed their plea to guilty; the case was presented to the magistrates and maximum fines were sought as well as full costs. There was no mitigation in respect of the offences but the case was put by the defence that if the company were fined to the maximum, three members of staff would be made redundant that day so that the fines and costs could be paid. The magistrates, while accepting that the case was serious, took account of the fact that it was a high unemployment area and they could not impose maximum fines. They took the view that to do so would place people who were innocent of the offences and actions of the company out of work. Fines and costs were imposed on the company, but far less than those sought. The fact that the managing director and his son arrived in separate Rolls Royce cars did nothing to dispel the view that the courts failed to administer fair justice.

11.4   Celia Wells[1] highlights the question of fines and the issue of others bearing the costs:

'British Rail was fined £250,000 and ordered to pay £55,000 prosecution costs for an admitted failure to ensure the safety of its employees and passengers following the Clapham rail collision in 1987. The judge was faced with an *acute problem* ... the fine could only be met either by increasing the burden on fare paying passengers or by reducing the finance available for improvement to the railway system.'

What may not be known and therefore not considered are the salaries and bonuses paid to senior management, particularly in large organisations. Fines imposed for health and safety breaches should not be a burden on passengers, but should affect those in control. The loss of annual bonuses by all board members would focus their attitude for the future and deliver the penalty where it belongs.

---

1 Wells, C, *Corporations and Criminal Responsibilities* (Oxford University Press, 1994).

11.5   The subject of fines for corporate crime is the subject of a discussion by Smith[1] who states;

'... the fine imposed is ultimately borne by the shareholders who, in most cases are not responsible, in any sense, for the offence. If they really had any control over the directors and so over management of the company, this might afford some justification; but it is generally recognised that they have no such control over large, public companies ... Since the persons actually responsible for the offence may, in the great majority of cases, be convicted, is there any need to impose this additional penalty? Arguments in favour of corporate liability are that there may be difficulty in fixing individuals with liability where someone among the "brains" of the corporation has undoubt-edly authorised the offence. Corporate liability ensures that the offence will not go unpunished and that a fine proportionate to the gravity of the offence may be imposed, when it might be out of proportion to the means of the individuals concerned. The imposition of liability on the organisation gives all those directing it an interest in the prevention of illegalities, and they are in a position to prevent them, though the shareholders are not ...'

It is not only shareholders who see fines imposed for health and safety offences but also *organisations* that provide vital services to the public have to face the implications of heavy fines. For example, if a NHS health care trust, was fined, say, £40,000 with court costs of, say, £15,000, then the judge in passing sentence will take into account the importance of such a case because it raises issues not present in other cases. However, the lawyer representing the NHS trust would tell the court that every pound that the hospital is fined is a pound less spent on the care of the community. The outcome would be that the penalty would be very much less than that which would be imposed on a commercial organisation; in those circumstances, a financial penalty may not be the best option.

---

1 Smith and Hogan, *Criminal Law* Butterworths (9th edn, 1999).

11.6   This shows that there is a need to avoid placing a debit upon innocent shareholders and employees and means that there have to be alternative penalty options. The level of fines imposed for health and safety offences are deemed to be low and this has for some time been an area of concern for both the Health and Safety Commission (HSC) and experts who claim that there is a failing in the level of penalties. This was highlighted by Wells[1] who states that:

> 'The word *punishment* is dropped when corporations are the object of criminal enforcement and is replaced by the altogether less emotive *sanction*. This downgrades the whole status of a corporation being in court, which will be of concern in the event of an injury, but if there is a fatality then the status of that death is in effect downgraded further, albeit in a criminal court.'

---

1 Wells, C, *Corporations and Criminal Responsibilities* (Oxford University Press, 1994).

11.7   The debate is further developed by Wells[1] who identifies that:

> '... both Magistrates' and Crown Courts frequently require reports to be prepared for individuals, as well as the completion of a personal means form prior to sentencing. However, with corporate defendants, there is generally no attempt made to investigate the financial background or assets, before imposing fines. Courts accept a verbal description of the *organisation's* financial status and that of an individual if appropriate ...'

---

1 Wells, C, *Corporations and Criminal Responsibilities* (Oxford University Press, 1994).

11.8   The Law Commission[1] recommended (in the light of such concern) that there should not be scope for avoidance measures by unscrupulous companies or directors, and that enforcement action should act as a real deterrent, even in large companies and within groups of companies. Further, it should not be possible for holding companies to attempt to evade possible liability for health and safety offences through the establishment of subsidiary companies carrying on the group's riskier business which would be most likely to give rise to manslaughter charges. This includes the possibility that a subsidiary company within a large group of companies might have insufficient assets to pay a large fine, and that, in such cases, liability could not be transferred to its parent company. It is important that group structures should not be used as a mechanism for evasion. However, this very important aspect has not been addressed in the new corporate manslaughter and corporate homicide legislation.

---

1 *Legislating the Criminal Code: Involuntary Manslaughter*, 1996, Law Commission No 237, HMSO.

11.9   However, fines have taken on a new meaning in 2005 with the case of Transco (£15 million) where the penalty far exceeded the previous biggest fine on a company for a breach of health and safety regulations. That had previously been the £2 million penalty imposed on Thames Trains after the 1999 Ladbroke Grove rail disaster, in which 31 people died. The size of that fine was in relation to a profit of £390 million in 2004. Balfour Beatty, a railway maintenance company, was then fined £10 million for negligence which resulted in four deaths and 102 injuries in the Hatfield train crash.

Alternatives to fines

11.10   What should be the punishment for organisations found guilty of health and safety failures? If financial penalties do not deter management, what possible options will? The HSC's Revitalising Health and Safety strategy[1] commits it to looking for '*innovative*' penalties that could be added to the penalty options. Many of the possible options already exist within the criminal law system and range from financial penalties to personal liability.

---

1 June 2000, Department for the Environment, Transport and the Regions.

Imprisonment

11.11   The majority of directors of companies or principals in partnerships, trusts and other unincorporated organisations are law-abiding individuals. This means that they usually conduct their lives without recourse to the courts, and the criminal justice system is an alien place, reserved for those who carry out criminal acts such as theft and violence. It could be considered that breaches of health and safety legislation are outside of the public perception of criminal offences and therefore, prison is not generally seen as an appropriate option.

11.12   While any debate may indicate that senior management do not want to see a term of imprisonment as a punishment option, this is because they do not want to be in the unenviable position of facing a prison sentence for a workplace accident. A survey titled 'Directors respond to *'corporate killer'* label'[1] showed areas of concern and provided fuel to those who seek greater powers for the courts to increase workplace custodial sentences. The article states:

> 'Most industry leaders rank safety low on their list of business priorities, according to a British Safety Council (BSC)-MORI survey. The findings will disappoint the HSC, which has tried in recent years both to make a business case for safety and to make safety a board issue. The attitudes also fly in the face of increasing Government pressure to reduce workplace injuries and ill health.'

The article continues:

> 'Nearly 100 board directors (mainly chairs, presidents and managing directors) of FTSE 500 companies responded to the survey carried out in November 2001.When asked to list their three main corporate objectives, only one in six (16%) singled out improving safety in the working environment, although this represents a 3% increase on the 2000 survey. One in two manufacturing directors lists safety in their top three priorities. Across industry, generating profits for shareholders (84%) and increasing customer satisfaction (80%) continue to be the top objectives, with the desire for new products and services, maximising productivity and better training for staff all placed ahead of improving safety.
>
> Most of the directors interviewed are making preparations for the Government's proposed corporate killing legislation and only one in eight say they would be likely to, or would resign their directorships because of the new offences. The most popular preparations are demonstrating a commitment to health and safety (51%), setting up effective health and safety communications (41%), and appointing a health and safety director (35%).
>
> Four in five directors (86%) think loss of their company's reputation would be a long-term effect of a successful prosecution for corporate killing, and about half think it would create employee morale problems and raise insurance costs. Seven in 10 believe such legal action would have some effect on their companies' share prices and nearly two thirds believe that their institutional investors would demand corrective action.'

---

1 *Directors respond to 'corporate killer' label'*, Health and Safety Bulletin 307, April 2002.

11.13   Whatever the arguments and counter arguments, there will remain a case for custodial sentences for workplace accidents. This will be particularly relevant where there has been serious neglect on behalf of the most senior officials. The question that will have to be addressed is the level of custodial sentences and degree of culpability of the defendant on each occasion.

Director's bonus

11.14   Many businesses reward senior management for reaching corporate targets, generally focused on turnover and profit. Targets are set to meet corporate objectives and the reward system provides personal motivation to executives. In the case of a management failure in respect of health and safety, where the consequences are fatalities, serious accidents or risks to the health of others, there is the potential option of prohibiting director bonuses for a fixed period, which in some cases could be a substantial figure. The problem would be identifying who would carry the burden. This could be answered by delivering the penalty to all at board of director level, as they are all representatives of the 'corporate' body. They reap the rewards of profit and so should share the burden of failure. There may be a difficulty in imposing a collective sanction because of one person's failure. However, the option could be introduced to encourage senior management to take a greater interest and participation in health and safety.

Suspending management

11.15   Where individual managers are found to have failed, the option of suspending those individuals without pay may be effective. This would apply to management below director level who may disregard health and safety in their operational decisions in order to get the job done for some form of personal gain. This style of option has been proven to be an effective penalty as the author found in one situation that did not reach court. A manager was responsible for an operation that was being carried out for a fixed sum of money and he could receive a completion bonus that was linked to meeting the budget. If the job ran over the time limit his bonus would reduce quite rapidly and so he was under personal pressure to complete the operation on time. As the job progressed he identified a situation where corners could be cut, but which would be to the detriment of an employee if there was an equipment failure. He directed a change in the programme which resulted in the failure of the equipment; by sheer luck the employee was not injured, although the failure could have resulted in a fatality. The HSE Inspectorate, having investigated the incident, encouraged the company to impose a serious sanction on the manager. This was achieved by the removal of all bonuses, which amounted to several thousand pounds; he was also suspended from his post until he had undertaken and passed an accredited health and safety training course.

11.16   This was a new course of action and it saved regulatory time and expensive enforcement against the organisation, which in this case was not at fault, but upheld the ultimate duty under the HSWA 1974. Under the circumstances enforcement action had been a viable option and the message it sent to the boardroom was to review its bonus policy. It delivered an effective message to the manager who lost financially, along with damage to his personal credibility. In the wider sense it sent a strong message to all managers for the need to conform to corporate procedures and not to embark on frolics of their own.

Suspended sentences

11.17   It is already possible under the criminal law to impose a custodial sentence, then to suspend it. In these circumstances, for example, a sentence could be suspended for 18 months, during which time if there were further breaches of health and safety legislation, the organisation or individual would return to court and be sentenced for the new offence in addition to the original sentence.

Compulsory health and safety training

11.18   An option that could readily be adopted would be to impose compulsory health and safety training where there has been a health and safety failure. Peter Rogerson[1] provides an interesting argument where he states:

> 'Health and safety offences are generally dealt with by way of fines and remedy orders … This will usually reflect the seriousness of the offence, the degree of co-operation of the company concerned, the warnings given, the timeliness of the plea and the size of the resources of the organisation … specific charges are now often accompanied by additional charges of general failure under the 1992 Management of Health and Safety Regulations to undertake suitable risk assessments … But is this approach, particularly when dealing with small and medium enterprises, fulfilling the primary objective of the court, which is to prevent re-offending? Will a fine on the company or its management necessarily make the working environment any safer for its workers and visitors alike? Why do businesses commit health and safety offences? Clearly there are those driven by profit and greed. Such companies, quite rightly, deserve to be hit hard with the full weight of the law and often end up in the Crown Court for sentencing. Most, however, commit offences because of poor management, lack of resources, ignorance and confusion … we could look to other areas for inspiration. Courts are now able to direct offenders through the probation service to undertake training on alcohol awareness, anger management and drug abuse to name but a few … Can this principle be applied to companies and directors who commit health and safety offences? At the lower end the smaller organisations could have a health and safety training order, where, instead of a significant fine, the company would be required to send the executive named by the court (usually its most senior executive, director, partner or proprietor) on an approved health and safety management training course. Such a course could be one or two days and failure to comply would result in significant fines both for the company. Medium size companies could be given a health and safety training and action plan order, where, in addition to the training, the company would be required to work with an approved consultant … for a specified time … with the aim of creating a safety management system and instilling a "safety culture".'

---

1 Rogerson, P, 'Health and Safety Sentencing – a better way?' Magistrate Magazine, Summer 2002.

11.19   This option is commendable in its concept but does highlight some major hurdles. In particular, what type of health and safety training could be adopted? Is a one or two day training course a suitable option as opposed to a substantial fine? One course of action could be to suspend part of a fine to allow for training and safety management system development and if the organisation is prosecuted for health and safety breaches in the future, the suspended part of the fine would become payable along with any additional fines. Of course a company with a potential outstanding financial commitment could move vulnerable funds to a separate company thus making the payment unviable.

Community punishment orders

11.20   Community punishment orders, such as those already used in the criminal courts could be imposed. These require an individual to undertake unpaid work in the community at large for a predetermined period of time. Such an option may be useful where an appropriate fine would plunge a company into financial difficulties. The question arises as to who would physically carry out any such order, particularly where there were several directors, partners or trustees. It is claimed that such orders could enhance the company's image in the community, with those who carried out the work wearing corporate overalls or other protective clothing advertising their organisation. Such orders might result in the community work being carried out by innocent employees. This option, whilst it has some advantages, would require 'loopholes' to be plugged because it can be anticipated that many of those who breach health and safety law will not be averse to breaching punishment orders.

11.21   Any such order must be punitive as it would be replacing a fine, the latter having a negative effect on the company. The cost of community service would be borne by the company with the rehabilitative element being seen as giving something back to the community. Any such order should not require the consent of the convicted company prior to imposing the sentence. A report states:[1]

> 'Requiring a corporation to undertake unpaid work as a community service would no more involve unlawful forced or compulsory work than subjecting a corporation to an improvement notice or mandatory injunction requiring [...] Furthermore, a requirement of consent would be undesirable because it would provide too convenient a refuge for corporations wishing to pay fines rather than suffer a more severe type of sentence.'

---

1 www.corporateaccountability.org, *Corporate Harm and the Criminal Justice System: Proposals for Reform*, 2001.

11.22   The calculation of the value of the community service would include the cost of materials and labour and not the number of hours, as is the case with conventional criminal orders. Corporate orders would have to be subject to a two-year completion period.

11.23   The type of community service imposed upon an individual organisation would be dependent upon the skills and resources available and where possible have some relationship to the offence that had been committed. It would be important that any project should involve the senior management of the organisation and not be a burden to those at a lower level. There may be situations where other expertise would need to be brought into the project, and that would be encompassed within the financial restraints of the Community Service Order. The profile of any order will need to be within the means and capabilities of the organisation.

11.24   There would need to be a requirement for the organisation to prepare a report before it commences community service, setting out the plan of how it intends to comply with the order. The court will need to appoint an independent person to provide advice on the suitability of the plan. Upon completion of the community service order, a report should be prepared providing details of the work carried out so as to advise the court of completion of the order.

11.25   If an organisation completed the specified work in the allocated time frame to a satisfactory standard then it would have met its obligations. If the organisation fails to comply with the order, the court can revoke the community service order and fine the organisation up to one and a half times the original amount of the fine.

11.26   Possible corporate community service orders are described by Slapper and Toms:[1]

> '... soup kitchens for the homeless if it had previously sold adulterated food; sending its executives to do voluntary work in emergency rooms if they deliberately built cars that became fire bombs when hit from the rear; or requiring its board to work in Veterans Administration hospitals if the corporation profited from systematically falsifying test records on drugs, declaring them safe when they were not.'

Clearly the adoption of community service orders could be an option for the courts as a corporate punishment; however, there are some fundamental flaws in the concept that would need to be addressed.

---

1 Slapper, G, and Toms, S, *Corporate Crime* (Longman, 1999).

Company probation orders

11.27   Company probation orders could facilitate rehabilitation by forcing immediate changes in the company's decision-making, monitoring and personal incentive processes. There is also the important question as to who would undertake the planning and supervision. The order would focus on those who have the ultimate control because companies are often diverse and fragmented in their structure, particularly large enterprises. The scheme would be expensive to operate and courts may not have the knowledge and expertise of corporate law needed; corporate law is complicated and the consequences of a wrong outcome could be very damaging. It also raises issues under the Human Rights Act 1998, because restricting business operations could affect the operating viability of an organisation.

11.28   In Slapper and Toms[1] the corporate probation option is considered:

'Corporate Probation, which has been used in the USA since 1987, has the merit that it is an 'organisation-specific' sanction and helps strengthen the legal foundation of corporate liability, and avoids the conception of company crimes as crimes committed by individuals within companies.'

Corporate probation orders would be an amended version of the probation orders currently imposed on individuals in the criminal courts. The focus of such orders should be rehabilitative in nature but be seen by the public to be an effective punishment. In the criminal courts probation orders are generally imposed as an alternative to a custodial sentence, but as an organisation cannot be sent to prison, such an order should be imposed in addition to a financial or equity fine.

1 Slapper, G, and Toms, S, *Corporate Crime*, (Longman, 1999).

Fixed penalty notices

11.29   Another option could be fixed penalty notices for specific offences and a penalty point system modelled on the current driver's licence system. However, occupational health and safety is a complex subject affecting organisations involved in diverse activities and of varying sizes. Breaches of health and safety law are often based on an inspector's interpretation at the time of an inspection. The inspector would have to make a judgment on the spot and issue a fixed penalty notice. The management of the company would have the right of appeal and so a formal process of dealing with appeals would be required which would be costly to operate both in terms of time and financially. This is in comparison to a speeding offence where the evidence of a fixed or mobile camera provides proof. The process is straightforward as there is a defined speed limit and the breach is calculated by the excess speed. The penalty notice is issued, and in the majority of cases, the fine is paid. The issue of penalty points in driving cases is also straightforward in concept. There is a licence and a system to administer it in place. There is no such system in place for business or industry: organisations come and go and there is no formal registration scheme for non-incorporated businesses.

Equity fines

11.30   Courts could also have the power to impose 'equity fines' on limited companies. This would involve the court ordering a company to issue a specified number of shares, valued at a particular price, and place them into a fund. Again Slapper and Toms[1] make the following comments:

> 'A court should only be liable to an equity fine when two situations exist (1) the company must be a public limited company; and (ii) the courts should have assessed that the company might not pay the cash fine without passing the amount onto its workers or customers. The basis of any proposal would be as outlined below.

> (a)   Court power to impose an equity fine. When a court is sentencing a public limited company, and it has reasonable cause to believe that if it sentenced the company to a cash fine there would be unreasonable consequences on the company's employees or there is a real risk of bankruptcy, the court may sentence the company to an equity fine.

> (b)   Ordering a company to issue shares to court. When sentencing a company to an equity fine, the court shall order the company to issue shares, equal in sum to the cash fine that the court would otherwise impose on the company, into a fund set up by the court.'

Again there is an administrative burden problem where the cost to the courts of recovery of moneys through 'costs' awarded would be equitable.

---

1 Slapper, G, and Toms, S, *Corporate Crime* (Longman, 1999).

Penalty points

11.31   Penalty points could be introduced for health and safety offences. If a company was convicted of a serious health and safety offence(s), a company director would receive penalty points. These would need to be officially recorded through an endorsement on the company's registration form. While such a system could be adopted for limited companies, consideration would need to be given to extending it to partnerships, trusts and self employed persons. The proposal outlined by Slapper and Toms[1] would be based upon the following concept:

'(1)   Where a company director is found to be guilty of an offence listed below, the court must endorse the company registration form, with a number of penalty points which are attributable to each offence committed.

(2)   The number of penalty points, which the court should attribute to any offence, is: the number, or where a range of numbers is shown, a number within the range.

(3)   Any penalty points endorsed onto the company registration form as a result of the conviction of a director should count as the penalty points for that director alone.'

---

1 Slapper, G, and Toms, S, *Corporate Crime* (Longman, 1999).

Health and safety v insurance cover

11.32   Sanctions that will impose themselves could come about through insurance. Employers' liability insurance is compulsory for all employers and there is a need to have liability insurance for those who are not employed but can be affected by the organisation. Insurance companies are already imposing restrictions on organisations through increasing premiums. Businesses that carry risks to employees and/or others not employed face premium increases of 40% to 60% and in a growing number of instances, an inability to obtain cover at any cost. The Hazards[1] campaign proposes that companies should publish their record on health and safety and publish the name of their insurers, to prevent them from evading the requirement of having employers' liability insurance and to make it easier for those seeking injury or illness compensation.

---

1 www.hazardscampaign.org.uk

11.33   Since 1975 the HSE has been the enforcing authority for the Employer's Liability (Compulsory Insurance) Act 1969 (ELCIA 1969). The field of responsibility includes premises allocated to local authorities for HSWA 1974 enforcement as well as premises normally inspected by the HSE.

11.34   Under the ELCIA 1969 employers are obliged to:

●   insure against liability for injury or disease to an employee arising out of and in the course of his/her employment in Great Britain;

●   display the certificate of insurance at his or her places of business;

●   produce the certificate or send a copy when required to do so by an authorised inspector;

●   send the certificate or copy in response to a Notice served on behalf of the HSE;

- permit an authorised inspector to inspect his policy or copy provided that reasonable notice has been given.

With certain specified exceptions, an employer carrying on business in Great Britain is required to insure against liability for injury or disease to any employee, arising out of and in the course of his/her employment in Great Britain, in that business. The principle of using the insurance industry to penalise bad performance and reward good performance in companies' health and safety practices was initially thought to be sound. However, it has been shown that where a company finds its insurance premiums raised as a result of poor health and safety performance it can simply approach a different insurance company, which is often willing to undercut the original quote.

11.35   As an outcome of numerous large insurance claims in recent years, the insurance underwriters have begun to review their client base in terms of risk liability. This is coupled with the fact that the number of underwriters providing cover for employers' liability insurance has dramatically reduced. These factors are having an impact on business where 'risk' is having a direct effect on premiums with dramatic increases; in a growing number of cases, businesses are unable to obtain cover at any cost. Another factor that will impact on premiums is the proposal that hospitals will charge for treatment where there is a workplace incident.

NHS injury at work costs

11.36   The Personal Injuries (NHS Charges) Amounts) Regulations 2007[1] came into force on 29 January 2007, allowing the NHS to recover costs from insurance companies for treating patients in all cases where personal injury compensation is paid. Hospitals are already able to recover the costs of treating people injured in road traffic accidents (RTA) where they have successfully claimed compensation for their injuries.

---

1 SI 2007/115.

11.37   This new legislation means that companies will have to pay hospital bills for workplace injuries in line with the costs recovered, as is the case following a road accident where there is a liability to pay for ambulance transport and emergency NHS treatment. This follows a study[1] undertaken by the Health Department's economists who found that employer liability for accidents and diseases and public liability for accidents are the most common types of personal injury claim. This means that the taxpayer has been subsidising the medical treatment for these accidents. The study identified that employers' liability insurance is costing an estimated £42m for inpatient and £12m for outpatient treatment; there is also a £4m cost of emergency ambulance transport. It is considered that public liability accidents will generate similar figures. It was concluded that it would be difficult to quantify the costs of work-related diseases due to the complexities of treatment and time frames, and this area would require further study as would the identification of types of accidents.

---

1 *The Recovery of National Health Service Costs in Cases Involving Personal Injury Compensation: A Consultation*, Department of Health, September 2002.

11.38   The proposal focuses on any business which has potential liabilities for personal injury, which can be an employer, a producer of goods or the undertaking of business in a public place. This means that there will be an impact on insurance companies who will have to apportion costs to clients, as they will face a recovery of costs bill estimated to be in the region of £100m to £120m. Where insurance is not compulsory, it is anticipated that responsible businesses will carry insurance cover, such as contractor's all risk insurance, which includes an element of public liability cover. There are potential consequences in that undertakings that are required to carry insurance cover may not do so, leaving those injured covered by medical treatment, but the NHS unable to recover costs. However, this would be a legal requirement and failure to insure would result in enforcement action. The expectation is that higher insurance premiums to cover NHS costs should encourage undertakings to review health and safety management systems and risk control measures.

11.39   The introduction of such a scheme could impact on small business and the consultation document stated:

> 'The vast majority of businesses in the United Kingdom employ fewer than 50 people and are therefore classed as small businesses. More than two thirds of these small businesses are sole proprietorships and partnerships comprising only the self-employed owner manager(s) and comprising only an employee director ... Where any business is run on a tight margin the impact of any increase in either compulsory or voluntary insurance premiums will be unwelcome. However, the small business attracts responsibilities for the safety and well being of people who come into contact with it in just the same way as any other business and should be encouraged to both reduce that risk wherever possible and to make sensible and prudent provision for meeting the costs of any accidents should they nevertheless occur.'

11.40   The concept underlying the new law is that it is considered unacceptable that taxpayers have had to pay for the medical treatment of someone injured at work simply because employers have failed to take adequate steps to protect their workforce. In addition to recovering funds it is hoped that employers will take steps to prevent employees being injured and that the law will provide the impetus to improve health and safety. The scheme will not introduce any more extra regulations for businesses as it will be based on the current road traffic accident scheme which recovers the money through the insurance company. Under the current scheme, where an injured person makes a personal injury compensation claim, their insurer or representative has a legal obligation to inform the Compensation Recovery Unit (CRU) of the claim and to provide additional information to the CRU on whether the injured person was treated in a NHS hospital. NHS costs are only recoverable if the injured person actually receives a compensation payment, which can take on average 18 months to be settled. However, it is anticipated that there will be an increase in insurance premiums of between 5–8%.[1]

---

1 Federation of Small Business information.

11.41   The NHS Injury Costs Recovery (ICR) scheme will apply to injuries only; diseases are excluded from the scheme unless the disease has been contracted as a direct result of an injury that falls within the scope of the scheme. Costs of treatment given by general practitioners in the primary care setting are not included in the scheme.

11.42   A reduction in the charges will be made where the compensation claim payment has been reduced to take account of contributory negligence. Contributory negligence is where the injured person acknowledges, or is deemed to have, some responsibility for the injury. In such cases a reduction in the compensation payment recognises the element of the injured person's own responsibility. There are no patient confidentiality issues because the insurer and the NHS body are required by law to provide this information, which in any case will almost always be information that the injured person has provided themselves as part of their compensation claim. The CRU will use the hospital attendance information to apply a national tariff and calculate charges due to the NHS trust. The tariff is currently set at a flat rate fee of £505 for treatment without admission or £620 per day for treatment with admission, and there is a ceiling of charges for any one injury, currently set at £37,100.

11.43   One of the key new features is that ambulance service costs will also be recoverable where there has been a personal injury compensation claim. This will include all ambulance transportation used by the injured person who has made the claim, such as the first journey to Accident and Emergency and any subsequent transfers to other hospitals. It is interesting to note that air ambulance costs will only be recoverable in Scotland.

Part 3

Directors' Responsibilities for Health and Safety

Chapter 12

Management of Health and Safety

Introduction

12.1 The corporate manslaughter offence is focused upon the management of health and safety, and any failure that evolves from an act or omission by management within the corporate structure itself. The structure generally encompasses the main board directors, executives or others identified as being in control of the organisation. It follows that every company should have a safety management system, which should be an integrated part of the company's day-to-day activities. This will enable management to encompass within its activities a seamless system to ensure the safety and health of all its employees. This must be equal to all other business functions such as finance, manufacturing, marketing and distribution.

12.2 It is recognised that companies not only vary in size and complexity, but also vary by industry and even by constitution. This means that there will be varying hazards that can affect those employed as well as those who are not employed, such as contractors or members of the public. It is, therefore, the responsibility of those at board level who set the policy and standards of the organisation to create a safe working environment. This is achieved in part by identifying the hazards, controlling the risks and monitoring the effectiveness of their control procedures.

Corporate governance

12.3 During the 1980s Polly Peck, British Commonwealth, BCCI and Robert Maxwell's Mirror Group News International were victims of poorly managed business practices that led to the failure of those companies. As a result, the Cadbury Committee was established by the UK Stock Exchange. The membership of the committee included representatives from the senior level of British industry. Their task was to develop a code of practice that would provide guidance in defining and applying internal controls to limit the risks of financial loss, whatever the cause.

The Cadbury Committee Report

12.4   The committee produced a report[1] in 1992 and a code of best practice. The recommendations of the code were not mandatory, but all UK quoted companies listed on the UK Stock Exchange, must now clearly state whether or not the code has been followed, and if it has not, then they must explain why. The report focused on corporate governance by identifying that there was a need for a clearly accepted division of responsibilities at the head of a company. The objective was to ensure a balance of power and authority, such that no individual had an unfettered decision-making power.

---

1 *The Financial Aspects of Corporate Governance*, The Cadbury Committee, December 1992.

12.5   The focus of the report was on the role of directors, both in their boardroom function and as individuals, and it identified a need to introduce thorough reporting and control measures. Risk management was not identified as an official duty for directors; however, there is a requirement for board members to include a formal statement confirming compliance with the code, which raises the profile of risk management overall.

12.6   A key objective of the code was to make directors and non-executive directors aware of the need for boardroom confirmation that their companies are protected from major losses resulting from inappropriate working practices. A problem that was identified in obtaining full support from the boardroom was that it was generally considered that risk management was linked to insurance. This was a situation that had to be addressed, as boardroom members could not absolve their responsibilities to a third party.

12.7   There are three key points for risk management: identification, evaluation and control, which encompass all aspects of corporate activities and include safety management. Hazards need to be identified and controlled with an audit system to identify compliance, all as an integrated part of a safety management system. The code identified that the responsibility for health and safety within a corporation was at boardroom level, where directors, who are the pinnacle of the corporate safety culture, provide leadership of the organisation.

Turnbull Guidance

12.8   Following the Cadbury report and code the *Combined Code of the Committee on Corporate Governance*[1] was published in 1999 and applied to listed companies on the London Stock Exchange (some 2,700 companies). The code focuses on corporate governance which, whilst centred upon the financial aspects of an organisation, is linked to corporate losses in the wider context. That includes health and safety which is a major risk factor for all organisations and where there is a need for board control.

The document (known as the 'Turnbull Guidance', named after the chairman of the committee, Nigel Turnbull) provides a structure for assessing the effectiveness of a company's risk and control process which encompasses health and safety as a key factor in the management process.

---

1 *Combined Code of the Committee on Corporate Governance*, Institute of Chartered Accountants, 1999.

12.9   The guidance identifies risk assessment as a boardroom issue and determines that the company should have clear objectives and make sure that they have been communicated to employees so as to provide effective direction on the identification and assessment of risk. This should ensure that significant internal and external health and safety risks are identified and assessed, and that there is knowledge by management and others within the company as to what risks are acceptable to the board.

12.10   Control is a key factor within management and that requires the board to have clear strategies for dealing with the significant risks that have been identified. This is established within the company's culture, code of conduct, human resources, operating procedures and policies that support the overall business objectives, including risk management. Senior management has to demonstrate, through its actions as well as its policies, the necessary commitment to ensure competence and integrity so as to develop a culture of trust within the company. The control element needs to ensure that responsibilities and accountability are clearly defined and that decisions are made and actions taken by the appropriate people and in a diverse organisation, effectively co-ordinated.

12.11   Board members must communicate to their employees what is expected of them and define in detail the scope of their freedom to act and make decisions. This would include internal and outsourced activities regarding health and safety. The management must ensure that the people in the company as well as its providers of outsourced services have the competence to fulfil the company's objectives in supporting the management of the organisation's health and safety risks. Because risks within an organisation are subject to constant change there need to be controls in place that can reflect new or changing risks, or operational deficiencies.

12.12   Information and communication are vital to any organisation and it is important that management and the board members receive timely, relevant and reliable reports on health and safety issues that could affect the business

251

objectives. The sources should evolve from both inside and outside the organisation providing information that allows for decision-making and management review of health and safety. There will also need to be periodic reporting procedures, including half-yearly and annual reporting where matters relating to health and safety are on the agenda. This should identify that there are effective communication channels that will allow individuals to report suspected breaches of laws, regulations or concerns in respect to health and safety.

12.13   To ensure compliance there is a requirement to have systems structured within the organisation's overall business operations that are accessed by senior management, to monitor the effectiveness of the policies, processes and activities related to health and safety. These processes are required to review the company's ability to re-evaluate risks and make suitable amendments as an effective response to changes. That in turn requires there to be a system to monitor any follow-up procedures so to ensure that the appropriate changes or actions are carried out in response to changes identified through risk management. The systems will allow the board or board committees to ensure the effectiveness of the ongoing processes of risk and control matters, which should include identifying any significant health and safety issues and the degree of risk. To complete the control process there need to be specific arrangements for management to report to the board on health and safety risk and control matters.

12.14   The statement 'good governance is good business' is the foundation of corporate governance, encompassing the management of financial and operating risks within an organisation. An important ingredient within the organisation's operations is health and safety and as such must occupy an equal place within an organisation's activity.

The Hampton Report

12.15   The government commissioned a report[1] with the remit of examining the regulatory authorities in identifying what their objectives were and how they carried them out. There was a focus on regulation, inspection and prosecution process and overlap of regulatory bodies. Businesses saw the regulatory burden as a negative often with multiple organisations requiring the same information and, in the case of health and safety, confusion over where the Health and Safety Executive (HSE) and local authorities have jurisdiction. Many businesses do not know which regulations apply to them and therefore act in ignorance.

---

1 Hampton, Phillip, *Reducing Administrative Burdens: effective inspection and enforcement*, March 2005.

12.16   Hampton's final report, *Reducing Administrative Burdens: effective inspection and enforcement*, is concerned primarily with regulatory functions at the national level and the Government's role in coordination and target setting.

- Continuing the trend towards consolidation of regulatory functions at national level (rather, as in 1974, when Robens had recommended the integration of inspectorates to form the HSE).

- Placing greater emphasis on advice in preference to inspection to secure the improvement of regulatory outcomes, particularly for small and medium enterprises (SMEs).

- Joint working, information and cross training of staff involved in inspection and enforcement.

- Ensuring more widespread use of robust risk assessment schemes to programme inspections, so that no inspection takes place without a reason.

- Strengthening of penalties.

- Better incentives to improve compliance.

- A national regulators' forum would be established to oversee the coordination of effort through 'best value' and help to set national priorities for regulation.

- Responsibility for environmental health and trading standards would be removed from local authorities to a new national body.

12.17   The focus of the Hampton review has been to identify ways in which the administrative burden of regulation on businesses can be reduced, while maintaining or improving regulatory outcomes. It was found that the regulatory bodies that were reviewed carry out more than 3 million inspections each year involving 63 national regulators and 468 local authorities. The review looked at how the structure of the UK's regulatory system affects the ability of regulators to minimise administrative burdens when interacting with, and importantly encouraging compliance from, businesses.

12.18   It was identified that the requirement for official form completion with regard to health and safety is very limited, generally to the Reporting of Injuries, Diseases and Dangerous Occurrences Regulations (RIDDOR) following an incident.

12.19   There was also concern about inconsistent practice and decision-making between regulators and this will be of concern to those inspected by the HSE. It was found that the current regulatory system involving health and safety provides much that is good, and there are many examples of excellent, innovative practice. However, there are fundamental concerns that the use of risk assessment in regard to inspection is not consistent. Regulators do not give enough emphasis to providing advice in order to secure compliance and regulators lack effective tools to punish persistent offenders and reward compliant behaviour by business. This in turn discourages business-responsive behaviour.

12.20   Everybody involved in health and safety understands that risk assessment is an inbuilt part of the risk management process and helps organisations to focus resources where they are required. It is also understood that risk assessment should be an essential tool for directing regulatory resources where they can have the maximum impact on outcomes. The objective is that the undertaking of risk assessments would make regulators take proper account of the nature of businesses. This would encompass all external factors affecting the risk the business poses to its employees and to those who are not employed but could be affected by the business's activities. Using this information, regulators can direct their resources where they can do most good and they can plan effective inspections and end unnecessary inspections on less risky businesses. The outcome would be to identify businesses which are identified as requiring more inspections, and release resources to improve broader advice services.

12.21   A major factor for businesses is that there must be proper sanctions against illegal activity in order to prevent businesses operating outside the law and gaining a competitive advantage. At present there is no incentive for many businesses to comply as it is in a business's interest to pay the fine rather than comply. This is especially true where a business feels able to shrug off the risk of prosecution on the basis of damage to its reputation. The evidence is that if businesses do not face an effective deterrent for illegal activity they will be tempted to break the law. There are also major concerns that penalties have fallen far short of the commercial value of the regulatory breach and, in the case of the HSE, for health and safety offences prosecuted the average fine in 2003–04 was £4,306. The compelling evidence is that if penalties do not reflect the advantage gained by a company in breaking the law, dishonest businesses are given further incentive to breach regulations, and undercut companies who are complying. A knock on effect that evolves from ineffective penalties can be unnecessary levels of inspection of compliant businesses.

12.22   The HSE can trace its origins back to 1833. Today the principal national regulators are the Health and Safety Commission (HSC) and the HSE. Both organisations were established by the Health and Safety at Work etc Act 1974 (HSWA 1974). The HSC and the HSE are responsible for protecting all citizens against the risks to health or safety arising out of work-related activities, covering the whole of the UK with the exception of Northern Ireland. The HSC submits proposals for new or revised regulations and approved codes of practice. Both the HSE and local authorities carry out enforcement activity, under the supervision of the HSC. The main inspectorate arm of the HSE is the Field Operations Directorate and about 50% of inspections are reactive in response to an accident or particular incident.

12.23   The HSE has for years focused on assessing every workplace for which it is responsible against criteria for risks to employees and the public, and the competence of site management in managing these risks. This programme has enabled inspection to be focused in the right areas. Throughout that time the

HSE has built up its database to enable a risk-based approach to be followed. However, databases need to be maintained, updated and added to and if the number of inspections declines the database will deteriorate until it is ineffective.

12.24   If regulatory risk assessments have been properly used, businesses being inspected will generally be the riskiest and present the most complicated problems. The division of health and safety between the HSE and local authorities dates back to 1974 and whilst it has been amended since, the fundamental split between 'factories' (HSE) and safer premises (local authorities) remains.

12.25   The HSC has less specific powers but it can advise both HSE and local authorities on inspection activity. It can request annual reports from each local authority, and take over failing authorities. There is a further complication with boundary problems between the HSE and local authorities and that causes problems both in inspection, where standards and activity vary widely, and in the level of enforcement. Premises are divided between the HSE and local authorities, with the HSE generally taking the more dangerous premises, and the local authority the safer ones.

12.26   The report clearly identifies that the HSE, whose remit extends to the safety of workers and the public in workplaces, should evolve to encompass other bodies with a similar remit, including aspects of public safety. This would require the HSE to take responsibility for the planned Gangmasters Licensing Authority and the Engineering Inspectorate, which is part of the Department for Business, Enterprise and Regulatory Reform, whose remit is the safety of overhead power lines.

12.27   Local authority regulators, because of the types of business they see, tend to be effective at providing business advice. Overall, local authorities carry out four times as many inspections as national regulators following guidance provided by a national regulator or a government department. District and unitary authorities employ Environmental Health Officers (EHOs). Nationally there are 408 environmental health officers in England, Scotland and Wales. EHOs are professionally qualified local government officials who inspect premises for food safety and health and safety.

12.28   Regulatory compliance is through inspection which is carried out on a number of businesses. For regulatory advice the HSE operates particularly helpful advice websites and there is a wealth of information in the form of leaflets, booklets, guidance and approved codes of practice. However, it has been found that business knowledge of regulations, even well-established regulations, is low.

12.29   It is important that inspectors and regulatory staff have input into the discussions when regulations are be developed and drafted. This means that those involved in the process of developing new regulations should be required to follow the principles of enforcement so that they have a full understanding as to how the inspection and prosecution process is implemented. Where existing systems of inspections or penalty objectives can be used to meet new regulatory requirements, then they should be used. The focus is on goal-based regulation as opposed to prescriptive regulation and regulations should, where possible, be 'self-enforcing'. This means that regulations should be developed to cater for self-enforcement.

Corporate memory

12.30 Modern work practices mean people move jobs more frequently. This results in the detail of accidents and incidents that have occurred in an organisation often being forgotten or lost. It is a very important issue because if the causes of accidents and incidents are not in the memory of new staff, including directors and senior managers, past lessons have not been learned and acted on leaving an organisation's safety management system exposed to failure.

12.31 Trevor Kletz[1] identified some interesting points about corporate memory which are applicable:

'The following actions can help us remember the lessons of the past. If we have paid the high price of an accident we should at least turn it into a learning experience:

- Include in every instruction, code and standard, a note on the reason it was introduced and accounts of accidents which would not have occurred if it had been followed;

- Describe old accidents as well as recent ones in safety bulletins and newsletters and discuss them at safety meetings: *giving the message once is not enough*;

- Follow up at regular intervals to see that the recommendations made after accidents are being followed, in design as well as operation;

- Remember that the first step down the road to the next accident occurs when someone turns a blind eye to a missing blind;

- Never remove equipment before you know why it was installed. Never abandon a procedure before you know why it was adopted;

- Include important accidents of the past in the training of undergraduates and company employees;

- Before experienced people retire, get them to write down their know-how, especially the information that younger and less experienced people are not aware of;

- Devise better retrieval systems so that we can find, more easily than at present, details of past accidents, in your own and other companies, and recommendations made afterwards ...'

---

1 Kletz, T, Safety and Health Practitioner, December 1996.

12.32   Kletz further identifies the significance of an effective system when he states:

> 'In a typical factory it is often hard to find anyone who has been there for more than ten years. After a while people move, taking their memories with them, and the lessons learnt after an accident are forgotten ... The present enthusiasm for down sizing makes the problem worse; we can manage without the advice and experience when everything seems to be going well, until we fall into the hole in the road that no one knew was there, except old Joe who retired early.'

He further identifies a good example for management to learn from the past such as with the Aberfan disaster in 1966. The village in South Wales was the scene of a colliery tip slide that engulfed part of the village with the result that 144 people were killed, most of whom were children. The underlying cause of the disaster was that the tip had been located over a stream on sloping ground. This is a classic management failure highlighted through an extract from the official report:[1]

> '... forty years before it occurred, we have the basic cause of the Aberfan disaster recognised and warned against. But, as we shall see, it was a warning which went largely unheeded ... Tip slides are not a new phenomena. Although not frequent, they have happened throughout the world and particularly in South Wales for many years, and they have given rise to an extensive body of literature available long before the disaster ... In 1939 there was a tip slide at Cilfynydd in South Wales ... Its speed and destructive effect were comparable with the disaster at Aberfan, but fortunately no school, house or person lay in its path ... It could not fail to have alerted the minds of all reasonably prudent personnel employed in the industry of the dangers lurking in coal tips ... the lesson if ever learnt, was soon forgotten ... In 1944 another tip at Aberfan slid 500–600 feet. Apparently, no one troubled to investigate why it had slipped, but a completely adequate explanation was to hand ... it covered 400 feet of a totally unculverted stream ... Why was there this general neglect? Human nature being what it is, we think the answer to this question lies in the fact that ... there is no previous case of loss of life due to tip stability.'

---

1 Kletz, T, Safety and Health Practitioner, December 1996.

257

Corporate safety culture

12.33   Any organisation is only as good as its culture and if there is a sound safety culture then it has reduced its exposure to accidents and incidents. A corporate safety culture is one that encompasses all areas of the oganisation, from the top [board or managing director] to the most junior of staff. It is not an add on but is the way the business operates on a day-to-day basis and safety has an equal standing to output and profit.

12.34   The important factor when looking at a good culture is to identify leadership management where there is a commitment to safety and that involves the clear adoption of safety attitudes and practices. It will not be sufficient to make bold statements or produce systems if there is a perceived lack of safety management and ownership from the senior management. Such statements and procedures will be rendered as meaningless where the management actions do not match the words and will not aid the development of a safety culture within an organisation.

12.35   Perhaps the most difficult concept for many in senior management positions is that effective safety management will create an environment where worker safety takes precedence over all other matters, including production. This requires the active involvement of senior management as a motivational force for both line management and employees. The objective is to promote the concept of safe activities being associated with good safety performance and the more that safety management is fully integrated into the running of the business (the overall management system) the more effective the organisation will be. A fully integrated system works with the organisation including senior management, the individual managers, supervisors and employees who work within the organisation and the work that is done. They all have equal importance and overlap with each other to equal proportions.

12.36   Senior management will need to focus on a number of proactive activities including giving positive recognition for a good job or performance and empowering subordinates within the decision-making process. This will develop middle management and supervisors with a sense of ownership and ensure continued professional development which in turn leads to effective participation, supportive and trust relationships and – most important – ownership in the organisation.

12.37   There are a number of key issues[1] that apply to all organisations and are imperative for the health and safety culture of any organisation to eliminate if possible, any harm to any person.

- Health and safety must be adopted as part of the organisation's business plan.

- Leadership is the *key,* and that must come from the board.

- Systems that are compatible and understandable must be adopted.

- Everybody in the organisation must know and understand the health and safety standards senior management require.

- Senior management must communicate with those in the organisation to obtain feedback.

- Contractors, part-time and agency staff must be integrated into the corporate system.

- Ownership of safety, health and environment includes everybody from the top to the bottom of the organisation.

12.38   The workforce needs to see a positive corporate culture and that requires clearly defined lines of what is, and what is not, acceptable behaviour. It follows that worker safety will be higher when supervisors have the appropriate authority to influence decisions that affect the safety of those under their supervision. To achieve this, senior management needs to encourage involvement and participation between management, supervisors and employees with regard to health and safety. Therefore, managers and supervisors have different but complimentary roles in the management of health and safety in the workplace. Managers have a wide range of influence over corporate outcomes while supervisors have a narrower focus of influence in the day-to-day activities; being closer to the workforce they will have a greater direct involvement with health and safety issues. The provision of suitable training is a requirement for management to identify and manage so as to develop their employees' skills to enable them to undertake their duties in a competent and safe manner. The individual should fit the job and the job should fit with the employee's abilities. This is a people matter and it must be given the highest priority.

12.39   Safety suggestions[1] and ideas raised by the workforce should get serious attention and consideration. Obtaining this information is so often achieved through an anonymous system because many workers do not want to be identified for putting forward a suggestion. In large organisations with a large workforce management can obtain an input from safety and health committees which will help address health and safety issues. In smaller organisations more care is required in obtaining information as people cannot seek support from a committee situation. It must be remembered that people are involved, people do the work and people get harmed and so they are an important factor. Organisations with a positive health and safety culture will have a high level of morale that has evolved through good safety management. It is shown through accident data that low morale is directly related to management failure to adopt safe systems of work and involve lower levels of management and the workforce in health and safety issues.

1 Welham M, Risk S, *The Poacher and the Gamekeeper*, Total Control (Anglia) Ltd, 2004.

12.40   The evidence clearly shows that ownership of a health and safety culture starts with senior management and they need to be seen to be actively leading and participating in the organisation. Ownership will be measured by a greater priority afforded to safety and the belief that all accidents are preventable. It is a key factor that in organisations where there is a culture of open communication there is a greater trust in management.

12.41   Trust of senior management is linked into numerous aspects of the organisation, including the quality of communication, staff performance and behaviour, problem solving and co-operation. This means that managerial behaviour is important in the development of trust in the employee-manager relationships.

Management structure

12.42   For an organisation to be effective there has to be a management structure with clear responsibilities and reporting lines. It follows that all members of that organisation must have a clear understanding of reporting lines and the extent of their authority. Good organisations have effective structures with safeguards that allow staff with real concerns to be able to express them. An organisation that has the 'open management' philosophy can identify health and safety issues and deal with them before being exposed to management failure.

12.43   It follows that all organisations have a management structure no matter its size. Larger organisations will have a more defined and detailed line management combined with responsibilities and generally have three main levels of management. The first is the corporate (senior level) management, which includes directors or others at a similar level in an organisation. The second level is the middle management who are the interface between the senior management and the supervisory level of management. The third level comprises the first-line managers often known as supervisors, team leaders or foremen. The senior managers are the key influence on an organisation's safety management and it is imperative that they are proactive in establishing the safety culture in the organisation. The key to effective management is that the tiers of management must overlap particularly with regard to communication. See **Figure 4**.

Figure 4:

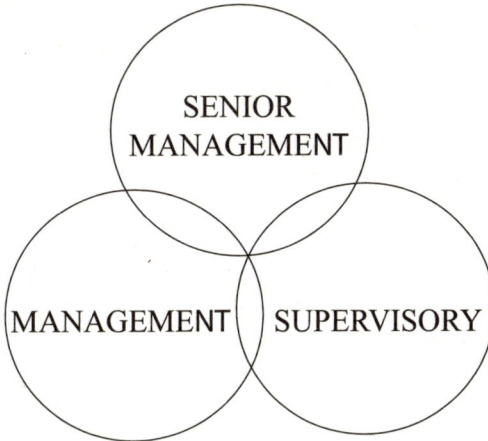

12.44   The more senior a manager the more his position will be concerned with strategy, for example, making long-range plans, formulating policy, modifying the organisation's structure, and initiating new ways of doing things. Decisions at this level usually have a long-term perspective. Middle-level management, such as site, factory or general managers, are primarily concerned with interpreting and implementing the corporate policies and programmes, and they usually have a moderately long-term perspective of one to three years. Low-level managers, such as supervisors and team leaders, are primarily concerned with operational matters, for example structuring, co-ordinating and facilitating work activities, and that occurs on a day-to-day basis. It is imperative that these three levels of management interface regularly with constructive two-way communication and shared information.

Senior management responsibilities

12.45   Senior management duties require them to develop the organisation's rules and regulations and regularly update them. It is also important that both management and staff comply with them and the employees must be seen to be involved, as the rules will protect them. As part of an effective safety culture, management must be visible and undertake formal inspections of the workplace or sites at regular and frequent intervals. Face-to-face communication provides an effective overview of the workplace reality as paperwork audits are not always effective when dealing with people. It is essential that management does not condone unsafe acts and it is important that management is involved with the thorough investigation of all accidents and near misses. They must also ensure that there is a system for record keeping and passing on lessons learned from incident investigations to all staff.

12.46 Management must encourage good housekeeping and environmental conditions as well as provide good and relevant training to ensure a competent workforce, and that includes everybody employed in the organisation. A high priority must be given to safety at any company meeting and it is imperative that in larger organisations there is an active safety committee involving a high-ranking safety advisor, preferably at board level. This shows that there is a commitment to safety through management which will have a powerful influence on workforce safety motivation.

12.47 Through active leadership, workplace safety initiatives combine with worker motivation to promote co-operation so as to develop a positive organisational willingness to co-operate in order to achieve the organisation's goals.

12.48 It is well known that organisations with clear safety objectives tend to be more productive, particularly where the workforce helps to develop interventions rather than simply playing a passive role of compliance. A decentralised approach to safety management has been shown to be the most effective way in which management can promote workforce safety motivation. This also aids the development of a culture where workers take ownership and responsibility for safety and become actively motivated to take personal initiatives in safety.

12.49 The senior management of any organisation sets the standards for how health and safety will be adopted and requires leadership management that is positive and invokes trust and ownership. Failures occur when senior management says one thing but does another, or uses fear motivation or bullying techniques to obtain an objective. Safety and health within an organisation should not be a stand-alone, add on concept, but should be integral to the corporate culture and be seen to be as important as competitiveness, marketing and profitability. In the 'senior management leadership' concept, the three elements of the management must show leadership, trust-ownership and safety which are interlinked as being of equal significance and importance. See **Figure 5**. This is important because if there is a failing in one of the elements then the balance is offset and the concept of senior management leadership is ineffective.

12.50 A critical point of management failure often occurs when there is no management of change, particularly when there are takeovers or mergers. Health and safety may take a reduced presence with individuals in new roles and with new responsibilities placing their focus on fulfilling the new role and meeting the objectives or targets. Often such changes mean a dilution in numbers of staff and those remaining being given additional duties and that can have an impact on safety within the organisation. These changes are often implemented quickly with little communication passing from senior management, leaving staff without a clear understanding of the impact on them and the organisation. This affects individual performance, particularly if individual competencies are weak and workload is increased. The analysis of safety

Figure 5:

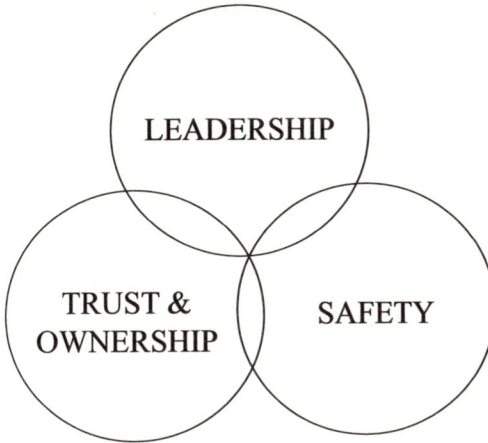

critical tasks and competencies is vital to eliminate potential hazardous situations. In order to reduce the impact of such changes, good effective communication is essential and there must be strong management to make the change happen and to ensure that everyone has the right knowledge and skills.

Middle management responsibilities

12.51 While the senior management can be described as the 'controlling minds' of the organisation, middle management are tasked with implementing the senior management's objectives. The middle management have an essential role to play in the communication path as the senior management find it more difficult to spend time with the workforce as the company grows. It is essential, therefore, that middle management clearly understands that health and safety ranks as a corporate performance measure on the same level as production output and profitability. At all levels of management and supervision the link between good safety and good business must be clear. They must appreciate the effect poor health and safety performance can have on corporate reputation, the possible loss of revenue if customers lose trust and the reduction in profits in the longer term as insurance premiums increase.

Supervisory management responsibilities

12.52 Effective supervisors and team leaders must recognise that health and safety is an integral part of the corporate culture and adopt the concept of openness, participation and teamwork. They hold an important place in the corporate management structure, being involved in planning and influencing decision making whilst controlling the workforce. They fill the gap between senior and middle management and those carrying out the work activities. They need to be fair, participative and value the workforce they are responsible for. To be effective, supervisors and team leaders must communicate and display management skills, in particular, when difficult or complex issues have to be dealt with and they will generally have more detailed knowledge of hazards and the risk involved. Providing that they recognise that safety is a major part of their job they should have the trust of the workforce and, in turn, they should have the trust of management. A failure in this important link can be failure in corporate health and safety practice and could be seen as management failure.

Employees' perceptions

12.53   Employees adopt the values and beliefs of their organisations and it has been shown that an organisation with positive and proactive management engaging with the workforce performs better. People are the key element of an organisation and the social support given to them by managers and supervisors is important, particularly with regard to safety measures in the workplace. Management which has an interest in its employees and treats them with respect regarding their work, will find a workforce that feels appreciated as individuals with a belief that their contribution is valuable to the organisation.

12.54   Evidence shows that companies that have good safety records tend to be more productive and efficient and it requires positive management leadership to convince the workforce that the developments of a positive health and safety culture can improve performance and efficiency. It should be a corporate policy to adopt the 'STOP' culture so that workers are encouraged to stop work if they consider an operation puts them or others at risk of harm.

12.55   High levels of open communication and interaction between workers and management can be identified with positive leadership management. It follows that participative management and time spent by management communicating at the worksite are associated with good safety performance. Top performing companies provide direct and immediate channels of communication and positive employee/management interaction using some form of immediate feedback to motivate their employees.

12.56   It is the employees' perceptions of organisational support and quality of communication that will lead to employees' being willing to engage in safety discussions and enhance safety commitments, which in turn will reduce accident rates. It is also shown that supervisors who use a more participative management style and place importance on team work recognise safety as an important aspect of their role. Supervisors who do not value their staff and do not have a participatory attitude will have safety low on the agenda, if at all. They will operate in an environment of distrust and have a policing system of supervision.

12.57   It is evident that there is a need to integrate senior management, middle management, supervisors and employees into a closed loop style of working. This means that communication flows down through the chain of command and feedback flows back up. In this way senior management will have knowledge of the thinking of the workforce who in turn will have knowledge of the thinking of the senior management. This is valuable as senior management will want the workforce to progress their action plans and the workforce will respond better if it knows why the action plans are being implemented.

Work practice developments

12.58   Work practice developments have been significant in the world of work. Many companies now use contractors to carry out functions that were previously done by direct employees. This has become known as contractorisation[1] and if not managed properly, could lead to increased risks to the workforce and the public. The restructuring of business has resulted in extensive outsourcing of functions which were previously done in-house. Many very large companies have reduced staff numbers with the result that either relatively large specialist companies do much of this outsourced work or it is undertaken by small firms or the self-employed.

---

1   Welham, M, HSE Paper on Contractorisation, 2002.

12.59   A definition of contractorisation used by HSE is:

> 'The process of restructuring or other initiatives carried out by an organisation to enable contractors to be used to replace or augment directly employed staff in performing functions.'

A further development is a wider use of so-called partnering and alliancing arrangements as a response to problems with the adversarial nature of many contracts. This approach can work well but requires a good deal of effort on both sides. This extends to the self-employed including consultants, agency workers and peripatetic or mobile workers. With the advent of more sophisticated information technology systems, many work from home. These workers often do not have the benefit of support and advice from a health and safety organisation and therefore rely on client companies to provide this.

12.60   Contractorisation may lead to less supervision by people who are knowledgeable about the hazards of the plant; contractors may not have access to comprehensive health and safety advice or training; contractors may be under more stress because of the uncertainty of future work; commercial pressures may be allowed to outweigh health and safety considerations and sometimes the riskier work is outsourced. On the other hand, business reorganisation may lead to more efficient working and better health and safety management. Also clients may be able to adopt good health and safety practice from specialist contractors.

12.61   It is therefore evident that the modern world of work includes more contractorisation and different methods of working pose a challenge to both industry and the regulator to ensure risks to health and safety are properly controlled. Court cases have shown that the client will always retain some duties in respect of the health and safety of his employees, the contractor's employees and the public.

Chapter 13

Management of Road Risk

Introduction

13.1   Driving at work covers a wide and diverse range of vehicles. Company representatives driving for an organisation, thousands of van and lorry drivers all ply our roads and could fall under the law of corporate manslaughter in the event of a fatal accident. This means that road risk is a very real problem and it is one that must be managed. Driving at work comes under road traffic offences as well as the Health and Safety at Work etc Act 1974 (HSWA 1974) and there will be cases under the corporate manslaughter offence.

13.2   An article in the Guardian in 2005 bore the headline 'Working drivers responsible for 1,000 road deaths a year.' The article was based on new research undertaken by the Transport Research Institute at Edinburgh's Napier University, the results of which were published in a report, *Factors Influencing the Behaviour of People who Drive at Work*. The report identifies that employees who regularly drive for work are much more likely than other road users to cause accidents. The report shows that employees cause around 1,000 deaths a year, which is almost a third of the UK's annual toll of 3,221 road deaths. These drivers break speed limits, get fined, pick up penalty points and crash more often than other drivers. The causes are determined to be tight deadlines, work-related stress, fatigue, use of mobile phones and lack of driver training for staff.

13.3   Steve Stradling,[1] professor of transport psychology in the Transport Research Institute at Edinburgh's Napier University found that:

- 30% of work drivers questioned had been involved in one or more accidents in the previous three years.

- 56% of their crashes occurred while they were driving for work.

- 15% had been caught speeding during work time over the same period and 10% had been flashed by speed cameras while driving in their leisure time.

- 63% had received penalty points.

- 60% admitted slowing down when they saw cameras, then speeding up for the rest of their journey.

1 Reported by Denis Campbell in *The Observer*, 13 November 2005.

13.4   In the same article it was reported that Edmund King, executive director of the RAC Foundation, considered that some accidents involving work drivers occurred because staff are put under greater pressure by their employers:

> ' "Ten years ago, a salesman may have had to make six calls a day; now it's ten. So when you get in your car, there's more of a temptation to put your foot down," said King. "An employee may hit congestion, be late for a client and miss a sale as a result." '

One of the fundamental problems is that management fails to set realistic targets for those on the road and does not provide training in how to cope with the deteriorating conditions that are evolving on a daily basis. The time/target problem is further compromised with the number of road traffic incidents causing loss of life and blockages on major routes.

Road haulage and transport companies

13.5   Fatal road accidents involving road haulage or transport companies have been the focus of public concern. The law states that the case of *R v*

Adomako[1] provides the basis that involuntary gross negligence manslaughter includes 'motor manslaughter' but as the Road Traffic Act 1988, s 1 specifically covers causing death by dangerous driving, unless the car has been used as a weapon, the charge against the individual driver should usually be one under the Road Traffic Act legislation. In a situation where death has resulted from a road traffic accident and is found to have been caused by a defective vehicle, an investigation can determine if the company, through one of its controlling officers, was responsible for any lack of maintenance of the vehicle concerned. This means that a transport manager might be identified as a 'controlling officer' of the company and if that person has been grossly negligent with regard to the maintenance of a vehicle under their control then that person as well as the company may be open to be prosecuted for manslaughter, following a fatal accident that has occurred because of the dangerous condition of that vehicle.

---

1 [1994] QB 302.

13.6 In 2006 the Health and Safety Commission (HSC)[1] granted the Metropolitan Police powers to visit freight operating companies and enforce provisions of the HSWA 1974. This comes as part of a project to improve road safety which has been devised by the police and Transport for London (TfL), the Freight Operators Recognition Scheme (FOPS). It is a three-year pilot project aimed at encouraging freight operators in London to implement policies and procedures to improve safety, reduce environmental impact and improve efficiency.

---

1 HSB November 2006, No 353.

13.7 The police believe health and safety management failings are an underlying cause of a significant number of accidents. In 2005, there were 3,260 collisions involving goods vehicles, and they accounted for 17% (36) of fatalities on London roads. Experienced Metropolitan Police officers will assist businesses in tackling issues such as illegal use of mobile phones, unsafe vehicles, excessive driver hours and unfit or incompetent drivers. They will also give guidance on areas of legal compliance. The Health and Safety Executive (HSE) plans to second a staff member temporarily to the FOPS scheme to provide training on HSE enforcement policy and techniques of safety management auditing, and to monitor police performance.

13.8 The HSE is now working on a programme, in co-operation with the Department for Transport, to improve understanding of the health and safety management aspects of road risks. It hopes that the FOPS work will contribute to this programme by illuminating links between road-safety violations and employers' safety management failures.

Transport cases

13.9   Workplace manslaughter has already had an impact on transport through a number of cases. Generally these are cases where a driver is involved in a fatal accident and there is a link back to management who have failed to manage the road driving aspect of their business. The cases to date show that, for example, driving hours are often the result of undue pressure placed on drivers to deliver. The driver who breaks the law is open to prosecution but there is now more emphasis on work instructions given by management and whether they exceed what is deemed acceptable and do not put drivers or others at risk. The following cases provide examples of management failure.

Roy Bowles Transport case

13.10   The directors of Roy Bowles Transport were prosecuted for corporate manslaughter. The incident occurred when one of their employees, a driver of an articulated lorry, fell asleep at the wheel allowing his vehicle to crash into the back of an empty skip lorry. As a result it crossed the central reservation landing on top of a Ford Mondeo. Seven vehicles were involved in the resulting pile up, with two people killed. Stephen and Julie Bowles, directors of the company, were accused of being grossly negligent in allowing their driver to spend more that 60 hours a week at the wheel and so breaking the law on driving hours. They were convicted of two charges of manslaughter in that they knew or should have known that the driver, Andrew Cox, was in a *dangerously exhausted state*. Sir Derek Spencer, QC for the prosecution told the court that Mr Cox was an accident waiting to happen and he often worked 60 hours or more without taking proper breaks. He earned a basic wage of £160, but when overtime was added that figure regularly rose to £500 a week. There was a newspaper report that claimed that there was a corporate manslaughter conviction, but that is incorrect.

On 19 November 1999 at the Old Bailey, Stephen and Julie Bowles as directors of the company were each given 12-months prison sentences suspended for two years. Cox, the driver, was jailed for 30 months. This again shows that if directors have knowledge of the activities of their employees and know that by an individual's actions there could be risk to others, they must shoulder responsibility when things go wrong. They were accused of being *grossly negligent* in allowing their driver to spend more than 60 hours a week behind the wheel and breaking the law on driving hours. A report[1] states:

> 'Stephen Bowles and his sister Julie were convicted of two charges of manslaughter, after the court was told that they knew, or should have known, that the driver, Andrew Cox, of Colnbrook, Buckinghamshire, was in a dangerously exhausted state'.

The Bowles case identifies an issue in that only a company can be guilty of corporate manslaughter, with individuals guilty of manslaughter. With no other evidence available the conclusion is drawn that the company was found guilty of the corporate offence with the two individuals being identified as the controlling minds and being found guilty of manslaughter as individuals and sentenced.

---

1 Health and Safety Bulletin, Jan/Feb 2000.

The Paul Browning case

13.11   Paul Browning, a lorry driver, was undertaking deliveries when he killed a man while driving and at the same time composing a text message on his mobile telephone. His concentration was on the message and not the road and he veered into a lay-by where his heavily laden lorry collided with the man. Paul Hammond was standing beside his mother's car talking to her when the lorry struck and dragged him along the road, killing him instantly. On 14 February 2001 at a special hearing at Southend Crown Court, Browning received a five year prison sentence for killing the pedestrian.[3] This is not an *at work* prosecution although Browning was at work at the time. He was sending the message to his girlfriend and not his employer; had that been the case then the company could have been implicated in the offence and faced potential manslaughter charges (see **13.10** above). Every day drivers who are *at work* are using hand held mobile phones to undertake business communications, and there is a growing use of text message phones and e-mail communications used by drivers while *at work* and probably whilst continuing to drive. Companies and their drivers can in the future face corporate manslaughter charges if the offence is committed whilst at work.

Keymark Services

13.12   Following a crash on the M1 in Northamptonshire on 27 February 2002 Melvyn Spree[1] was charged with manslaughter and pleaded guilty to the manslaughter and unlawful killing of Neil Owen and Benjamin Kwapong. Lorry driver Steven Law who worked for Keymark Services had fallen asleep at the wheel and crashed into seven vehicles.

The investigation found that Keymark Services drivers were told to falsify records so they could work longer hours and appear they were complying with the law. The reality was that there was a risk that any of the drivers might fall asleep at the wheel. It was found that at the time of the crash Mr Law's tachograph actually showed his truck at rest at Keymark's depot on the Isle of Sheppey. Following the police investigation all of the company's 10 full-time drivers were prosecuted for a total of 400 different offences of breaching driving regulations and falsifying vehicle records. The drivers were fined for the offences. Three other part-time drivers received official cautions.

At a hearing at Leicester Crown Court in October, Melvyn Spree, 47, from Sheerness, in Kent, admitted the manslaughter and unlawful killing of Mr Owen and Mr Kwapong. Keymark Services pleaded guilty to the manslaughter of the two men.

Melvyn Spree was jailed for seven years for his company's role in a road crash in which three men were killed. Spree's fellow director Lorraine March was jailed for 16 months for conspiracy to falsify driving records, while the company's secretary, 24-year-old Clare Miller, was given 160 hours of community service for the same charge.

---

1 Leathley, A, *The Times*, 20 November 1999.

The Produce Connection case

13.13   A company was fined £30,000 for breaching health and safety legislation as a result of one of its workers dying in a car crash after working 76 hours in four days.

The case is thought to be the first of its kind in the UK because the company involved, The Produce Connection[1] admitted breaching health and safety legislation even though the employee died outside working hours. Mark Fiebig had worked four 19-hour days – starting early in the morning and finishing late at night. He died when his car drifted into the path of an oncoming lorry as he drove home from work in October 2002.

The court heard that Fiebig was thought to be suffering from 'chronic fatigue' and had fallen asleep at the wheel. Prosecutor Pascal Bates said Fiebig had worked 11 days without a day off prior to his fatal crash. During that time he had worked on average 17 hours a day and was getting three to four hours' sleep a night. Bates said other staff were working similarly long hours.

He added:

> 'Workers were paid by the hour. For payroll purposes a daily note was kept of each worker's working hours. [The farm manager] had to be aware, and so did other management.'

Judge Gareth Hawksworth said the company had failed to properly monitor the hours its employees were working. The company admitted failing to ensure the health of workers and the public. Along with the £30,000 it was also ordered to pay £24,000 costs.

---

1 *The Independent*, 15 February 2001.

Wincanton Group

13.14   Following the death of an employee on 11 August 2003 the Wincanton Group Limited pleaded guilty to breaches of the HSWA 1974. The accident involved one of their employees, Michael Brookman who was repairing a lorry which had broken down on the hard shoulder of the northbound M5 in Gloucestershire when the accident happened. At the broken down lorry Brookman found that he did not have the right parts to repair the vehicle and so he left the lorry on the hard shoulder and went to collect the spares he needed. It was seven and a half hours later when he returned to carry out the repair work. It was whilst Brookman was working on the vehicle that a heavy goods vehicle (HGV) travelling along the motorway collided with the lorry and crushed Brookman to death.

The court accepted that Wincanton was not responsible for the accident which killed Brookman, but identified that the company failed to ensure that there was a system in place for training mechanics to carry out roadside repair work safely. Evidence was given to highlight the fact that the firm's mechanics should have been provided with training on assessing roadside risks and implementing a system of work to deal with them safely. The court heard that when Brookman realised that he did not have the correct parts to carry out the repair work, and being unsure how long it would take to retrieve the necessary parts, he should have organised for the vehicle to be removed from the hard shoulder.

An important point was that when Brookman was at the broken down lorry he parked his rescue van in front of the vehicle. Had he been provided with sufficient training, he would have realised that parking his rescue van in front of the lorry was unsafe. He should have parked the van at a sufficient distance behind the lorry, with its hazard lights activated. Following the accident the company had provided suitable safety training for all of its mechanics.

The Wincanton Group Limited was fined £10,000 under the HSWA 1974, s 2 and was ordered to pay prosecution costs of £2,051. At a separate hearing, Alan Mottershead, the driver of the HGV that collided with the lorry Brookman was repairing was jailed for two-and-a-years for causing *death* by dangerous driving after he admitted to falling asleep at the wheel moments before the crash.

Hough Green Garage Ltd

13.15   On 31 December 2003 Scott Allen, an employee of Hough Green Garage Ltd, was recovering a single-deck Volvo B 10 B bus in Liverpool when, as he worked underneath the unsupported vehicle, the air-suspension system failed suddenly and the bus body fell down on him, crushing him to death.

The HSE's investigation found that the garage had trained and encouraged Allen and other employees to work under unsupported buses and to employ an unsafe method of raising the bus body using the vehicle's air-suspension levelling valve. It was not known why Allen was raising the bus at the time of the accident: it was considered that he may have been trying either to prevent the back from grounding as he moved it up onto a recovery trailer, or to remove the brakes, which were stuck. In either case, the system of work was unsafe.

Hough Green Garage and its managing director, David Farrell, denied breaching health and safety legislation but the jury convicted the company of two breaches of the HSWA 1974, s 2(1) for failing to ensure its employees' safety, by training and encouraging them to:

- go under buses without first propping, packing or otherwise supporting the bus body; and

- use the air-suspension levelling valve to raise the suspension and gain additional clearance between the bottom of the bus and the ground.

The company was also convicted of the Management of Health and Safety at Work Regulations 1999, reg 3 in that it failed to carry out a suitable and sufficient risk assessment for roadside vehicle recovery.

Following the trial, on 17 October 2006 the judge fined the company £60,000 for the first breach (s 2) and £30,000 for the second. The judge fined Farrell £10,000 and £4,000 for the two offences by virtue of the HSWA 1974, s 37 after the jury decided that he consented to his company committing those offences. The company was fined a further £6,000 for a breach of the Management of Health and Safety at Work Regulations 1999, reg 3. The judge ordered the garage and Farrell to pay £20,000 and £15,000 costs respectively.

Nightfreight (GB) Ltd

13.16   On 6 February 2002 at Nightfreight's Willenhall site in Staffordshire, Neil Prestage, a lorry driver who worked for WA Rainbow, a franchise of Nightfreight, was on the telephone, standing on the ground near the raised-deck platform of a loading bay when he was hit by a Nightfreight shunt driver reversing an empty trailer into the bay ready for the next shift.

The HSE's investigation found that the company Nightfreight (GB) Ltd,[1] had ignored previous advice on traffic management at this and other sites around the country. They also found that the risk assessment was generic and not specific enough to the site and the activities performed there. The company failed to enforce the strict requirement that people should stay off the ground unless they had legitimate activities. The company also failed to ensure that drivers always used banksmen; instead, it was left to the employees to use one if somebody was about, otherwise they continued without assistance. In addition, general health, safety and transport management at the site was not sufficiently rigorous.

Nightfreight pleaded guilty to breaching the HSWA 1974, s 3(1) in that it had failed to ensure the safety of non-employees. Judge Mitchell fined the company £150,000 and ordered it to pay £91,000 costs. He found that the company had fallen well short of accepted standards and highlighted other aggravating factors, including the loss of life, the absence of a specific risk assessment, the previous HSE warnings, and the significant number of people exposed to risks, including employees as well as non-employees. Mitigating factors including Nightfreight's early guilty plea, full co-operation with the investigation, and timely and effective response were taken into account. Nightfreight claimed that it had spent almost £0.5 million on health and safety improvements since the injury.

---

1 HSB December 2006 No 354.

John Payne – Lane Croup

13.17   John Payne[1] was driving a lorry when it crashed into a line of stationary traffic on 17 October 2005 on the M3 near Basingstoke in Hampshire. As a result he killed 23-year-old Trinity Taylor, whose car was at the back of the queue, and severely damaged six other vehicles. Prior to the crash, Payne's attention was focused on the cab's mobile phone and he failed to notice the queue of traffic, which was visible for 900 metres. He was travelling at 47 mph when he crashed into the traffic and the 7.5-tonne lorry rolled over the top of Taylor's Peugeot 106; she died from chest and head injuries at the scene.

At court, the prosecution described how Payne had told William Fowell, the driver's mate, that he wanted to find out how to use the phone, which was in a cradle, and then started punching in numbers to the keypad. Payne, who worked for transport firm Lane Croup, was delivering jacuzzis and baths.

Payne had admitted causing death by dangerous driving at an earlier hearing. On 7 August 2006, Recorder Michael Brodrick sentenced Payne to four years in prison. He also disqualified him from driving for seven years and ordered him to take an extended driving test.

---

1 HSB October 2006 No 352.

R&B Drivers

13.18   Raymond Knapman and Robert Legg, who ran Plymouth-based agency R&B Drivers, were convicted of criminal offences following a collision between two articulated goods vehicles on 6 December 2003.[1] Mark Chadbourne, supplied by R&B, had exceeded his legal driving hours when he drove into another lorry.

Judge Brodrick, sentencing at Winchester Crown Court in January 2006, jailed Knapman for two and a half years after he admitted eight counts of obtaining property by deception by taking money from hauliers for drivers' services when he knew they had already exceeded their legal hours working for another company. He also admitted breaching HSWA 1974, s 3 in that as a self-employed person he failed to ensure the safety of non-employees. Legg was fined £1,000 with £1,500 costs after pleading guilty to the same HSWA 1974, s 3 charge.

An employment tribunal in Exeter banned Raymond Knapman for the maximum term of 10 years, and Robert Legg for five years, following an application by the Department of Trade and Industry under the Employment Agencies Act 1973, s 3A, which allows a tribunal to issue an order prohibiting a person from running an employment agency or business for a specified time if it is satisfied that, on account of misconduct or for any other sufficient reason, the person is unsuitable to do so.

R&B, which supplied 40 to 50 drivers to firms across the country, consistently provided drivers that had already worked a 12-hour shift for one company to work a 12-hour night shift for another. The police identified that there was scant regard for the safety of their drivers and the public at large. They determined that they encouraged law-breaking on a massive scale while realising large financial benefits. The Crown Court heard that drivers said they had told Knapman that they had fallen asleep at the wheel and some had taken caffeine tablets to stay awake. The outcome was that he punished some drivers with fewer shifts if they refused to work.

---

1 HSB No 360 July 2007.

Foreign lorries

13.19   The Transport & General Workers' Union, the Freight Transport Association (FTA) and the Road Haulage Association (RHA) have raised concerns about the increasing evidence that shows vehicles visiting the UK are less roadworthy than in the past. Evidence also shows that the number of road traffic offences by foreign lorries is increasing, notably drivers' hours breaches and overloading; and that foreign lorries are now involved in a disproportion-ately high number of accidents. Richard Turner, FTA chief executive, said:

> 'The number of foreign lorries working in the UK is constantly rising – something like one in seven of the heaviest vehicles on our roads is from overseas. It is vital that the operating conditions of these vehicles, and the behaviour of their drivers, match the high standards we expect of our home fleet.'

13.20   The Road Haulage Task Group, FTA and RHA have called for foreign lorries working in the UK to be required to register details of ownership and vehicle records in order to assist the work of UK enforcement authorities. At present VOSA and the police have instant access to information about UK-based vehicles but little or no information regarding foreign vehicles. This is particularly relevant when the prospect of UK companies facing a corporate manslaughter charge is increasing and there are no such implications for foreign companies.

The white van

13.21   The government is to spend £1.3 million on providing driving lessons for some of the UK's 200,000 van drivers, to make them more considerate behind the wheel. They will also teach 'white van man' – the stereotypical aggressive driver – how to reduce fuel consumption by using the right gears and better braking. Launching the scheme, the then Transport Secretary Alistair Darling said:

> 'I think I've been driven mad on a number of occasions … if we can persuade the driving population as a whole to drive better, you'll get a cleaner, safer, cheaper drive, and that must be a good thing.'

Company cars

13.22   Companies with employees using their own cars on business are responsible for ensuring such vehicles are 'fit for the purpose' and need to maintain records to show that this has been done.[1] Failure to do so could make senior managers liable in the event of a serious accident involving staff and that will include possible prosecution for corporate manslaughter. It is estimated that about 5 million people currently use their own cars on business in the UK, and government figures show there are around 20 road deaths a week involving people at work.

---

1 Adele Burton, Fleet special issue, 7 September 2006.

277

13.23   The workplace encompasses employees who use their own cars when on business and that makes the employer responsible for ensuring their health and safety in these circumstances. This applies even where drivers have taken cash in place of a car, because the company employing them has a duty of care to them while on business, in particular by ensuring that the vehicle they are using is fit for purpose. In the case where employers use rental cars for employees to undertake their workplace activities the responsibility for ensuring the vehicle is fit for purpose rests solely with the rental company.

13.24   The problem arises where an employer, knowing or believing a vehicle to be in an unsafe condition, orders an employee to drive the vehicle and there is a fatal accident; then there could be a case of causing death by dangerous driving. Businesses most at risk are small and medium-sized enterprises (SMEs) where the directors or senior management may not be aware of the Health & Safety Executive (HSE)'s Driving at Work guidelines and regulations affecting staff when travelling on business.

13.25   Guidelines such as the HSE's are now becoming a legal requirement and businesses must adopt formal procedures to ensure employees' cars are roadworthy. They can opt for an alternative company transport policy such as using company provided vehicles (e g rented cars) for employee use. This means that employees do not use their own cars other than to get to and from work.

Dangerous activity

13.26   Road traffic accidents account for the majority of lost lives in any sector. If people driving at work who are involved in road traffic accidents were included in the annual HSE health and safety statistics, the figures would be considered unacceptable by the public. The reality is that people are at work and they are having accidents and because it is not a high priority for the HSE, sitting as it does in the road traffic figures, many do not consider it as part of their health and safety obligations.

13.27   In an article John Maslen[1] states:

'Driving is one of the most dangerous activities, in health and safety terms, that employees undertake, yet it is often dismissed as no more than an inconvenient break until the next appointment or meeting.'

To support that statement he provides some interesting figures:

'In 2004, the latest year for which figures are available, 3,221 people died on Britain's roads, a further 31,130 were seriously injured and another 246,489 received slight injuries a grand total of 280,840 people, or 64 an hour, all day every day.

About 183,858 of those injuries occurred in cars, either to drivers or passengers, and official research by the Work-related Road Safety Task Group suggests one-third of those involved were at work at the time. In fact, according to safety experts at the Royal Society for the Prevention of Accidents, car and van drivers who cover 25,000 miles a year as part of their job are at about the same risk of being killed at work as workers in construction and quarrying.'

He continues:

'Experts warn of the iceberg effect, where the £1,000 cost of accident repair is more like £5,000 when you include replacement cars, missed appointments and so on. Safer drivers tend to look after their cars better too, so firms get lower maintenance costs and reduced fuel bills of more than 10% in some cases ... Despite this, a study of 1,000 motorists by the Institute of Advanced Motorists earlier this year revealed that seven out of 10 said their employers neither offered nor required medical check-ups, a driver risk assessment or training on basic vehicle safety checks. And six out of 10 said they had not been offered, or been required to take, a basic eyesight test.'

1 Maslen, John, *Accountancy Age*, June 2006.

The Department for Transport

13.28   The Department for Transport has published a document entitled *Driving at Work*,[1] which lists the key issues companies need to think about when it comes to staff transport. There is a focus on the requirement to carry out risk assessments to ensure the health and safety of employees, while they are at work, and to other people who may be affected by an organisation's work activities.

1 www.majorhazards.gov.uk INDG 382 *Driving at Work*.

13.29   Following a fatal at work road accident the police use the Road Death Investigation Manual, which states that all road deaths should be treated as unlawful killings until proved otherwise. The best defence for any organisation is not to have any road related accidents and crashes. In adopting this approach staff need to be trained to be road safe and the company must ensure that it has done everything it can to meet its duty of care to drivers. The savings will be in money and lives, a valuable contribution if it could avoid the potential of a corporate manslaughter prosecution.

Legal changes

13.30   Corporate manslaughter and corporate homicide will encompass any organisation who employs staff who drive as part of their work. The driving context means those who drive a car as a way of doing their business, such as nurses doing home visits, sales representatives or a manager or director visiting another part of the organisation. The more accepted workplace vehicles of vans and trucks are included and there are prosecution cases as examples. The police, when attending a traffic accident will determine if any of the drivers are at work and where they are, take the investigation to the company.

13.31   When investigating a potential case of corporate manslaughter the police and the HSE will look into every aspect of a company's fleet policy and procedures. This means that if the police find the fleet manager has been negligent, such as failing to ensure that the fleet was fit for purpose and roadworthy, drivers were correctly licensed, competent and familiar with their vehicles, they could also face prosecution. Depending on the corporate structure it may be the fleet manager's responsibility to advise the board members of legislative and policy changes regarding company car drivers.

13.32   Fleet managers may be well aware of the work-related road risk management issues, but are often less aware of what practical measures can be taken to manage them. For many managers it will be getting the message across to senior managers and board members, to emphasise that the organisation needs to manage the risks faced by its employees on the road that will be difficult.

Management of road risks

13.33   It is the directors and senior management who have the responsibility to evaluate whether work-related road safety is being managed effectively. This means that where somebody who is employed drives any form of transport there must be a driving management system in place. The HSE[1] provide guidance for management to focus on and key issues include but are not limited to the following.

---

1 *Driving at Work – Managing work related road safety* HSE INDG 382.

The driver

13.34

- Drivers, who are employees, are an important part of a company's driving policy and procedures. They must be provided with information and understand what is expected of them.

- Management must be satisfied that drivers are competent and capable of doing their work in a way that is safe for them and other people.

- Management must ensure that the employees have relevant previous experience.

- It must be identified whether the job requires anything more than a current driving licence, valid for the type of vehicle to be driven.

- Company recruitment procedures must include appropriate pre-appointment checks such as taking up references.

- Management must check the validity of the driving licence on recruitment and periodically thereafter.

- In particular management must check the validity of any LCV/PSV driving entitlements as part of the recruitment procedures and periodically thereafter. Such entitlements may not have been restored after a period of disqualification.

- Management must ensure that their at-work drivers are aware of company policy on work-related road safety, and that they understand what is expected of them.

- It may be relevant for policy documents to be accompanied by written instructions and guidance and/or training sessions or group meetings.

- The company policy must specify what standards of skill and expertise are required for the circumstances of the particular job.

- Management must ensure that these standards are met.

Driver training

13.35   Management must ensure that all drivers of company vehicles or driving on behalf of company are properly trained. Therefore, management must ensure that they:

- evaluate whether those that drive at work require additional training to carry out their duties safely;

- provide induction training for drivers;

- arrange for drivers to be trained giving priority to those at highest risk, eg those with high annual mileage, poor accident records, or young drivers.

Drivers' skills

13.36   There are some essential drivers' skills which management must ensure are known and adopted. Money has to be budgeted for training and should include refresher training. Topics to be addressed include:

- Identify whether drivers need to know how to carry out routine safety checks such as those on lights, tyres and wheel fixings.

- Ensure that drivers know how to correctly adjust safety equipment, eg seat belts and head restraints.

- Drivers must know how to use anti-lock brakes (ABS) properly.

- Drivers have a responsibility to check washer fluid levels before starting a journey.

- Drivers must know how to ensure safe load distribution, such as when undertaking multi-drop operations.

- It is essential that drivers know what actions to take to ensure their own safety following the breakdown of their vehicle.

- Management must provide a handbook for drivers giving advice and information on road safety.

- Management and drivers must be aware of the dangers of fatigue.

- Drivers must know what they should do if they start to feel sleepy.

- Drivers must be fully aware of the height of their vehicle, both laden and empty.

Health and fitness

13.37 A very important management function is to ensure that your drivers are sufficiently fit and healthy to undertake the driving task required of them and not put themselves or others at risk. Some factors include:

- Management must ensure that drivers of heavy lorries, for which there are legal requirements for medical examination, have the appropriate medical certificate.

- Although there is no legal requirement, management must decide whether those at-work drivers who are most at risk should also undergo regular medicals.

- Management must ensure that staff who drive at work are aware that they must be able satisfy the eyesight requirements set out in the Highway Code.

- The company policy must identify that staff should not drive, or undertake other duties, while taking a course of medicine that might impair their judgment.

The vehicle

13.38   Management are responsible for all vehicles driven by staff for work purposes and must ensure that they are fit for the purpose for which they are used. This includes company management cars. Management issues include:

- The determination of which vehicles are best for driving and public health and safety when purchasing new or replacement vehicles.

- The vehicle fleet is suitable for the job in hand.

- Consider providing leased or hire vehicles.

- Ensure that privately owned vehicles are not used for work purposes unless they are insured for business use and, where the vehicle is over three years old, they have a valid MOT certificate.

- Vehicles are maintained in a safe and fit condition.

- There are adequate maintenance arrangements in place.

- Ensure maintenance and repairs are carried out to an acceptable standard.

- Planned/preventative maintenance is carried out in accordance with manufacturers' recommendations.

- Ensure that drivers know how to carry out basic safety checks.

- Ensure that vehicles do not exceed maximum load weight.

- Ensure that goods and equipment which are to be carried in a vehicle are properly secured and not allowed to move around freely or fall from the vehicle.

- Windscreen wipers are inspected regularly and replaced as necessary.

- Safety equipment is appropriate, properly fitted and maintained.

- Seatbelts and head restraints are fitted correctly and function properly.

- Drivers have access to information that will help them reduce road risks.

- Take account of ergonomic considerations before purchasing or leasing new vehicles.

- Provide drivers with guidance on good posture and, where appropriate, on how to set their seat correctly.

The journey

13.39   Management must plan routes thoroughly and where possible use the safest routes which are more appropriate for the type of vehicle undertaking the journey. Motorways are the safest roads and although minor roads may be fine for cars, they are less safe and could present difficulties for larger vehicles. Route planning must take account of overhead restrictions such as bridges, tunnels, level crossings, and other hazards which may present dangers for long or high vehicles. Other issues that must be managed include:

- Driving at work schedules are realistic. The Highway Code recommends that drivers should take a 15-minute break every two hours. Professional drivers must of course comply with drivers' hours rules.

- Periods when drivers are most likely to feel sleepy are planned for in work schedules.

- There are effective procedures to stop employees from driving if they feel sleepy even if this might upset delivery schedules.

- There are regular checks of tachographs to ensure drivers are not cutting corners and putting themselves and others at risk.

- Drivers are not put under pressure and encouraged to take unnecessary risks, eg to exceed safe speeds because of agreed arrival times.

- Drivers can make an overnight stay, rather than having to complete a long road journey at the end of the working day.

- Avoid periods of peak traffic flow.

- Make sufficient allowances for new trainee drivers.

- Advise staff working irregular hours of the dangers of driving home from work when they are excessively tired.

- Consider eliminating long road journeys or reduce them by combining with other methods of transport, for example by train to a point for local distribution by van or lorry.

Weather conditions

13.40 Management must give sufficient consideration to adverse weather conditions, such as snow or high winds, when planning journeys. This may mean that journey times and routes have to be rescheduled to take account of adverse weather conditions. Other management factors include:

- Vehicles are properly equipped to operate in poor weather conditions such as being fitted with anti-lock brakes.

- Drivers understand the action that they should take to reduce risk.

- Drivers do not feel pressurised to complete journeys where weather conditions are exceptionally difficult.

13.41   It is very clearly a matter for management to manage its driving activities. With the police reviewing if the driver was at work following a road vehicle accident any failings may involve not only the driver but also the company. Some of the cases above show how the link can and will be made.

Chapter 14

Accident and Incident Investigation

Introduction

14.1   The evidence required to prove a case of corporate manslaughter will be that of management failure. Such a charge will follow an incident with fatalities and therefore it is vital that every organisation investigates accidents and incidents and acts upon the findings. Accidents and incidents have many causes and what may appear to be bad luck, such as being in the wrong place at the wrong time, can, on analysis, be seen as a chain of failures and errors that lead almost inevitably to an accident or incident; this is often called the Domino effect. There may be concerns about litigation following an accident or incident which may make an employer think that it is better not to investigate, but failings cannot be rectified if it is not known what went wrong! The fact that there was a thorough investigation into an accident and that there was remedial action to prevent further accidents would demonstrate to a court that an organisation has a positive attitude to health and safety. The investigation findings will also provide essential information for the insurers in the event of a claim.

14.2   Learning lessons from near misses can prevent costly accidents both in terms of loss of life, equipment, premises and financial implications. The Piper Alpha oil platform, *Herald of Free Enterprise* ferry capsize and the numerous rail crashes that have occurred are examples of situations where management had failed to recognise, and act on, previous failings in the system. This means that there is a real need to investigate accidents or incidents for a number of reasons.

Legal reasons for investigating

14.3   There are legal reasons for investigating which include the following.

- To ensure the organisation is operating within the law and in particular to comply with the Reporting of Injuries, Diseases and Dangerous Occurrences Regulations 1995 (RIDDOR).[1]

- The Management of Health and Safety at Work Regulations 1999, reg 5,[2] requires employers to plan, organise, control, monitor and review their health and safety arrangements. Health and safety investigations form an essential part of this process.

- Following the Woolf Report on civil action, employers are expected to make full disclosure of the circumstances of an accident to the injured parties considering legal action and that can only be achieved through an accident investigation.

---

1 SI 1995/3163.
2 SI 1999/3242.

Valuable information can be gained from an investigation to gain an understanding of how and why things went wrong and of the ways people can be exposed to substances or conditions that may affect their health. It will provide an overview of what really happens and how work is really done. Workers may find short cuts to make their work easier or quicker and may ignore rules; management needs to be aware of what is happening. Senior managers will be able to use the information to identify deficiencies in an organisation's risk management, which will enable improvement in the management of risk in the future and to learn lessons which will be applicable to other parts of the organisation.

14.5   This will have the positive result of preventing business losses due to disruption, stoppage, lost orders and the costs of criminal and civil legal actions. Employee morale and attitude towards health and safety will improve and they are likely to be more co-operative in implementing new safety precautions if they have been involved in any decisions and can see that problems are dealt with. There will be a development of managerial skills which can be readily applied to other areas of the organisation.

RIDDOR

14.6 For those accidents and dangerous occurrences that are reportable under the provisions of RIDDOR, this information must be notified to the Incident Contact Centre (ICC). Although phoning is the quickest and most convenient way of informing the enforcing authorities, whether the Health and Safety Executive (HSE) or local authority (LA), a report can be sent via e-mail or by conventional mail.

Sydney Dekker option

14.7 Through his book, *The Field Guide to Human Error in Accident Investigation*, Sydney Dekker[1] explains that rather than place the blame for an accident on human error, an investigation should consider that it is a symptom of trouble deeper inside a company system. He suggests that to explain failure, do not try to find where people went wrong, but find how people's assessments and actions made sense at the time, given the circumstances that surrounded them. It must be considered that complex systems are basically safe but they need to be protected from unreliable people.

---

1 Ashgate, 2002.

14.8 Dekker explains that to understand failure, we must first understand our reactions to failure. Following an accident the questions that most people would ask are: 'How could they not have noticed and how could they not have known?'

Generally investigations examine what people could have done to prevent the incident and what people should have done, or failed to do, to prevent the incident. The problem is that investigations explain a part of the past, yet are conducted in the present and thus are inevitably influenced by it. One of the most important factors is that of hindsight. In terms of an accident it provides a means of being able to look back, from the outside, on a sequence of events that lead to an outcome that is already known. It provides almost unlimited access to the real situation that surrounded people at the time. The objective is to pinpoint what people missed and should not have missed; what they did not do but should have done.

14.9 Accident reports generally describe in fine detail the routes and options that the people in question did not take and so in order to explain why a failure occurred, errors are looked for. Explaining failure and making wrong judgments is possibly a good place to start. However, these decisions, judgments, perceptions are bad or wrong or inaccurate only from hindsight. When viewed from the inside of a situation, decisions, judgments and perceptions are just that: decisions, judgments and perceptions. The outcome will be that a bad outcome will equate to a bad process and bad processes sometimes lead to bad outcomes however, good processes also sometimes lead to bad outcomes.

14.10   It is important to consider that with many accidents people were doing exactly the sorts of things they would usually be doing which are the things that usually lead to success and safety. This would indicate that people are doing what makes sense given the situational indications, operational pressures and organisational norms existing at the time and accidents are seldom preceded by bizarre behaviour.

14.11   The point of an investigation is not to find where people went wrong but to understand why their assessments and actions made sense at the time. People have goals and they are in a situation to get a job done, to achieve a particular aim. People have knowledge and they use it to interpret what goes on around them. It is people's goals and knowledge together that determine their focus of attention.

'Near miss' incidents

14.12   There are numerous incidents that occur everyday in workplaces where nobody is harmed, often due to good luck; this is what is termed as a 'near miss' incident. The reporting of near misses is to be encouraged so as to learn from them and provide remedies before somebody is harmed. Therefore, investigating near misses is valuable and it is much easier than investigating accidents. A constructive investigation is not an end in itself, but the first step in engineering out future accident or incidents. This means that a good investigation will enable general lessons to be learned which can be applied across an organisation. The investigation should identify why the existing risk control measures failed and what improvements or additional measures are needed. It should be seen as a learning opportunity before somebody is harmed.

The decision to investigate

14.13   Having been notified of an accident/incident and been given basic information on what happened, management must decide whether it should be investigated and if so, to what extent. It is the potential consequences and the likelihood of the accident or incident recurring that should determine the level of investigation, not simply the injury or ill health suffered on this occasion. The causes of a near miss can have potential for causing injury and ill health and when making decisions lessons must be learned.

Details of the accident must be recorded in an accident book and there needs to be a decision as to the scale of the investigation. Management must decide who will carry out the investigation, the resources required and brief the investigation team.

14.14   There are potentially four levels of investigation which are appropriate for an accident/incident. While line management and supervisors are active participants in undertaking investigations they should have a level of competence for what is required. This means that they should have some training and be familiar with the corporate accident investigation requirements.

1   In a minimal level investigation, the relevant supervisor will look into the circumstances of the event and try to learn any lessons which will prevent future occurrences.

2   A low level investigation will involve a short investigation by the relevant supervisor or line manager into the circumstances and immediate, underlying and root causes of the accident/incident, to try to prevent a recurrence and to learn any general lessons.

3   A medium level investigation will involve a more detailed investigation by the relevant supervisor or line manager, the health and safety adviser and employee representatives and will look for the immediate, underlying and root causes.

4   A high level investigation will involve a team-based investigation, involving supervisors or line managers, health and safety advisers and employee representatives. It will be carried out under the supervision of senior management or directors and will look for the immediate, underlying, and root causes.

14.15   Senior management have responsibility for the organisation and they need to ensure that they have staff that can undertake the investigation and that they are suitably informed of the outcomes of all aspects of the investigation, the findings and remedial proposals. It may well be that senior management are the only people who can direct the financial expenditure to put in place remedial actions.

The investigation

14.16   With any investigation it is essential that the management and the workforce are fully involved. Depending on the level of the investigation, the size of the organisation, the supervisors, line managers, health and safety professionals, union safety representatives, employee representatives and senior management/directors should have an involvement, even if it is only a watching brief. As well as being a legal duty, it has been found that where there is full co-operation and consultation with union representatives and employees, the number of accidents is half that of workplaces where there is no such employee involvement.

14.17   The investigation team must include people who have the necessary investigative skills to gather and record information and skills in interviewing, evaluating and analysing. Management must ensure that the team has sufficient time and resources to enable them to carry out the investigation efficiently. It is essential that the investigation team is either led by, or reports directly to a senior manager with the authority to make decisions and act on their recommendations.

14.18   The key element of an investigation will involve an analysis of all the information available. That will include the scene of the incident, the accounts of witnesses and risk assessments, procedures and instructions, to identify what went wrong and determine what steps must be taken to prevent the accident or incident from happening again. It is important for everybody involved to be open, honest and objective throughout the investigation process. Preconceived ideas about the process, the equipment or the people involved in an accident or incident may obscure the real causes. A good investigator will question everything and avoid blaming individuals.

No blame

14.19   Attempting to apportion blame before the investigation has started is counterproductive, because people become defensive and unco-operative. Only after the investigation has been completed is it appropriate to consider whether any individuals acted inappropriately. It is important to note that investigations that conclude that operator error was the sole cause are rarely acceptable. Underpinning the 'human error' there will be a number of underlying causes that created the environment in which human errors were inevitable. For example:

- inadequate training and supervision;
- poor equipment design;
- lack of management commitment;
- poor attitude to health and safety.

The root causes of accidents or incidents are almost inevitably management, organisational or planning failures.

Action following an accident or incident

14.20   There are three key elements that must be adopted immediately following an accident and incident:

1   Emergency response:

- take prompt emergency action (e g first aid, alert emergency services if appropriate);

- make the area safe (in some cases this may need to be done first).

2   Initial report:

- preserve the scene as the authorities may want to investigate; if it is a fatal accident/incident the police will attend and until advised otherwise it is a crime scene;

- record the names of the people, equipment involved, the names of the witnesses and open an accident/incident file;

- report the accident/incident to the person responsible for health and safety who will decide what further action (if any) is needed. Management must be informed and be proactive in supporting those dealing with the incident.

3   Initial assessment and investigation response.

4   Report the accident/incident to the regulatory authority if appropriate.

If there is a death then the police must be informed followed by the HSE or LA. The site must be made safe but left undisturbed until advised otherwise because it is a potential crime scene.

Management system failings

14.21   If the investigation identifies that errors with failings of company policies and procedures contributed to the accident or incident, then careful consideration must be given as to how to deal with the information. Human factors or failings must be addressed if there is to be value in the investigation. The whole objective of an investigation is to learn the lessons from the failure and to take appropriate action to prevent recurrences, through suitable risk control measures. This will not be achievable unless the workforce trusts management enough to co-operate and participate in the investigation and subsequent processes.

14.22   Placing the blame on one or more individuals is counter-productive and runs the risk of alienating the workforce and undermining the safety culture, crucial to creating and maintaining a safer working environment. This is particularly important if the workforce believes that management has failed in its role and is a contributory cause of the accident or incident and see the blame being put on the workforce.

14.23 A senior manager must speak to those involved and explain how the investigation has identified that their action(s) contributed to the accident/incident. In a non-confrontational situation they should be invited to explain why they did what they did. This may not only help a better understanding of the reasons behind the immediate causes of the accident or incident, but may indicate areas showing an underlying cause. These could cover a range of topics such as that the production deadline was short, and removing the guards saved valuable time or that the workload is too great for one person.

14.24 Management has to make a formal decision about what course of action needs to be taken with individuals. There are reasons for considering that unless there was a deliberate and malicious violation or sabotage of workplace safety precautions, it may be counter-productive to take disciplinary action against those involved. Management must adopt a fair and just system where people are held to account for their behaviour, without being unduly blamed. In any event, management must recognise that the regime of supervision and monitoring of performance should have detected and corrected unsafe behaviours.

Influencing human behaviour

14.25 When considering how to avoid human failings, bear in mind the fact they do not happen in isolation. If human failings are identified as a cause of an accident/incident, consider the following factors that can influence human behaviour.

1   Job factors:
   - the evaluation of how much attention is needed for the task because both too little and too much could lead to higher error rates;
   - other activities going on that divide attention or distract from the prime task;
   - inadequate procedures or instructions are provided;
   - no evaluation of time available for the task.

2   Human factors:
   - physical ability to undertake a task to include factors such as size and strength;

- sufficient competence comprising knowledge, skill and experience;
- individual factors such as fatigue, stress, morale, alcohol or drugs.

3   Organisational factors:

- work pressure, long hours;
- availability of sufficient resources;
- the quality and competence of supervision;
- management's real belief in health and safety and a positive safety culture.

4   Plant and equipment factors:

- the clarity and simplicity of reading and understanding controls;
- is the equipment designed to detect or prevent errors (such as that with the different-sized connectors which are used for oxygen and acetylene bottles to prevent errors in connecting the hoses)?
- is the workplace layout safe and user-friendly?

Every organisation has people engaged in some form of activity and while technology and automation has taken over many riskier activities, people are often controlling the equipment and have to make decisions that a machine is unable to do. This may well be a weak link and needs to be addressed. Whatever the failing it will be people who make the decisions and the outcome if there is an accident or incident will affect people.

Positive approach

14.26   An organisation that has a positive and proactive health and safety culture will reduce the potential of high costs in terms of finance and resources following accidents/incidents. If there is an accident/incident it needs to be investigated and outcomes recorded and this also applies to contractors and subcontractors. Co-operate with the authorities if they are involved. Be proactive in monitoring performance so as to reduce the likelihood of there being an accident/incident. Remember that if there have been injuries or a fatality then there is a human element. The injured parties and/or family etc must be kept informed as to what is being done.

14.27   The initial purpose of the investigation is to prevent similar accidents in the future and to determine if any health and safety laws have been breached. At this point if the HSE or LA officer considers that there is evidence of a serious individual offence then the police will be notified and they will take the lead in the investigation for any individual offences.

14.28   Some investigations are straightforward and progress can be made within a reasonable time. Others are more complex and the decision as to whether to prosecute may be delayed until after the inquest. If there has been an injury or fatality the inspector will speak to the family involved and keep them informed about progress. The amount of detail about the case that can be given throughout this period may be limited if a prosecution is likely to follow. The case cannot be discussed and the inspector is not allowed to answer questions. During this period the case is 'sub judice' which precludes information being used or discussed prior to the case reaching court.

Authorities' accident investigation

14.29   As the result of an accident in connection with work, the HSE or LA can undertake an investigation. Priority will be given to fatal and serious accidents and will be dependent upon the availability of resources. The HSE or LA will investigate to determine the cause and whether there were breaches of health and safety legislation. If during their investigation the HSE or LA discover evidence that could make an individual culpable of a more serious offence, the case can be referred back to the police. This will include cases of individual reckless killing and/or perverting the course of justice. In the event of an accident it is expected that an undertaking will carry out its own investigation so as to identify the cause and introduce appropriate measures to ensure that it does not reoccur.

14.30   The authorities will collect evidence that will form the basis of a prosecution case if such an option is adopted. Evidence consists of witness statements; documentation; physical evidence and evidence of the previous character of the organisation and/or individuals.

14.31   Inspectors have the power to take possession of any article or sub-stance in the premises, which appears to have caused or be likely to cause danger to health and safety. The owner of the item is given a 'Taking into Possession Notice' identifying the item and stating that the object has been taken under Health and Safety at Work etc Act 1974 (HSWA 1974), s 20(2)(i) powers. If the item cannot be moved the inspector can still take possession and will require that nobody touches or tampers with it, as it could be evidence for a prosecution. The powers under HSWA 1974, s 20 extend to premises, or enable any part of them to be left undisturbed for as long as is reasonably necessary for the purposes of an investigation. A notice to this effect can be issued if there is any doubt about compliance. As part of the investigation an inspector can require any documents to be produced which may be relevant to the investiga-tion. To fulfil the above procedures an inspector can take a police officer to the premises to enter and take possession of the items.

Witness statements

14.32 Witness statements are taken from those having first hand knowledge of what occurred, who have seen or been part of the accident. Information obtained will aid determination of the sequence of events and the witness's ability to judge the risks and avoid the risks. This may be in the form of training, instruction and supervision. Management will also be interviewed because of their background knowledge of the systems of work that were in place and any control measures in place to ensure safety. Those being interviewed should be treated with courtesy and, where possible, the interview should be conducted in a private room; if that is not possible, then a quiet private area should be sought. The inspector will explain why a statement is being taken and how it could be used in due course. All statements should be written and signed in ink, and any alterations should be identified, crossed out and initialled by the person being interviewed. There are safeguards for the witness, who cannot be intimidated by the inspector to alter or withdraw evidence through bribery, threats or improper pressure.

Voluntary statement

14.33 An investigation requires the gathering of witness evidence and this can include obtaining voluntary witness statements. When obtaining a voluntary statement an inspector would not invoke the HSWA 1974, s 20 powers and would simply ask the witness to provide information, which is written down, signed and dated. The witness is under no obligation to make the statement and no warnings or cautions are made. However, if the inspector deems the evidence important to the investigation the HSWA 1974, s 20 power could be used if the witness is reluctant to provide a statement.

Involuntary statement

14.34 Under the HSWA 1974, s 20 (2)(j) an inspector can compel a person to answer questions. That person is required to sign a declaration of the truth of those answers, but the answers will not be admissible against that person or their spouse. Inspectors may not refer to their HSWA 1974, s 20 powers so as not to be seen to be repressive or authoritarian, but if challenged they will produce their warrant and declare their powers. All witnesses are entitled to have another person present at the interview; that person cannot become involved in the discussions between the witness and the inspector or influence what is being said. It is intended to be a comfort factor for the witness. If the inspector does not wish the other person to be present they can invoke their HSWA 1974, s 20 powers to exclude the person while still requiring the witness to make a statement. The witness can request a copy of their statement; however, if a defence solicitor requests a copy it will only be provided if the witness gives written and signed authority for it to be made available. The statement is sent to the witness, leaving it to them to forward to their legal representative who may have been provided by the organisation; the witness may be against the statement being forwarded to such a person, fearing that it may be passed on to the organisation. If a witness has a visual or hearing impediment, reading difficulties or is non English speaking there may be another person present to assist.

14.35 Because it is a written statement the inspector will talk through what information is sought and make notes. The statement is then written on a form LP7 and continuation form LP8, preferably using the witness's own words, reflecting what was actually said. If during the interview the witness gives evidence that could incriminate them, the inspector will terminate the interview and caution the witness. To continue gathering evidence from a witness in this situation will require the statement to be taken under Police and Criminal Evidence Act 1984 (PACE) rules.

PACE statement

14.36 A statement is taken from anybody who could be prosecuted and that can include directors or other officers of a company. Questioning will be done under the Police and Criminal Evidence Act 1984, s 67(9) which places a duty on persons other than police officers who are charged with the duty of investigating offences or charging offenders to have regard to any relevant provisions of the PACE Code of Practice. The interviews are tape-recorded and the person to be interviewed is advised to have a solicitor to accompany them. As this interview is voluntary, the person being interviewed can leave at any time and does not have to answer the questions. Unlike the police, the HSE or LA inspectors do not have powers of arrest. In the interview there will be two members of the investigating team, a PACE tape recording machine and a selection of tapes that are sealed in cellophane wrapping. When the witness and their solicitor are in the room and seated, the procedure will be explained to them and one of the investigators will unwrap two tapes and place them in the machine. Both tapes record at the same time so that there are two identical tapes. One tape is called the *master tape* and as soon as it is taken out of the machine it is sealed in its container in a manner that does not allow access to the tape. The seal is signed by the person being interviewed and is held at the investigating inspector's offices. The tape remains sealed and can only be opened in court should there be a dispute over the content on the other tape. The other tape is the *working tape* and is retained by the inspectors who will have it transcribed into a typed transcript. A typist will identify each person speaking and what they say. On long interviews this can amount to many pages and it is from this interview that the investigators and legal team will extract any appropriate evidence.

14.37   The HSE and LA will generally undertake a PACE interview at their offices. They may have portable systems and can undertake the interview at a company office but there may be a reluctance to do so due to possible interruptions. The police will conduct such interviews at a police station and as such this will not be a pleasant experience. The person being interviewed will be taken to an interview room which are stark and comprise basic furniture which is generally attached to the floor. It must be remembered that the police deal with all manner of people and offences and they do not make special allowances for senior corporate managers who are being investigated for their part in a potential corporate or individual manslaughter prosecution.

14.38   At the commencement of an interview the machine is switched on and a noise emits indicating that it is working. When the noise stops every person in the room will be asked to identify themselves and a caution is issued to the person being interviewed in the following terms:

> 'You do not have to say anything. But it may harm your defence if you do not mention when questioned something which you later rely on in court. Anything you do say may be given in evidence.'

Minor deviations are permissible, provided that the sense of the caution is preserved. If the person being interviewed is unclear of what has been said the investigator can explain what the caution means. Once the caution is given the person is advised that they are not under arrest or obliged to remain at the interview and may seek legal advice if no solicitor is present.

14.39   The interview will continue with questions being asked and answers sought until the investigators have sufficient information, whereupon they will end the interview. Both tapes are removed and sealed. In a long interview there may be a number of tapes. The comfort of the person being interviewed is taken into consideration and comfort breaks, refreshments and private access to legal advice is available. The person being interviewed is entitled to a copy of the tapes and a form LP 74 is provided which gives details of how and where to apply for copies of the tape/s. It may well be the case that copies of the tapes are provided at the time of the interview.

14.40   Being interviewed for potential corporate or individual manslaughter offences will not be a pleasant experience and may be done over more than one day. The author experienced a situation where a senior manager was invited to interview at a police station. The person being interviewed thought it would be a straightforward and quick process and had allowed an hour. Arriving at the police station and after being taken through the explanation of what was going to happen, the individual, accompanied by his lawyer, was interviewed. In line with the requirements of breaks for comfort, food and drink and to consult with the legal adviser, the individual eventually left the police station at quarter to nine that night. Such is the manner of the police investigation process.

Small businesses

14.41   No matter the size of the organisation there is a duty to report accidents and to investigate the cause and outcome. This should not be confused with the requirement to maintain an accident report which records basic details about all types of workplace accidents.

14.42   Most directors and managers of small organisations do not investigate accidents and are therefore exposed to further accidents with the same causes. Where there is a fatal accident the failure to have adopted accident investigation in the management system could leave a company as well as its senior management exposed to legal action.

14.43   An accident investigation form and details of contents should be determined by each organisation, but to provide an overview of the sort of details required a basic Accident Investigation Form and guidance for completion is in **Appendix 1**.

Chapter 15

Directors' Responsibilities for Health and Safety

Introduction

15.1   There needs to be a risk management process established within all organisations. The degree of risk management required depends upon the size of the organisation and the complexity of the work activities. For example, the level of requirement at an oil refinery will differ in context to that of a supermarket or an office block. The potential for a serious incident is more probable at a refinery than at a supermarket and the consequences would generally be more severe. However, every organisation needs to have an effective risk management process and it needs to be specific to the organisation. An 'off the peg' system is not the answer because it means that a few simple questions have been answered and does not require much thought. It is the thought process that makes the difference because there will have been a genuine effort to identify hazards, assess and manage the risks.

Directors' responsibilities for health and safety

15.2   Some years ago the Health and Safety Commission (HSC) introduced a guidance document[1] for board members of all types of organisations. The objective of the guidance is to ensure that risks to employees and others affected by the organisation's activities are properly managed. The focus is on company directors to establish effective management of health and safety risks with the emphasis on the following key issues:

- Maximise the well being and productivity of all people working for an organisation.

- Stop people getting injured, ill or killed through work activities.

- Improve the organisation's reputation in the eyes of customers, competitors, suppliers, other stakeholders and the wider community.

- Avoid damaging effects on turnover and profitability.

- Encourage better relationships with contractors and more effective contracted activities.

- Minimise the likelihood of prosecution and consequent penalties.

The guidance is not compulsory and organisations are free to take other action, but if they follow the guidance they will generally be doing enough to comply with the law, and in the legal sense the guidance can be used to illustrate good practice.

---

1 HSC, *Directors' Responsibilities for Health and Safety*, 2001.

15.3   The six action points identify that the board needs to accept formally and publicly its collective role in providing health and safety leadership for their organisation. The board needs to ensure that all of their decisions reflect its health and safety intentions, as described in the health and safety policy statement. It needs to recognise its role in engaging the active participation of workers in providing health and safety and needs to ensure that it is kept informed of and alert to, relevant health and safety risk management issues. The HSC recommends that boards appoint one of their number to be the health and safety director.

15.4   It is the last action that has provoked most comments and concerns as many directors and organisations see the appointed director as being the 'scapegoat' for the board when things go wrong. There is no intention for there to be an individual exposed for the failings of the board, providing that the individual who has responsibility for health and safety has not been negligent. The director appointed, should ideally be the chairman, chief executive or the head of an organisation, so as to ensure that there is in place an effective and positive 'voice' for health and safety at the most senior level. It follows that management has to be seen to demonstrate its commitment to safety which will encompass a wide range of factors. This will include management behaviours from the development of a safety programme to the quality of employee management relations. This guidance will be replaced by The Institute of Directors Health and Safety Commission jointly produced guidance *Leading Health and safety at Work – Actions and Good Practice for Board Members,* October 2007. See **15.12** below.

Management of risk

15.5   Every organisation has different circumstances surrounding its hazard risk activities. A large organisation may expose its employees and those not employed to minimum risk, while a small organisation may have a high hazard activity with the subsequent high-level risks. Therefore, all organisations require safety management systems that are developed specifically to meet the organisation's needs, all based upon a number of basic principles.

A key factor is the requirement for management to develop a system that is not only ownership which shows commitment, but also knowledge, and it is the knowledge of a particular industry and organisation that is important.

15.6   In addition to the lack of management knowledge in respect to accidents both large and small, involving both employees and those not employed there are cases where management do not accept responsibility for accidents. This issue is identified by Denis Smith[1] who states:

> 'Despite the presentation of data which shows that health and safety makes financial as well as moral sense, there are still clear barriers to making the necessary step change. The first is that managers show a clear reluctance to blame themselves for accidents, despite research that shows the importance of latent managerial error in accident generation. Why then would managers be willing to accept many of the non-intangible costs associated with accidents such as, opportunity costs, loss of reputation and the like? While they are more likely to acknowledge the more tangible costs of damage, compensation, loss of production, loss of product and raw materials, it is unlikely that they will accept that the management function has been instrumental in creating these costs indeed, the search for scapegoats serves to legitimise management actions. Secondly, many organisations have shown clear reluctance to change their procedures and systems in the wake of accidents occurring elsewhere because they believe that it couldn't happen to them.'

He continues:

> '... management plays a central role in the process of failure by providing the environmental and cultural conditions in which operator error occurs.

> Management, after all, is responsible for the development of standard operating procedures and is an important element in the development of a safety culture. It is also important to note that many managerial decisions have a long latency period before their implications are known, thus embedding an error cost within the system. Such strategic decisions can obviously play a major role in system safety.'

This is clearly a poignant statement, especially when reviewing a subject such as corporate manslaughter. Disregard and non-acceptance of management failure will expose an organisation not only to accidents but also to charges under the proposed offence.

---

1 Smith, D, *The Health and Safety Practitioner*, February 1998.

15.7   The Management of Health and Safety at Work Regulations 1992[1] were implemented as a result of EC Directive 89/391 EEC on the introduction of measures to encourage improvements in the safety and health of workers at work. The original Regulations were revoked and replaced with the Management of Health and Safety Regulations 1999.[2] These Regulations extend that requirement to all employers (and the self-employed) and to all workplaces covered by the Health and Safety at Work etc Act 1974 (HSWA 1974) from the simplest office to the most hazardous process.

---

1 SI 1992/2051.
2 SI 1999/3242.

15.8   The first step is to recognise the hazards and risks that are found in a particular work environment, which leads the employer to identify hazards and ensure that arrangements are in place to combat the risk. These arrangements should include the effective planning, organisation, control, monitoring and review of the preventive and protective measures. There is a requirement for employers to undertake health surveillance, which means having regard to the risks to their health and safety that are identified by the assessment. The employer has a duty to obtain health and safety assistance by appointing one or more competent persons to assist with health and safety issues within the organisation. That person shall be regarded as competent where he has sufficient training and experience or knowledge and other qualities to enable him properly to assist. It is also a duty for the employer to provide procedures to manage serious and imminent danger and for danger areas. These can include a written emergency action plan and a procedure for identifying foreseeable events that need to be covered. Employers have to provide information to employees that is relevant, understandable and achievable for:

(a)   any risks to their health and safety identified by the assessment; and

(b)   the preventive and protective control measures.

15.9   Estimates attribute up to 80% of accidents to human factors with human error being an element in many major incidents. In the past placing blame for incidents on human error was seen as a viable explanation and beyond the control of an organisation's management. This is not acceptable and the human element needs to be managed in the same way and with the same seriousness as technical and systems failures.

15.10   The management of health and safety must review the types and causes of human failures and develop ways of reducing them. Management needs to develop better design of tasks, equipment and procedures. Critical issues for many organisations are operational issues that include shift work and the potential implications, communications with shift workers, employee's perception of risk, their behaviour and the need for a positive safety culture.

15.11   Management will need to examine:

- *The job*: what people are being asked to do, such as workload, task, environment, controls and procedures.

- *The individual*: the person doing the job, their competence, skills, personality and attitudes.

- *The organisation*: the health and safety resources, the corporate culture, work systems and communications.

All of these elements must overlap to integrate equally. An imbalance caused by one taking precedence over another will focus priorities and expose others as being less important. The key is to maintain an equal overlap. See **Figure 6**.

Figure 6:

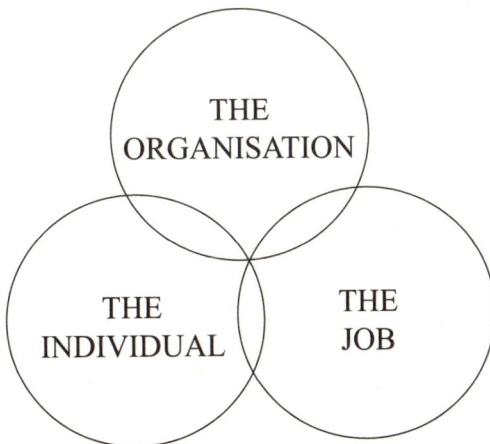

Risk assessment

15.12   The Management of Health and Safety at Work Regulations 1999, reg 3 states:

> '(1)   Every employer shall make a suitable and sufficient assessment of –
>
>> (a)   the risks to the health and safety of his employees to which they are exposed whilst they are at work; and
>>
>> (b)   the risks to the health and safety of persons not in his employment arising out of or in connection with the conduct by him of his organisation ...'

Because of the importance of risk assessment in organisations the Health and Safety Executive (HSE) produced a guidance leaflet, *Five Steps to Risk Assessment* (updated in 1999) which contains information on good practices. While not compulsory these are of help to management in understanding what is required and how to set about organisation risk assessments. The leaflet contains a blank risk assessment form that can be adopted by most businesses and industries, focusing on types of hazards, who might be harmed, is the risk adequately controlled and what further action is necessary to control the risks. The guidance sets the basis for employers and self-employed to assess the risks in the workplace with the aim of ensuring that there are sufficient precautions taken to make sure that no-one gets hurt. It explains that accidents and ill health can affect a business, through lost output, machinery damage, increased insurance costs or court action.

15.13   The fact that risk assessment is enshrined in law means that risks have to be assessed and controlled. Failures that cause deaths at work could show a management failure to heed advice and adopt safe practices. This in turn would be an evidential factor in potential corporate manslaughter prosecutions.

15.14   Employers have to identify the capabilities and competencies of its staff and provide training where necessary with the emphasis on health and safety. This can be achieved by providing adequate health and safety training when staff are recruited and when they are exposed to new or increased risks.

Health and safety assistance

15.15   Organisations differ in size, location, type and management structure, and they will involve a range of hazards from very low to very high, providing a wide range of risks that have to be managed. It follows that the law pertaining to health and safety can also be complex and may not be readily understood by management; they may consider that their role is much wider than health and safety law. The senior management of many organisations will argue that it is not financially viable to employ a competent health and safety professional. However, that does not preclude utilising the services of a health and safety consultant, providing that person is competent.

15.16 Under the Management of Health and Safety at Work Regulations 1999 every employer shall appoint one or more competent persons to assist him in organising the protective and preventative measures which have been identified in consequence of an assessment as to the measures he needs to take in order to comply with the relevant statutory provisions which require an employee to be 'qualified or trained', and other provisions require that certain things may only be done 'by or under the supervision of a competent person'. These phrases are usually left undefined and it may well be that the burden is on the employer to show in any given case that the person who performed the task in question was qualified, trained or competent as the case may be. The possession of some formal certification or qualification would no doubt assist in discharging this burden but it may also be shown that the person concerned has pursued some approved course of training or instruction as well as possessing practical experience of the work. The existence of a safety officer with details of his functions and powers, would be one of the things an employer would refer to in the written statement of his general policy on health and safety at work, as required by HSWA 1974, s 2(3), being part of the organisation and arrangements in force for the carrying into effect of that policy.

15.17 In most cases, the ideal appointment will be made in-house, from persons who are familiar with the organisation, its corporate structure, products, hazards and problems. If no such person is readily available, a suitable person may be trained into the job. However, there will be occasions when a suitable external consultant will be needed, and, in such circumstances the employer must be quite clear of the precise nature of the need, and the role to be played. Responsibilities should be determined, time scales laid down, performance monitored and fees agreed. Before an appointment is made, appropriate checks should be made on the consultant's qualifications, experience and professional standing through membership of one of the professional bodies identified below.

15.18 Competence can in part be identified through professional qualifications such as the National Examination Board in Occupational Safety and Health (NEBOSH), British Safety Council (BSC) and university diplomas or a NVQ Level 4 in Occupational Health and Safety. To underpin this there needs to have been workplace activity to form experience. There are higher postgraduate levels of study which are generally undertaken at a university and linked with this formal and practical experience and knowledge will be membership of a professional body. The body that represents health and safety professionals is the Chartered Institution of Occupational Safety and Health – IOSH[1] and this organisation can be contacted to verify an individual's Chartered Membership and status.

---

1 www.iosh.co.uk.

Employees' health and safety duties

15.19   It must not be forgotten that employees also have health and safety duties when at work and that means that every employee has to use any machinery or equipment in accordance with any instruction and training in the correct use of the equipment. The employee is required to inform his employer or any other employee if there is any work situation where it is considered that there could be a serious and immediate danger to health and safety. If this is done the employer has to investigate the situation and act appropriately, as it is the employer who has the ultimate responsibility for health and safety in the organisation.

Safe system of work

15.20   The term 'safe system of work' is broad based and includes the precautions that have to be made to account for the safety of the workers at all times, and that includes having sufficient persons to do the job, and that those persons are competent to undertake the work tasks. In addition it extends to safeguarding non-employees who may be affected by the activities of the organisation.

15.21   The definition of a 'safe system of work' is most effectively dealt with by the examination of cases that have progressed through the appeals system. While not definitive, it does provide the details of what the management failed to do, the actions of the employee and the legal determination.

General Cleaning Contractors Ltd v Christmas

15.22   A leading case for safe systems of work is that of *General Cleaning Contractors Ltd v Christmas*,[1] an appeal to the House of Lords in 1952. This is the case of a window cleaner employed by General Cleaning Contractors Ltd who was cleaning the outside of the windows of a club. There were no fittings to which he could attach a safety belt so he stood on the sill of the window, a method commonly used by his colleagues. A defective sash window fell on his hand, causing him to let go and fall. He was awarded damages against both the employer and the occupier of the premises. However, the decision against the occupier was reversed on appeal because the defective window was not an unusual danger of which the occupier was bound to warn the window cleaner.

The employer appealed to the House of Lords, which ruled that where the practice of ignoring an obvious danger had developed, it was not reasonable to expect the individual employee to take the initiative in devising a system of work against the danger. This is regardless of the fact that other systems of work were not practical. General Cleaning Contractors Ltd were still obliged to consider the situation, to take reasonable steps to provide a system that would be reasonably safe having regard to the dangers inherent in the operation and to ensure that its employees were instructed on how to prevent accidents in their work, including providing the implements. The employer had not done so and had not discharged its duty to the employee and therefore the appeal was dismissed.

This is a case that explains the relationship between the duty of care owed by employers and the obligations on workmen to take reasonable care for their own safety. Those at work are not in the position of employers when taking decisions.

It is the responsibility of the employer to take the initiative in devising and using precautions and the workman is not expected to do so himself. If a man is doing work as specified and expected by his employer and there has been a failure to take adequate precautions, then the blame should not rest on the man. The main issue is whether the employer has taken responsibility with reasonable care to provide a safe system of work for the employees. Where a practice of ignoring an obvious danger has developed then it is not the workman's responsibility to devise a system to overcome it. As to the decision as to what is reasonable, the employer must take into account the conduct and long established practices in the trade.

Lord Oaksey, who highlighted the key issues in the case said:

> 'It is the duty of an employer to give such general safety instructions as a reasonably careful employer who has considered the problem presented by the work would give his workmen. ... It is well known to employers ... that their workpeople are very frequently, if not habitually, careless about risks which their work may involve. It is ... for that very reason that the common law demands that employers should take reasonable care to lay down a reasonably safe system of work. Employers are not exempted from this duty by the fact that their men are experienced and might, if they were in the position of an employer, be able to lay down a reasonably safe system of work themselves. Workmen are not in a position of employers. Their duties are not performed in the calm atmosphere of a boardroom with the advice of experts. They have to make their decisions on narrow sills and other places of danger and in circumstances where dangers are obscured by repetition.'

Lord Reid said in the same case:

> 'Where the practice of ignoring an obvious danger has grown up I do not think that it is reasonable to expect an individual workman to take the initiative in devising and using precautions. It is the duty of the employer to consider the situation, to devise a suitable system, to instruct his men what they must do and to supply any implements that may be required.'

The general consensus of the legal ruling and commentators is that the definition of what is a safe system of work is broad and open to interpretation. It is therefore a matter of fact and will be a matter for a judge and jury to determine. It does, however, place the duty for the development of a safe system of work with the employer. It further places the duty on the employer to inform the employees of what is required.

---

1 [1952] 2 All ER 1110.

Paris v Stepney Borough

15.23   An unusual case involved a member of staff who had a partial disability and following a failure in the management of health and safety, became completely disabled. The case was the House of Lords appeal in 1951 of *Paris v Stepney Borough Council*.[1] A one-eyed garage worker become completely blind after a chip of metal entered his good eye. It was not usual practice for Stepney Borough Council to provide protective goggles to its employees working in garages on the maintenance and repair of vehicles and so no protective equipment had been given to Mr Paris.

After the accident he claimed damages from his employer, alleging negligence. The claim was successful in the High Court but the Court of Appeal reversed the decision. Mr Paris then appealed to the House of Lords who held that where an employer is aware that an employee has a disability which while it does not increase the risk of an accident occurring it does increase the risk of serious injury, special precautions should be taken if the employer is to fulfil its duty to take reasonable care for the safety of its employee. The condition of Mr Paris's eyes, the employer's knowledge of his condition, the likelihood of an accident occurring and the gravity of the consequences should an accident occur were all to be considered in determining whether the employer took reasonable steps to protect its employee's safety. It was determined that Stepney Borough Council owed a special duty of care to Mr Paris and had been negligent in failing to supply goggles to him, even though such equipment was not given to other employees.

In the same case Lord Morton stated:

> 'There are occupations in which the possibility of an accident occurring to a workman is extremely remote, while there are other occupations in which there is a constant risk of accident. Similarly, there are occupations in which if an accident occurs, it is likely to be of trivial nature, whilst there are other occupations in which ... the result ... may well be fatal ... there has to be in each case a gradually ascending scale between the two extremes ... the more

serious the damage which will happen if an accident occurs, the more thorough are the precautions which an employer must take.'

---

1 [1951] 1 All ER 42.

Morris v West Hartlepool Steam Navigation Go Ltd

15.24   Lord Reid further clarified the duty of the employer in 1956 in the case of *Morris v West Hartlepool Steam Navigation* Co *Ltd*:[1]

> 'It is the duty of an employer in considering whether some precautions should be taken against foreseeable risk, to weigh, on the one hand, the magnitude of the risk, the likelihood of an accident occurring and the possible seriousness of the consequences if an accident does happen, and, on the other hand, the difficulty and expense and any other disadvantage of taking precaution.'

A high standard of care must be applied when the employer knows that there are particular risks and where the employer knows of risks of which others are ignorant. His conduct should be judged upon that knowledge.

---

1 [1956] 1 All ER 385.

Nilsson v Redditch

15.25   An example of an employer's duty to provide a safe system of work based upon widespread custom and practice balanced against unreasonable cost is in the Court of Appeal case of *Nilsson v Redditch Borough Council.*[1] Redditch Borough Council employed Nilsson as a dustman, where black plastic bags were used for rubbish collection. The accident happened when Mr Nilsson was swinging a bag up into the collection lorry and was nicked on the leg by a piece of glass that had worked its way through the bag. The incident caused him to slip and fall, injuring his shoulder. He argued that the council was negligent for failing to provide a safe system of work and it was in the proceedings that Mr Nilsson raised the issue of the use of wheelie bins as an alternative.

The question was to identify whether the employers had taken reasonable steps to provide a system that was reasonably safe, having regard to the dangers necessarily inherent in its operation. The court was required to consider the extent to which the system used was widespread or of long-standing. If it was found to be both, then Mr Nilsson would have a heavy burden to establish a breach of duty of care. Where a claimant raises the point that an alternative

311

system of work should have been adopted, that alternative must be judged comparatively, taking into account issues of practicability and commercial viability as well as safety.

The Court of Appeal held that Mr Nilsson had not been able to show that the bin bag was unsafe. It was found to be a system in widespread use across the country, and this provided evidence that the system was reasonably safe. Waite J considered that there had not been enough evidence adduced to enable a proper comparison of the competing bin bag and wheelie-bin systems in respect to practicability, commercial viability, safety and extent of use elsewhere. This case identifies the importance of a system being commonplace and generally accepted as a system which is safe. The rubbish system was used throughout the country and to replace the system would have cost a lot of money.

---

1 1994, unreported.

Stokes v Guest, Keen and Nettlefold (Bolts and Nuts) Ltd

15.26   Another important case involving the requirement for proper safe systems of work was the case heard in the High Court, Birmingham Assizes in 1968 of *Stokes v Guest, Keen and Nettlefold (Bolts and Nuts) Ltd*.[1] Mr Stokes died from scrotal cancer and it was established on the balance of probabilities, that this was induced by contact with mineral oils during the course of his employment as a tool setter and that his work had played a part in the development of cancer. An action was brought by Mrs Stokes who alleged negligence and breach of duty by the company to provide a safe system of work. It was contended the company knew or should have known that contact with mineral oils could lead to a risk of cancer and should have warned Mr Stokes of the dangers of the material, instructed him on safe working practices, provided protective measures and conducted periodical medical examinations. Even though the company had employed a medical officer since 1941, no warnings or information were provided about the potential risks of mineral oils. No medical examinations were conducted, despite recommendations to the contrary since that date and a Factory Inspectorate leaflet on the dangers of scrotal cancer in 1960. The medical officer considered that medical examinations were unnecessary because of the low incidence of the disease.

The High Court held that an employer must meet the standards of a reasonable and prudent employer and follow recognised and general practice. The practice must have been followed for a substantial period in similar circumstances without mishap unless in the light of common sense or newer knowledge it is clearly bad. Where there is developing knowledge concerning the safety of workers, however, a reasonable and prudent employer should keep reasonably abreast of it and not be slow to apply the new knowledge. If the employer had a more than average knowledge of the risks, more than average precautions should be taken. When determining what action to take, the risk of injury occurring and its consequences should be weighed against the effectiveness, expense and inconvenience of that action. Where the employer falls below the standards to be expected of a reasonable and prudent employer, it has been negligent. In situations where a task requiring a special skill is delegated to an employee such as a medical officer, the individual's performance should be judged by the standards relating to that skill to the extent of his abilities. However, more general principles should be used to judge the non-medical aspects of the medical officer's work, such as advice concerning economic and administrative considerations. Applying these tests, the High Court held that the company's medical officer was negligent in failing to conduct medical examinations of employees at risk of developing scrotal cancer and failing to issue a notice drawing attention to that risk, and the company was vicariously liable for that negligence.

Employers who are responsible for the health and safety of their employees should keep up to date with developing knowledge in the various fields of potential illness that their employees may be exposed to as a result of their work. A subjective element was imported into the test to be applied to employers, in that when determining the liability of the employer, it is necessary to take into account the amount of knowledge and awareness of developments in the law that the employer actually has. Where an employer has a greater than average knowledge of the risks, he should put into place precautions which reflects this greater level of knowledge.

In the case Swanwick said:

> '... the overall test is still the conduct of the reasonable and prudent employer, taking positive thought for the safety of his workers in the light of what he knows or ought to know; where there is a recognised and general practice which has been followed for a substantial period in similar circumstances without mishap, he is entitled to follow it, unless in the light of common sense or newer knowledge it is clearly bad; but, where there is developing knowledge, he must keep reasonably abreast of it and not be too slow to apply it; and where he has in fact greater than average knowledge of the risks, he may be thereby obliged to take more than average or standard precautions. He must weigh up the risks in terms of the likelihood of injury occurring and the potential consequences if it does; and he must balance against this the probable effectiveness of the precautions that can be taken to meet it and the expense and inconvenience they involve. If he is found to have fallen below the standard to be properly expected of a reasonable and prudent employer in these respects, he is negligent.'

---

1 [1968] 1 WLR 1776.

Ward v T E Hopkins and Sons Ltd

15.27   The focus has been on the employer's requirement to provide a safe system of work but there are situations where there is some failing on behalf of the employee, such as in the Court of Appeal case of *Ward v T E Hopkins & Sons Ltd*.[1] This was the case of Mr Ward who was employed by a building company on a job that required him to empty a well of water. He and another workman and a director of the company built a platform down inside the well, from which they were using a petrol driven pump to remove the water. After an hour and a half usage, the pump was stopped; a haze of fumes was visible containing carbon monoxide. In the evening the director returned to the site and noticed the haze and the smell of fumes. The following morning he instructed Mr Ward and the other workman to go to the site but not to enter the well until he arrived. The two men arrived and ignoring the instruction entered the well, where they were overcome by the fumes. A doctor was summoned and although warned about the fumes, went down into the well to rescue the two men. Fumes overcame him and the rope that had been tied around him fouled on a pipe and he could not be pulled up. Mr Ward, the other workman and the doctor all died. The Court of Appeal held that in respect of the death of Mr Ward, the company had been negligent and had adopted a dangerous system of work. Even though the director had warned Mr Ward not to go down into the well, he had not been sufficiently clear about the danger involved and so did not discharge the company's duty. The fault was not entirely with the company and it was found that there was some contributory negligence on the part of Mr Ward.

These examples provided some of the cases that have progressed through the courts and offer some detail to show the failings within management to ensure health and safety.

---

1   [1959] 3 All ER 225.

HS(G) 65: Safety Management System

15.28   In order that directors and senior management as well as those involved in health and safety management within a corporation have information available to them, a practical guide: *Successful Health and Safety Management*[1] has been produced by the HSE. See **Figure 7**. The key elements of this guidance apply to any organisation, from multinationals to small enterprises, and comprise policy, organisation, planning, and measurement of performance, auditing and reviewing performance.

---

1   Successful Health and Safety Management HS(G) 65.

Figure 7: HSE HS (G) 65 Safety Management System

HSE HS(G) 65 SAFETY MANAGEMENT SYSTEM

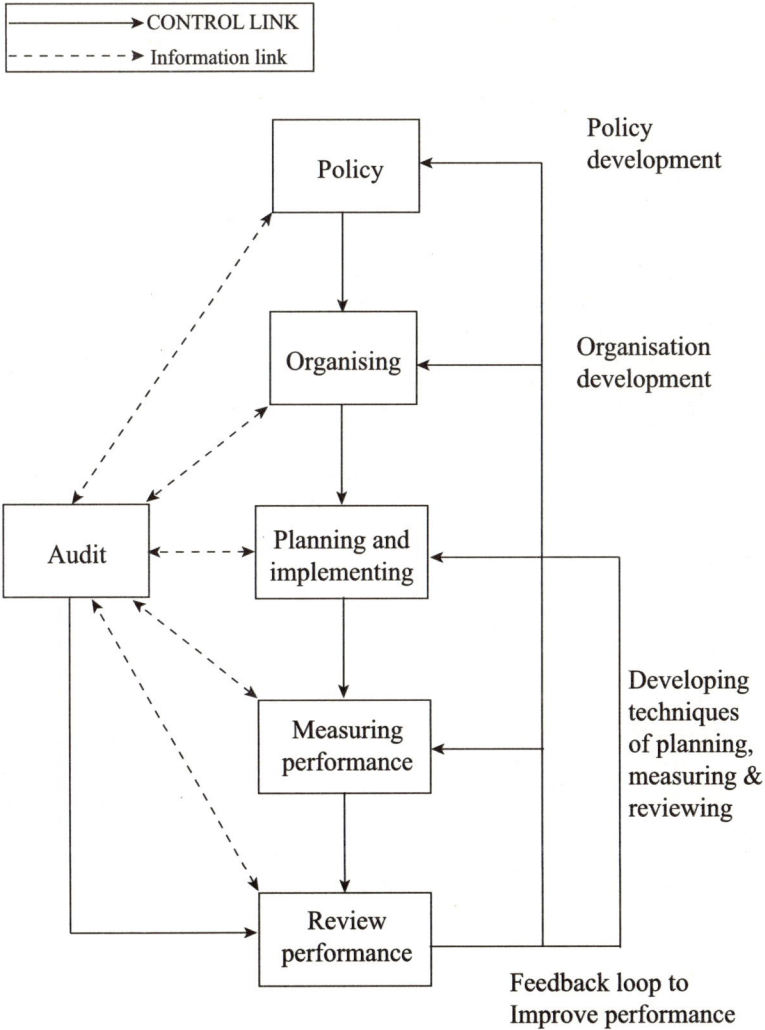

15.29 By adopting this system the directors and management have to establish a corporate policy with regard to health and safety, so as to ensure that all employees are motivated and involved in the organisation's vision, values and beliefs. This means that senior management has to provide leadership in the development of a positive health and safety culture.

15.30   Planning is an important part of an organisation's system as it is aimed at identifying hazards and minimising or removing risks. The onus is on the management of an organisation that creates the risk to control the risks and this is undertaken by risk assessments. The objective is to develop safe methods and procedures for working as part of a corporate health and safety culture.

15.31   The management, having undertaken the risk evaluation and mitigation process, need to ensure that what has been adopted is effective. This is achieved by the measuring of performance, which will identify strengths and weaknesses within the system. By analysis of the information, management can maintain effective control of the corporation's activities in respect to safety and health.

15.32   Management can monitor progress of the corporate safety system, through feedback from all levels of the workforce, either through union officials, safety representatives or others appointed as spokespersons, and if necessary, individuals who raise specific concerns. While this can be effective in theory, what happens in practice may provide a different story and therefore the system needs to be audited, preferably by an independent source, who can identify positive and negative outcomes. There should be access to every level of the corporation's workforce, including the chief executive or managing director, so that the safety management system is seen to be transparent within the organisation, and part of its culture.

15.33   The HS(G) 65 model provides a sound basis for the management of safety and can be used to evaluate failures in an organisation's activities. The example chosen is that of the sinking of the *Herald of Free Enterprise*. See **Figure 8**. The incident has been examined in some detail earlier (see **2.7**) and is a prime example of a management failure that led to a major disaster. The key elements of HS(G) 65 can be used to highlight some of the failures within premises/place, procedures, people, planning, risk assessment, communication, control, competence, monitoring and audit. The example given is not a complete review of the case, but provides easily identifiable evidence of senior management's failings. There was a lack of knowledge of what was occurring within the organisation, and more damning, where it was known what was being done, the activities were condoned. The example used proactively by an organisation can readily identify failings within the system, individuals and those in control.

British Standards Institution

15.34   An alternative, which corporations have adopted, is the *British Standards Institution Guide to Occupational Health and Safety Management Systems*.[1] This is designed to base health and safety management on the BS EN ISO

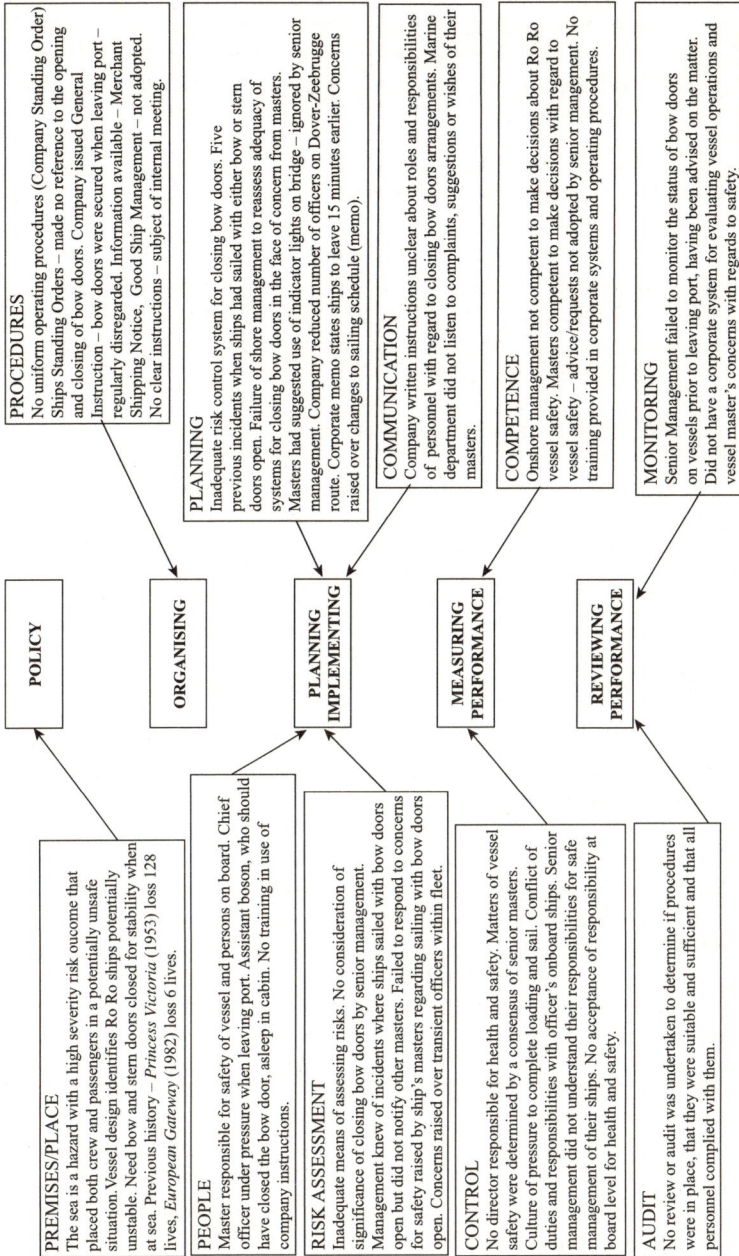

Figure 8:

POLICY

ORGANISING

**PLANNING
IMPLEMENTING**

**MEASURING
PERFORMANCE**

**REVIEWING
PERFORMANCE**

PROCEDURES
No uniform operating procedures (Company Standing Order) Ships Standing Orders – made no reference to the opening and closing of bow doors. Company issued General Instruction – bow doors were secured when leaving port – regularly disregarded. Information available – Merchant Shipping Notice, Good Ship Management – not adopted. No clear instructions – subject of internal meeting.

PLANNING
Inadequate risk control system for closing bow doors. Five previous incidents when ships had sailed with either bow or stern doors open. Failure of shore management to reassess adequacy of systems for closing bow doors in the face of concern from masters. Masters had suggested use of indicator lights on bridge – ignored by senior management. Company reduced number of officers on Dover-Zeebrugge route. Corporate memo states ships to leave 15 minutes earlier. Concerns raised over changes to sailing schedule (memo).

COMMUNICATION
Company written instructions unclear about roles and responsibilities of personnel with regard to closing bow doors arrangements. Marine department did not listen to complaints, suggestions or wishes of their masters.

COMPETENCE
Onshore management not competent to make decisions about Ro Ro vessel safety. Masters competent to make decisions with regard to vessel safety – advice/requests not adopted by senior mangement. No training provided in corporate systems and operating procedures.

MONITORING
Senior Management failed to monitor the status of bow doors on vessels prior to leaving port, having been advised on the matter. Did not have a corporate system for evaluating vessel operations and vessel master's concerns with regards to safety.

PREMISES/PLACE
The sea is a hazard with a high severity risk oucome that placed both crew and passengers in a potentially unsafe situation. Vessel design identifies Ro Ro ships potentially unstable. Need bow and stern doors closed for stability when at sea. Previous history – *Princess Victoria* (1953) loss 128 lives, *European Gateway* (1982) loss 6 lives.

PEOPLE
Master responsible for safety of vessel and persons on board. Chief officer under pressure when leaving port. Assistant boson, who should have closed the bow door, asleep in cabin. No training in use of company instructions.

RISK ASSESSMENT
Inadequate means of assessing risks. No consideration of significance of closing bow doors by senior management. Management knew of incidents where ships sailed with bow doors open but did not notify other masters. Failed to respond to concerns for safety raised by ship's masters regarding sailing with bow doors open. Concerns raised over transient officers within fleet.

CONTROL
No director responsible for health and safety. Matters of vessel safety were determined by a consensus of senior masters. Culture of pressure to complete loading and sail. Conflict of duties and responsibilities with officer's onboard ships. Senior management did not understand their responsibilities for safe management of their ships. No acceptance of responsibility at board level for health and safety.

AUDIT
No review or audit was undertaken to determine if procedures were in place, that they were suitable and sufficient and that all personnel complied with them.

1400, the environmental systems standard to identify common areas in the overall management system. The system comprises a number of key elements and the focus of the adoption of the elements depends upon the size of the organisation and type of activities that are undertaken. This is based upon the hazards that are created or encountered by the corporation for those employed and those not employed, but who could be affected by those hazards.

---

1 British Standards Institution *Guide to Occupational Health and Safety Management Systems – BS: 8800: 1996*; *The BS EN ISO 140001 Occupational Health and Safety Management System.*

15.35   Companies adopting the BSI approach for their safety management system will require the management to review the company's current status in respect to health and safety. This initial review should determine the scope and adequacy of any system in place and identify a base line on which to develop an effective system, with a method of measuring progress.

15.36   The development of the occupational health and safety policy requires the organisation's senior management to define, record and endorse the policy. The policy should quantify the management's commitment as being an important part of the company's culture. This places the burden with the senior management, which should be endorsed by the chief executive or managing director.

15.37   Planning is identified as being a critical part of company policy and this includes health and safety requirements. To achieve this, management should set the performance standards, identify who is responsible and monitor progress.

15.38   The responsibility for health and safety lies with senior management, at board level. Therefore, the implementation of an occupational health and safety management system should be allocated to a board member, who has the authority to ensure its effectiveness within the company. To ensure that the occupational health and safety management system is effective, the performance outcomes need to be measured. This requires the system to be checked and supported by an effective method of introducing corrective action.

15.39   Senior management can introduce a management system, but they must ensure that the criteria they have set down in the policy and any subsequent changes made to that policy are being followed. This requires a senior management review of the policy, its effectiveness throughout the organisation and implementing any changes for continual improvement.

15.40   There is a need for senior management, however titled, to understand the changes that there will be when the new offence of corporate manslaughter becomes law. The implications for senior management of corporate manslaughter are far-reaching because instead of the manslaughter element, it is now a case of management failure and, it will be the degree of that failure that will determine the corporate and individual charges that could be laid.

15.41   Senior management at board level (or its equivalent) in an organisation will need to focus on its responsibilities. This clearly places the ownership of health and safety at the highest level of management in every organisation. It is therefore imperative that health and safety is adopted as an integral part of day-to-day activities and culture. This means that management will need to show that they take suitable and sufficient steps, to manage health and safety in the same way that they manage other aspects of the business. This is the situation no matter what the size of an organisation and it is a matter for those who create the risks to manage the risks. While having management systems in place is no guarantee that criminal sanctions will not be imposed, a court will take the level of positive health and safety management into consideration.

The people health and safety system

15.42   The two systems above are focused on the management of health and safety and a corporate structure that ensures that a formal system is in place and being adopted. While such systems are credible formats upon which any organisation can base its management they may fall short of being people factored. People are the embodiment of all organisations that have employees and it is the employees who are involved in accidents, near misses and illnesses. Management and supervisors are also people and they are involved in the management and supervision of people and have a different perspective on the workplace and activities. A people health and safety system could follow a structure such as that shown in **Figure 9**.

Senior management policy

15.43   Senior management are the 'controlling minds' of the organisation. They set the policies, objectives and the culture of the organisation. Whilst they have key issues such as profit/loss and productivity to contend with, they also have to encompass the people who comprise the workforce into a positive health and safety culture. This will encompass leadership management.

People in the organisation

15.44   People are the embodiment of the organisation and they need to be suitable for the job, trained and competent. Good communication will provide information and encourage feedback all of which are positive health and safety objectives.

Figure 9:

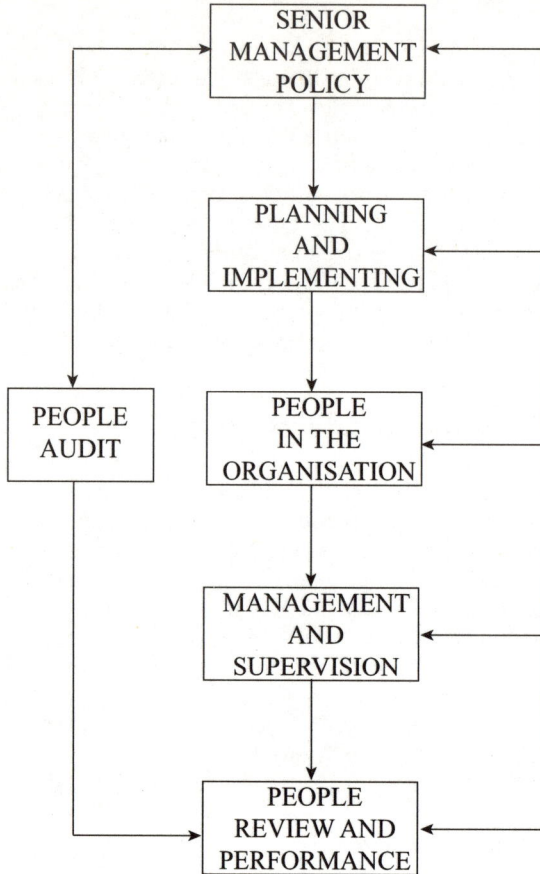

Management and supervision

15.45   Managers and supervisors plan and implement the objectives of senior management. The information they receive must be clear and concise as they are carrying out the will of the organisation.

People review and performance

15.46   Employees' objectives and performance need to be reviewed as a key element of culture ownership.

Positive outcomes

15.47   Positive outcomes involve meeting corporate objectives of profit/loss, productivity and no accidents or incidents. A focus on the positive by senior management is paramount as a tool of effective leadership management.

People audit

15.48   While systems are formally audited to ensure compliance there needs to be a 'people' audit to examine the reality. This means looking at the corporate structure in terms of people and obtaining a top down and bottom up perspective. People are involved, be it the managing director or the newest trainee, and all have key roles albeit with differing responsibilities.

Corporate audits

15.49   The main guidance on the requirement to audit is documented in the Health and Safety at Work Regulations 1999 which define auditing as:

> 'The structured process of collecting independent information on the efficiency effectiveness and reliability of the total health and safety management system and drawing up plans for corrective action.'

The audit process must, therefore, be conducted to confirm the arrangements that are in place to assure the safety of employees, contractors, the public and other parties that may be affected by an operation's activities and products. The principal elements of a safety management system must be confirmed by the audit process. This will include a review of:

- leadership and commitment;
- policy and strategic objectives;
- organisation, responsibilities, resources, standards and documents;
- hazard and effects management;
- planning and procedures;
- implementation and monitoring;
- audit;
- management review.

15.50   The Occupational Health and Safety Assessment Series (OHSAS) is a guideline that provides generic advice on the application of OHSAS 18001.[1] It provides the details of the underlying principles of 18001 and describes the intent, typical inputs, processes and typical outputs, against each requirement and is applicable to occupational health and safety (OH&S) rather than product and services safety. The specification gives requirements for an OH&S management system, to enable an organisation to control its OH&S risks and improve its performance. However, it does not state specific OH&S performance criteria, nor does it give detailed specifications for the design of a management system.

---

1 www.oshs-bs8800-ohsas-18001-health-and-safety.com

15.51 The specification of 18001 is applicable to any organisation intending to:

- establish an OH&S management system to eliminate or minimise risk to employees and other interested parties who may be exposed to OH&S risks associated with its activities

- implement, maintain and continually improve an OH&S management system;

- assure itself of its conformance with its stated OH&S policy;

- demonstrate such conformance to others;

- seek certification/registration of its OH&S management system by an external organisation; or

- make a self-determination and declaration of conformance with this OHSAS specification.

All the requirements in the 18001 specification are intended to be an integral part of any organisation's OH&S management system.

15.52 It is considered that the most effective safety audits require an extensive series of interview questions, commencing with interviews of the most senior management followed with interviews down through the management chain right through to the workforce, so as to confirm that the management safety messages and systems are well communicated and effective. To be effective, agreed audit actions must be drawn up and improvements implemented. Audits by third parties should be considered as a learning opportunity and should be welcomed by progressive companies. An effective internal audit programme is also essential to ensure systems are effective.

15.53 The objective of audits is to provide management with a detailed picture regarding the standards of health and safety management within the organisation. So audits and inspection are, essentially, confirmatory exercises which demonstrate that the health and safety management system is effective.

The level and detail of audits carried out will depend on the type of organisation and its confidence in the existing management system.

15.54   Information from audits enables both symptoms as well as the cause to be identified and appropriate action taken. It is important to take this balanced approach where employees see that they have a part to play in ensuring a safe and healthy workplace. Auditors and inspectors can obtain information from three sources:

● Interviewing individuals both about the operation of the health and safety management system and practices and their knowledge, understanding and perceptions of it.

● Examining documentation for completeness, accuracy and reliability.

● Visual observation of physical conditions and working practices to ensure conformity to legal and organisational standards.

It is very important for any audit to identify and promulgate positive outcomes and not to just focus on non-conformance.

Leadership management

15.55   Without leadership from senior management with regard to health and safety, there is no direction or motivation. That will render safety policies, statements and procedures ineffective. So in the spirit of corporate governance, mitigating corporate risk with regard to health and safety is a key issue for all directors and senior managers and needs to be addressed as an integrated part of the business culture. This requires positive leadership and as Jon Adair, a leading authority on leadership management, states:[1]

> 'You can be appointed a manager but you are not a leader until your personality and character, your knowledge and your skill in doing the functions of leadership are recognised by the others involved'.

---

1 Welham, M, Risk, S, *The Poacher and the Gamekeeper, Leadership for Risk Mitigation in Occupational Health and Safety*, Total Control (Anglia) Ltd, 2004.

15.56   The word 'leadership' conjures up a picture that can be all things to all people and who is a leader to one person can be seen as quite the opposite to another. However, a true leader will adopt health and safety management because in a world of continuing change, risk reduction and business improvement, there needs to be positive leadership. It can be argued that there are managers but few leaders and so the question, therefore, has to be: what is a

leader, what are the qualities and what are the personal attributes? The word
'leadership' carries some of the important attributes and these are identified as
follows.

Leadership

15.57

● **L**ead by example

● **E**ncourage ownership

● **A**ddress problems

● **D**evelop safety culture

● **E**nsure competence

● **R**esponsibilities identified

● **S**et standards

● **H**elp not hinder

● **I**nform and communicate

● **P**ositive and proactive

Lead by example

15.58   Leaders lead, managers manage and there is a difference. It is the
manager who leads that is the important factor. Possibly the most important of
the key requirements is for management, no matter the position within the
undertaking, to set an example. There is absolutely no point in having health and
safety policies and procedures and expecting staff to follow them if senior
management ignores or does not support them. This creates a 'one rule for us'
and 'one rule for them' situation and leadership becomes non-existent.

Encourage ownership

15.59   Ownership of health and safety by staff in an undertaking has changed
and one reason is that long-term permanent jobs are being lost. The problem is
compounded by the situation where many workers are, for example, contractors, agency personnel, subcontractors, casual staff, etc. People arrive, do a
work task and leave at the end of their allotted time and are less likely to be
flexible and have little or no loyalty to the undertaking. Good leadership
management can encourage ownership, to draw staff into the 'team' even when
they are not direct employees.

Address problems

15.60   Senior management must address problems that arise with health, safety and welfare issues. Faced with critical problems the leader will address problems and not 'sweep them under the carpet' hoping that they go away. A leader will acknowledge that high-level responsibilities cannot be delegated and so the leader can establish control and maintain leadership and encourage staff interaction in problem solving.

Develop safety culture

15.61   A leader will ensure that as part of corporate governance, health and safety will be integrated as part of the corporate structure and not as an 'add on'. Reference is often made to a company's 'safety culture' and it is probably the most difficult environment for senior management to develop. A key objective is that there must be an environment where staff are not afraid to say 'no' or 'stop – it is not safe'. They must be able to take such action and know that they will be supported and that the leadership culture will allow it, without redress. A leader will recognise that an open culture will get staff on-board with health and safety and move away from a blame culture where management looks for a junior member of staff to 'carry the can' when there is an incident, particularly if there is 'blood on the floor'.

Ensure competence

15.62   Competence is derived from a combination of work experience and formal training. An organisation cannot flourish if members of the staff are not competent in the tasks that they are required to do. This particularly extends to health and safety advice because senior management is relying on the information that they receive and will act on. A leader will endeavour to obtain the highest level of competence in his health and safety advisor and will support the use of specialised expertise when required. In a developing area such as health and safety, a leader will acknowledge that his staff need to maintain their professional competence and encourage development. To lead by example, senior managers should undertake safety management training.

Responsibilities identified

15.63   Senior management are responsible for health and safety within the organisation and must ensure that policies and procedures are complied with. The saying 'the buck stops at the top' is an important aspect of health and safety leadership management with regard to the workplace. A leader will have unrestricted access to health and safety advice and adopt business decisions to encompass any issues that may affect the corporate activities. The health and safety professional should only provide advice to the organisation and a leader will acknowledge that it is the responsibility of line managers to enact the requirements.

Set standards

15.64   It is a matter for the senior management at board level, or its equivalent to set the standards and determine the policies for the organisation. The standards must be the highest that the organisation can aspire to and they may be structured with milestones with realistic targets to be attained. Standards can be generated in-house or through external sources and good management will ensure that the most appropriate are identified and adopted. Leadership management, having set the objectives, will have to monitor achievement and modify the standards if required.

Help not hinder

15.65   Leadership management will adopt a style that helps and encourages staff. Senior management who micro manage, in other words get involved in the fine detail of day-to-day management, hinder a health and safety culture. A leader will be able to delegate and provide effective support when needed. Leadership management adopts careful but unobtrusive monitoring and provides effective support when required.

Inform and communicate

15.66   There is nothing worse than no information – only perhaps limited information poorly presented. Staff can generally cope with bad news and delight in good news and so it is imperative that a good leader will be able to communicate at all levels. This can involve staff and public which means that the leader is the face and personality of the organisation and being a good communicator is a very important aspect.

Positive and proactive

15.67   In business, possibly the most difficult task for senior management is to maintain a positive and proactive approach at all times. Business activities fluctuate with both positive and negative outcomes and it is for a good leader to react in a way that, in times of adversity, remains positive and through proactive actions leads the team and the business to achieve successful outcomes.

15.68   It is important to identify that managers manage often by the position that they hold and the perceived or real power that they hold over subordinates. A leader does not have to invoke 'power' but can motivate all in an organisation. Good health and safety is good for business and a leadership manager is a good business motivator.

15.69   The ultimate challenge for a safety leader is to predict where the next accident could occur and put in place measures to prevent it happening. Unlike a healthy bottom line in a profitable company, the results of good safety leadership are non-events and so a safety leader's task is never ending.

The Institute of Directors Health and Safety Commission Guidance

15.70   In 2001, the HSC issued guidance for directors. However, following a re-examination of the issue in 2006, the Commission determined that new guidance was needed to build on the progress made since the earlier publication, to do more to get the health and safety message over at board level and to use that as a key part of maintaining and improving the health and safety performance of organisations.

15.71   At the May 2006 meeting of the HSC the Commission asked the HSE to work with 'key stakeholders to produce authoritative guidance' on directors' responsibilities for health and safety. This led to the IoD being asked to take the process forward, with the HSE providing the secretariat (which has been done in co-operation with the IoD). A Steering Group was formed to undertake the work which involves making sure that the revised Guidance is noticed, read and put into practice which in turn means being produced in language that directors use and understand.

IoD Steering Group

15.72   Michael Large, one of the two Vice Chairmen of the IoD's own Board, was chosen to chair the steering group. Members of the Steering Group (and their nominating organisations) are:

- Michael Large (Institute of Directors) – Chairman
- Dr Peter Doyle (Confederation of British Industry)
- Eva Garland (National Council for Voluntary Organisations)

- Dr Rowland B Hopkinson (NHS Confederation)

- Bud Hudspith (Trades Union Congress)

- Richard Jones (Institution of Occupational Safety and Health)

- Paul Lankester (Local Government Association)

- Mike Welham (Federation of Small Businesses)

- Professor Frank Wright (University of Warwick)

- Alan Morley (HSE-Secretary)

In addition representatives from the IoD and HSE have attended the meetings to provide information and observe.

Steering Group development

15.73   The Steering Group has held a number of meetings since being formed and the IoD held a seminar in October 2006, just after the first meeting of the Steering Group. Many stakeholders were invited and the results of that seminar were considered by the Steering Group. New Guidance[1] was prepared for consultation and the Steering Group considered the responses. Following HSC approval the guidance was launched at the end of October 2007.

---

1 The Institute of Directors Health and Safety Commission jointly produced guidance *Leading Health and Safety at Work – Actions for Board Members*. The Guidance can be accessed at *www.iod.com/hsguide* or *www.hsa.gov.uk/ leadership*.

15.74   The IoD and HSC will have jointly produced the guidance *Leading Health and Safety at Work – Actions for Board Members*. The document draws reference to the corporate manslaughter and corporate homicide legislation and it is important to note that this guidance may be considered 'relevant' by the courts.

15.75   The guidance is designed to be a senior management tool which provides information for effective leadership of health and safety to be used by directors, governors, trustees, officers and those who hold senior positions in an organisation. It applies to organisations of all sizes and occupational type. The structure of the guidance includes an introduction to health and safety at board level; a four-point agenda, comprising actions and best practice; a checklist of key questions for the board; a summary of legal liabilities and a check list of key actions.

15.76   The important message is that health and safety should appear regularly on the agenda for board meetings. Whilst the chair or CEO should set the direction for effective health and safety management through effective leadership, some boards may find it useful to nominate one of their number to be the 'champion' of health and safety. The presence on the board of a health and safety director can be a strong signal that the issue is being taken seriously and that its strategic importance is understood. All board members should be seen to be taking the lead in communicating health and safety duties and benefits throughout the organisation. Options may include the appraisals of senior managers as part of an assessment of their contribution to health and safety performance. Non-executive directors should act as scrutineers ensuring that the processes to support boards facing significant health and safety risks are robust.

15.77   To take responsibility and leadership of health and safety, members of the board must ensure that:

- health and safety arrangements are adequately resourced;
- they consult competent health and safety advisers;
- health and safety is a factor when deciding senior management appointments;
- appropriate risk assessments are carried out;
- employees or their representatives are involved in decisions that affect their health and safety.

It is a board responsibility to consider the health and safety implications when introducing new processes, new working practices or new personnel, dedicating adequate resources to the task and seeking advice where necessary. Board decisions must be made in the context of the organisation's health and safety policy; therefore, it is important to 'design-in' health and safety when implementing change.

15.78   The board should review health and safety performance at least once a year and the review process should:

- examine whether the health and safety policy reflects the organisation's current priorities;
- examine whether risk management and other health and safety structures have been effectively reported to the board;
- report health and safety shortcomings, and the effect of all board or management team decisions made;
- decide actions to address any weaknesses and a system to monitor their implementation.

To obtain an independent review of the organisation there should be external auditing and reporting of health and safety performance. The board should ensure that any audit is perceived as a positive management and boardroom tool.

Fatal accident procedure

15.79 In the unlikely event of a workplace fatal accident it will be a time of great stress and trauma for those involved so clear and concise management, both offshore and onshore, will be required. Senior management must be notified as soon as possible and the organisation's Emergency Plan must be activated.

Criminal Defence Team

15.80 As soon as the company is notified of a fatal accident senior management must advise the appointed Criminal Defence Team (CDT). They will appoint lawyers to represent the company and those involved in the accident.

It is important to have a legal team with workplace manslaughter experience as many legal organisations may not have the required expertise.

Anybody required to attend a PACE interview under caution must have a CDT lawyer with them. The lawyer will provide support and guidance before and during interview and have important defence information after the interview.

Site of accident

15.81 The police and HSE will be notified as soon as possible and will allocate staff to go to the site to commence an investigation. The police will be in the lead of the investigation and the location of the accident will be a crime scene. Those who were at the site or directly privy to the accident could be witnesses and some could be potential suspects.

It is imperative that the scene is left untouched until advised otherwise by the police/HSE. The removal or destruction of evidence could result in a prosecution for perverting the course of justice.

Internal investigation

15.82 Management will organise and carry out an internal accident investigation following the organisation's Accident Investigation procedure. All or some of this information could be legally privileged and therefore legal advice must be obtained before any information gathered in this investigation is made available to anybody other than the organisation's management or the legal representatives.

Crime scene

15.83   When the police arrive on site Detectives and Crime Scene Investigators will gather evidence and take photographs. Police officers will interview all those involved at the scene and take into possession equipment and documents that could be relevant to their investigation. This will be done in conjunction with HSE inspectors.

Police investigation

15.84   The police will be investigating on behalf of the Coroner but will also be considering the possibility of a prosecution for corporate manslaughter or corporate homicide (England/Scotland). They will also be looking at the actions of individuals for possible prosecution for gross negligence manslaughter.

Police/HSE powers

15.85   The police and/or the HSE can take into possession any document or item of equipment and that includes computers. The police have powers of arrest and the HSE have powers of entry. It is therefore crucial that everybody co-operates fully with the authorities at all times. However, all communications with the authorities must be documented as part of the internal investigation record process.

Possible conflict of interest

15.86   As the investigation continues the situation could arise where an employee is investigated as a possible suspect. At this point the decision will have to be made as to whether the individual can be represented by the company CDT or would be required to seek their own separate legal representation. This is a situation where there is a conflict of interest between the corporate body itself and an individual working for the corporate body.

An investigation by the authorities is generally a lengthy process which can take many months and may even exceed a year. Individuals may be requested to provide witness statements, which are just that, an individual's account of what they saw and heard first-hand. If during the process of giving a voluntary witness statement the interviewers consider that the individual is giving information that could be incriminating, then the interviewers will stop and organise a PACE interview.

Legal action options

15.87   Once the investigation is completed the police hand the case file to the Crown Prosecution Service (CPS) for evaluation for possible prosecution. They have criteria to follow in that there must be sufficient evidence to provide a realistic prospect for a successful prosecution and conviction. They must also decide whether it is in the public interest to proceed with a prosecution. This will apply whether it is a corporate manslaughter case or an individual to be prosecuted for gross negligence manslaughter.

If the decision is to prosecute then the court process will be followed. The outcome from a guilty verdict would be an unlimited fine with regard to a corporate offence and possibly a custodial sentence for an individual found guilty of gross negligence manslaughter. It is important to note that it is very difficult to prove the individual offence but such convictions are on the increase.

If the decision is not to prosecute then the file is handed to the HSE who then take primacy and can bring charges against the company and/or individuals. With regard to a successful prosecution under the HSWA 1974 there is an unlimited fine both for the company and any individual found guilty of a HSWA 1974 offence.

With the introduction of the new offence it will be wise to have an action plan in place to deal with the unplanned should it ever be required.

Index